Food, Nutrition, and the Young Child

FOURTH EDITION

Food, Nutrition, and the Young Child

Jeannette Brakhane Endres

Southern Illinois University, Carbondale

Robert E. Rockwell

Southern Illinois University, Edwardsville

PRENTICE HALL, Englewood Cliffs, New Jersey 07632

Editor: Linda Sullivan
Production Supervisor: Custom Editorial Productions, Inc.
Production Manager: Francesca Drago
Cover Designer: Cathleen Norz
Cover Photograph: © 1993 Hunter Freeman/San Francisco
Photo Editor: Debbie Fullerton

This book was set in Palatino by The Clarinda Company and printed and bound by
Book Press. The cover was printed by Phoenix Color Corp.

Macmillan Publishing Company
866 Third Avenue, New York, New York 10022

Macmillan Publishing Company is
part of the Maxwell Communication
Group of Companies.

Maxwell Macmillan Canada, Inc.
1200 Eglinton Avenue East
Suite 200
Don Mills, Ontario M3C 3N1

Library of Congress Cataloging-in-Publication Data

Endres, Jeannette Brakhane, 1941–
    Food, nutrition, and the young child / Jeannette Brakhane Endres,
  Robert E. Rockwell.
      p. cm.
    Includes bibliographical references and index.
    ISBN 0-02-333721-4
    1. Children—Nutrition.   2. Day care centers—Food service.
  3. Nursery schools—Food service.   I. Rockwell, Robert E.
  II. Title.
  RJ206.E63   1994
  649'.3—dc20   93-25602
                                                                       CIP

Printing: 2 3 4 5 6 7   Year: 4 5 6 7 8 9 0

Chapter Opening Photographs: By Robert M. Wagner (Chapter 1); courtesy of The
Nutrasweet Co. (Chapter 2); by Robert E. Rockwell (Chapters 3, 6, 8, 9); by Janet K.
Kniepkamp (Chapters 4, 5); courtesy of USDA (Chapter 7).

To
Alicia Christina, Teri Lynn, Robert Joel, Amanda Sue,
Kathryn Lee, and Michael Wayne

Preface

The purpose of *Food, Nutrition, and the Young Child* is to provide an easy-to-read book about food and nutrition as it applies to the care of the child from birth through eight years of age. It provides ways to integrate food and nutrition into the early childhood setting.

MAIN FEATURES

The book begins with basic nutrition principles in Chapter 1. As suggested by the reviewers, Chapter 2 was added to apply the principles of food and nutrition to everyday life for the care provider.

The book specifically addresses the child who is cared for in home day-care, preschool or full-day-care centers with emphasis on protecting the child's health by providing the tools to assure the care provider and parents that the child is growing and developing normally. Since the last edition there have been significant national policy statements encouraging the establishment of child care programs at the work site. The text addresses the arrangement of the child care facility to provide a place where mothers may come during the day to breast-feed their baby.

Benefits for professors and students include an easy-to-read text that covers the newest information for the infants, toddlers, preschoolers, and young children on: what foods to provide; when to provide the foods; how to encourage a nutritious food intake; how to arrange the eating situation to facilitate use of the situation for learning activities; what food and nutrition problems are seen in each age group; and strategies for involving parents.

NEW FEATURES

New to the fourth edition of *Food, Nutrition, and the Young Child* is:

Chapter 1

- Detailed description of LDL/HDL cholesterol in relation to cardiovascular disease
- Energy calculations related to activity
- The effect of alcohol intake on the adult diet

Chapter 2

- Dietary Guidelines for Americans
- Food Guide Pyramid and Guide to Daily Food Choices
- Incorporation of additional servings of fruit, vegetables, and grains into the diet
- Discussion of *Healthy People 2000: Health Promotion and Disease Prevention Objectives* as applied to early childhood care
- New labeling legislation

Chapter 3

- Expanded discussion of breast-feeding benefits for mother and infant
- Eight steps taken by center to promote breast-feeding
- Effect of diet during pregnancy on infant
- Identification of children high risk for food and nutrition problems
- Guidelines for use of microwave in infant feeding
- Description of new formulas and use of cow's milk during infancy
- Preparation of infant formulas to prevent lead poisoning

Chapter 4–5

- Update of eating patterns recommended for children using the new Food Guide Pyramid
- Incorporation of the new Recommended Dietary Allowances into diets of toddlers and preschoolers
- Use of low-fat diets for children after the age of 2 years
- Sweeteners

Chapter 6

- Low fat-diets for 6–8 year-olds
- Role of center in promoting *Healthy People 2000* objective for oral health
- Snack foods that are less cariogenic

Chapter 7

- Seven Steps to Successful Ethnic Menus
- Use of the "Children Food Safety Kit: A Health Professional's Guide to the Issues"
- Expanded role of the community dietitian in providing consultation to the care provider

Chapter 8

- Explores a variety of programatic approaches used in early childhood programs

Chapter 9

- New strategies for involving parents and teachers as partners in nutrition education

METHOD OF RESEARCH

The text is up to date, reflecting numerous new research publications from professional journals, industry, and governmental agencies. In addition, the authors have tested the concepts presented in the book in day-care and preschool centers. Of particular interest in this context was the testing of the ethnic menus that led to the development of the Seven Steps to Successful Ethnic Meals.

With the publication of *Healthy People 2000: Health Promotion and Disease Prevention Objectives* and with the Dietary Guidelines for Americans and the Food Guide Pyramid, the text incorporates the most recent information on dietary guides and standards available today. The text reflects the newly increased emphasis on the need for additional servings of fruit, vegetables, and grain products in dietary intakes of the young child.

ACKNOWLEDGMENTS

We wish to acknowledge the efforts of those who helped in the research, diet analysis, and preparation of the fourth edition of *Food, Nutrition, and the Young Child*. These include Meri Devore, who formatted table after table and corrected data errors; Denise Ivey, who researched and stayed late to help in preparation; researcher Kay Glass; graduate assistant Christine Norris for her computer expertise as well as research skills; Kathy Long for her typing and computer tutoring; and administrative secretaries Marilyn Griffith and Beverly Robbins, who put up with the disruption in the office.

We are also grateful to the reviewers: Linda Aiken, Southwestern Community College; Linda Herring, Itawamba Community College; Sally Fogg Jennings, St. Louis Community College; John Worobey, Rutgers University; and Jessie Zola, Milwaukee Area Technical College.

J. B. E.
R. E. R.

Brief Contents

1 Nutrition: What Is It? 1

2 Foods For Health 35

3 The Infant (Birth to 12 Months) 59

4 The Toddler (1 to 3 Years) 101

5 The Preschooler (3 to 5 Years) 143

6 The 6- to 8-Year-Old 183

7 The Menu 203

8 Integrating Food and Nutrition Concepts into the Early Childhood Curriculum 245

9 Parent Involvement in Nutrition Education 285

   Appendixes 315

   Glossary 363

   Index 369

Contents

1 Nutrition: What Is It?   1

What Is Nutrition?   1
     Social Factors   1
     Economic Factors   2
     Cultural Factors   2
     Emotional Factors   3
Eating Disorders   3
Nutrients in Foods   4
Energy   6
Fats   8
     Sources   8
     Cholesterol   11
     Recommendations   11
     Fat Substitutes   12
Carbohydrates   13
     Function   14
     Sources   14
     Sugar and Disease   16
Proteins   16
     Function   17
     Sources   17
Alcohol   17
Vitamins   18
     Fat-Soluble Vitamins   19
     Water-Soluble Vitamins   22
     Toxicity   23
Minerals   23
     Macrominerals   25
     Trace Elements   28
Water   30

Supplements   31
Summary   31
Discussion Questions   32

2   Foods for Health   35

Guides and Standards   35
Dietary Guidelines for Americans   35
A Guide to Daily Food Choices   36
National Health Objectives for the Year 2000   39
Recommended Dietary Allowances (RDA)   44
Food Labeling   45
Personal Dietary Intake and Exercise Patterns   49
How Does Your Diet Compare?   50
Exercise and Energy   53
Guidelines for Vegetarians   53
Exercise Concerns and Cautions for Children   55
Summary   55
Discussion Questions   56

3   The Infant (Birth to 12 Months)   59

Physical Characteristics Related to Food   59
Critical Periods   60
Anthropometric and Laboratory Measures Related to
Nutrition   60
Measuring   60
Recording   66
Interpreting   68
Laboratory Measurements   70
Nutritional Needs   71
Prenatal Period   71
Lactation   71
Bottle-feeding   77
Supplementation   82
Solid Foods   83
Infant Feeders   84
How Much Food?   84
First Finger Foods   86
The Cup   87
Eating With Utensils   87
Evaluating the Diet   87
Health Concerns   88
Iron-Deficiency Anemia   88
Lactose Intolerance   88
Food Allergies   89
Gastrointestinal Tract Disturbances   89
Nursing Bottle Caries   90

Exercise and Physical Fitness for Infants   91
Policies of the Infant Center   92
Summary   93
Discussion Questions   94
Appendix 3-A   Resources for Lactating Mothers   97
Appendix 3-B   Special Supplemental Food Program for
    Women, Infants, and Children   98

4   The Toddler (1 to 3 Years)   **101**
Growth and Development   101
Developmental Skills   105
Psychological and Social Characteristics   106
Nutritional Needs   109
    Energy   110
    Protein   111
    Minerals   111
    Other Nutrients   113
    Supplementation   113
Food Guide for the Toddler   114
    Fruits and Vegetables   117
    Meat and Meat Alternates   118
    Breads and Cereals   119
    Milk and Milk Products   121
Eating and Care Provider's Role   121
    Bottle or Cup   122
    Commercial Toddler Foods   123
    Serving Food to the Toddler   123
    Equipment   125
    Eating Behavior   125
Nutrition-related Health Concerns   127
    Anemia   127
    Obesity   128
    Dental Caries   134
    Cardiovascular Disease   135
    Lactose Intolerance   135
Exercise and Physical Fitness   136
Summary   138
Discussion Questions   139

5   The Preschooler (3 to 5 Years)   **143**
Weight and Stature   144
Child Development Skills   145
Energy and Nutrient Needs   147
    Energy   147
    Protein   148
    Fat   148
    Minerals/Vitamins   148

Food Needs   150
   Fruits and Vegetables   153
   Meats and Meat Alternatives   153
   Breads and Cereals   155
   Milk and Milk Products   156
Supplementation   156
Eating Behavior   157
   Equipment   159
   Location   160
Special Concerns Related to Dietary Intake   161
   Snack Foods   161
   Fast Food   164
   Sweeteners   164
Vegetarian Diet   168
   Is the Vegetarian Diet Safe for Children?   169
   Natural? Organic?   169
   Additives   171
   Diet and Hyperactivity   171
Exercise and Physical Fitness   172
Summary   176
Discussion Questions   176
Appendix 5-A   Equipment and Play Materials for
   Preschoolers   179

6   The 6- to 8-Year-Old   183

Weight and Stature   183
Energy and Nutrient Needs   184
   Nutrients   184
   Dietary Supplementation   185
Food Needs   186
What Influences Eating Patterns?   189
   Media   189
   Family   189
   School   189
   Snack Foods   190
Nutrition-related Health Concerns   193
   Dental Health   193
   Cardiovascular Diseases   194
   Obesity   196
Exercise and Physical Fitness   196
   Components of Fitness   196
   Frequency of Physical Education Classes   196
   Parent's Role   198
Summary   198
Discussion Questions   199

7   The Menu   **203**

What Food to Serve Children   205
  The Infant   205
  The Toddler and Preschooler   209
  CACFP Food Requirements   209
  CACFP Questions Frequently Asked   209
  Coordinating Center and Home Food Intake   215
Planning Menus with Staff   217
  Food Service Supervisor's Contribution   217
  Availability of Foods   218
  Teacher's Contribution   218
Styles of Food Service   224
  Planning Cycle Menus   224
  Child Nutrition Labeling   229
Cultural Food Patterns   230
Menu Checklist   231
Good Management Principles   232
  Planning the Menu   232
  Ordering and Purchasing Food   232
  Controlling Supplies   233
  Preparing Food   233
  Analyzing Costs   233
Sanitary Practices   233
  Organisms   234
  Personnel Sanitation   235
  Food Handling   238
  Microwave Ovens   239
  Care Providers and Food Service   240
Parent Participation   240
Community Dietitian   241
  Qualifications Expected   241
  Training   241
Summary   242
Discussion Questions   242

**8   Integrating Food and Nutrition Concepts into the
Early Childhood Curriculum**   **245**

Programmatic Approaches to Learning   245
  Cognitive-interactionist Approach   246
  Other Approaches   248
  Programmatic Insights   249
Goals and Objectives for Nutrition Education   250
Teaching Children to Eat Nourishing Food   251
  Food Group Reference   251
  Teaching a Nutrition Concept   253
  Teaching about Nutrients   256
  Strategies for Incorporating Nutrition Education   258

The Menu   259
    Use of Food from the Menu   260
    Developmental Areas   264
Objectives and Nutrition Education   267
    Ten Steps   268
    Lesson Plans for Preschoolers   270
Recipes for Nonreaders   276
    Use of a Recipe for Nonreaders   276
Cooking in the Classroom   279
Summary   279
Discussion Questions   281

9   Parent Involvement in Nutrition Education   285
Why Involve Parents?   285
    First Steps in Getting Parents Involved   287
    Ways in Which to Use Parent Contributions   290
Evaluation of Parent Involvement   295
Recognition   296
Summary   297
Discussion Questions   298
Appendix 9-A   Center Feeding Chart   300
Appendix 9-B   Notes for Parents of 3- to 18-Month-
    Old Infants   301
Appendix 9-C   Notes for Parents of 18- to 24-Month-
    Old Toddlers   302
Appendix 9-D   Parent Report Form   303
Appendix 9-E   Sign In and Out Form   304
Appendix 9-F   Sample Agenda for Preplanning, Con-
    ducting, and Evaluating a Family Workshop   305
Appendix 9-G   Letter to Parents   312

Appendixes   315
  I.   Nutritive Values of the Edible Parts of
    Foods   316
  II.   Recommended Dietary Allowances (RDA),
    Revised 1989   348
  III.   Daily Values (DV)   350
  IV.   Dietary Screening Aids   352
  V.   Weight-for-Stature Charts for Prepubertal Girls
    and Boys   356
  VI.   Sources of Funding for Food Service   361

Glossary   363

Index   369

Nutrition: What Is It?

LEARNING OBJECTIVES

Students will be able to:
- Define nutrition.
- List factors that influence food and nutrient intake.
- List the basic nutrients and their uses in the body.
- Describe the specific effects of alcohol and fat consumption.
- Identify foods that supply major nutrients.
- State the recommended use of nutritional supplements.

Before we study the use of foods and nutrition in early childhood settings, we need a basic knowledge of foods and their nutrient content. The mass media inform us daily of the latest nutrition controversy, and information on topics such as cholesterol, fat, sugar, fiber, and dietary supplements is often confusing. Parents are concerned not only about their children's dietary intake but about their own as well. They turn to the care provider for advice and accurate information. For this reason, factual information about food and nutrition is an essential part of the early childhood curriculum and should be understood by all care providers. Chapters 1 and 2 are especially for you! Using knowledge of basic nutrition principles in your daily food selection will help you have the energy and right combination of nutrients necessary to meet the demands of your profession. In addition, you will be providing a good role model for parents and children.

WHAT IS NUTRITION?

Nutrition is the science of food and how it is used by the body. Nutrition can also be defined as all the processes by which a child or adult consumes, digests, absorbs, transports, and uses food substances, and excretes end products as waste. *Nutrients* are substances found in food that must be supplied to the body. When you eat food, your body takes in the nourishment necessary to live, grow, maintain good health, and have energy for work and play.

Most people do not eat only for nourishment. Therefore, the study of nutrition must also be concerned with the social, economic, cultural, and psychological implications of food and eating.

Social Factors

Food plays a large part in our social lives. Whether we go to the ballpark, the zoo, the movies, or a party, or stay at home reading a book or watching television, food serves a social role. Rare is the social gathering at which food is not served or sold.

1

Economic Factors

The cost of living has had an impact on food purchasing. Economic constraints limit the amount and type of food some individuals or families can afford. The wider the variety of foods eaten, the more likely the diet is to contain all the nutrients essential for good health.

Some families with limited economic resources may not be able to purchase a wide variety of foods, and, therefore, they may have more difficulty acquiring a wide variety of nutrients. Low-income families without adequate transportation may have access only to small grocery stores with limited food selections.

Sometimes parents can afford to purchase a wide variety of foods, but time constraints make buying foods from restaurants the economical choice. Food purchased at restaurants can adequately meet nutritional needs, but families may repeatedly choose to eat only a few selected items from fast-food restaurants. Nutrient intake may be limited if foods are not selected carefully.

Thus, variety can be limited either because of the economic inability to purchase nutritious foods or because of repeated purchases or preparation of only a few nutrient-specific food items from restaurants.

Cultural Factors

The cultural and ethnic customs of our society influence the food we eat, and ethnic groups in the United States follow various dietary patterns and food preferences. A person's cultural heritage often determines whether a particular food will be eaten, regardless of its nutrient value. However, this country's wide variety of cultures and food habits can make eating interesting and enjoyable as well as a learning experience for children.

Two of the most popular ethnic cuisines are Asian and Italian foods. Asian cuisine typically emphasizes vegetables, fruits, and rice or noodles but only small amounts of meat and milk products. Italian cooking is characterized by liberal use of pastas, tomato sauces, and bread. Italian cuisine also emphasizes vegetables and fruits, as well as meats and cheeses. Milk is seldom consumed except in coffee.

Middle Eastern food is also a popular ethnic choice. Food dishes from this culture may include yogurt, rice, lamb, and curried foods. Members of the Moslem religion do not eat pork products.

Jewish customs, including dietary laws, are observed in varying degrees in this country by Orthodox, Conservative, or Reform denominations. Some families place great value on traditional rituals of the Jewish religion and observe the dietary laws under all conditions. Dietary laws prohibit the use of meat and milk at the same meal, and separate dishes and utensils must be used for preparing and serving meat and dairy products. Orthodox Jews use only the forequarter of animals such as cattle and sheep. Animals and poultry are slaughtered by a ritual butcher (schochet) according to specified regulations. The meat is then koshered. Jewish persons who follow religious customs do not eat pork products.

In the United States, region also plays a part in what foods are eaten and how they are prepared. In the South, for example, cooks season liberally with bacon and salt pork, and hominy grits, hot biscuits, corn bread, and rice are common accompaniments to meals that may include fried meats and fish, and greens and many varieties of dried beans. Southern cooking may also be high-fat in its traditional recipes.

The United States also has a thriving vegetarian population. Vegetarians, for a variety of religious and personal reasons, may restrict meat, milk, and eggs from their diets. Vegetarian diets are discussed in Chapters 2 and 5.

The foods prepared in these differing cuisines vary widely in nutritional value. Asian food is generally low-fat and low-cholesterol, although some foods are deep-fried. Italian food is typically low-fat unless heavy cream and oil are used in pasta sauces. Mexican food can be spicy and high-fat if not modified.

The American Diabetes Association and the American Dietetic Association have published a series on practices, customs, and holidays related to various ethnic groups [1]. See Chapter 7 for the Seven Steps to Successful Ethnic Meals.

Emotional Factors

Emotional factors such as stress or excitement can trigger over- or undereating. Food may be used as an emotional weapon or crutch. One individual can use rejection or acceptance of specific foods or meals as a method to control the behavior of another.

Students going home from college for vacation who are determined to stay on their diets often find themselves overeating foods prepared by parents. Some nutritional deficiencies cause apathy and depression and are accompanied by a loss of appetite; however, these deficiencies are rare, and variations in the amount of food consumed from day to day are usually normal.

Almost every parent believes at some time that his or her child exhibits eating problems. This occurs when the child refuses to eat vegetables or meat, eats too many sweets, or does not seem to eat enough food. In many cases, eating behavior is a way for children to assert their individuality. A child may have a temper tantrum if the family runs out of a favorite cereal. Another child learns that refusing to eat will usually upset the family and may even result in a reward, a "bribe," for improved behavior. Most of these situations are short-lived and have few consequences. Psychologists often disagree about the cause and cure of eating whims expressed by children, but whatever the cause, psychological aspects of food consumption that originate in early childhood often continue throughout life.

EATING DISORDERS

The eating problems discussed earlier are generally minor and disappear without affecting growth and development. Eating disorders that cause obesity or starvation should be identified and treated through specially designed programs now available at health clinics (contact local or state health departments).

Obesity is believed to be influenced by early childhood eating and exercise patterns as well as genetic factors. Emphasis must be placed on the prevention of obesity. Although there are hundreds of weight loss programs, only 10% to 15% of obese adults are successfully treated and maintain the desired weight loss.

Some persons who have a strong fear of becoming overweight practice self-starvation. This condition is known as *anorexia nervosa*. Its cause is not known, and in fact it may have multiple causes. It is unclear whether factors related to childhood eating behavior have any effect on later eating disorders. The mass media's campaigns for thinness, specific foods, exercise programs, dietary supplements, and "pill popping" certainly influence some sufferers of anorexia. Some persons, especially women and teenaged girls, take drastic action to control their weight.

Persons diagnosed with anorexia nervosa severely limit food intake to the point where they lose excessive amounts of body weight. They complain of being "too fat" when in fact their body weight is below recommended levels. They believe they "need more exercise" even though they exercise excessively. A constant preoccupation with food may also cause some persons to go on eating binges, gorging on well-liked foods, only to force themselves to vomit or take diuretics and laxatives to bring the weight back down; this condition is called *bulimia*. Extreme thinness provides anorectic and bulimic persons with a sense of control over their lives. Immediate medical, dietetic, and psychiatric measures are needed when anorexia nervosa or bulimia is suspected.

NUTRIENTS IN FOODS

Nutrients are found in foods. Foods may contain a few or many nutrients, and each nutrient has specific uses in the body (see Figure 1–1).

Because all foods do not contain the same nutrients or equal amounts of any one nutrient, it is important to understand which foods and quantities of food can provide the combination of nutrients to promote optimal health.

The body requires six nutrient classes to ensure adequate nutritional status and to maintain good health:

Fat	Protein	Minerals
Carbohydrate	Vitamins	Water

Alcohol also provides energy, but the body does not require alcohol for adequate nutrition.

The primary function of some nutrients is to provide calories, or energy; others enable the body to grow new cells and tissues. Essential nutrients are especially important for children while they grow and for the repair of injured

**Figure 1–1
Nutrients are found
in foods.**
Photo courtesy of
USDA.

tissue for people of any age. Fat, carbohydrate, and protein provide energy/ calories,* whereas vitamins, minerals, and water help regulate metabolic processes, including energy metabolism, but do not provide energy. Other nutrients function either as part of tissue and biochemical compounds or as regulators of body functions.

Some nutrients are needed in large quantities and others in smaller quantities, but each functions in a specialized manner. The task of providing nutrients to the body in the amounts necessary to ensure adequate nutritional status may seem overwhelming. However, there are shortcuts to selecting the proper nutrients. Using food guides and standards will help you select a variety of foods to obtain the nutrients needed for health and life. Because each nutrient is found in a wide variety of foods, the wider the variety of foods eaten, the more likely that the diet will contain all essential nutrients.

---

* Kilocalories, or "calories," are a way of measuring the amount of potential energy in a foodstuff. A calorie is the basic unit for measuring the energy that will raise the temperature of 1 gram of water 1 degree centigrade. One calorie is a small amount of energy compared with what the human body needs each day; therefore, the term kilocalorie (kcal) is used. A kilocalorie represents a unit that stands for 1000 times as much energy as a calorie represents. When, in everyday conversation, we talk about "calories," we actually mean kilocalories. The proper shortened form of kilocalorie is Calorie, spelled with a capital C.

ENERGY

The World Health Organization publication *Energy and Protein Requirements* states that energy requirement is

> that level of energy intake from food which will balance energy expenditure when the individual has a body size and composition, and level of physical activity, consistent with long-term good health; and which will allow for the maintenance of economically necessary and socially desirable physical activity. In children and pregnant or lactating women the energy requirement includes the energy needs associated with the deposition of tissue or secretion of milk at rates consistent with good health. [2]

Obviously, if energy intake is above or below that which is required by the body over a period of time, the child or adult will gain or lose body weight. When you eat too many foods that contain large amounts of potential energy in relation to the amount of energy you actually use, the excess is stored as fat. One indication of excess fat stores in the body is when an individual weighs more than what the charts estimate to be a desirable body weight (DBW) in relation to that person's sex, age, height, and body frame. Desirable body weight can be calculated with the following formulas:

For women: Allow 100 pounds for first 5 feet of height. For each additional inch over 5 feet, add 5 pounds (for each inch under, subtract 5 pounds).

For example, at 5'5":   100 pounds (for first 5 feet)
$$\underline{+25} \text{ pounds (for remaining 5 inches)}$$
125 pounds = DBW

For men: Allow 106 pounds for first 5 feet of height. For each additional inch, add 6 pounds (for each inch under, subtract 6 pounds).

For example, at 6':   106 pounds (for first 5 feet)
$$\underline{+72} \text{ pounds (for remaining 12 inches)}$$
178 pounds = DBW

An individual may weigh up to 20% more than the DBW and still be within normal limits depending upon proportion of muscle to fat, frame size, and age. These formulas are guides. Table 1–1 shows ranges of suggested weights for adults.

Calculating your caloric needs can be easy.

1. First determine whether you are very inactive, sedentary, moderately active, or very active.
2. Depending upon your activity level, you need from 10 to 25 kcal per pound of DBW. Men need more energy than women, so they need to use the upper end of the range.

    13–14 kcal/lb (30–31 kcal/kg) = very inactive/obese
    15–16 kcal/lb (35–38 kcal/kg) = sedentary
    17–19 kcal/lb (37–41 kcal/kg) = moderately active
    20–23 kcal/lb (44–50 kcal/kg) = active/strenuous

Table 1–1 Suggested weights for adults.

Height*	Weight in Pounds[†,‡]	
	19 to 34 Years	35 Years and Over
5'0"	97–128	108–138
5'1"	101–132	111–143
5'2"	104–137	115–148
5'3"	107–141	119–152
5'4"	111–146	122–157
5'5"	114–150	126–162
5'6"	118–155	130–167
5'7"	121–160	134–172
5'8"	125–164	138–178
5'9"	129–169	142–183
5'10"	132–174	146–188
5'11"	136–179	151–194
6'0"	140–184	155–199
6'1"	144–189	159–205
6'2"	148–195	164–210
6'3"	152–200	168–216
6'4"	156–205	173–222
6'5"	160–211	177–228
6'6"	164–216	182–234

*Without shoes.

[†]Without clothes.

[‡]The higher weights in the ranges generally apply to men, who tend to have more muscle and bone; the lower weights more often apply to women, who have less muscle and bone.

Source: Derived from National Research Council, National Academy of Sciences: Diet and health: implications for reducing chronic disease risk, 1989.

3. DBW (Desirable Body Weight) × kcal per pound; e.g., DBW is 125 pounds and you are sedentary: $125 \times 13 = 1625$

The information today suggests that for adults, body shape as well as weight is important to health. Excess fat in the abdomen (apple shape) is believed to indicate greater health risk than fat in the hips and thighs (pear shape). Look at your profile in the mirror or check your body shape this way:

Measure around your waist near your navel while you stand relaxed.
Measure around your hips over the buttocks, where they are largest.
Divide the waist measurement by the hip measurement to determine your waist to hip ratio.

Example:
   Waist = 28 in.
   Hips = 40 in.
      28 ÷ 40 = less than "1"
   Waist = 39 in.
   Hips = 37 in.
      38 ÷ 37 = more than "1"

Research in adults suggests that ratios close to or above 1 are linked with greater risk for heart disease.

Nutrients that provide energy, or heat, are fat, carbohydrate, and protein. Energy, or the calories, supplied by foods and beverages are approximately 9 kcal/g from fat; 4 kcal/g from carbohydrate; 4 kcal/g from protein; and 7 kcal/g from alcohol. Appendix I lists not only the calories but also the nutrient composition of various foods.

A brief look at nutrients in foods follows; however, for a more complete discussion, see additional nutrition textbooks [3,4] and Chapter 2 for a discussion of foods to meet your energy needs.

FATS

Fats, oils, waxes, and related substances are collectively known as *lipids*. Fats function to provide energy, or heat, for the body. Of all the nutrient classes, fats provide the most concentrated form of energy, supplying 9 kcal/g (29 g = 1 ounce). Fat also supplies a good padding or protection for the liver, heart, and kidneys, the body's vital organs. In addition, fats comprise an essential part of many body tissues such as the brain, bone marrow, and cell membranes. Certain vitamins (A, D, E, and K) are soluble only in fatty substances. Before they can be absorbed from the intestinal tract, these vitamins must be incorporated into a tiny droplet containing fat. In summary, fat provides (1) an energy reserve, (2) insulation and padding for body organs, (3) a vehicle for the absorption of certain vitamins, (4) essential fatty acids, and (5) a component of certain body tissues.

Sources

Fats are frequently found in our favorite foods for good reason: They enhance flavor and allow us to feel satisfied. Fats can be found in both animal and plant foodstuffs; for example: butter and margarine; whole milk; eggs; oils such as corn, soybean, peanut, and cottonseed; and even in the leanest muscle tissue. All fried foods, including popular snack chips, contain fat. Most of the fat eaten in the American diet comes from fats and oils, meats, poultry and fish, and dairy products. Other foods that provide energy from fat include mayonnaise, whipped cream, chocolate, nuts, avocados, and coconut.

Fats consist mainly of fatty acids, which can be classified as saturated or unsaturated. Fatty acids have a variety of structures as shown in Figure 1–2. Foods containing fat will have all of these fatty acids in various amounts as shown in Figure 1–3.

The number of carbon atoms in a fatty acid may vary from a few to 20 or more. Note that the number of hydrogen atoms compared to carbon atoms differs among the three fatty acids in Figure 1–2. The fatty acids shown have 16 or 18 carbon atoms and 2 oxygen atoms, but they have different numbers of hydrogen atoms.

Saturated fatty acids have a maximum number of hydrogen atoms attached to every carbon atom. Therefore, we say that these fatty acids are "saturated" with hydrogen atoms. Saturated fatty acids (Figure 1–2a) are usually solid at room temperature and especially so when refrigerated. The exceptions are some "tree oils" such as palm oil and coconut palm-kernel oil. Other foods containing a high proportion of saturated fatty acids are meats, butter fat, and shortening. Saturated fatty acids and dietary cholesterol tend to increase total cholesterol and therefore the risk of cardiovascular disease [5,6].

Monounsaturated fatty acids have one unsaturation where 2 hydrogen atoms are missing in the middle of the molecule, 1 from each of 2 adjoining carbon atoms (Figure 1–2b). Olive oil, peanut oil, and canola oil are good sources of monounsaturated fatty acids.

Polyunsaturated fatty acids (Figure 1–2c) have more than one unsaturation. These fatty acids are found in the oils of vegetable and cereal products, such as soybeans, canola, corn, cottonseed, and safflower. Oils can contain some proportion of all three fatty acids: saturated, monounsaturated, and polyunsaturated. Seafood is an especially rich source of polyunsaturated fatty acids.

Figure 1–2 (a) Saturated, (b) monounsaturated, and (c) polyunsaturated fatty acids.

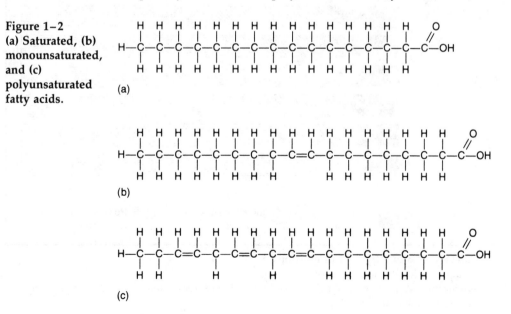

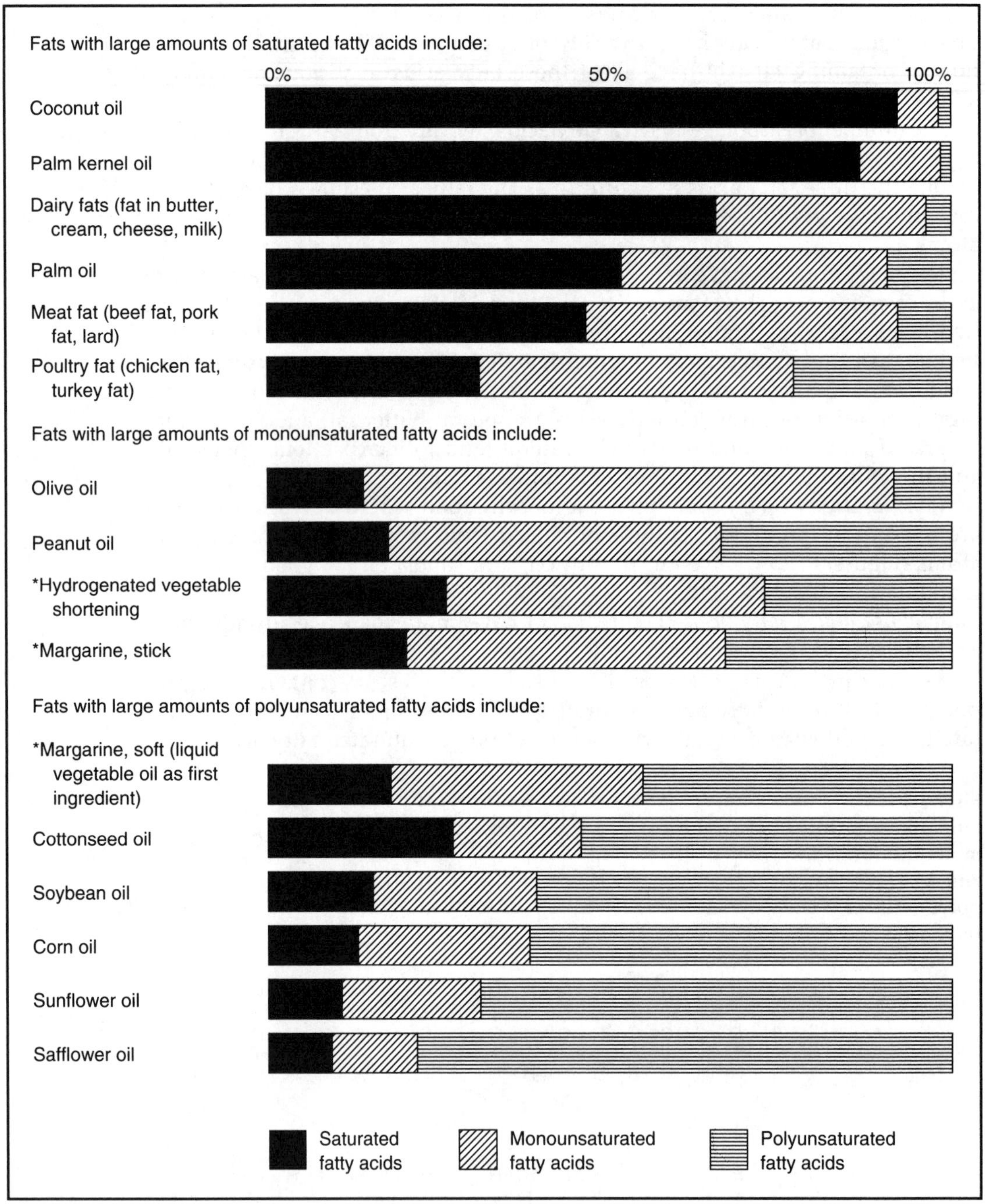

Fats with large amounts of saturated fatty acids include:

Fats with large amounts of monounsaturated fatty acids include:

Fats with large amounts of polyunsaturated fatty acids include:

Figure 1–3   Dietary fat and fatty acid proportions.
*The amounts of unsaturated fatty acids in these foods vary.
Source: U.S. Department of Agriculture, Human Nutrition Information Service: Preparing foods and planning menus, Home and Garden Bulletin No. 232-8.

Vegetable oils are made solid, or saturated, through *hydrogenation,* a process used by manufacturers to add hydrogen to oils. Generally, the more hydrogen added, the harder the fat or margarine. The name given to this product is *hydrogenated vegetable fat.*

Cholesterol

Cholesterol belongs to the category of lipids called *sterols.* It does not contribute energy and unlike fat is not measured using calories. All the cholesterol you need is made in the liver, and the cholesterol you eat is absorbed and carried to the liver. Cholesterol helps carry fat through the blood vessels to the various parts of the body where it is needed for energy or where it is stored—sometimes "on the hips."

Since fat and water (water is a major ingredient of blood) do not mix, cholesterol is carried through the blood in packages or clusters of molecules called *lipoprotein,* lipid plus protein. Most of the cholesterol in the body is carried by three types of lipoprotein: high-density lipoprotein (HDL), low-density lipoprotein (LDL), and very low density lipoprotein (VLDL). VLDL carries fat from the liver to other parts of your body. VLDL is converted to LDL after it unloads fat wherever it is needed or stored. Because of its structure, LDL tends to get stuck or clog the vessels as it travels through the blood vessels back to the liver. The result is a blood clot. HDL, the "good cholesterol," finds and rescues the LDL and takes it back to the liver.

Usually this carrier system works well: The liver sends out cholesterol and HDL rescues the LDL. However, when you eat too much fat or when you are genetically predisposed to making high levels of cholesterol, VLDLs are made in great quantities. The VLDLs are converted to LDLs, which may accumulate in the vessels if HDL is not available. The result is heart disease or clogged arteries.

In summary, low-density lipoprotein (LDL) is believed to be a risk factor in the development of heart disease. High-density lipoprotein (HDL) may protect against cardiovascular disease. The more HDL one has, the lower the total cholesterol and, theoretically, the lower the risk of heart disease. You can maintain or increase your HDL blood level by not smoking, by maintaining correct weight for height, by exercising, and by consuming a diet that does not contain too much cholesterol or fat.

When you go for a health screening, the laboratory may provide information not only on your serum cholesterol level, but also on the amount of LDL cholesterol and HDL cholesterol in the blood. Total serum cholesterol refers to the sum of HDL, LDL, and VLDL cholesterol in the bloodstream. Medical experts consider a total serum cholesterol level below 200 milligrams per deciliter (mg/dl) to be desirable [5].

Recommendations

The Dietary Guidelines for Americans [7] advise people in the United States to consume diets low in total fat (30% of calories) and saturated fats (10% of calo-

Table 1–2   Food substitutions to lower dietary fat and cholesterol.

Eat Less:	Eat More:
Vegetables cooked in butter	Vegetables stir-fried in oil
	Fresh fruit
Croissants, cakes	Low-fat whole grain cereals
Sour cream	Plain low-fat yogurt
Ice cream	Ice milk or frozen yogurt
American or cheddar cheese	Low-fat cheese, skim ricotta, or skim-mozzarella
Whole or 2% milk	Skim or 1% milk
Bologna	Sliced turkey or chicken, tuna, fish, or lean roast beef
Barbecued ribs	Chicken barbecued without the skin
Heavily marbled beef, such as sirloin or New York cuts	Lean beef cuts with all fat removed, such as flank steak, rump steak, or London broil
Butter	Reduced-calorie margarine
Lard, meat fat, or shortening made from animal fat	All-vegetable shortenings
Palm oil, coconut oil	Soybean, corn, sunflower, and safflower oils
Regular (bottled) salad dressing	Oil plus water, vinegar, and seasoning; reduced-calorie or fat-free salad dressing

ries) with polyunsaturated fatty acids containing no more than 10% of calories. When the labels show the total grams of fat, saturated fat, and unsaturated fatty acids, the care provider can determine whether a product can be included in the diet. Cholesterol levels in the diet should be at no more than 300 mg per day. Chapter 2 discusses how this prescription translates into food usage.

Instead of worrying about the specific amounts of certain fatty acids in the diet, concentrate on choosing foods generally low in fat, such as fish, lean meat, and chicken with the skin removed; skim milk; and low-fat yogurt, margarine, and salad dressings. These low-fat foods can be substituted for whole milk, sour cream, and high-fat spreads (i.e., butter, mayonnaise). Table 1–2 lists foods to substitute when trying to lower dietary cholesterol and fat levels.

A diet that contains a low level of fat, especially saturated fat, and cholesterol appears to reduce one of the risks of heart disease [5].

Fat Substitutes

The desire of Americans to reduce their fat intake has encouraged manufacturers to market fat substitutes developed through new technology. Many of these substitutes enable food products to taste like fat without real fat.

The first fat substitute approved for marketing was Simplesse, made from egg white or whey protein (milk) by a special method, called microparticulation. The proteins are cooked and blended to produce tiny particles. The tongue perceives this protein product as rich and creamy like fat but with only 3 to 4 calories per gram instead of the 9 kcal/g that fat provides. The body digests this protein like any other protein substance. Since this fat substitute is protein, foods containing Simplesse cannot be fried at high temperatures. Protein always changes when subjected to high temperatures.

Olestra is a manufactured sucrose polyester product that tastes like fat. The body doesn't digest, absorb, or recognize it as a foodstuff. The Food and Drug Administration considers Olestra an additive, and testing continues on this product to determine its safety. It can withstand heat and has the potential to produce low-fat fried snack foods.

Stellar is a modified cornstarch. It is produced by an acid hydrolysis technology. Manufactured as a crystalline powder, Stellar is converted to a "cream" through a shearing process for use in finished products. As such, it contains 25% Stellar and 75% water and replaces fat on a 1:1 basis. Stellar provides only 1 kcal/g (from complex carbohydrate). Stellar can be used by manufacturers in baked goods.

When this textbook was written, "cellulose gel" (Avicel) was frequently seen on labels of low-fat or fat-free products, especially salad dressings and processed cheese food. It is a microcrystalline cellulose that provides the body and mouth-feel properties of fat in a variety of fat-free formulations, including salad dressings and frozen desserts. Cellulose gel has been used in the food supply for years and is considered safe.

Healthy People 2000 [8] has directed industry to manufacturer more products that comply with the Dietary Guidelines for Americans [7]: "Increase to at least 5,000 brand items the availability of processed food products that are reduced in fat and saturated fat." The products being developed today are primarily lower fat products using newer technology for fat replacements.

CARBOHYDRATES

At least 50% of the calories in your diet should come from complex carbohydrates. Carbohydrates come in different sizes. Simple sugars (glucose and fructose) are called *monosaccharides* because they contain one single unit. *Disaccharides* (sucrose or table sugar) contain two saccharides or two simple sugars (e.g., glucose plus fructose). The more complex forms of carbohydrate, or starches, contain many units of sugar and are called *polysaccharides*. Breads and cereals, fruits and vegetables, dairy products, and legumes contain complex carbohydrates.

Monosaccharides and disaccharides make up about half of the total digestible carbohydrate intake. These are found in fruits (sucrose, glucose, fructose, pentoses) and milk (lactose). Sugars in soft drinks, candies, jams, jellies, and sweet desserts are mainly sucrose and high-fructose corn syrup.

Complex carbohydrates, which constitute the other half of digestible carbohydrate intake, are starches found predominantly in cereal grains and their products (flour, bread, rice, corn, oats, and barley), potatoes, legumes, and a few other vegetables [6]. Carbohydrates are converted to glucose in the digestive processes before being absorbed and used as a readily available supply of energy.

Function

Carbohydrates provide less energy than fat, yielding only 4 kcal/g. One ounce of fat (2 tablespoons of oil, margarine, or butter) provides approximately 220 kcal, whereas 2 tablespoons of flour or sugar (carbohydrate) provide approximately 100 kcal.

Carbohydrates function primarily as a source of readily available energy, since only a relatively small amount can be stored in the liver and muscle tissues. In addition, some carbohydrates act as body regulators or contribute to the structure of certain cells. If intake of carbohydrates exceeds energy needs, carbohydrate is converted to fat and stored.

Sources

High-fructose corn syrup is used commercially in soft drinks, baked products, and table syrup, and has replaced sucrose (table sugar) in many commercial products. It should not be confused with crystalline fructose, which does not appear to raise blood sugar levels in normal individuals, although it does provide energy in amounts similar to table sugar and high-fructose corn syrup.

The carbohydrate most frequently seen on the table is sugar, or sucrose, a disaccharide, also found naturally in many fruits. However, the carbohydrate found most frequently in foods, especially grains and potatoes and other fruits and vegetables, is starch, a more complex form that takes longer to be broken down by the digestive system when compared with sucrose and high-fructose corn syrup. Carbohydrates from grains and cereal products are the world's primary source of food, vital to the survival of many persons. The Dietary Guidelines for Americans [7] specifically encourage using sugar in moderation and increasing intake of complex carbohydrates and fiber.

Fiber is considered a carbohydrate. Complex carbohydrates (polysaccharides) make up the group of starches and dietary fibers. Dietary fibers are mainly indigestible complex carbohydrates in plant cell walls (cellulose, hemicellulose, and pectin) and a variety of gums, mucilages, and algal polysaccharides. Insoluble fiber, such as bran, helps move material through the intestinal tract through a process called peristalsis. Soluble fiber found in fruits, vegetables, and oats provides bulk to the stools and may affect the development of certain diseases. Table 1–3 lists the dietary fiber content of some common foods.

The use of fiber in the diet has been advocated to decrease the incidence of atherosclerosis, coronary and aortic disease, appendicitis, disease of the colon, and diabetes. In the United States, high-fiber diets have been used successfully

Table 1–3   Dietary fiber in selected foods.

Product	Serving Size	Dietary Fiber (g)
Fruits		
Apple, raw, w/skin	1 fruit	2.8
Blackberries, raw	½ C	4.5
Prunes, canned	⅓ C	5.8
Prunes, dried	3 fruits	3.7
Banana, raw	½ med	1.0
Boysenberries, canned	½ C	5.6
Figs, dried	1 med	3.7
Pear, canned	½ C	3.7
Red raspberries, canned	½ C	9.1
Strawberries, raw	¾ C	2.0
Vegetables		
Artichoke, fresh, cooked	½ globe	7.6
Asparagus, frozen spears	¾ C	4.8
Brussels sprouts, cooked	½ C	3.9
Corn, cooked	½ C	3.9
Corn, creamed, canned	½ C	5.1
Okra, frozen	½ C	3.0
Peas, green, young, canned	½ C	7.9
Pumpkin, canned	¾ C	3.3
Squash, winter, raw (acorn)	¼ squash	4.3
Turnip, green, frozen	½ C	3.7
Legumes		
Beans, butter, cooked	½ C	4.4
Beans, kidney, canned	½ C	7.9
Beans, pinto, cooked	½ C	5.3
Peas, black-eyed, cooked	½ C	12.4
Beans, white, cooked	½ C	5.0
Breads/Cereals		
Bread, pumpernickel	1 slice	4.3
Bread, whole wheat	1 slice	1.4
All Bran	⅓ C	8.6
100% Bran	⅓ C	9.1
Wheat germ, plain	¼ C	5.5

Source: Data from Anderson, W.: Plant fiber in foods, Lexington, KY, 1986, The HCF Diabetes Research Foundation, Inc.

to treat persons with colon disease. However, there is no evidence that our consumption of less dietary fiber than people of other countries has led to the development of colon disorders. The claims for a high-fiber diet look promising but are still under investigation. A high-fiber diet causes larger stools and more frequent bowel movements. It is also consistent with current ideas about energy conservation; that is, we should eat more cereal grains directly rather than indirectly from animal products. Foods high in fiber include bran, whole-grain breads and cereals, most fruits and vegetables, nuts, and legumes.

Sugar and Disease

There is no substantial evidence that table sugar (sucrose) intake causes hyper-activity, cardiovascular disease, cancer, or obesity. Sucrose, whether eaten in a sucker or on presweetened cereal, does not cancel the nutritive value of any food or of the total diet. However, consuming sucrose can contribute to tooth decay, so it is important to restrict intake of sticky carbohydrate foods that feed the bacteria which cause tooth decay.

Nutritionists are often asked whether sugar should be excluded from the diet. The nutrient density of the food in relationship to the total diet must be considered. If a food supplies a high proportion of nutrients in relation to the amount of energy, it is a nutrient-dense food; conversely, if it contains a high proportion of energy, or calories, in relation to the amount of nutrients, it is a calorie-dense food. For example, an orange juice ice pop is more nutrient-dense than a sugar-laden soft drink.

A person who requires large amounts of energy because of exercise or growth can consume more foods that are energy-rich or calorie-dense than a person who is sedentary. The quantity of nutrients needed by an individual remains relatively constant for the same age-sex group. Diets for the elderly and for young children, which are relatively low in kilocalories, need to contain nutrient-dense foods unless extra energy is expended.

PROTEINS

Proteins play an important role in the growth, restoration, and maintenance of body tissues. They contribute 15% of the total body weight. Proteins are made up of about 20 different chemical structures known as *amino acids*. Those manufactured in the body are identified as nonessential amino acids, whereas those supplied by proteins in animal or plant foods in the diet are known as essential amino acids. The Recommended Dietary Allowance [9] for protein is 0.8 g per kilogram (2.2 lb) or 0.36 g per pound.

All of the essential amino acids are found in a complete protein. Proteins that contain all the essential amino acids, such as those from animal sources, are known as complete proteins, or high-quality proteins. Proteins found in foods from plants lack one or more of the essential amino acids and are therefore called incomplete proteins.

Because the body can manufacture many of the amino acids, only seven or eight must come from the daily dietary intake. The consumption of protein in the United States does not appear to be below recommended levels. In fact, persons consume more protein than is needed to meet the daily recommended allowances [10,11].

Function

Unlike fat and carbohydrate, the primary function of protein is not to supply energy or heat. The principal functions of protein are for growth, maintenance and repair of body tissues, regulation of water balance, help in maintenance of the proper acid base balance within the body, and formation of enzymes, antibodies, and hormones. When sufficient carbohydrates and fats are consumed, excess protein is converted to fat and stored as fat.

Sources

Good sources of complete protein include meats, eggs, and milk. Foods that provide high-quality protein are often also high in fat. However, choosing lean cuts of beef, poultry, and pork, as well as fish, skim milk, and legumes, can provide high-quality protein with only small amounts of fat.

Complementary proteins can be formulated from plant sources to form complete proteins. Two or more foods that contain incomplete proteins and, alone, do not have all the essential amino acids, are combined to form a complete protein containing all the essential amino acids.

A mixture of proteins from grains, legumes, seeds, nuts, and vegetables eaten over the course of the day will complement one another in their amino acid profiles. It is not necessary that complementation of amino acid profiles be precise and eaten at exactly the same meal. The following food combinations supply complementary proteins:

Baked beans and brown bread	Vegetable pizza with whole wheat crust
Lentil soup with rice	Granola with cereal, nuts, and seeds
Hopping John (black-eyed peas or beans and rice)	Tamale pie with beans
	Chili with beans and crackers
Split pea soup with bread or crackers	Peanut butter sandwich

Foods containing low-quality protein are supplemented with milk, meat, and eggs that contain higher quality protein:

Iron-fortified cereal, hot or cold, with milk	Cheese vegetable casserole
Iron-fortified cereal cooked with milk	Cheese souffles
Cheese sandwich	Chili with beans and added meat
Toast and eggs	

ALCOHOL

Alcohol provides 7 kcal/g but is not considered a carbohydrate, protein, or fat. It is a drug. The Committee on Diet and Health of the National Research Council does not recommend alcohol consumption:

> It is not recommended that you drink alcohol. If you drink alcoholic beverages, limit the amount you drink in a single day to no more than two cans of beer, two small glasses of wine, or two average cocktails. Pregnant women should avoid alcoholic beverages [5,6].

Persons who consume too much alcohol increase their risk of developing heart disease, high blood pressure, chronic liver disease, some forms of cancer, neurological diseases, and nutritional deficiencies [5]. Heavy use of alcohol can lead to fatty liver, alcoholic hepatitis, and cirrhosis of the liver. The risk of cancers of the oral cavity, pharynx, esophagus, and larynx increases if the person also smokes.

Ethanol (the alcohol we drink) is produced by the fermentation of glucose in foods such as sugar, fruit, or cereal grain. For this fermentation to happen, certain enzymes in yeast must be present and oxygen must not be present.

Alcohol is not digested. It is absorbed quickly throughout the length of the gastrointestinal tract including the stomach. It is water soluble and disperses throughout the body fluids. Less than 5% is lost in the breath and urine. Because these amounts are in equilibrium with amounts in the blood, they are used as a legally valid measure of the amount in the blood. A blood concentration of 0.1% is evidence of intoxication; one of 0.4% is usually fatal. The body uses alcohol immediately as a source of energy in preference to fatty acids and glucose; alcohol therefore spares other energy sources and indirectly contributes to fat storage.

Most people are considered light drinkers when they consume 0.01 to 0.21 of an ounce (less than ¼ oz) of alcohol a day.

1 oz of whiskey (80 proof)	= 0.40 oz alcohol
1 12 oz beer	= 0.42 oz alcohol
3½ oz table wine	= 0.42 oz alcohol

A light drinker would have a beer *every other* day, while a moderate drinker would have a beer each day, and a heavy drinker at least two cocktails or two beers each day. The *Eat for Life* [6] guidelines indicate that alcohol is not to be avoided if you use it responsibly in limited amounts, but should not be used during pregnancy.

Caffeine or coffee intake does not decrease the absorption of alcohol. Alcohol may depress appetite and therefore food intake; it may displace food in the diet, thus lowering the intake of nutrients. In addition, even moderate drinking carries some risks in circumstances that require good coordination and judgment such as driving and especially caring for children.

VITAMINS

Vitamins, like minerals, do not produce energy. Unlike minerals, they are organic and contain carbon compounds; but because they usually are not broken down to carbon dioxide and water (the end products of metabolism), they provide no useful energy. The body cannot manufacture vitamins, yet vitamins are essential for life. They are needed in only small amounts. Their role is to regulate biological reactions required for normal metabolism (chemical changes involved in using nutrients for the functioning of the body) of amino acids, fats, and carbohydrates. Vitamins are used to produce energy and synthesize tissues, enzymes, hormones, and other vital compounds.

Table 1–4 groups vitamins into those soluble in fat and those soluble in water and provides major functions and sources of vitamins.

Fat-Soluble Vitamins

Fat-soluble vitamins A, D, E, and K are retained by the body. Any conditions that limit fat intake will limit the consumption of fat-soluble vitamins. No one food contains all the vitamins needed, but eating a wide variety of foods from the basic food groups, including fats and oils, will provide an adequate intake. In the past, vitamins A and D were not available in necessary quantities in the general food supply, and certain foods (for example, fluid milk and other dairy products) had to be fortified.

Vitamin A is required for bone growth, reproduction, stability of cell membranes, healthy linings of skin and mucous membranes, and visual processes. Vitamin A is essential in preventing night blindness. Vitamin A is required in direct proportion to the weight of the individual; Appendix II lists the Recommended Dietary Allowances (RDA) for each age group based on average weights.

The preformed sources of vitamin A include animal products such as butter, liver, and whole milk. Nonfat milk and margarine are often fortified with vitamin A, as are liquid skim, low-fat, and whole milk. Liquid skim and low-fat milk are fortified with the same amount of vitamin A as whole milk, although dry skim milk may not be fortified.

The body converts certain carotenoids to vitamin A. Beta carotene is often referred to as a "precursor" of vitamin A. Fruits and vegetables contain no preformed vitamin A but contain specific precursors the body converts to vitamin A. The use of foods such as dark green, yellow, and orange vegetables—greens, broccoli, and carrots—may play a role in decreasing the incidence of certain cancers in the population [5]. More research into the cancer-fighting mechanisms is needed. *Hypercarotenemia* is caused by very large intakes of beta carotene resulting in yellow-orange pigmentation of the skin. This condition is not harmful but may be seen in children who consume large amounts of carrots.

Vitamin D, also called calciferol, is important in regulating the metabolism of calcium and phosphorus. It helps in absorption of calcium and phosphorus from the intestine so that proper mineralization of the bones and teeth can proceed. Requirements for vitamin D are not specifically known, but Appendix II provides the RDA for each age group.

Vitamin D can be obtained from food and by the action of the ultraviolet rays in sunlight. Generally, if enough sun is available, deficiencies will not occur. Those persons who cannot get outside in the sun, as well as rapidly growing infants and children, need a food source of vitamin D. Fish-liver oils, egg yolk, liver, cream, fatty fish, and fortified milk and margarine are sources. Growing children who follow strict vegan diets (without milk) risk insufficient vitamin D

Table 1–4   Major functions and sources of selected vitamins.

Vitamins	Functions	Sources
Fat-soluble Vitamins		
A	Promotes normal growth of bones, epithelial cells,[*] and tooth enamel; aids in visual adaptation	Liver, kidney, butter, cream, egg yolk, deep yellow and green leafy vegetables, orange fruits and vegetables
D	Regulates absorption and use of calcium and phosphorus; aids in building and maintaining bones and teeth	Direct exposure of the skin to sunlight, fortified milk, margarine, cereals and breads, fish liver oils, small amounts in egg yolk, butter, liver and some fish such as tuna, salmon, herring, sardines
E	Serves as an antioxidant[†] to reduce the oxidation of vitamin A, unsaturated fatty acids, and vitamin C; helps prevent bursting of red blood cells	Germs of grains, vegetable oils such as corn, soybean, cottonseed, safflower, and coconut; margarine; dark green leafy vegetables; nuts; legumes
K	Required for synthesis of prothrombin needed in normal blood clotting	Main source is synthesized by the intestinal flora; alfalfa, dark green leafy vegetables, liver, egg yolk
Water-soluble Vitamins		
Ascorbic acid (vitamin C)	Promotes formation and maintenance of bone matrix, cartilage, dentin, collagen, and connective tissue; cell wall integrity; acts in metabolic processes of some amino acids; absorption and use of iron; conversion of folic acid into its active form, folinic acid	Citrus fruits and juices, cantaloupe, strawberries, kiwi, grapefruit, watermelon, tomatoes, cabbage, green leafy vegetables, broccoli, green peppers, cauliflower, turnips, fresh potatoes
Thiamin (vitamin B_1)	Coenzyme[‡] required in carbohydrate metabolism for energy production	Whole-grain products, enriched rice, legumes, nuts, liver, pork, green leafy vegetables

[*]Cells that line the surfaces of cavities and tubes in the body.

[†]Inhibitor of reactions promoted by oxygen.

[‡]Small molecule that works with an enzyme to promote the enzyme's activity.

[§]Large protein molecules that help with the formation of chemical bonds.

[‖]Fat-related substances that contain sterols. Sterols are compounds composed of carbon, hydrogen, and oxygen atoms arranged in rings with side chains attached.

[#]Formation of glycogen, which is the storage form of carbohydrate in animals.

[**]Amino acids are building blocks of protein.

Table 1–4   (Continued)

Vitamins	Functions	Sources
Riboflavin (vitamin B$_2$)	Part of the enzymes[§] and coenzymes that accept transfer hydrogen during metabolism; aids in the production of corticosteroids[‖] in the adrenal cortex, the formation of red blood cells in bone marrow, glycogenesis,[#] breakdown of fatty acids	Milk, cheese, eggs, enriched breads and whole grains, green leafy vegetables, fish, organ meats, lean meats, yeast
Niacin (nicotinic acid)	Constituent of coenzymes[‡] involved in the metabolism of carbohydrate, fat, and protein	Yeast, wheat germ, whole grains, soybeans, corn, peanuts, meat, liver, kidney
Pyridoxine (vitamin B$_6$)	Required for metabolism of amino acids[**] and use of carbon dioxide, amino, and sulfur groups	Yeast, wheat germ, whole grains, soybeans, corn, peanuts, meat, liver, kidney
Folacin (folic acid)	Required for blood cell formation; coenzyme for use of carbon and hydrogen	Dark green leafy vegetables, mushrooms, organ meats, whole grains, yeast, legumes, orange juice, lemons, bananas, strawberries, cantaloupe, asparagus, lima beans
Vitamin B$_{12}$	Necessary for normal growth, maintenance of healthy nervous tissue, and for normal blood formation; concerned with metabolism that involves single-carbon units; aids in providing energy for the central nervous system; converts folacin into active form	Liver, kidney, meat, fish, poultry, eggs, milk and milk products; primarily found in animal products
Biotin	Required in enzyme systems involving carbon dioxide; releases energy from carbohydrate and fatty acids; metabolizes fatty acids; deaminates protein	Liver, yeast, cauliflower, nuts, chocolate, legumes, egg yolk, milk
Pantothenic acid	Component of coenzyme A for energy metabolism and steroid and cholesterol synthesis	Liver, kidney, yeast, egg yolk, peanuts, whole grains, lean beef, milk, potatoes, tomatoes, broccoli, fish, poultry, legumes; smaller amounts in other fruits and vegetables

intake, but selection of fortified soy milk and other foods can ensure an adequate supply.

Vitamin E protects vitamins A and C and unsaturated fatty acids from oxidation, a process in which oxygen reacts with and destroys these substances. It is therefore called an *antioxidant*. According to the Committee on Diet and Health from the Food and Nutrition Board [5] even though countless newspaper and magazine stories have touted vitamin E supplements as an effective cancer-preventive measure, studies fail to find any connection between the amount of vitamin E people eat and their risk for cancer.

Vitamin E and polyunsaturated fatty acids are present in the same foods, so increasing the amount eaten of one will increase the other. Vitamin E is found in vegetable and seed oils, shortening, egg yolk, margarine, butter, whole grains, and green leafy vegetables.

Vitamin K is associated with blood clotting. Deficiencies are uncommon except in newborn, especially premature, infants, whose intestinal tracts are free of bacteria (a source of the vitamin) and who must rely on maternal stores. The main sources are intestinal bacteria and foods such as dark green vegetables, wheat bran, soybeans, cauliflower, and tomatoes.

Water-Soluble Vitamins

B vitamins are found in many foods. Because many of the B vitamins are found in combination with one another as well as with other nutrients such as protein and minerals, a deficiency of one B vitamin is rare. There are eight B vitamins: thiamin, riboflavin, niacin, and pantothenic acid are involved primarily in the energy-releasing function of the body, whereas biotin is used for energy storage, pyridoxine for protein metabolism, and folate and B_{12} for blood manufacturing. Each of the B vitamins is involved in many complex steps in the metabolic processes of the body.

The RDA for each B vitamin is listed in Appendix II, and food sources are shown in Table 1–4. In general, the B vitamins associated with releasing energy are needed in larger quantities by persons who have higher energy intakes. B vitamin deficiencies caused by lack of dietary intake are rare today.

Another water-soluble vitamin, vitamin C, or ascorbic acid, is found in many drink mixes and gelatin products in a form chemically identical to the vitamin C found in citrus fruits and many vegetables. Although all water-soluble vitamins can be lost from the diet if the cooking juices are not retained, vitamin C is the most unstable. It can be destroyed by copper cookware, heat, and especially alkaline solutions. Vitamin C is oxidized in the air and preserves or protects other substances. In this manner, it prevents fruits from turning brown during food processing.

Scurvy, rarely seen today, is the well-known deficiency disease associated with inadequate vitamin C in the diet. Its symptoms include pinpoint hemorrhages or bleeding under the skin along with weakness. Vitamin C is, therefore, believed to be needed for proper functioning of connective tissue, the intercellular cement that holds body tissue together and helps support it. In addition, when taken with iron-rich foods vitamin C facilitates the absorption of iron. The other exact roles of vitamin C are not completely understood; however, 3% of the population have been found recently to have low serum levels of vitamin C. This vitamin will be monitored in the future [10].

The mean intake reported [11,12] is over 125% of the RDA for both children and adults. Most people have little difficulty acquiring the adult recommended amount of 60 mg because many foods are fortified with vitamin C. Citrus fruits are the best sources, along with broccoli, cantaloupe, and greens. See Table 1–4 for additional sources. Smokers should take additional foods high in vitamin C (100 mg) because smoking seems to affect the metabolism of vitamin C, and serum levels are lower in smokers [9].

Foods eaten for their water-soluble vitamins should be handled carefully. If possible, vegetables should be steamed to preserve water-soluble vitamins, or the liquid should be used in gravies and soups. Vegetables should be cooked for short periods to retain full nutritional value.

Toxicity

Excessive intakes of water-soluble vitamins are excreted in the urine and present little problem of toxicity. However, a number of adverse effects have been reported from excessive (greater than 1 g/day) intake of vitamin C [13]. Fat-soluble vitamins, especially vitamin A, are more likely to cause toxicity because the excess will be stored in the body and can reach dangerous levels.

MINERALS

A mineral is technically defined as an inorganic element containing no carbon that remains as ash when food is burned. Minerals cannot be broken down any further. As many as 40 kinds of minerals may exist, but only 17 are known to be essential to human nutrition (see Table 1–5).

Minerals comprise only 4% of total body weight. Macrominerals are required in relatively large amounts, whereas trace elements, or microminerals, are needed in very small amounts. The macrominerals are calcium, phosphorus, potassium, magnesium, sulfur, sodium, and chlorine. Iron, zinc, selenium, molybdenum, iodine, cobalt, copper, manganese, fluorine, and chromium are microminerals.

Mineral functions can be classified as either structural or regulatory. Structural minerals are part of cell tissues or substances. Regulatory minerals help regulate acid-base balance, muscle contractibility, and nerve irritability and also act in coenzyme systems.

An important consideration today is whether the increased consumption of processed and refined foods in which the trace element concentrations have been reduced or altered will eventually lead to major disease problems. No evidence exists that this has been the case.

Table 1–5 Major functions and sources of selected minerals.

Minerals	Functions	Sources
Macrominerals		
Calcium	Strengthens structure of bones and teeth; promotes clotting of blood; promotes water balance; plays a role in the contraction and relaxation of muscle fibers and transmission of nerve impulses; maintains the function of the cell membrane	Milk and milk products, green leafy vegetables, clams, oysters, legumes, almonds, sesame seeds, broccoli, water, dried beans
Phosphorus	Involved in calcification of teeth and bones; acid-base balance; energy metabolism	Liver, meat, eggs, fish, poultry, milk, dairy products, whole grains, legumes, nuts, refined cereals
Magnesium	Catalyst to biological reactions within the cell; aids in the regulation of nerve impulses and muscle contraction	Whole grains, legumes, nuts, green leafy vegetables, meat, molasses, soybeans, cocoa
Sulfur	Component of protein, thiamin, and biotin; involved in oxidation-reduction reactions; activates many enzymes; participates in several detoxification reactions	Meat, eggs, dairy products, nuts, legumes
Sodium	Promotes acid-base balance, water balance, nerve and muscle activity	Table salt, leavenings, monosodium glutamate, soy sauce, condiments, milk, cheese, eggs, sauerkraut, cured ham, fish, water, green leafy vegetables
Potassium	Catalyst in many biological reactions, especially protein synthesis and glycogen formation; promotes water balance, nerve and muscle activity	Bananas, dates, apricots, oranges, cantaloupe, tomatoes, dark green leafy vegetables, liver, meat, milk, fish, bamboo shoots, prunes
Chlorine	Provides hydrochloric acid of gastric juice; acid-base balance; activity of muscles and nerves; water balance	Table salt, egg yolk, meat, cereals, legumes, water
Microminerals		
Iron	Carrier of oxygen and carbon dioxide; constituent of hemoglobin in blood and myoglobin in muscles; required element for many enzymes	Organ meats, meat, oysters, leafy green vegetables, legumes, enriched cereals, dried apricots, prunes, peaches, raisins, egg yolk, nuts, whole grains
Iodine	Part of thyroxine, a thyroid hormone that influences growth and rate of metabolism	Iodized table salt, seafood, water, milk, cheese, eggs (if the animal's diet is high in iodine)

Table 1–5   (Continued)

Minerals	Functions	Sources
Manganese	Essential for normal bone development; activates enzymes; temperature regulation, nerve and muscle activity, and protein synthesis; enhances thiamin storage in the body	Whole grains, legumes, nuts, green leafy vegetables, meat, tea, coffee
Copper	Required for use of iron and enzymes in energy metabolism; necessary in the formation of nerve walls and connective tissue	Liver, shellfish, nuts, legumes, mushrooms, whole-grain cereals, gelatin
Zinc	Constituent of hormones and insulin; promotes enzyme activity in metabolism; associated with wound healing; mobilizes vitamin A from liver stores	Seafood, liver, meat, wheat germ, yeast, legumes
Fluorine	Provides resistance to development of dental caries	Water and beverages prepared with water, naturally occurring or fluoridated
Chromium	Required for metabolism of blood glucose, fatty acid synthesis, insulin metabolism	Meat, whole grains, corn oil
Selenium	Antioxidant; substitutes for some of the functions of vitamin E	Seafood, meats, grains
Molybdenum	Aids in oxidation reactions	Organ meats, legumes, whole-grain cereals
Cobalt	Aids in maturation of red blood cells (as part of vitamin B_{12} molecule)	Organ meats

Macrominerals

Calcium.   "Maintain adequate calcium intake" is one of the dietary guidelines recommended by the Committee on Diet and Health [5] to reduce risk of loss of bone mass. Osteoporosis is related to low calcium intakes. Since human bones reach their maximum mass at about age 25 to 30, children, teenagers, and young adults must get calcium-rich foods throughout these years.

Calcium is found in the body in amounts larger than any other mineral; it is found primarily in the bones and teeth, where it is part of the hard structure. A specific level of calcium is required in tissues and blood. If this level falls, the body takes calcium from bones to restore the tissue and blood levels. Calcium in the tissues and blood acts as a cementing substance, holding cells together, and is used to transmit nerve impulses, to control the movement of substances into and out of cells, and to regulate muscle contractions. Calcium also is used in the blood-clotting mechanism and in the absorption of B_{12}. Factors that make calcium more available to the body:

- Need increases absorption, e.g. pregnancy
- Small amounts taken throughout the day
- Presence of lactose, a milk sugar in milk
- Vitamin D present in the diet
- Acid conditions in the stomach

Factors that hinder calcium availability:

- A high-protein diet may cause calcium to be excreted
- Lack of physical exercise in persons confined to bed
- Phytic and oxalic acids, which bind calcium
- Excessive dietary fat may move calcium through the body too rapidly for absorption

Phytates are present in whole-grain cereals, oxalates in foods such as greens, rhubarb, and chocolate, but harmful effects of these substances depend on the quantity consumed. Fortunately, dietary calcium is plentiful, especially in dairy products, compared with the amounts of phytic and oxalic acid. Chocolate milk is a rich source of calcium; it can be low in fat and has been shown not to promote tooth decay, so serve chocolate milk for variety in the center.

The need for calcium remains throughout life, with the highest intake (1200 mg) required for the female to 25 years of age. The adult (25–51) RDA [9] is 800 mg, the quantity usually obtained from two glasses of milk and a variety of other foods. Milk and dairy products are the best sources of calcium; broccoli, okra, dried beans, and peas are other sources of the mineral.

Osteoporosis and osteomalacia are two bone abnormalities related to calcium. Osteoporosis is a loss in total amount of bone, and osteomalacia is the loss of calcium and phosphorus crystals from the bone. Adequate consumption of food high in calcium in childhood and adolescence appears to be needed not only for growth and development, but possibly to assure high bone density and greater latitude for maintenance of skeletal integrity in the face of bone loss in later years. Calcium is withdrawn from bone and excreted after menopause.

Older adults absorb less calcium than younger adults. In general, children in the United States consume the recommended allowance of calcium. However, women 18 years and older have been shown to consume less than the recommended allowance [12].

Women start to lose calcium around 30 years of age. This process is accelerated in women right before and after menopause. The use of estrogen after menopause seems to stop the bone loss completely. Without estrogen therapy, women during menopause and after can take calcium plus vitamin D supplementation to possibly slow bone loss [5,6].

Phosphorus.   Like calcium, phosphorus is found in large amounts in bones and teeth. This mineral gives rigidity to bones and teeth and performs more functions than any other mineral element in normal cell metabolism and functioning.

Phosphorus is involved in the metabolism of carbohydrate, fat, and protein. It is part of many enzyme systems and plays an important role in the energy metabolism of muscle.

Requirements for phosphorus are the same as those for calcium. Consuming large amounts of antacids may interfere with phosphorus absorption and result in phosphorus depletion. An equal intake of calcium and phosphorus is recommended.

Sources of phosphorus include foods containing calcium and protein. Persons generally need to be more concerned about getting enough calcium than phosphorus. Soft drinks are often overlooked as sources of phosphorus, and frequent intake of these beverages can disrupt the body's calcium-phosphorus balance.

Sodium.   The principal element in extracellular fluids, sodium is involved primarily in regulating the acid-base balance in body fluids. Along with potassium, it is important in regulating the body fluid volume. The cells work to keep sodium on the outside of the cell membrane (extracellular) and potassium on the inside (intracellular). If the amount of sodium in the blood changes, the fluid balance of the body is affected.

Many Americans regularly eat more than 2 teaspoons of salt per day (2400 mg sodium). A safe and adequate supply for adults is less than 1 teaspoon of salt (1200 mg sodium). The sodium or salt described here is that included in foods as well as the salt added to foods after preparation.

There is no RDA for sodium. The kidneys conserve sodium, filtering any excess from the blood into the urine. Too much sodium may lead to an increase in blood volume and extra pressure on the arteries, causing the heart to work harder to pump blood and the blood pressure to rise in persons who are particularly sensitive to sodium. Excessive intake of sodium, primarily from table salt (sodium chloride), has been implicated in hypertension (higher blood pressure) but only for those who have been shown to be sensitive to sodium. There is some evidence that excessive consumption of salt-preserved or salt-pickled foods increases the risk of stomach cancer. Some evidence links salt intake itself to stomach cancer, although the evidence is not as persuasive as the connection between high salt intake and hypertension [5]. The Dietary Guidelines for Americans [7] recommends using sodium "in moderation."

The *Diet and Health* [5] guidelines state:

> Limit the amount of salt (sodium chloride) that you eat to 6 grams (slightly more than 1 teaspoon of salt) per day or less. Limit the use of salt in cooking and avoid adding it to food at the table. Salty foods, including highly processed salty foods, salt-preserved foods, and salt-pickled foods, should be eaten sparingly, if at all.

Sodium is found naturally in greater quantities in animal foods than in plant foods (Figure 1–4). Cured meats, sausages, canned soups and vegetables, soy sauce, and steak sauces have a high sodium content. Salting of food at the table is unnecessary, except for the athlete who has just lost water and sodium through perspiration. Because over-the-counter drugs may also be a source of sodium, labels should be read carefully.

Figure 1–4   Control sodium levels by limiting use of table salt.

Potassium.   Potassium is an essential mineral that maintains intracellular fluid balance. It is a component of lean body tissue. The need for potassium increases during growth of lean tissue. Potassium is lost when muscle breaks down because of starvation, protein deficiency, or injury. Nerve and muscle cells are rich in potassium. Sodium and potassium ions exchange places during nerve transmission and muscle contraction. Therefore, they keep the heart beating regularly. Several studies have shown that groups of people who eat low-potassium diets have an increased incidence of high blood pressure and heart disease. Diets high in potassium and low in sodium can lower blood pressure. An intake of 3.5 g/day of potassium is associated with lower blood pressure and fewer deaths from strokes [6]. Extreme dieting (liquid-protein diets) may lead to loss of potassium and can cause heart abnormalities.

There is no RDA for potassium, and the daily intake may range from 1900 to 5600 mg. Sources include fruits and vegetables, such as bananas, tomatoes, citrus juices, and potatoes. Following the Food Guide as recommended in the Dietary Guidelines for Americans and consuming five servings of fruits and vegetables will provide all the potassium necessary [7].

Trace Elements

Iron.   Iron is probably one of the most widely known elements. Certain populations in the United States, including children, have an iron intake less than the recommended level [9]. Iron is found in the blood as part of hemoglobin in red blood cells and myoglobin in muscle tissue. Its best-known task is in providing oxygen to the cells of the body. It is also part of enzyme systems.

Iron must be absorbed to be usable. Absorption is enhanced by acids and the presence of vitamin C. When there is a physiological need for iron and when iron is presented in a certain chemical form, it is absorbed more readily. Iron from meats, fish, and poultry, called *heme iron,* is more readily absorbed than the nonheme iron of plant origin found in vegetables, legumes, and grains. As with calcium, phytic acid, found in bran, binds iron and forms an insoluble complex that is difficult to absorb. At current levels of fiber consumption, decreased absorption because of phytates and oxalates is not a problem [14]. Likewise, fiber may cause food to move through the intestinal tract too quickly, reducing the time needed for complete digestion of foods and iron absorption.

Women need 15 mg per day and men 10 mg. Pregnant women need more iron (see Appendix II). Iron-deficiency anemia may be seen in young children after 6 months of age and in adolescents, especially girls. A low iron intake can lead to iron-deficiency anemia, which lowers the blood's oxygen-carrying capacity.

Good sources of iron include liver and other organ meats, red meat, whole-grain or enriched and fortified cereals, oysters, clams, dried beans, some fruits, and dark green vegetables. Although the iron from plant sources is poorly absorbed, absorption can be increased by eating a small amount of meat and eating foods high in vitamin C with the meal.

Iodine.   Iodine is necessary for the proper functioning of the thyroid gland; without iodine, the thyroid enlarges to capture what little iodine is available in the blood. This enlargement, or goiter, is seen as a swelling in the neck.

The RDA for iodine is 150 μg per day for adults. The major source of iodine is iodized salt. Seafood also contains iodine, and iodine is used by some manufacturers as a dough conditioner. Although iodized salt costs a penny or two more than the noniodized form, this small investment goes a long way toward preventing goiter, especially when seafood is not eaten frequently.

Zinc.   Present in every tissue, zinc is essential as a component for enzymes involved in vital metabolic pathways. It is necessary for normal growth, prevention of anemia, general repair of all tissues, and wound healing.

The RDA is 15 mg for adult males and 10 mg for females (Appendix II). Zinc deficiency has been noted in children, and it appears that regular intake of zinc through diet, particularly during periods of growth and stress, is necessary. Sources include red meats, milk, liver, poultry, eggs, fish, and seafood, especially shellfish.

Selenium.   Selenium is a trace element that has recently been studied as the underlying condition predisposing people to the development of a cardiomyopathy called Keshan disease, affecting Chinese children. It also is related to the destruction of hydroperoxide and is related to the metabolic activity of the antioxidant vitamin E. The RDA for selenium has just been established, and food sources include seafood, kidney and liver and to a lesser extent other meats [9].

WATER

Water is an extremely important nutrient. For a child, the proportion of body surface area to body mass is much larger than for an adult; thus, children need proportionately more fluid. The water lost by evaporation from the young child accounts for more than 60% of that needed to maintain the body compared with 45% for the adult. However, it is difficult to determine how much water a child needs, because surface area, activity, and other foods consumed are all contributing factors.

Adults lose about 1½ quarts (1.4 L) of fluid per day through urine, feces, and perspiration. At least this much should be replaced from food and beverages each day. A greater quantity of liquids should be taken frequently in warm weather or during strenuous exercise. Anyone who refuses liquids, is vomiting, or has diarrhea can rapidly become dehydrated. Water is also important for proper elimination. One of the first factors to be considered when a child or adult complains of constipation is the amount of fluids consumed. A recommended practice for anyone is to drink 1 to 2 quarts or liters of liquids per day (Figure 1–5).

Figure 1–5
It is important to drink an adequate amount of water each day.
Photo courtesy of The NutraSweet Company.

SUPPLEMENTS

There are few, if any, quick solutions to gaining and maintaining good health. "Popping pills" appears an easy solution to losing weight or making up nutrients missed in dietary intake. However, benefits are largely unproven. Nutrients function together; therefore, an excess intake of one may create a greater need for others. In addition, the use of pills is inappropriate modeling behavior for persons involved with young children. Unless a specific deficiency has been diagnosed in laboratory and clinical tests, the habitual intake of large doses of vitamins and minerals should be discouraged [6,9].

"Avoid taking dietary supplements in excess." [6] For healthy people eating a varied diet, a single daily dose of a multiple vitamin-mineral supplement containing 100% of the RDAs is not known to be either harmful or beneficial. High-potency vitamin and mineral supplements should be avoided. These include protein powders, single amino acids, fiber, and lecithin.

Many organizations including the American Dietetic Association [15] recommend no vitamin or mineral supplement for healthy people eating a varied diet. Those persons who may need supplements include women with excessive menstrual bleeding; women who are pregnant or breast-feeding; people with very low caloric intakes; some vegetarians; newborns; and people with certain disorders or diseases or who are taking medications that may interfere with nutrient intake, digestion, absorption, metabolism, or excretion.

SUMMARY

- Nutrition is the science of food and how it is used by the body. The study of nutrition involves the social, economic, cultural, and emotional factors that affect the intake of food.
- There are six classes of nutrients with specialized functions in the body.
- Dietary fat, carbohydrate, and protein are major nutrients that have specific functions but also supply heat, or energy, to the body.
- Each of the nutrients is found in a wide variety of foods. Therefore, the wider the variety of foods one eats, the more likely the diet will contain all essential nutrients.
- HDL and LDL cholesterol are related to heart disease and may be altered by diet.
- Consider activity when calculating energy needs. Increasing exercise may allow for an intake of more food.
- Alcohol contributes 7 kcal/g and may affect dietary intake.
- Supplementing the diet with large amounts of vitamins and minerals is not advisable. Megadoses of specific nutrients should be prescribed only after appropriate clinical and laboratory tests confirm the need.

- Applying the basic principles of nutrition to your personal diet provides experience in learning what factors to evaluate in diets of children in the center, and practicing good nutrition principles helps care providers to be good role models for parents and children.

DISCUSSION QUESTIONS

1. Describe the nature, functions, and use of the essential nutrients.
2. Which of the nutrients supply energy to the body, and which one supplies energy most efficiently?
3. In addition to the specific nutrients found in foods, which other factors must be considered when the subject of nutrition is studied?
4. Are there consequences of exceeding nutrient requirements?
5. Why should you as a care provider practice the principles of good nutrition?
6. What is the role of alcohol in the diet?
7. Should I be concerned about the amount and kind of fat in my diet?
8. Has the government promoted the development of new food products by industry?
9. Name at least two culturally diverse foods you have eaten not included in the text that would be classified as high-fat and low-fat.

REFERENCES

1. Diabetes Education Care and Practice Group: Ethnic and regional food practices, a series: Chinese-American food practices, 1990; Navajo food practices, 1991; Mexican American food practices, 1989; Jewish food practices, 1989, Chicago, 1990, Am Diet Assn and Am Diabetes Assn.
2. WHO (World Health Organization): Energy and protein requirements, Report of a Joint FAO/WHO/UN Expert Consultation, Technical Report Series 724, Geneva, 1985, World Health Organization.
3. Rolfes, Sharon R., and DeBruyne, Linda K.: Life span nutrition: conception through life, St. Paul, 1990, West Publishing Co.
4. Whitney, Eleanor N., Hamilton, Eva M. N., et al.: Understanding nutrition, ed. 5, St. Paul, 1991, West Publishing Co.
5. National Research Council: Diet and health: implications for reducing chronic disease risk, Report of the Committee on Diet and Health,

Food and Nutrition Board, Commission on Life Sciences, Washington, DC, 1989, National Academy Press.
6. Institute on Medicine, Committee on Diet and Health, Food and Nutrition Board: Eat for life: the food and nutrition board's guide to reducing your risk of chronic disease, Woteki, C.E., and Thomas, P.R. (editors), Washington, DC, 1992, National Academy Press.
7. U.S. Department of Agriculture and U.S. Department of Health and Human Services: Nutrition and your health: dietary guidelines for Americans, Home and Garden Bulletin No. 228, Washington, DC, 1990, U.S. Government Printing Office.
8. U.S. Department of Health and Human Services, Public Health Service: Healthy people 2000: health promotion and disease prevention objectives, Washington, DC, 1990, U.S. Government Printing Office.

9. National Research Council, Subcommittee on the 10th Edition of the RDAs, Food and Nutrition Board, Commission on Life Sciences, Recommended dietary allowances, Washington. DC, 1989, National Academy Press.

10. Public Health Service, National Center for Health Statistics: DHHS-USDA nutrition monitoring in the United States—a progress report from the Joint Nutrition Monitoring Evaluation Committee, DHHS Pub. No. (PHS) 86-1255, Hyattsville, MD, 1986, Department of Health and Human Services.

11. U.S. Department of Agriculture Nationwide Food Consumption Survey: Continuing survey of food intakes by individuals. Men 19–50 years, 1 day, 1985, Report No. 85-3, Nutrition Monitoring Division, Human Nutrition Information Service, Hyattsville, MD, 1987, U.S. Department of Agriculture.

12. U.S. Department of Agriculture Nationwide Food Consumption Survey: Continuing survey of food intakes by individuals. Women 19–50 years and their children 1–5 years, 4 days, 1985, Report No. 85-4, Nutrition Monitoring Division, Human Nutrition Information Service, Hyattsville, MD, 1987, U.S. Department of Agriculture

13. Rivers, J. M.: Safety of high-level vitamin C ingestion, Ann. N. Y. Acad. Sci. 498:445–454, 1987.

14. Whitney, E. N., Cataldo, C. B., and Rolfes, S. R., Understanding normal and clinical nutrition, ed. 3, St Paul, 1991, West Publishing Co.

15. American Dietetic Association: Recommendations concerning supplement usage: ADA statement, 87:1342–1343, 1987.

2

Foods for Health

LEARNING OBJECTIVES

Students will be able to:
- Describe tools to promote health and prevent disease:
    Dietary Guidelines for Americans
    A Guide to Daily Food Choices
    National Health Promotion and Disease Prevention Objectives
    Recommended Dietary Allowances
    Labels
- Evaluate dietary and exercise patterns using forms provided.
- Write a vegetarian diet using favorite foods.
- Explain when exercise should not be used for preschoolers.

Since the last edition of this textbook, a consensus regarding dietary guidelines has been reached. Although individual groups still promote guidelines for specific needs, the following sections summarize general guidelines for promoting health and preventing disease through sound nutrition and exercise principles.

GUIDES AND STANDARDS

The U.S. Department of Agriculture (USDA) and the U.S. Department of Health and Human Services (DHHS) have been involved in and supportive of efforts to encourage changes in certain eating habits. Health problems such as obesity, heart disease, and cancer have been linked to overconsumption of foods containing certain nutrients. Many health professionals believe that the public needs guidance in avoiding excessive consumption of foods with nutrients that appear to be implicated in these disease states.

Dietary Guidelines for Americans

The Dietary Guidelines for Americans provide the following general recommendations:

- Eat a variety of foods.
- Maintain desirable weight.
- Choose a diet low in fat, saturated fat, and cholesterol.
- Choose a diet with plenty of vegetables, fruits, and grain products.
- Use sugar only in moderation.
- Use sodium in moderation.
- If you drink alcoholic beverages, do so in moderation [1].

The publication also includes a Guide to Daily Food Choices [2]. This Guide has been developed to integrate and replace other food guides such as the Basic

Four Food Guide and provides specific amounts of food from food groups to help plan a diet for an individual or a group.

A Guide to Daily Food Choices

The Guide to Daily Food Choices was developed because not every food contains all the nutrients necessary for life. For example, milk approximates the perfect food, but even it has less fiber, vitamin C, and iron than recommended for children or adults.

The U.S. Department of Agriculture, in order to help consumers remember the Guide, developed a Food Guide Pyramid (Figure 2–1). In this text the term *Food Guide* will be used when referring to the Guide to Daily Food Choices.

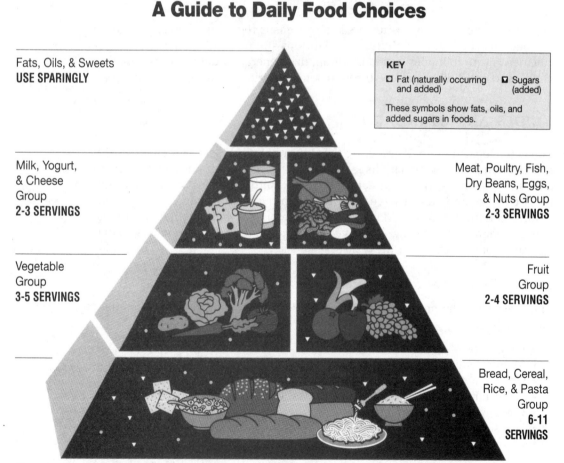

Food Guide Pyramid
A Guide to Daily Food Choices

Fats, Oils, & Sweets
USE SPARINGLY

KEY
▫ Fat (naturally occurring and added)   ◪ Sugars (added)
These symbols show fats, oils, and added sugars in foods.

Milk, Yogurt, & Cheese Group
2-3 SERVINGS

Meat, Poultry, Fish, Dry Beans, Eggs, & Nuts Group
2-3 SERVINGS

Vegetable Group
3-5 SERVINGS

Fruit Group
2-4 SERVINGS

Bread, Cereal, Rice, & Pasta Group
6-11 SERVINGS

Figure 2–1   The Food Guide Pyramid.
Source: U.S. Department of Agriculture/U.S. Department of Health and Human Services.

The Pyramid has been developed to help consumers plan a nutritionally sound diet and to promote good eating habits among children and adults. The pyramid illustrates at a glance the food groups that should be included in a healthful diet and in what proportions.

The bread, cereal, rice, and pasta group is at the base of the pyramid and should be the basis of the diet. Grain-based foods are rich in complex carbohydrates including fiber, vitamins, and minerals, and should make up the bulk of the diet in six to eleven servings per day. The phrase "five a day" is used frequently to refer to the five fruits and vegetables that are next on the list of priorities. Depending on your age, from two to three servings from the dairy products group and meat and meat alternates group are recommended. Fats, oils, and sweets take up the least space at the pyramid's narrower tip because they should be given lowest priority in a healthful meal plan. The Food Guide has been modified in this text to reflect updated knowledge and information for vegetarians and those who do not consume milk. Figure 2–2 provides serving sizes for adults.

Table 2–1 gives suggested daily servings for meal plans for a variety of special preferences (no meat, no milk, and no legumes). It is important to choose a variety of foods from each food group. To ensure adequate intake of all nutri-

Figure 2–2 What counts as a serving?

Bread, Cereal, Rice, & Pasta: 6–11

- 1 slice of bread
- 1 oz of ready-to-cook cereal
- ½ C of cooked cereal, rice, or pasta
- 3 or 4 small plain crackers

Vegetables: 3–5

- 1 C of raw leafy vegetables
- ½ C of other vegetables, cooked or chopped raw
- ¾ C of vegetable juice

Fruits: 2–4

- 1 medium apple, banana, or orange
- ½ C of chopped, cooked, or canned fruit
- ¾ C of fruit juice

Milk, Yogurt, and Cheese: 2–3

- 1 C of milk or yogurt
- 1½ oz of natural cheese
- 2 oz of process cheese

Meat, Poultry, Fish, Dry Beans, Eggs, & Nuts: 2–3

- 2–3 oz of cooked lean meat, poultry, or fish
- ½ C of cooked dry beans, or 1 egg.

Table 2–1 Guide to Daily Food Choices modified for special preferences.

Food Group (quantity/serving)	Recommended (servings/day)	No. Meat (servings/day)	No. Milk (servings/day)	No. Legumes (servings/day)
Vegetables	3–5	4–5	3–4	3–4
½ C dark green	1	1½	3	2
½ C other	2	3	0	1
Fruit	2–4	3	3	3
¾ C vitamin C-rich juice	1	1	1	1
½ C canned fruit		1	1	1
1 medium fresh fruit	1	1	1	1
Whole-grain Cereal	6–11	9	6	6
1 slice bread				
1 oz cereal				
Milk	2–3	2	0	2
8 oz milk or yogurt				
1 oz cheese				
1½ C cottage cheese				
Meat and Alternates	2–3	3	5	3
Animal sources		0	3	3
3 oz meat, poultry, fish				
1 egg				
Legumes/Nuts		3	2	0
2 tbsp peanut butter				
½ C lentils or beans				
1 oz nuts				

ents, the dietary plans emphasize multiple servings of whole-grain cereals, green and yellow vegetables, and legumes.

Vitamin E, vitamin B_6, magnesium, zinc, and folacin should be included in the diet in greater quantities now that the Food Guide is based upon more servings from the fruits, vegetables, and grains [3]. Table 2–2 shows good food sources of these nutrients.

Only whole-grain breads and cereals are included in calculations for the Guide to Daily Food Choices for this text. Many bread and cereal products have been "enriched" in order to replace nutrients found in the bran portion of whole-grain cereals that is removed during the milling process. Enriched rice and bread have substantial quantities of iron, thiamin, riboflavin, and niacin vitamins. However, fiber and other vitamins and minerals are more abundant in whole-grain products than in enriched products (Appendix I).

Table 2–2   Good sources of vitamin E, vitamin B$_6$, magnesium, zinc, and folacin

Vitamin E (>2.0 IU/ serving*)	Vitamin B$_6$ (>0.2 mg/ serving)	Magnesium (>20 mg/ serving)	Zinc (>1.0 mg/ serving)	Folacin (>25 µg/ serving)
Nuts	Meat, poultry,	Milk	Milk	Liver
Vegetable oils	fish	Meat, fish	Meat, poultry	Beans
Wheat germ	Legumes	Nuts	Seafood	Leafy greens
Leafy greens	Wheat germ	Legumes	Legumes	Asparagus
		Leafy greens	Whole-grain	Broccoli
		Wheat germ	cereals	
		Wheat cereal	Wheat germ	

*A serving equals 3 oz meat, poultry, fish; 2 eggs; ¾ C cooked beans or legumes; 1 oz nuts; ¾ C cooked vegetables or 1 C raw; 1 C milk; 1 tbsp wheat germ; 1 oz dry cereal; ¾ C cooked cereal or pasta; 1 slice bread; 1 tbsp vegetable oil.

Source: Modified from King, J. C., Cohenour, S. H., Corruccini, C. G., et al.: Evaluation and modification of the basic four food guide, J. Nutr. Educ., 10:27–29, 1978.

National Health Objectives for the Year 2000

Nutrition-related objectives are included among the 297 objectives for the country published in *Healthy People 2000* [4]. The Dietary Guidelines for Americans are reflected in the nutrition objectives. The national objectives are statements about changing and improving health behaviors including food and nutrition behaviors. Certain population groups such as children, pregnant women, and women who breastfeed are targeted for behavior change. Organizations such as child-care centers are encouraged to participate in health promotion activities by focusing on key areas of concern.

The following are examples of objectives that relate to the Dietary Guidelines for Americans. Those objectives relating specifically to the child will be included in the respective chapters.

Eat a Variety of Foods

- Increase to at least 90% the proportion of school lunch and breakfast services and child care food services with menus that are consistent with the nutrition principles in the Dietary Guidelines for Americans.
- Increase to at least 85% the proportion of people aged 18 and older who use food labels to make nutritious food selections. (Baseline: 74% used labels to make food selections in 1988.)
- Increase calcium intake so at least 50% of youth aged 12 through 24 and 50% of pregnant and lactating women consume three or more servings daily of foods rich in calcium, and at least 50% of people aged 25 and older consume two or more servings daily. (Baseline: 7% of women, 14% of men aged 19 through 24, and 24% of pregnant and lactating women consumed three or

Eat a variety of foods.
Photo courtesy of USDA.

more servings, and 15% of women and 23% of men aged 25 through 50 consumed two or more servings in 1985–86.)

Maintain Desirable Weight

- Reduce overweight to a prevalence of no more than 20% of people aged 20 and older and no more than 15% among adolescents aged 12 through 19. (Baseline: 26% for people aged 20 through 74 in 1976–80, 24% for men and 27% for women; 15% for adolescents aged 12 through 19 in 1976–80.)

Special Population Targets

	Overweight Prevalence	1976–80 Baseline	2000 Target
Low-income women		37%	25%
Black women		44%	30%
Hispanic women		(not available)	25%

- Increase to at least 50% the proportion of overweight people aged 12 and older who have adopted sound dietary practices combined with regular physical activity to attain an appropriate body weight. (Baseline: 30% of overweight women and 25% of overweight men for people aged 18 and older in 1985.)

- Increase to at least 30% the proportion of people *aged 6 and older* who engage regularly, preferably daily, in light to moderate physical activity for at least 30 minutes per day. (Baseline: 22% of people aged 18 and older were active for at least 30 minutes 5 or more times per week and 12% were active 7 or more times per week in 1985.)
- Increase to at least 20% the proportion of people aged 18 and older and to at least 75% the proportion of children and adolescents aged 6 through 17 who engage in vigorous physical activity that promotes the development and maintenance of cardiorespiratory fitness 3 or more days per week for 20 or more minutes per occasion. (Baseline: 12% for people aged 18 and older in 1985; 66% for youth aged 10 through 17 in 1984.)
- Increase to at least 40% the proportion of people *aged 6 and older* who regularly perform physical activities that enhance and maintain muscular strength, muscular endurance, and flexibility.

Choose a Diet Low in Fat, Saturated Fat, and Cholesterol

- Reduce dietary fat intake to an average of 30% of calories or less and average saturated fat intake to less than 10% of calories among people aged 2 and older. (Baseline: 36% of calories from total fat and 13% from saturated fat for people aged 20 through 74 in 1976–80; 36% and 13% for women aged 19 through 50 in 1985.)
- Increase to at least 5000 brand items the availability of processed food products that are reduced in fat and saturated fat. (Baseline: 2,500 items reduced in fat in 1986.)
- Increase to at least 90% the proportion of restaurants and institutional food service operations that offer identifiable low-fat, low-calorie food choices consistent with the Dietary Guidelines for Americans. (Baseline: About 70% of fast food and family restaurant chains with 350 or more units had at least one low-fat low-calorie item on their menu in 1989.)

Choose a Diet with Plenty of Vegetables, Fruits, and Grain Products

- Increase complex carbohydrate and fiber-containing foods in the diets of adults to five or more daily servings for vegetables (including legumes) and fruits, and to six or more daily servings for grain products. (Baseline: 2½ servings of vegetables and fruits and 3 servings of grain products for women aged 19 through 50 in 1985.)

Use Sodium in Moderation

- Decrease salt and sodium intake so at least 65% of home meal preparers prepare foods without adding salt, at least 80% of people avoid using salt at the table, and at least 40% of adults regularly purchase foods modified or

Choose a diet with plenty of vegetables, fruits, grains, and cereals. Photo courtesy of USDA.

lower in sodium. (Baseline: 54% of women aged 19 through 50 who served as the main meal preparer did not use salt in food preparation, and 68% of women aged 19 through 50 did not use salt at the table in 1985; 20% of all people aged 18 and older regularly purchased foods with reduced salt and sodium content in 1988.)

If You Drink Alcoholic Beverages, Do So in Moderation

- Increase the proportion of high school seniors who associate risk of physical or psychological harm with heavy use of alcohol. In 1989, 44% of students surveyed associated risks with alcohol; the target for 2000 is for 70% of high school seniors to associate risk with alcohol.
- Reduce alcohol consumption by people aged 14 and older to an annual average of no more than 2 gallons of ethanol per person. (Baseline: 2.54 gallons of ethanol in 1987.)

To be sure the above behaviors or objectives are implemented, some education is needed. This education begins with the care provider implementing the following objectives:

- Increase to at least 75% the proportion of the nation's schools that provide nutrition education from *preschool* through 12th grade, preferably as part of quality school health education.
- Increase to at least 50% the proportion of worksites with 50 or more employees that offer nutrition education and/or weight management programs for employees. (Baseline: 17% offered nutrition education.)

These national objectives in *Healthy People 2000* [4] aim for measurable changes in what Americans eat as well as increased access to healthier food products by the year 2000. Encouraging attention to healthy choices in diet, exercise, weight control, and other risk factors for disease are major themes throughout the objectives. The 21 nutrition objectives addressed by *Healthy People 2000* can be summarized as follows:

Health Status

- Reduce coronary heart disease deaths.
- Reverse the rise in cancer deaths.
- Reduce the prevalence of overweight.
- Reduce the prevalence of growth retardation.

Risk Reduction

- Reduce dietary fat and saturated fat intake.
- Increase intake of vegetables, fruits, and grain products.
- Increase weight loss practices.
- Increase calcium intake.
- Decrease salt and sodium intake.
- Reduce iron deficiency anemia.
- Increase breastfeeding.
- Decrease baby bottle tooth decay.
- Increase food label use.

Services and Protection

- Standardize nutrition labeling.
- Increase the number of reduced fat and saturated fat processed food products.
- Increase low-fat, low-calorie menu choices.
- Increase school meals and child-care food service menus that are consistent with the Dietary Guidelines for Americans.
- Increase home-delivered meals for older adults.
- Increase nutrition education in schools.
- Increase worksite nutrition/weight management programs.
- Increase nutrition assessment, counseling, and referral by clinicians.

The national objectives for the year 2000 offer a blueprint of the changes that need to be effected over a course of 10 years. Dietary factors contribute substantially to the burden of preventable illness and premature death. Once-prevalent nutrient deficiencies have been replaced by excesses and imbalances, primarily fat and saturated fat, that are now associated with leading causes of death: heart disease, cancer, and stroke.

Attaining the year 2000 objectives will require a concerted national effort with new initiatives and intensified efforts at many levels and within many sectors. Care providers of young children can initiate activities to publicize and promote the national objectives to their advisory boards and parents. Many state health departments have begun the process of developing state objectives for the year 2000 using the national objectives as a model. Eventually, all states and territories are expected to follow suit. Care providers can receive help from state organizations.

Achievement of these objectives will require individual and collective action. Individual citizens, families, and professionals in government, business, industry, labor, education, professional and voluntary organizations, and the media are all being called upon to play an active role to promote a safer, healthier, and more productive nation.

Recommended Dietary Allowances (RDA)

The tools discussed in the preceding section—the Dietary Guidelines for Americans, the Guide to Daily Food Choices, and *Healthy People 2000* [4]—help you look primarily at food intake and provide a method to measure whether *food* choices promote health and prevent disease. The Recommended Dietary Allowances (RDA) [5] is the tool or standard used to evaluate *nutrients* in the diet, especially for groups such as day-care centers, group homes, or schools.

To ensure that the best possible diet has been planned for groups of individuals or for the menus served in preschool or day-care facilities, dietitians often rely not only on guides but also on the RDA [5]. They compare the nutrients from foods on the menu with the RDA. Although food guides answer the question, "Am I getting enough of the right foods?", the RDA best answers the question, "Are the diets or menus providing groups of children with the nutrients needed to meet their needs?"

The 1989 RDA table is found in Appendix II. It lists levels of nutrients considered essential to meet the known nutritional needs of practically all healthy persons. The RDA is based on the judgment of the Food and Nutrition Board and on available scientific knowledge. The allowances are recommendations, not average requirements, and most individuals require less of a nutrient than the RDA values.

The RDA does not provide a definite answer about whether the nutrient needs of an individual are met by a certain dietary intake. For example, if you eat a diet with 45 g of protein daily, the only way to know whether your protein intake is greater or less than your protein requirement is to measure in a laboratory the nitrogen-containing protein waste products lost in urine and feces. Such laboratory tests are rarely necessary. However, the risk of a deficiency increases when intake of a particular nutrient falls below the RDA. Over a period of time or across population groups (for example, children in day-care centers), statements can be made about the extent to which a given group meets the RDA. Using the RDA to evaluate a diet does not allow the dietitian to say a diet is deficient in nutrients but only that the diet did not meet the RDA for the period in question.

Computerized programs have been developed to calculate automatically nutrient intake recorded through dietary recalls or records. One such program, the Nutrient Dietary Data Analysis System [6], has been used for nutrient analysis in this text and for diets and menus nationally [7,8]. It was designed for research purposes and is based upon a large national database. Well-designed and maintained dietary data analysis systems can help the care provider or parent evaluate individual dietary intakes. Not only can an analysis estimate the energy/calories in the diet, but it can also determine how closely the diet or menu meets the Food Guide.

A list of computer programs is available from the Food and Nutrition Center [9] for use with personal computers. The brief description of each program will begin to help you select the best program for the money available. The care provider can call the National Agricultural Library (301-504-5719) for a computer program list.

Be sure that you see the program demonstrated AND THAT YOU ACTUALLY ENTER YOUR OWN DATA AND READ THE ANALYSIS YOU RETRIEVE. Only by entering your own data will you really be sure you know it meets your needs. Compatibility of the diet analysis program with your equipment is a major concern, but some other questions to ask before buying a diet analysis program include:

How long does it take to enter one diet or menu?
Do I have to look up codes for each food?
Do I have to convert cups to grams, tablespoons to ounces?
If I do not, how accurate are the program's calculations?
Does the program use the latest food data and RDA tables?
Where did the program get the database?
Do I have names and addresses of current users?
Can I add new foods/nutrients into the existing food database as these foods
    enter my region and appear on the menu?
Is the nutrient analysis for each food listed and not just the total nutrients for
    the diet or menu?
Is the percent (%) of calories from fat, carbohydrates, and proteins given?
Are the foods analyzed into lists of food groups as well as for nutrients?
Is the analysis readable and useful?

Food Labeling

Labeling is identified in this text as another tool to promote health and prevent disease. The Nutrition Labeling and Education Act of 1990 (NLEA) encourages implementation of *Healthy People 2000* objectives [4]. "Achieve useful and informative nutrition labeling for virtually all processed foods and at least 40% of fresh meats, poultry, fish, fruits, vegetables, baked goods, and ready-to-eat carry-away foods."

Americans are taking an active interest in what they eat. Not too long ago, maintaining a healthy diet took hard work. Some would say it still does take plenty of will-power. The growing number of readily available nutritious products has made life easier for people who are concerned about what they eat, but also somewhat confusing.

For all the choices in the new nutrition marketplace, however, there is also a sizable risk. The new era in health consciousness rests precariously on public confidence and understanding. Marketers and producers may take advantage of public interest by making false, misleading, or simply overwhelming claims about their products.

The goal is simple: a food label the public can understand and count on, that will bring them up to date with today's health concerns. It has three objectives: (1) to clear up confusion; (2) to help us make healthy choices; and (3) to encourage product innovation, so that companies are more interested in producing healthier foods to go inside the package, instead of merely tinkering with the words on the label.

The food label was always meant to help us make healthy diet choices. The problem with the label prior to 1992 was that it was better at helping prevent beriberi and pellagra than heart disease and cancer.

The proposed regulations were not developed until 1991, and as this text goes to press, the implementation of the final regulations are not complete. The following list provides some points on labeling rules:

1. Nutrition labeling is mandatory. Virtually all processed foods have nutrition labels.
2. Raw fruits, vegetables, and seafood have voluntary labeling. However, if the FDA finds that stores are not labeling these raw foods, the program will become mandatory.
3. Information on the amount of cholesterol, saturated fat, complex carbohydrates, sugars, fiber, and calories from fat are included because today's health concerns involve these nutrients.
4. The FDA has developed Daily Values (DV) to replace the U.S. RDA on the food label. Appendix III shows the values used in calculating percentages on the label.

While the following text describes the label, refer to Figure 2–3 to identify the components. Check labels on the containers to determine the way information relates to your eating pattern.

Serving Size.   Reference amounts have been standardized for food categories in quantities customarily consumed. These amounts will be expressed on the label in common household measures. For example, to determine the serving size for a loaf of sliced bread, a producer would simply count the number of its slices closest to the "bread reference amount," which is 55 grams; that will usually be two slices. Let's say a producer wished to slice the bread very thin and have only 20 grams per slice; then one serving would have to be listed as three or more slices.

Prior to 1992, a single-serving container such as a 12-ounce can of a soft drink was often labeled as two servings, lowering the calories per serving as stated on the can. Since the can was sold in a single-serving container with the assumption

Figure 2–3   A food label.

Nutrition Facts	
Serving Size ½ cup (114 g)	
Servings per container 4	
Calories 260 Calories from fat 120	
Amount per serving	**% Daily Value***
Total Fat 13 g	**20%**
Saturated Fat	**25%**
Cholesterol 30 mg	**10%**
Sodium 660 mg	**28%**
Total Carbohydrate 31 g	**11%**
Sugars 5 g	
Dietary fiber 25 g	**0%**
Protein 5 mg	

Vitamin A 4%   •   Vitamin C 2%   •   Calcium 15%   •   Iron 4%

*Percents (%) of a Daily Value are based on a 2,000 calorie diet. Your Daily Values may vary higher or lower depending on your calorie needs.

Nutrient		2,000 Calories	2,500 Calories
Total Fat	Less than	65 g	80 g
Sat. Fat	Less than	20 g	25 g
Cholesterol	Less than	300 mg	300 mg
Sodium	Less than	2,400 mg	2,400 mg
Total Carbohydrate		300 g	375 g
Fiber		25 g	30 g

1g Fat = 9 calories
1g Carbohydrate = 4 calories
1g Protein = 4 calories

that it would be consumed in one sitting, not two or three, the serving size should have been listed as one 12-ounce serving.

Descriptors.   In the past, marketers have used the FDA-defined terms of "low," "reduced," and "diet" to describe the level of calories; and "free," "very low," and "reduced" to describe the level of sodium in their products. Descriptive claims were not defined for other nutrients until 1992.

To communicate effectively, every manufacturer and marketer after 1992 must work from the same "dictionary," rather than invent their own descriptors. A descriptor will have only one meaning defined by FDA. This new "dictionary" contains core terms:

- Free
- Light or Lite
- High
- More
- Low
- Less
- Source of
- Reduced
- Lean and Extra Lean

And because consumers read these claims to help choose a healthy diet, foods labeled with a descriptor that also contain other nutrients at levels known to be less healthy will be required to bring that fact to the consumer's attention. For example, if a food making a low-sodium claim is also high in fat, the claim must state "see back panel for information about fat and other nutrients." Producers can lower the fat content in a food such as sour cream and still use the name sour cream.

Messages.   Consumers are seeking to learn more about healthy eating, and food producers and marketers are eager to help. But without rules or guidelines, even the best intentions are more likely to mislead than lead. The law requires that messages can be approved only where there is significant scientific agreement, and then only in a form most likely to give the consumer the full story. NLEA considered messages linking a nutrient to a health topic. The topics referenced on the labels include:

- Saturated Fat and Cholesterol and Coronary Heart Disease
- Fat and Cancer
- Sodium and High Blood Pressure
- Calcium or Osteoporosis
- Fiber-containing Foods and Cancer
- Grain Products, Fruits, and Vegatables and Cancer
- Fruits, Vegetables, and Grain Products that Contain Fiber and Risk of Coronary Heart Disease

PERSONAL DIETARY INTAKE AND EXERCISE PATTERNS

In Chapter 1 you learned to calculate your energy needs and determine if your weight exceeded the suggested weights for adults. This section helps you look at diet and exercise to maintain, gain, or lose weight. Looking at your own dietary pattern is one of the most important steps in improving your diet. You will need a sheet of paper and pencil to record your current eating habits. Nutritionists use either a diet record or 24-hour dietary recall.

Diet records are usually sent home with individuals who are asked to record everything they eat and drink for one or more days. A 24-hour dietary recall is usually taken by a trained person (following a specific protocol) during an interview session. Both are means of collecting information about dietary intake to determine the nutrient content of one or more diets. Appendix IV includes forms for recording dietary intake.

For the purpose of analyzing your own dietary intake, you may combine the two methods. For example, you may keep a record for two days preceding or following the 24-hour recall. Just write down all the foods and beverages eaten, when these foods were eaten, how prepared (for example, frying, steaming), and the amount consumed. In addition, when dietary habits are studied in order to modify an undesirable pattern, you may want to include where the food was eaten, with whom the food was eaten, and your mood or feeling when the food was eaten. How much and the kind of exercise you participate in may also be important in controlling eating behavior (Figure 2–4).

Recording the amount of food eaten and your exercise patterns will make you more conscious of what you eat. However, this is true only if the recording or

	Food and Exercise Record				
Amount of Food/ Duration of Exercise*	Description	Time	Where/With Whom (location of eating/exercise)	Mood†	Kcal Consumed/ Expended‡
2 C	Popcorn	3:30–4:00	Watching TV	b	+200
½ hr	Walked 1½ miles	4:00–4:30	Park/alone	c	−160

*May calculate activity in minutes at miles per hour.
†a = anxious, b = bored, c = content, d = depressed, e = angry, h = happy, t = tired. May be omitted when recording for a child.
‡Record calories for foods eaten only if those expended in exercise are not available.

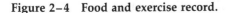

Figure 2–4   Food and exercise record.

recall is completed in the time interval immediately following food intake. When taking a 24-hour recall, it is best to start with foods that have just been consumed and then to work back to foods consumed at this time yesterday.

Now take a look at the diet. How can you evaluate it? If you continue to eat this way, will your food intake ensure good health and prevent nutritional deficiencies? How do you know? What standard did you use? You now have the tools to evaluate your food and nutrient intake.

Check your diet. How many different kinds of food did you consume? Five? Seven? Ten? Fifteen? In general, the wider the variety of foods eaten, the more likely the diet is to be adequate. At least 12 to 15 different items chosen from a wide variety of foods, not fortified foods, are needed to meet the RDA. However, if a diet consists of candy, soft drinks, and other foods with low nutritional value or density, the diet will be inadequate, no matter how varied. Remember that all persons throughout life have the need for the same nutrients, but the amounts may vary. Nutrient needs can change depending on age, sex, size, activity, and state of health.

How Does Your Diet Compare?

You will find it easier to compare your diet to the Food Guide if you first list the food groups and then compare the number of servings of each food consumed with the recommended quantity. A 24-hour dietary recall for a 20-year-old woman is recorded on Table 2–3, column 1. On examining the diet, you may note that you eat more or less frequently and that your choice of foods differs from the example given. Many combinations of foods can supply the nutrients the body needs to function properly. It appears to have all the constituents so commonly discussed (e.g., vitamin C in juice, protein in beans, eggs, and fish). Note that it does not meet the Food Guide recommendation for 6 servings of grains.

The diet was also compared with the RDA (Figure 2–5) by using a computer. The results show that intake of vitamin D, B_6, and zinc are less than the RDA. One additional serving of whole wheat bread or brown rice would have increased the intake of B_6. Consuming more milk would increase vitamin D and zinc.

You can manually complete a 24-hour recall by listing the foods from the diet and converting them to nutrients found in the food composition table (Appendix I). The major nutrients for each food can be totaled and compared with the RDA (Appendix II) and a percentage calculated.

Computerization provides a much easier method for analyzing the nutrient content of the diet. However, use of the Guide to Daily Food Choices does an adequate job of determining if your diet meets most nutritional needs.

A person's dietary intake may not be judged adequate or inadequate based on an evaluation of 24-hour recall. However, the 24-hour recall can help you make decisions on how to modify your own dietary intake or help you determine whether a child needs further evaluation of nutritional status.

Table 2–3   Comparison of sample diet to A Guide to Daily Food Choices.

			Servings			
		Protein Foods				
Consumed Quantity of Food in Sample Diet	Milk	Meats, Poultry, Fish	Dried Beans and Peas, Eggs, Nuts	Fruits	Vegetables	Breads, Cereals, Rice, and Pasta
7:00 A.M.						
¾ C orange juice				1		
1 scrambled egg		1				
2 slices whole wheat toast						2
8 oz milk (2%)	1					
1 tsp margarine						
12:00 P.M.						
1 C cooked beans			2			
1 C cooked cabbage					2	
1 piece corn bread						1
½ C fruit cocktail				1		
3:00 P.M.						
8 oz milk (2%)	1					
½ C raw carrots					1	
6:30 P.M.						
3 oz salmon loaf		1				
¾ C creamed potatoes					1	
1 C broccoli					2	
1 slice whole grain bread						1
2 tsp margarine						
10:00 P.M.						
8 oz coffee						
1 large apple				1		
Total	2	4		3	6	4
Daily Food Guide	2–3	2–3		2–4	3–5	6–11
Difference	0	+		0	+	−

*Count ½ cup cooked dried beans or peas as a serving of vegetables or as 1 ounce of the meat group.

Percent Energy Distribution:

Fat	28%
Carbohydrate	56%
Protein	19%

Total		Nutrient	%RDA
1874.0	KCAL	ENERGY	85%
89.7	GM	PROTEIN	195%
12309.3	IU	VITAMIN A	380%
200.8	IU	VITAMIN D	50%
18.5	IU	VITAMIN E	231%
294.6	MG	VITAMIN C	491%
431.0	MCG	FOLACIN	239%
16.1	MG	NIACIN	108%
2.1	MG	RIBOFLAVIN	164%
1.5	MG	THIAMIN	139%
0.9	MG	VITAMIN B6	58%
2.5	MCG	VITAMIN B12	127%
1413.3	MG	CALCIUM	118%
1887.6	MG	PHOSPHOROUS	157%
17.2	MG	IRON	114%
353.1	MG	MAGNESIUM	126%
8.9	MG	ZINC	74%

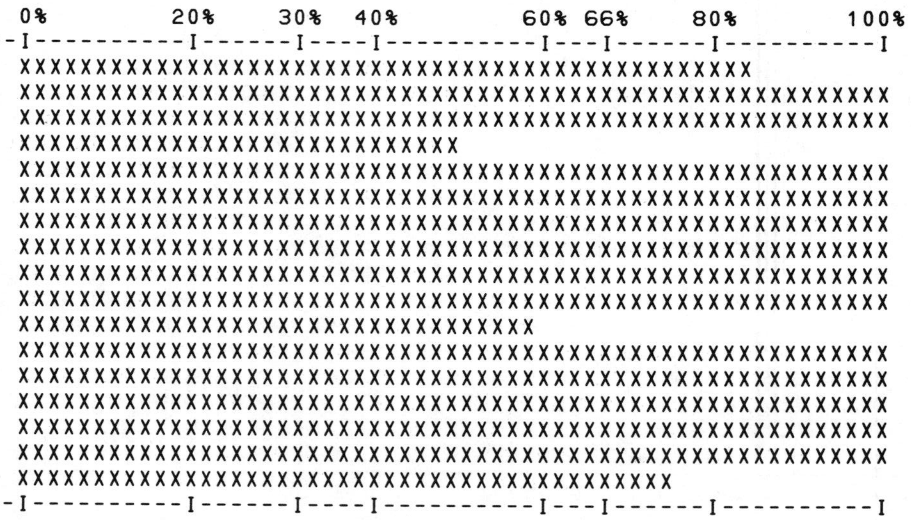

(Bar chart scale: 0% 20% 30% 40% 60% 66% 80% 100%)

Figure 2–5 Nutrient analysis of woman's diet in Table 2–3.
Source: NDDA Laboratory, Southern Illinois University at Carbondale.

Exercise and Energy

What about your output of energy? You don't have time to exercise? You can't put forth the time and effort of the jogger you watch each day? Only 90 minutes of brisk exercise per week or 30–45 minutes of vigorous exercise three times a week is recommended as a minimum amount. Exercising every day establishes a habit and can more easily become part of your daily routine. Gardening, house cleaning, and other routine exercises have been shown to improve cardiovascular fitness. Be sure to have a physical examination before you begin any exercise program.

Exercise does affect the amount of energy you need. What you eat and how much you exercise must be considered together when evaluating your dietary intake. Sitting quietly for one hour may burn only 80 to 100 calories while walking 3.5 mph may burn from 350 to 450 calories per hour depending upon the size of the individual.

An additional benefit of exercise is that it keeps the body's appetite control mechanism functioning properly. A person may miss internal cues for hunger and satiety without exercise. Weight loss through diet and exercise is likely to be 98% fat, whereas diet alone produces a weight loss of 75% from fat and the remainder from muscle tissue.

You are now ready to record what you eat along with how much you exercise on a form similar to the one presented in Figure 2–4. A 3- to 7-day record can better help you determine changes required in your diet and exercise patterns.

GUIDELINES FOR VEGETARIANS

Vegetarian diets may help some individuals more easily meet the Dietary Guidelines. The guidelines for vegetarian diets are presented here to encourage you to plan a menu for yourself using the information you have learned in Chapters 1 and 2.

According to the American Dietetic Association [10], vegetarian diets are healthful and nutritionally adequate when appropriately planned. It is important to choose a wide variety of foods from the major food groups and to include a good food source of ascorbic acid (vitamin C) with meals to enhance iron absorption. Special attention should be given to children who are following a vegetarian diet. The growing child's nutrient needs are especially high. Careful planning can allow the child to meet the requirements while following a vegetarian diet, especially one containing dairy products, eggs, and soy products.

Recommendations for selecting vegetarian diets include [10,11]:

- Keep the intake of calorie-dense foods, such as sweets and fatty foods, to a minimum.
- Choose whole or unrefined grain products instead of refined products whenever possible.
- Use a variety of fruits and vegetables including a good food source of vitamin C to enhance iron absorption.

- If milk products are consumed, use low-fat varieties.
- Limit intake of eggs to two to three yolks per week to avoid excessive cholesterol intake.
- For vegans, use a properly fortified food source of vitamin B_{12} such as fortified soy milks or breakfast cereals, or take a supplement.
- For infants and children, ensure adequate intakes of iron, vitamin D, and sources of energy.
- Consult a registered dietitian or other qualified nutrition professional.

Well-planned vegetarian diets effectively meet the Dietary Guidelines for Americans.

Figure 2–6 Most children get all the exercise they need during play.
Photo by Robert E. Rockwell.

EXERCISE CONCERNS AND CAUTIONS FOR CHILDREN

With the increase in incidence of obesity, care providers are becoming concerned about energy balance as it affects not only energy intake but also energy expenditure. Positive energy balance produces weight gain in excess of needs for growth and development. When this happens, the care provider may turn to exercise to increase the young child's energy expenditure, especially when the child is at the 90th percentile height for weight. The child's parents may also be pressuring the care provider to modify the child's dietary intake and exercise patterns.

Caution regarding preschool exercise programs comes from both the early childhood and the health care professions. Elkind [12] feels that exercise programs at too early an age put infants and young children in inappropriate learning situations as well as expose them to risk of physical and/or psychological damage. Most children can get all the exercise they need by doing what they do naturally as they use their senses and movements to explore their world [12]. (See Figure 2–6.)

Further cautions come from the American Academy of Pediatrics [13]. After a 2-year study of preschool exercise programs, the academy concluded that infant exercise programs do nothing to improve a baby's physical fitness. The Academy advises general play until age 6. Exercise programs geared to children under age 3 do not enhance the development of the healthy child.

Structured exercise programs do not belong in the early childhood curriculum. Care providers should provide a physical environment that provides freedom of movement and exploration. Specific recommendations for physical fitness activity are provided in other chapters.

SUMMARY

- Consuming a variety of foods while following the Guide to Daily Food Choices allows the care provider to obtain the Recommended Dietary Allowances.
- Completing a daily record of what has been eaten and the amount and kind of exercise performed are steps in understanding an individual's total dietary intake needs.
- Structured exercise programs are not necessary for children under the age of 6.
- The *Healthy People 2000* objectives should help the care provider understand major nutrition-related concerns in the population and help the child-care center set goals and objectives for its programs.
- Labeling now addresses more clearly issues of importance to today's consumer.

DISCUSSION QUESTIONS

1. List the Dietary Guidelines for Americans.
2. Describe the guides and standards you can use to evaluate dietary intake.
3. What is the purpose of the Dietary Guidelines for Americans and the Healthy People 2000 objectives?
4. Is it possible to evaluate both dietary intake and exercise?
5. Discuss structured exercise programs for adults and children under age 6. What differences exist and why?
6. How can you use the objectives in *Healthy People 2000*?
7. Pick three labels from similar products and identify the nutrients in each. Which product would you rate nutritionally superior?
8. Describe a label you have seen which makes or relates to a health claim.

REFERENCES

1. U.S. Department of Agriculture and U.S. Department of Health and Human Services: Nutrition and your health: dietary guidelines for Americans, Washington, DC, 1990, U.S. Government Printing Office.
2. USDA Human Nutrition Information Service: Nutrition and your health: dietary guidelines for Americans, Home and Garden Bull. N. 232–8, Washington, DC, 1990, U.S. Government Printing Office.
3. DeLeeuw, E. R., Windham, C. T., Lauritzen, G. C., et al: Developing menus to meet current dietary recommendations: implications and applications, J. Nutr. Educ. 24:136–143, 1992.
4. U.S. Department of Health and Human Services: Healthy people 2000: health promotion and disease prevention objectives, Public Health Service, Washington, DC, 1990, U.S. Government Printing Office.
5. Food and Nutrition Board, National Research Council: Recommended dietary allowances, ed. 10, Washington, DC, 1989, National Academy of Science.
6. Endres, J., and Sawicki, M.: Guide for the use of the Nutrient Dietary Data Analysis System, Carbondale, IL, 1980, Southern Illinois University.
7. Sawicki, M., and Endres, J.: Energy and nutrient calculations using an optical character reader system, J. Am. Diet. Assn. 83:138, 1983.
8. Endres, J., Dunning, S., Poon S. W., et al.: Older pregnant women and adolescents: nutrition data after enrollment in WIC, J. Am. Diet. Assoc. 87:1011–1019, 1988.
9. Updegrove, N.: Microcomputer Software Collection, Food and Nutrition Information Center, Beltsville, MD, 1992, National Agricultural Library.
10. American Dietetic Association: Position of the American Dietetic Association: vegetarian diets, J. Am. Diet. Assoc. 88(3):351, 1988.
11. American Dietetic Association: Position of the American Dietetic Association: vegetarian diets—technical support paper, J. Am. Diet. Assoc. 88:352–355, 1988.
12. Elkind, D: Miseducation: preschoolers at risk, New York, 1987, Alfred A. Knopf, p. 13.
13. American Academy of Pediatrics: Sports and your child: a position statement of the American Academy of Pediatrics, Chicago, 1987, The Academy.

3

The Infant (Birth to 12 Months)

LEARNING OBJECTIVES

Students will be able to:
- Identify tools used to evaluate nutritional status.
- State advantages and disadvantages of breast milk for infants.
- Describe infant formulas.
- Discuss the introduction of solid foods during the first year.
- Evaluate an infant's dietary intake and feeding and eating skills.
- Discuss nutrition-related problems of the infant.
- State several components included in the policy statement related to nutrition in an infant center.

Some of you reading this for the first time may never have held or cared for an infant. On the other hand, some of you may have several children of your own and feel comfortable with the infants brought to the center for care. In either case, the recommended practices related to nutritional care should help you provide the best nutritional care for the young child in the center. You are urged to consult the references for an in-depth study of growth, development, nutritional needs, feeding practices, and common problems of the infant and to refer parents to local public health nutritionists or dietitians for additional guidance.

PHYSICAL CHARACTERISTICS RELATED TO FOOD

The child will never again grow so rapidly as during the first year. Each month during that year brings a new set of joys and problems for parents and care providers until finally the infant emerges at 12 months as an individual and "proper person" [1]. During the first year, the child depends on the care provider for physical, emotional, and social needs, and the cry is the main form of communication.

At birth the normal child is able to suck but cannot lift its head, roll over, or in any other way signal for food. When the infant is at least 8 months old, the experienced care provider can easily distinguish between the distress cry (for example, for food or a dry diaper) and the "I'm-bored-and-frustrated" cry, which often characterizes to the parent the 1-year-old "whiny or demanding child." By this time the child is finger-feeding and is well into eating with a spoon. Some of the eating behaviors expected of the child during the latter part of the first year of life are chewing and feeding finger foods, holding a bottle, drinking from a cup, holding a spoon, and attempting to feed self if a spoon is dipped into food.

Critical Periods

As a child grows, a care provider will note critical periods characterized by certain oral, adaptive, and gross motor skills. Table 3–1 summarizes normal feeding development during these critical periods for the infant to 12 months. Referring to the developmental milestones in areas related to feeding and nutrition, the care provider can observe the child's behavior in relation to the standard. Further evaluation is necessary to determine any delay. In infancy, critical periods have special meanings in relation to food intake. When a baby is born, a sucking reflex provides a method for obtaining nourishment. Not until the 3- to 5-month period does the sucking motion become modified enough for the infant to accept semisolid food from a spoon.

By 7 months, the infant has learned to chew. At this time the infant is developmentally ready to accept foods with a texture other than pureed. Table foods chopped, mashed, or cut in small pieces are well accepted. Experience with developmentally delayed children shows that if foods of varied textures are not offered at this time, the infant may refuse food, refuse to chew, or even vomit unfamiliar foods when they are offered. This is rarely the case with a child who is developing well and is allowed to interact with the family. This child will take food while being held by someone who is eating and will explore tastes and textures.

ANTHROPOMETRIC AND LABORATORY MEASURES RELATED TO NUTRITION

Among the measures that the care provider can use to determine the proper intake of food and nourishment are the anthropometric measurements of length and weight. These measurements should be accurately taken on a monthly basis in the center, or parents should arrange to attend local public health or private clinics for such measurements. Although it is advisable and recommended for the center to have a properly constructed measuring board, in some cases the changing table, a tape measure, and an immovable head piece have been used. In all cases, two persons are needed to measure an infant. Figure 3–1 shows the proper procedure.

Measuring

The infant is measured using "recumbent" length (the child is lying down).* The standards until age 2 are based on recumbent length, ideally measured on a table with an immovable head piece and movable foot piece. A measuring tape (preferably graduated in millimeters) runs along the table's length. The child is

---

*Measuring devices are available from Perspective Enterprises, Inc., Kalamazoo, MI, 49001 (800-323-7452) or Ward Cabinet Works, 114 Maureen Dr., Hendersonville, TN 37075.

Table 3–1 Stages of development for infants.*

Stage	Physical	Nutritional	Intellectual
Fetal: *Conception to birth*	Development of anatomic characteristics followed by growth and elaboration of all systems	Receives nourishment via placenta; maternal weight gain first trimester 1 to 2 kg with 0.4 kg per week gain for remainder of pregnancy	Brain grows to about 25% of adult size
Newborn: *Birth to 10 days*	Average weight—3.4 kg; average height—50 cm; average HC†—35 cm; has large head, round face and chest, prominent abdomen, and short extremities; loses weight	Seeks source of nourishment by rooting reflex from bottle or breast, consuming colostrum or prepared formula	Brain growth continues; coordination of senses and motor functions begins
Infancy I: *10 days to 2 months*	Regains birthweight; sitting height equal to 57% of body length; rapid growth of head and body	Continues to nurse mature breast milk or formula; not developmentally ready for solid food (orally or physiologically, e.g., renal solute load)	Inspection of surroundings begins; differentiation of self from others
Infancy II: *3 to 5 months*	Doubles birthweight; increases length; posterior fontanel closes; deciduous teeth begin erupting	Continues to be nourished by breast milk or formula; iron stores begin to be depleted	Attention span increases; hand-eye coordination begins
Infancy III: *6 to 9 months*	Subcutaneous fat reaches peak by 9 months; closure of anterior fontanel by 9 months	Oral mechanism ready to accept solid food; cereal introduced first in a very thin consistency; consistency thickened, as tolerated; new foods introduced, as tolerated	Imitation of others begins; understands a few words
Infancy IV: *10 to 12 months*	Triples birthweight; average HC† of 47 cm equals chest circumference; 6 to 8 teeth present	Tooth eruption progresses to tolerated transition from pureed to chopped foods; formula or breast milk recommended until end of the first year	First words; concept of object permanence develops; brain weight now about 75% of adult's

*This chart provides the health professional with a standard tool for assessing feeding levels.
†Head circumference.

Table 3–1 (Continued)

Stage	Gross Motor	Fine Motor	Reflex
Fetal: Conception to birth		Sucks thumb in utero	
Newborn: Birth to 10 days	Flexed adducted posture	Grasp reflex; palmomental reflex; inserts thumb when hand is brought to mouth	Sucking, rooting, gag, asymmetrical tonic neck reflex (ATNR) present; moro and tonic labyrinthine reflexes emerge
Infancy I: 10 days to 2 months	Flexed-abducted posture emerges; head extension in prone (60° at 3 months); head lag when pulled to sitting; midline positioning of head begins in supine; forearm propping	Grasp reflex continues; hands often open; ulnar side of hand strongest; mouthing of fingers and mutual fingering	Rooting (3 months) and sucking (2 to 5 months) disappear; phasic bite reflex present
Infancy II: 3 to 5 months	Extended-abducted posture emerges; extended arm position in prone; rolls prone to supine and back; head erect in supported sitting (6 months); sits propping on arms	Raking fingers; immediate approach and grasp on site, then eyes and hands combine in joint action; radial fingers begin to dominate	Grasp reflex disappears (4 to 6 months) and moro disappears (5 to 6 months); tonic labyrinthine disappears (6 months); symmetrical topic neck reflex (STNR) emerges at 6 months
Infancy III: 6 to 9 months	Rotational patterns emerge; sits erect with hands free; re-erects self in sitting and comes to sitting independently; pivots on stomach; pulls to standing; crawls on stomach	One hand approach to objects; transfers objects; thumb begins to move toward forefinger	Protective extension forward in upper extremities begins (9 to 10 months); phasic bite develops to munching
Infancy IV: 10 to 12 months	Independent mobility by crawling (9 months), creeping (12 months), or walking (12 to 15 months); pivots on hips in sitting; walks holding onto furniture	Finer adjustment of digits; inferior-pincer grasp; pokes with forefinger; beginning of voluntary release and neat pincer grasp with slight extension of wrist (10 to 11 months)	Protective extension sidewards in upper extremities begins at 7 months; STNR disappears (8 to 12 months); tilting responses in sitting begin at 7 and 8 months.

Table 3–1 (Continued)

Stage	Oral/Motor	Speech and Language	Social/Behavioral
Fetal: Conception to birth	Embryological development of oral structures: lips, tongue, hard palate, soft palate, peripheral muscles		
Newborn: Birth to 10 days	Rooting reflex; gag reflex; sucking (flexor tone in neonate); suckling, phasic bite reflex; palmomental reflex; smooth coordination of suck, swallow, breathing	Birth cry; cry becomes longer; strong, rhythmical breathing	
Infancy I: 10 days to 2 months	Suckling, phasic bite reflex, palmomental reflex continue	Smiles; visually localizes speaker; breath stream lengthens; coos (vowel sounds); uses special cry for hunger	Regards face; eye contact; smiles
Infancy II: 3 to 5 months	Suckling; cup-drinking; spoon-feeding begins; phasic bite reflex develops to munching	Controls breath stream; varies pitch; vocalizes vowel sounds (nonimitative); begins to babble (consonant sounds); responds to name	Laughs aloud; responds to talking
Infancy III: 6 to 9 months	Sucking; cup-drinking continues; more refined spoonfeeding; chewing	Recognizes some familiar names; plays peek-a-boo, pat-a-cake; stops to "no"; gestures to some familiar words or requests (come, byebye, up); babbles imitatively; jargons	Differentiates family members; fearful of strangers
Infancy IV: 10 to 12 months	Sucking, cup-drinking, spoon-feeding, and chewing continue	Follows simple verbal requests (put that down); understands simple questions (where?); attends to speech; gestures appropriately; first words (mama, dada, byebye); jargons	Plays peek-a-boo and pat-a-cake

Source: Modified from Harvey-Smith, M., et al.: Feeding management of a child with a handicap: a guide for professionals, Memphis, 1982, University of Tennessee Center for the Health Sciences.

Figure 3–1 Care providers measure length of infant. Photo by Robert E. Rockwell.

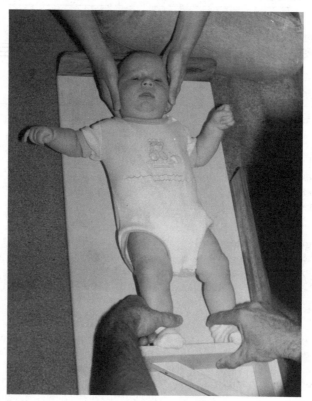

placed face up with the head brought against the head piece and is held there with gentle pressure. The head, shoulders, hips, and feet are oriented in a single line as they would be for a standing measurement. The knees are held flattened against the table, and the toes point upward. The movable board is brought against the bottom of the feet, heel touching board, with gentle pressure. Ideally, each measurement should be repeated at least three times with any necessary adjustments in body orientation. Immediate accurate recording of each of the three measurements is essential. The three measurements may then be averaged and recorded; in practice, it may not be possible to take three measurements.

Weight should be measured using a beam-balanced scale with nondetachable weights. The child should be wearing as little clothing as possible and should wear the same amount of clothing each month. For infants, scales weighing to the nearest gram are desirable. The balance of the scale should be checked before each weighing. An infant should be laid on the scale (if body size permits) or seated at the exact center of the scale [2, 3].

Individual charts for infants (for determining normal values) can aid in determining if the child is growing and developing at a satisfactory rate and can direct attention to unusual body size, which may be a result of disease or poor nutrition. The charts are intended to record the growth of the individual child; they were constructed by the National Center for Health Statistics (NCHS) in collaboration with the Centers for Disease Control [2, 3]. These data are appropriate for young girls and boys in the general U.S. population. Height and weight charts can aid both the care provider and the parent in making minor adjustments in the dietary intake of the child and should be provided for the parents. Girls' weight for length is charted in Figure 3–2, weight for age in Figure 3–3, and length for age in Figure 3–4. Similar charts for boys are found in Appendix V.

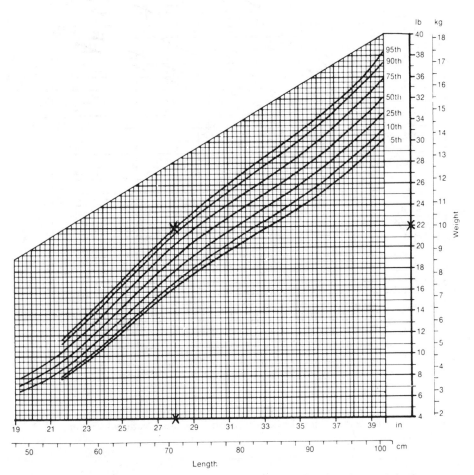

Figure 3–2 Girls' growth chart from birth to 36 months showing weight for length at 95th percentile.
Source: U.S. Department of Health, Education and Welfare, National Center for Health Statistics, 1979.

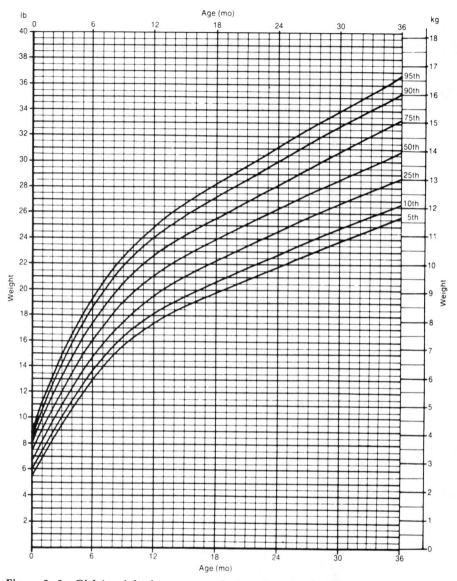

Figure 3–3   Girls' weight-for-age growth chart from birth to 36 months.
Source: U.S. Department of Health, Education and Welfare, National Center for Health Statistics, 1979.

Recording

First, take all measurements and record them. If three measurements are taken, the average should be plotted on the appropriate chart. For example, to plot a girl's length for age, find her age on the horizontal scale (Figure 3–4); then follow a vertical line from that point to the child's length measurement on the

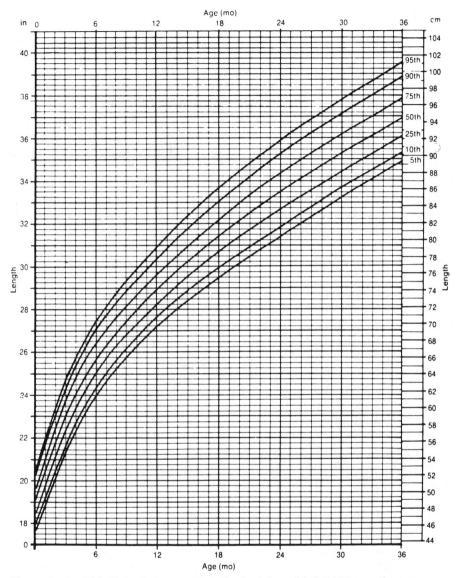

Figure 3–4   Girls' length-for-age growth chart from birth to 36 months.
Source: U.S. Department of Health, Education and Welfare, National Center for Health Statistics, 1979.

vertical scale. Indicate with a mark where the two lines intersect. When the child is measured again, join the new set of marks to the previous set by straight lines. Figure 3–2 shows one measurement for length (28 in.) and weight (22 lb) and is plotted on the weight for length chart. The child is at the 95th percentile of weight for length.

Interpreting

Many factors influence growth. Therefore, growth data alone must not be used to diagnose nutritional deficiencies, although measurements do allow you to identify unusual growth patterns in children. Each chart contains a series of curved lines, numbered to show selected percentiles. These refer to the rank of this measurement compared to a hypothetical group of 100 children. If a child's weight is taken and a mark is placed on the 95th percentile of weight for length (Figure 3–2), it means that only 5 children among 100 of the corresponding age and sex can be expected to have a weight for length greater than that recorded but 95 can be expected to have a weight for length less than that recorded. The charts were developed for infants who were primarily bottle-fed, and special consideration should be given to the breast-fed baby after 3 months.

If the child has been measured over a period of several months, compare the most recent set of marks with earlier sets for the same child. If the child's weight for height has jumped from one percentile level to another, you may also want to check the accuracy of the measurements and discuss any changes with the parents before referring the child for further evaluation. Rapid changes are less likely to be significant when they occur within the range from the 25th to the 75th percentile. Measurements that appear below the 25th or above the 90th may be normal and must be judged against previous and subsequent measurements and genetic and environmental factors that affect the infant.

Table 3–2 provides a quick reference of lengths and weights. If the child weighs more or less than indicated in the table, his or her measurements can be plotted on the length and weight charts to determine the individual child's pattern. The length and weight charts are more appropriate for regular use in the center over a long period.

In general, the normal full-term infant gains more than an ounce a day between the eighth and forty-second day of life, even the breast-fed baby. A baby who weighed 8 pounds at birth could weigh between 11 and 12 pounds when brought to the center at 2 months of age.

Table 3–2   Lengths and weights at 50th percentile for various ages.

	Weight (pounds)		Length (inches)	
	Males	Females	Males	Females
Birth	7¼	7	20	19¾
1 month	9½	8¾	21½	21
3 months	13¼	12	24	23½
6 months	17¼	16	26¾	26
9 months	20¼	18¾	28½	27¾
12 months	22½	21	30	29¼

Source: National Center for Health Statistics, Health Resources Administration, DHEW, Hyattsville, MD, 1977. Data from the Fels Research Institute, Yellow Springs, OH.

The Breast-fed Baby. Breast-fed infants grow less rapidly after the first 2 to 3 months of age according to recent data [4]. In fact, by 9 to 12 months more than half of those babies in your center who are breast-fed without the addition of other foods may have heights and weights below the 5th percentile [5]. The height and weight charts were standardized primarily on bottle-fed infants. However, most infants we see in the infant center by 6 to 9 months of age can be evaluated using the standard procedures for the growth chart because they have begun using more than ½ cup of other milk or formula and a substantial amount of solid foods have been introduced. When a breast-fed baby receives no more than ½ cup formula or other milk and has *not* begun solid foods, the child may begin weight gain with the other children, but by 3 months of age growth may be slower. If the child does not have frequent infections and is developing normally, do not become concerned.

Weight Gain Variation. Weight gain can vary depending on many factors other than whether the child is breast-fed. The height and weight of the natural parents can genetically affect their children. Short-statured parents are more likely to have a shorter child. Likewise, the premature infant, a child of multiple births (twins), and a low-birth-weight infant (birth weight of less than 2.5 kg or 5.1 pounds) will generally be smaller. Consequently, it is important to note the child's feeding record and family and medical history when a child enters your care so that you can accurately interpret the results of the measurements.

An additional anthropometric measurement taken by health professionals is skinfold thickness. Figure 3–5 shows the Lange Skinfold Caliper, which can be used to measure the amount of fat under the skin (subcutaneous fat). This measurement has been most widely used (1) in hospitals to determine the subcutaneous fat and nutritional status of a patient having surgery, (2) to monitor obesity in a clinical setting, and (3) in controlled research studies. We are not advocating the use of this instrument by every care provider. When a child has height and weight measurements that appear to need further evaluation, the dietitian or pediatrician will be able to provide additional information using the skinfold calipers. The care provider should understand the skinfold measurement as an additional tool to help evaluate the young child's total growth and development.

The use of skinfold thickness in the assessment of nutritional status of children is based on the assumption that increased subcutaneous fat, resulting from either high calorie intake or low energy expenditure, reflects a greater calorie reserve [6]. Measurement of skinfold thickness can provide an indirect estimate of body fat and may be used to screen children who are overweight or underweight. Along with length and weight, skinfold thickness should be taken at regular intervals during routine health checks by trained staff or when the child visits the health center.

Figure 3–5 Lange Skinfold Caliper. Cambridge Scientific Industries, P.O. Box 265, Cambridge, MD 21613.

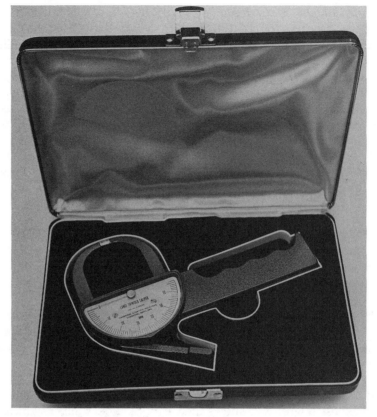

Laboratory Measurements

Measurements of hemoglobin and hematocrit are laboratory procedures that provide yet another index of nutritional status. Hemoglobin is the iron-containing protein in red blood cells and provides the bright red color. Hematocrit is a measure of the packed red blood cells after separating the solids from the plasma in the blood. When the red blood cells are few in number or are of poor quality, anemia is diagnosed. If the child has iron-deficiency anemia, the red blood cells will be small and light in color (indicating less hemoglobin) and will carry less oxygen than normal red blood cells.

Measurements of hemoglobin or hematocrit are often taken to determine nutritional risk factors for children in programs such as the Supplemental Food Program for Women, Infants and Children [7]. The first assessments are usually taken after children reach 6 months of age. For the 6- to 12-month-old infant the acceptable hematocrit value is 31%, and the acceptable hemoglobin level is 10 g/100 mL.

It should be emphasized that abnormal data from any one measure alone are not indicative of malnutrition. They must be coupled with other medical, laboratory, and dietary indexes before the parents or care provider becomes alarmed.

NUTRITIONAL NEEDS

Prenatal Period

A successful pregnancy is important for the health of the infant and is preparation not only for delivery of a healthy child but also for storage of energy and nutrients for lactation. Although the care provider may not be in a position to counsel the pregnant woman, knowledge of the nutritional needs during pregnancy can help the care provider understand problems that infants may be experiencing.

Prepregnancy weight and weight gain during pregnancy are two of the most important determinants of the outcome of pregnancy. Thin women need to gain more weight and obese women need to gain less [8]. The woman who has a normal prepregnancy weight should gain from 25 to 35 pounds during pregnancy. Maintaining the energy or the caloric content of the diet during pregnancy is essential. The scale is the best indicator of the need for energy or calories. During the prenatal visits, the dietitian or nutritionist will evaluate the past and current weight of the woman. If the pregnant woman comes into pregnancy underweight, her energy needs are greater. If she comes to pregnancy overweight, her needs are somewhat less. Telling every pregnant woman she should gain 25 to 35 pounds is no longer the best advice.

There are no special foods for pregnancy. The extra energy should be obtained from the food groups as indicated in Chapter 2. Additional servings of milk, grains, fruits, and vegetables as well as meats and alternate meat products will provide the necessary nutrients and energy stores for a healthy baby and the lactation period. Other recommendations for pregnant women include taking a low-dose iron supplement, but other vitamins and minerals should be given only for special needs based upon the woman's nutrition and health status.

Care providers who have the opportunity to discuss pregnancy care should emphasize the importance of early prenatal care. Women who wish to become pregnant should not restrict their food intake, and if they have a low weight for height, must make up for the deficit between usual energy intake and requirements of pregnancy.

Lactation

The nutritional needs of infants from birth to at least 4 months of age are unique, are well-documented, and can be met with breast milk or iron-fortified infant formulas. The care provider makes few decisions regarding the kind and amount of food to give the young infant. These decisions have already been made by the parents with the hospital staff. The care provider must support the mother in a decision to breast- or bottle-feed the infant. The care provider must be informed regarding the special needs of the lactating mother.

What are the benefits of lactation? What should the mother be eating while breast-feeding her infant? How should the center be prepared for the breast-feeding mother and her child? Human milk is the most appropriate food for human infants while simultaneously benefitting the lactating mother. Breast-feeding should become the established norm. Nursing for only a few weeks or months is better than not nursing at all. The positive factors are more extensively discussed in many publications [9–11] and should be stressed by the care provider:

- Nutritional superiority and easy digestibility.
- Breast milk changes to match the changing needs of the infant.
- Lower incidence of infection, illness, and allergy in breast-fed infants owing to the safety of breast milk and the presence of immunologic components [9].
- Opportunity for optimum mother-infant physical contact and/or bonding.
- Likelihood of a return of the uterus to prepregnancy condition.
- Likelihood for the mother to return to prepregnant weight within 2 to 6 months if maternal fat stores are used to supply part of the caloric needs for breast-feeding.
- Delayed return to ovulation for some women [12].
- May lessen the risk that mother will develop breast cancer [13].
- Improved chances for the preterm child to develop to maximum potential [10].

The woman who has a normal prepregnancy weight for height and has gained 25 to 35 pounds during pregnancy usually has little difficulty providing sufficient milk for her infant. Mothers are able to produce milk of sufficient quantity and quality to support growth and promote the health of infants—even when the mother's supply of nutrients and energy is limited. However, limited studies are available on lactating women who are severely underweight or malnourished and reports are conflicting [9].

Who Breastfeeds?   The incidence of breast-feeding in hospitals (Figure 3–6) had decreased from 59.7% in 1984 to 52.2% in 1989 [14]. Recent information showed that the rates of initiation of breast-feeding and of continued breast-feeding at 6 months of age, which had risen in the years from 1971 to 1982, declined in the years from 1984 to 1989. The rate for the breast-feeding of infants at 6 months of age declined 24% (from 23.8 to 18.1%) during the same period. Women who experienced the largest decreases in initiating breast-feeding were black; younger than 25 years old; low income; without a high school education; participants of the Special Supplemental Food Program for Women, Infants and Children; living in the East, North, or Central United States; and mothers of low-birth weight infants.

The *smallest* decreases occurred in the group of women who were college-educated whites or Hispanics, aged 29 or older, earning $25,000 or more, and having full-term infants. Care providers should encourage mothers to continue to breast-feed their children [14].

**Figure 3–6
Mother breast-feeds
infant.**
Photo by Robert E.
Rockwell.

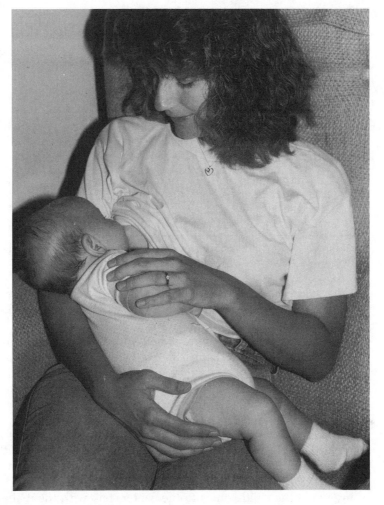

   Healthy People 2000 [15] states an objective of increasing to at least 75% the proportion of mothers who breast-feed their babies in the early postpartum period and to at least 50% the proportion who continue breast-feeding until their babies are 5 to 6 months old (Table 3–3).

   An important barrier to achieving this objective is the general absence of work policies and facilities that support lactating women. Large numbers of women discontinue breast-feeding between the time they must return to work (approximately 2 months) and the time the data are collected at 5 to 6 months. The care provider must try to influence these mothers as they begin to work again to continue several feedings a day. Given the large percentage of mothers of young children who work outside the home, your efforts to provide a good setting for breast-feeding, and your personal encouragment, will increase the number of mothers still breast-feeding at 6 months.

Table 3–3   Current and targeted incidences of breast-feeding by high-risk groups.

Mothers Breastfeeding Their Babies:	1988 Baseline	2000 Target
During early Postpartum Period		
Low-income mothers	32%	75%
Black mothers	25%	75%
Hispanic mothers	51%	75%
American Indian/Alaska Native mothers	47%	75%
At Age 5–6 Months		
Low-income mothers	9%	50%
Black mothers	8%	50%
Hispanic mothers	6%	50%
American Indian/Alaska Native mothers	28%	50%

Baseline data sources: Ross Laboratories Mothers Survey; for American Indians and Alaska Natives, Pediatric Nutrition Surveillance System, CDC.

Care of Breast Milk.   The milk can be collected in containers and, if refrigerated, can be safely used within 24 hours [11]. Breast milk may be frozen for longer periods; however, freezing and thawing can destroy its cellular structure. If freezing the milk, do so immediately after hand or mechanical expression into a container (such as a disposable bottle liner). Before use, place the frozen milk in the refrigerator for several hours to thaw, or defrost in warm water. After thawing, do not refreeze. The thawed milk may need to be mixed to distribute the cream.

Center Assistance for Breast-feeding Mothers.   The center staff can assist the breast-feeding mother by verbally reassuring the mother of the center's support for her effort. Working women may pump their breasts in order to leave milk with their child at the center. If mothers seem hesitant to continue breast-feeding when the child comes to the center, talk with them about expressing their milk using a breast pump. The LaLeche League International has information that can help you and the mother learn to easily express breast milk [16] (Figure 3–7).

Specifically, the center can:

1. Provide a room or screen a portion of a room for working mothers to feed infants during their breaks.
2. Provide the opportunity and space for mothers to express milk.
3. Provide access to hand or mechanical pumps for use by mothers. (See Figure 3–8.)
4. Provide refrigerator space for expressed milk so the infant can be fed during the day if the mother is not available.
5. Provide literature and referrals for the mother; for example, topics might include techniques of maintaining milk supply, resources for using or

Figure 3–7
Mothers can
express their breast
milk using a pump.
Photo by W.E.G.
Studio.

renting breast pumps, and names of other breast-feeding mothers. (See Appendix 3–A for sources of educational materials.)

6. Encourage the mother not to begin using pacifiers or supplemental bottles unless a feeding pattern has been established. Bottle-feeding may cause nipple confusion and decrease milk supply.

7. Refer low-income families at nutritional risk to the Special Supplemental Food Program for Women, Infants and Children (for more information, see Appendix 3–B).

8. Keep primary care providers aware of your center's facilities to help breast-feeding mothers so the health professional will lend stronger support.

Limitations of Breast-feeding.   Although breast-feeding is strongly recommended, it is not appropriate for babies whose mothers use drugs such as cocaine, PCP, or marijuana; who consume more than minimal amounts of alcohol; or who receive certain therapeutic or diagnostic agents such as radioactive elements and cancer chemotherapy. Women who are HIV-positive should also avoid breast-feeding.

A few of the complaints about breast-feeding reported by mothers [17] are more frequent feedings during the first weeks, milk leakage from the breasts, enlarged breasts, more gradual weight loss, less rest for mother during first weeks, and less opportunity for fathers (or other family members) to participate in feeding the infant. A mother whose job requires traveling must be accompanied by a babysitter.

Figure 3–8 One type of breast pump. The Avent Breast Pump courtesy of MacNeil Baby Care Limited, 5161 Thatcher Road, Downers Grove, IL 60515.

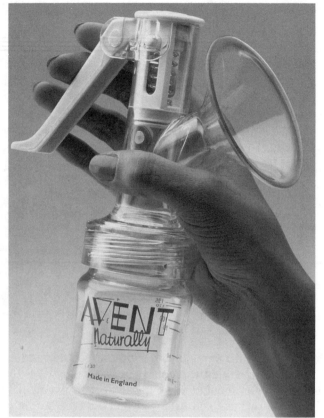

Nutrition/Exercise during Lactation. Do you recommend to the nursing mother that she must drink plenty of fluids, curtail exercise, and eat more food? Drinking at least 6 to 8 glasses of liquid per day is recommended for all adults, and there is little evidence [18] that increasing fluid intake much above 32 ounces per day actually increases milk production. The woman may exercise and in fact may even have a higher milk volume [19].

There is some debate whether the lactating woman needs as much energy as prescribed in the RDAs [20]. Mothers produce about 3 to 3½ cups of milk per day (750–800 mL/day). The production of three cups of milk accounts for approximately 500–600 additional calories. Increased maternal energy intake has not been linked with increased milk production among well-nourished women [9, 21].

The vitamin content of breast milk depends upon the mother's current vitamin intake and her stores, but concentrations of calcium, potassium, and other major minerals are not affected by the diet. Lactating women should eat more fruits, vegetables, and grains that have higher concentrations of vitamins and minerals. Advise women who choose to decrease their energy intake to include foods rich in calcium, vitamin B_6, folate, zinc, and magnesium. Energy intake should be at least 1800 kcal/day. Intakes below 1500 kcal/day are not recommended [9]. Depending upon the choice of foods for the mother's diet, breast-feeding may or may not be more costly than bottle-feeding [22].

Bottle-feeding

The most important thing for care providers to remember when bottle-feeding is always to hold the baby close to the body and focus attention on the child. Feeding should provide not only food but a feeling of security and love. There should be no "propped" bottles in the center (Figure 3–9). Any signal that the bottle-fed baby is satisfied should cause the care provider to stop feeding even if only 1 ounce (30 mL) of formula remains in the bottle. Forcing the last ounce into the baby may set the pattern for overeating for the toddler, preschooler, and adult. This can be associated with "cleaning your plate" or forcing the last bite of mashed potatoes—patterns that may lead to obesity.

Formula.   If formula is to be used, an iron-fortified commercially prepared formula is the complete food for the infant. Iron-fortified formulas contain vitamins and iron; therefore, no supplements are necessary. If fluoride is not available in the water supply, supplemental fluoride should be given. Most formulas come in ready-to-serve, concentrated, or powdered form.

After 3 months of age, relatively few infants consume more than 1 quart of formula, although large infants may require more energy to meet their needs. Table 3–4 provides a formula for calculating daily energy and protein needs and lists recommended allowances of vitamins and minerals. Regular formulas for infants supply 20 kcal per ounce, and 32 ounces of formula supply 640 kcal (20 kcal per ounce × 32 ounces). If the child is bottle-fed at 6 months of age and doesn't eat solid foods, more than 1 quart of formula would be necessary to meet the child's energy needs. The American Academy of Pediatrics recommends that the amount of formula or cow's milk should be limited to less than a quart or a liter (33.8 fl oz) per day [23]. This means that solid foods should make up part of the child's diet at 6 months of age.

A 3-month-old can be expected to weigh between 12 and 13 pounds (Table 3–2). The energy needs would be approximately 590 to 650 kcal (12–13 lb × 49.1 kcal/lb). A quart of formula (640 kcal) would meet the needs of the average baby of this weight. Obviously, if the child is larger, solid foods may be needed to meet energy needs. Somewhere between 4 to 6 months of age, solid foods are usually introduced to meet the physical as well as the social and psychological needs of the child.

A 6-month-old weighing 16 to 17 pounds needs 44.5 kcal per pound or approximately 715 to 750 kcal. Since caloric needs have begun to exceed that supplied by breast milk or 1 quart of formula (640 kcal), supplemental food should be offered.

**Figure 3–9
Always hold the
baby close during
feeding.**
Photo by Robert M.
Wagner.

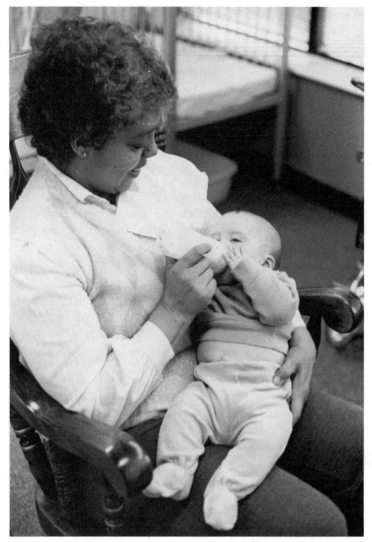

A wide variety of formulas are available on the market. The composition of these formulas is given in Table 3–5. Some formulas are designed for children who are allergic to milk. Premature infants may have a specific formula not shown in the list. Compare the formulas to human milk and regular cow's milk.

Whole Cow's Milk.   Fresh whole cow's milk or evaporated milk is not an acceptable alternative to human milk as long as milk or formula supplies the major source of calories. Protein content of cow's milk is above the acceptable range, and the carbohydrate content is lower than in commercially prepared formulas or breast milk. The amount of fat is consistently high in cow's milk, whereas the

Table 3–4 Recommended dietary allowances for infants.

Nutrient	0–6 Months*	6–12 Months†
Resting Energy	kg × 108	kg × 98
Equivalent	(lb × 49.1)	(lb × 44.5)
Protein (g)	kg × 2.1	kg × 1.6
(g/day)	13	14
Vitamin A (μg RE)	375	375
Vitamin D (μg)	7.5	10
Vitamin E (mg -TE)	3	4
Vitamin K (μg)	5	10
Ascorbic acid (mg)	30	35
Folate (μg)	25	35
Niacin (mg NE)	5	6
Riboflavin (mg)	0.4	0.5
Thiamin (mg)	0.3	0.4
Vitamin B_6 (mg)	0.3	0.6
Vitamin B_{12} (μg)	0.3	0.5
Calcium (mg)	400	600
Phosphorus (mg)	300	500
Iodine (μg)	40	50
Iron (mg)	6	10
Magnesium (mg)	40	60
Zinc (mg)	5	5

*Weight 6 kg (14 lb), height 60 cm (24 in).
†Weight 9 kg (20 lb), height 71 cm (28 in).

Source: Based on Food and Nutrition Board, National Academy of Sciences—National Research Council: Recommended dietary allowances, revised 1980.

fat content of breast milk increases as nursing continues. Breast milk is lower in fat content when nursing begins and higher at the end of the breast-feeding period.

The low-income, high-risk infant should be given breast milk or iron-fortified formula as the most reliable source of calories and iron until 1 year of age. For the diets of other infants, we agree with the American Academy of Pediatrics [23], which has stated,

Although many mothers will continue to breast-feed or formula-feed their babies through the first year of life, there is at present no convincing evidence from well-designed research studies that feeding whole cow's milk after 6 months of age is harmful if adequate supplementary feedings are given.

On the basis of knowledge of the types of solid foods commonly given to infants and the composition of these foods, it has been reported that the protein, fat, and carbohydrate content of the diet will probably remain within desirable limits if the transition to whole cow's milk is made after the infant is consuming the equivalent of at least 1.5 jars of strained foods (about ¾ cup) daily. If whole

Table 3–5   Composition of milk and infant formulas.

Name of Product	Energy Contribution		
	Carbohydrate (%)	Protein (%)	Fat (%)
Human milk	41	6	30 to 55
*Whole milk	30	21	49
*2% low-fat milk	38	27	35
*Skim milk	57	38	5
Goat's milk	26	20	54
†Enfamil	41	9	50
‡Isomil	41	10	49
‡Nursoy	40	12	48
§Alimentum	41	11	48
§Nutramigen	54	11	35
§Pregestimil	41	11	48
‡Prosobee	40	12	48
†Similac	43	9	48
†Similac PM 60/40	41	9	50
†S-M-A	43	9	48
‡iSoyalac	39	12	49
‡Soyalac	39	12	49
†Gerber	43	9	49
†Carnation Good Start	44	10	46
Carnation Follow-up	53	10	37

*Not recommended for infants <12 months.
†Milk-based formula.
‡Milk-free formula made with soy protein.
§Milk-free formula.

Sources: Data on human milk from Composition of foods, Agriculture Handbook No. 8-1., U.S. Department of Agriculture, Agricultural Research Service, revised 1976; data on whole, 2%, and skim milk from NDDA Laboratory, Southern Illinois University at Carbondale, 1980; data on formula composition provided by formula companies, 1992.

cow's milk and strained foods are used, the infant will probably not be receiving adequate iron (see *Supplementation* later in this chapter).

Skim and Low-Fat Milks.   Skim and low-fat milks are unacceptable alternatives to human milk during infancy. Skim milk provides 38% of calories from protein and 5% from fat, and "2 percent" milk provides 27% of calories from protein and 35% from fat. Thus, both are too high in protein, and skim milk is too low in fat in comparison with prepared formulas or human milk (6% to 12% protein, 30% to 55% fat).

Infants fed skim milk as the main source of calories generally are not able to consume the daily energy allowance and probably have to mobilize stores of body fat to meet energy needs. This is potentially dangerous, because it depletes energy reserves, and any illness that interferes more than briefly with food intake may become life-threatening.

Preparation of Formulas.   It is important in the infant center to remind care providers of the proper method to be used in preparation of all formulas. When preparing formulas from concentrate or powder, it is necessary to follow carefully the instructions on the can of formula. Since most city water supplies are clean, it is not necessary to sterilize water unless water is obtained from a private well.

Lead.   There is a hazard of lead contamination during infant formula preparation [24]. Studies show that infants were poisoned after they took formula prepared from tap water from lead pipes. Lead is most concentrated in the morning when water has not been used during the night, and lead becomes concentrated when water is boiled. Three rules for preparation of formula to prevent lead contamination include:

- Do not boil water for formula. Most water supplies are safe.
- Flush the water system with cold water 2 minutes or use bottled water.
- Discard any lead-based kettles that might be used.

Sterilization.   Most large centers will be required to use sanitary dishwashing techniques and bottles will be washed with hot soapy water, thoroughly rinsed, and sanitized. However, it may still be advisable to sterilize the bottles used for infant formula if many of the children in the home or center are suffering from acute infections.

Preparation of single feedings may be preferable to preparation of all feedings for a 24-hour period if only one or two infants are in the center. It is advisable in a center with only a few infants to purchase disposable bottles of ready-to-feed formula or prepare single bottles of formula for use during the first 2 to 3 months of life to ensure the child's safety. Often powdered formulas are convenient if the infant is at the center for a short time. Formula should be used in the 24 hours following preparation (Chapter 7). Breast-fed babies should have a supply of mother's milk in the freezer in case of emergency or to be used when the mother is delayed in returning to the center.

Microwave.   There has been at least one reported case [25] where a mother put formula into a disposable plastic liner of a baby bottle, sealed the bottle with the rubber nipple, and microwaved it for 1 minute. She removed the bottle from the oven and a few seconds later the liner exploded, resulting in burns to the infant's abdomen and thigh.

Reasons for not using the microwave with babies milk:

- Formulas at relatively high temperatures may lose some of the vitamins.
- Expressed breast milk may lose protective properties.

- Bottles stay cool while formula is hot, burning baby's mouth.
- Steam buildup in tightly closed containers can cause explosion.

If you do use a microwave for any food given to an infant, check to be sure that containers AND milk/food warmed in the microwave is not too hot. Containers not designed for the microwave often absorb heat. USE ONLY CONTAINERS DESIGNED FOR THE MICROWAVE!

Supplementation

If the infant is not regularly exposed to sunlight, the infant should be given a supplement of vitamin D each day. Fluoride supplements should be provided to breast-fed infants if the fluoride content of the household drinking water is low. Not until the breast-fed baby is taking other foods but at least by 6 months of age when table foods have become part of the diet, the infant should be given foods rich in bioavailable iron or a daily low-dose oral iron supplement [26].

If the mother decides not to breast-feed, iron-fortified infant formula is recommended for infants as an alternate and predictable source of iron in place of an iron supplement. If the infant is fed a commercial formula without supplemental iron or is fed cow's milk, supplemental iron should be used.

Once a child has started eating solids, iron-fortified cereal can provide a source of iron. One-half cup of iron-fortified dry cereal will provide over 50% of the recommended amount of iron. Mothers generally feel more comfortable feeding infant cereals than providing medicinal iron.

Gastrointestinal disturbances such as diarrhea or constipation and certain feeding problems have been attributed to formulas containing iron. There is little evidence, however, that this is a significant problem.

Although the RDA for specific nutrients is presented in Table 3-4 the care provider need worry little about the acquisition of specific nutrients by infants who are breast- or bottle-fed with iron-fortified formula. In summary, by 6 months of age children should be receiving [27]:

Breast milk with iron supplements and vitamin D if necessary
Iron-fortified formula only (supplements already added to formula); or
Formula (non-iron-fortified) with addition of iron-fortified infant cereal; or
Breast milk with iron-fortified infant cereal and vitamin D supplement if
    necessary; and
Fluoride if:
    (1) water is not given infants who are breast-feeding;
    (2) fluoridated water is not used for dilution of concentrated formula; or
    (3) ready-to-feed formula is used without additional water from a fluoridated supply.

The use of fluoride as a supplement remains controversial. Parents should consult their pediatrician for recommendation on fluoride supplementation.

SOLID FOODS

Currently there is a debate over whether solid foods should be introduced before the age of 6 months. Years ago mothers were told that they might introduce cereals at the first or second week or even the second day of life. This theory has now given way to the introduction of solid foods at a later time—4 to even 6 months. Most parents are providing their infants with some solid foods at approximately 4 months of age. It is probably better if this food is limited to iron-fortified infant cereal. If formula or cow's milk is limited to 1 quart (0.96 L) per day, when solid foods are introduced depends more on the weight or appetite of the baby than on an arbitrary age of 4 or 6 months.

By the age of 4 months, some infants are physiologically capable of accepting foods from a spoon and transferring them from the front of the mouth to the back for swallowing. Some children at this time will be able to sit in a high chair or baby seat and lean forward with mouth open indicating a need or desire to eat.

Turning the head, closing the mouth, and pushing food away should be signals to you that the infant is satisfied (Figure 3–10). Thus, the infant now has

Figure 3–10   Baby signals care provider to stop feeding.
Photo courtesy of USDA.

some control over how much is consumed. The parent or care provider who is responsive to the child's needs should stop feeding when the baby is satisfied and thereby prevent the possibility of overfeeding.

When introducing solid foods, parents often wonder what dietary restrictions they should apply to their children's diets. However, much of the nutrition information for adults is not appropriate for infants. The following guidelines are consistent with the positions of the American Academy of Pediatrics, Committee on Nutrition, and the American Dietetic Association. The guidelines can be used by care providers and parents to safeguard infants from overly restrictive diets.

- Build to a variety of foods.
- Listen to your baby's appetite to avoid overfeeding or underfeeding.
- Don't restrict fat and cholesterol.
- Don't overdo high-fiber foods.
- Sugar is okay, but in moderation.
- Sodium is okay, but in moderation.
- Babies need more iron, pound for pound than adults.*

Infant Feeders

For a child with normal development, cereals and other pureed foods should never be put through a bottle with a large opening or into an infant feeder. In essence, this is force feeding. Unfortunately, this type of feeding is usually provided by overanxious parents of young infants whose needs would be met by formula or breast milk alone. The extra energy provided by foods may lead to excessive weight gain. Parents who are using bottles with large holes in the nipple or infant feeders should be discouraged from such practice.

How Much Food?

Table 3–6 provides a guide to the amount of foods for infants, with the energy contribution of each item. In this case small amounts of cereal were added when formula intake reached 32 ounces (960 mL).

Table 3–7 illustrates the nutrient needs and food intake of one 5-month-old infant. Formula provides most of the calories and protein, which in this case is several grams higher than recommended. Note that single-grained infant cereal (rice) is used. High-protein cereal is unnecessary when infants are taking formula.

---

*Dietary guidelines for infants were developed by Gerber Products Company and based on American Academy of Pediatrics, Committee on Nutrition, 1989.

Table 3–6 Guide to amounts of foods for infants.

Age (months)	Weight	Foods*	Energy (kcal)
Up to 1	Up to 9 lb (9 lb × 49 kcal/lb = 441 kcal)	22 fl oz formula	440
2 to 3	Up to 12 lb (12 lb x 49 kcal/lb = 588 kcal)	30 fl oz iron-fortified formula	600
4 to 5	Up to 14 lb (14 lb x 49 kcal/lb = 686 kcal)	30 fl oz iron-fortified formula 8 tbsp dry baby cereal	600 83 683
6 to 7	Up to 16 lb (16 lb × 44.5 kcal/lb = 712 kcal)	30 fl oz iron-fortified formula 5 tbsp dry baby cereal 4 fl oz baby fruit juice 5 tbsp baby vegetables	600 52 56 15 723
8 to 9	Up to 18½ lb (18½ lb × 44.5 kcal/lb = 823.25 kcal)	32 fl oz iron-fortified formula 6 tbsp dry baby cereal 4 fl oz baby fruit juice 7 tbsp baby vegetables 6 tbsp baby fruit 3 tbsp baby meat, cooked legumes, or tofu	640 62 56 23 61 47 889
10 to 11	Up to 20 lb (20 lb × 44.5 kcal/lb = 890 kcal)	32 fl oz iron-fortified formula 6 tbsp dry baby cereal 4 fl oz fruit juice 8 tbsp vegetables 8 tbsp fruit 1 oz meat or equivalent meat alternate	640 83 56 24 76 75 954
12	Up to 22½ lb (22½ lb × 44.5 kcal/lb = 1001 kcal)	32 fl oz formula 8 tbsp dry baby cereal 6 fl oz fruit juice 10 tbsp vegetables 8 tbsp fruit 2 oz meat or equivalent	640 83 84 30 76 150 1063

*Because variation in individual recipes creates difficulties in calculating calorie content of homemade foods, commercial foods were used. "Table foods" should begin around 6 months of age. This guide may be used in screening dietary intakes of infants to help identify those with very excessive intakes. Activity levels can make a big difference in requirements, and a healthy infant may eat more or less. The infant who consumes more milk may need fewer other foods. Use table as a guide, not a rule!

Table 3–7   Nutritional needs and diet for 5-month-old infant (weight 6.4 kg [14 lb]; height 26 in.).

Nutritional Needs

Requirements

Calories	691 kcal (kg × 108 kcal or lb × 49.1 kcal
Protein	13 g (kg × 2.1 g)
Iron	6 mg

Food intake provides

Infant Food	Amount	Energy	Protein	Iron
Cereal*	9 tbsp dry	93 kcal	2.0 g	11.5 mg
Formula†	30 oz	600 kcal	12.0 g	10.8 mg
TOTAL		693 kcal	14.0 g	22.3 mg

Food Pattern for 5-Month-Old Infant

Time	Food	Amount
7:00 A.M.	Formula	6 oz
7:30 A.M.	Cereal with formula	5 tbsp + 3 oz formula
11:30 A.M.	Formula	6 oz
3:00 P.M.	Formula	2 oz
6:00 P.M.	Cereal with formula	4 tbsp dry + 2 oz formula
	Formula	6 oz
10:00 P.M.	Formula	5 oz

*Nutrient values for rice.
†Infant formula provides 20 kcal/oz standard dilution.

Source: Calculations from NDDA Laboratory, Southern Illinois University at Carbondale.

First Finger Foods

At 6 to 7 months the infant will also enjoy finger foods and will be eager to self-feed. Acceptable finger foods include hard toast (whole wheat), grapefruit and orange sections, other cooked fruits and vegetables, corn bread, whole wheat crackers, bite-sized pieces of soft pretzels, and soft cheese. Experiment, do not overcook vegetables and fruit, and omit foods that may cause choking. Young children when hungry will try a variety of cooked foods such as carrots, green beans, and cooked dried beans; young children enjoy even stronger-flavored vegetables—turnips, broccoli, cabbage, and cauliflower. Often children will eat these foods warm or cold. Before the meal, when the infant is particularly hungry, try placing a stick of cooked vegetable, warm or cold, on the child's tray instead of crackers or bread. You may be surprised to find that the child readily accepts these foods.

Fresh blackberries and strawberries, as well as more common fruits such as oranges, grapefruit, peaches, kiwi, pears, and apricots, are all acceptable and provide the child with a variety of tastes. The most important point is that variety introduced now will set the pattern for food habits throughout life.

THE CUP

The child can approximate lips to the rim of a cup by 5 months and can begin drinking from the cup by 6 months. No more than 2 to 3 tablespoons should be put in the cup when the baby is learning to drink. Two tablespoons are much easier to clean up from the floor than 4 ounces. A refill is also more rewarding for the child and the care provider or parent.

EATING WITH UTENSILS

At about 8 to 10 months of age, baby will be interested in using a spoon for feeding. Use a spoon with a flat, wide bowl for easier scooping; a dish with sides also makes scooping easier. Remember to be prepared for spills and messes that accompany the first attempts at self-feeding. It is best to place a vinyl or plastic cloth underneath the high chair or to spread papers on the floor. At 6 to 8 months, when baby is learning to experiment with foods, give the child every opportunity to learn about foods and how to eat them. These exciting learning experiences are expressions of independence and should certainly be encouraged and enjoyed. Try to understand and even see some humor in the sweet potatoes on the nose, chin, and hair. Adopting the child's perspective rather than an adult's helps make the experience tolerable and even enjoyable.

EVALUATING THE DIET

The following presents two diets for a 9-month-old infant. One of the diets uses whole milk. Whole milk could be continued as demonstrated in the Modified Menu, but the use of formula would ensure a balanced diet. The addition of vitamin C-rich foods, elimination of "junior" foods, and substituting at least one of the cookies with more nutrient-dense grain products improves the diet for the infant. Strained and chopped meats were retained on the diet since the infant may not be able to chew meat.

Current Menu	*Modified Menu*
Breakfast	*Breakfast*
Rice cereal, 3 tbsp	Rice cereal, 3 tbsp
Applesauce, ¼ C	Applesauce ¼ C
10:00 A.M.	*10:00 A.M.*
Whole milk, 8 oz	Iron-fortified formula, 8 oz
12:00 noon	*12:00 noon*
Vegetables and chicken, 1 jar	Steamed broccoli, 2 tbsp
Mashed potatoes and gravy, ½ C	Ground chicken, 1 oz
Whole milk, 1 C	Mashed potatoes, ½ C
	Iron-fortified formula, 8 oz

3:00 P.M.	*3:00 P.M.*
Whole milk, ½ C	Iron-fortified formula, 4 oz
Oatmeal cookie, 1	Graham cracker, 1
5:30 P.M.	*5:30 P.M.*
Strained peas, 1 jar	Cooked carrots, 2 tbsp
Junior vegetables and ham, 1 jar	Chopped/ground ham, 1 oz
Whole milk, ½	Iron-fortified formula, 4 oz
Oatmeal cookie, 1	Whole wheat bread, ¼ slice
	Margarine, ½ tsp
8:00 P.M.	*8 P.M.*
Ice cream, ½ C	Frozen yogurt, ½ C
Per day: 1100 cal, 39 g pro,	Per day: 990 cal, 35 g pro
126 g car, 52 g fat,	118 g car, 43 g fat,
4 mg iron	12.2 g iron

HEALTH CONCERNS

The care provider may be confronted with questions regarding iron-deficiency anemia, lactose intolerance, and food allergies. Perhaps even more common are concerns about constipation, diarrhea, and spitting up or vomiting.

Iron-Deficiency Anemia

The diagnosis of iron-deficiency anemia is left to the physician or health clinic. However, the care provider can help prevent the onset of iron-deficiency anemia by being informed of the foods that contain iron and helping parents see the importance of using sources of iron for prevention of this problem.

The RDA for iron for the young infant, birth to 6 months of age, is 6 mg; for the 6- to 12-month-old child it increases to 10 mg (Table 3–4). The full-term baby's iron stores are depleted by 6 months of age, and this occurs earlier for preterm infants. Iron-deficiency anemia often becomes apparent after the first 6 months of life and through the preschool years. As discussed earlier, if iron-fortified infant formula is used, iron is already in the formula and is a constant, predictable supply. If the baby is breast-fed, is fed a commercial formula without supplemental iron, or is fed cow's milk, iron-fortified infant cereal or supplemental iron should be used [27].

Lactose Intolerance

Lactose is the natural sugar in milk that is digested with the help of an enzyme called lactase. Breast milk has a high concentration of lactose, and full-term infants nearly always tolerate lactose well, even if they are from populations where there is a high prevalence of lactose intolerance among adults. When lactose intolerance occurs in infancy, it is usually temporary, a secondary symptom of illnesses that affect the intestinal mucosa (lining), producing diarrhea. When lactose intolerance is suspected, it should be confirmed by a physician before being treated by feeding a lactose-free formula. Unlike the infant, older children may have less of the enzyme lactase and may develop an intolerance to lactose [28].

Food Allergies

The gastrointestinal tract is permeable to macromolecules (larger molecules) during early infancy, at least to 7 months of age. If some proteins are not completely broken down to amino acids, the protein may be absorbed intact and a food allergy produced. If solid foods are introduced after 6 to 7 months of age, allergies present little problem. It is recommended that the use of commonly allergenic foods (eggs, cow's milk, soy protein) be delayed until after 6 months.

Foods should be introduced into the infant's diet one at a time, and the food should be continued for several days. Single foods are preferable to mixtures of foods in the early months (for example, peas would be a more appropriate choice than mixed vegetables). If allergic symptoms appear when this procedure is followed, it is easy to identify the food. If allergic symptoms appear after mixed vegetables are eaten, it is impossible to tell which vegetable caused the reaction. Children with a family history of allergies are more susceptible to allergies and should be fed single-grain cereals and individual vegetables and fruits. If no symptoms occur, mixed foods may be offered. Mothers of potentially allergic infants should be encouraged to breast-feed, since infants are rarely allergic to breast milk. Common food allergy symptoms include hives, rashes, vomiting, excessive gas, and diarrhea. In addition, a wide variety of other symptoms including respiratory problems may result from an allergy. If allergies are diagnosed, a dietitian can help parents find cookbooks and other materials to assist them in preparing allergen-free meals [29].

Gastrointestinal Tract Disturbances

Parents often come to care providers complaining that the child is constipated or has diarrhea. The definition, incidence, and treatment of constipation are all subjects of dispute. It is generally agreed that a hard, dry stool passed with straining characterizes constipation, not the frequency of the stool. Some babies may have a stool only three or four times a week. A daily stool is unnecessary. Constipation rarely occurs in breast-fed infants who receive adequate milk or in non-breast-fed infants who receive an adequate diet [29].

Stools of breast-fed infants shortly after birth usually appear loose and are frequent; however, it is not uncommon for a totally breast-fed infant to have no stools for 1 or 2 days. When solid foods are introduced, stools change in appearance and frequency.

When solid foods have been introduced, mild constipation may be alleviated by increasing use of whole-grain cereals, fruits, or vegetables. Check the child's current diet, including fluid intake, and modify it with food and additional fluids. With the decreased consumption of milk, other fluids may not be sufficient to meet the child's needs. If repeated episodes of constipation occur, an evaluation of the infant's diet by a health professional should be made and appropriate counseling given.

Diarrhea is the passage of frequent, unformed, or watery stools. The term usually implies a change from the infant's usual stool pattern. Acute diarrhea is frequently brief in duration—1 to 4 days—and represents a problem primarily with water and electrolyte (especially sodium and potassium) balance. If the infant is not severely dehydrated, an attempt should be made to feed the infant while treating diarrhea. However, foods that have been recently added to the diet should be avoided. If the infant is dehydrated, the pediatrician will prescribe replacement therapy for water and electrolytes. An infant is likely to become very irritable if given inadequate calories for long periods.

When mild diarrhea lasts for more than 3 days, attention should be focused on providing adequate calories and nutrients and on maintaining water balance. The mother should consult a physician. Diarrhea accompanied by a temperature over 101° F, diarrhea accompanied by vomiting that lasts more than 24 hours, or severe diarrhea with stools more than 10 times per day with a large volume of water lost requires immediate medical attention [30].

Spitting up, or regurgitation, is the return of small amounts of food during or immediately after eating. Vomiting is more complete emptying of the stomach, especially when it occurs some time after feeding. Spitting up should not concern the care provider or parent. A limited amount of regurgitation is a normal occurrence in the first 6 months of life. It can be kept to a minimum by burping the baby during and after each feeding, handling the baby gently, allowing the baby to nap on the side or abdomen after feeding, and making certain that the head is not lower than the body during naps. Spitting up usually diminishes by 8 months. Vomiting is common in infancy and is associated with many problems that vary widely in severity. A physician should always be consulted.

Nursing Bottle Caries

The use of a bottle as a pacifier may contribute to development of nursing bottle caries or baby bottle tooth decay (BBTD), a condition that can destroy the baby teeth. The condition occurs when the child's teeth are exposed to carbohydrates for long periods, such as when the child falls asleep with the bottle in the mouth. Sweetened drinks, fruit juices, formula, and breast milk can all cause caries. The baby should be held while taking the bottle.

If mother and baby sleep together, nursing on demand through the night may also lead to caries because the breast milk may pool in the mouth and remain in contact with the teeth for an extended period of time. Preferably, juices should be unsweetened and not offered until the infant is able to drink from a cup.

Genetic predisposition to caries may also contribute to the occurrence of nursing bottle caries. Characteristics of children at risk for development of caries can be identified in the preschool or infant center. Some of the characteristics of children include [31]:

- Living in a single parent household.
- Sleep difficulties.
- Strong temper.
- Taking the bottle to bed to an older age (1 to 2 years).
- Parents have received less advice regarding weaning.
- Less use of fluoride supplementation.

Some pediatricians advise wiping the teeth after each feeding; however, this may be impractical for the baby's care provider. The center can recognize the above profile and educate parents. The nutritionist or dietitian along with the care provider can offer educational programs emphasizing [32]:

- The risk factors.
- The appearance of the teeth.
- The specific steps to help the child sleep without a bottle.
- The role of parent and center in preventing BBTD.

EXERCISE AND PHYSICAL FITNESS FOR INFANTS

The National Association for the Education of Young Children suggests the following physical fitness activities for infant center care providers:

If you have time, you can play physical fitness games with babies for a minute or two once or twice a day. Move the arms gently in a rhythmic pattern. Make the legs "ride a bike." Firmly holding the baby under the arms, boost the infant slightly above your face so the child can laughingly look down at you. Hold the baby under the arms in a standing position on the lap and dance the child briefly up and down.

Encourage sluggish babies, but don't force them. For example, motivate the sedentary crawler by holding an attractive toy inches in front of the child to see if the child will creep to get it. Don't tease, though, if the baby appears to be frustrated. It seems pompous to call this a "curriculum." These are the things most mothers have done for centuries. But it is part of what people trained as infant workers are shown how to do because all these activities in gentle moderation are good for babies [33]. The following movement skills were observed during a visit to an infant-at-risk program [34]:

- Tumbling.
- Care provider exercising extremities during diaper changing.
- Doing pull-ups on walker.

**Figure 3–11
Infant interacts
with care provider.**
Photo by Robert E.
Rockwell.

- Scooting, crawling, and climbing up and down an incline board.
- Pushing bolster.
- Care providers holding babies by waist or hands, walking them around.
- Pushing a toy wagon.
- Care providers encouraging babies to reach out or crawl for objects.
- Playing with pop-up pets.
- Squeezing soft animals.
- Care providers and babies playing pat-a-cake before mirror.
- Watching overhead mobiles in cribs.
- Care providers placing babies on tummy, raising them up and down.
- Care provider and baby rolling ball while seated.

Structured exercise programs in infant care centers that serve children age 6 weeks through age 1 are not necessary. An encouraging care giver (Figure 3–11) and a physical environment that permits freedom of movement and exploration are enough to help infants develop their natural abilities.

POLICIES OF THE INFANT CENTER

One soon realizes that nutritional care of the infant, especially the very young, is quite different from care of the preschooler. This is not only because of the infant's nutritional needs, but also because parents come with definite ideas on how, when, and what their babies should be fed. Their methods may not always be best for the infant.

Center policies regarding feeding are best understood when put in writing and explained to parents. In addition, the child's pediatrician or the health clinic should be notified of the established practices. However, a policy should not be arbitrary; it should have a foundation in the nutrition literature and be necessary for the health and well-being of the infant. This chapter has cited numerous references to assist the care provider. It is important that parents see the center working with other community agencies and resources as an extension of the primary health care given to their infant. Parenthood is often frightening, and sources of information are varied and confusing. The center should not be an additional source of frustration to the parents.

The written feeding policy should include statements regarding basic nutrition for the infant. It should say when and how food will be introduced, where children will be fed, and who will feed them. Likewise, the availability of breast-feeding facilities (see *Center Assistance for Breast-feeding Mothers*) for mother and infant and policies regarding illness and formula preparation should be included. If possible, the mother or father who decides to bottle-feed the infant should also be given the opportunity to come to the center and feed the baby.

The center should be equipped to keep records on each child so that care providers are well aware which child is receiving supplementation and what the supplement contains. If the supplementation is not in line with good nutritional principles, the parent should be consulted as well as the health agency or pediatrician. If regular vitamin and mineral preparations are provided, they should be given by parents. Forms for recording routines and feeding schedules are presented in Chapter 9.

SUMMARY

- Height, weight, skinfold thickness, hemoglobin, and hematocrit, along with dietary intake, are measurements used to evaluate nutritional status of young children in community settings. Appropriate use and interpretation of results are important for the care provider.
- Breast-feeding is the preferred method of feeding infants from birth to 12 months of age.
- Iron-fortified formula given through the first year of life supplies the birth to 12-month-old child with all known essential nutrients (except fluoride) without the addition of vitamin and mineral supplements.
- For the infant who is not "at risk," there is no convincing evidence from the research that feeding whole cow's milk after 6 months of age is harmful, but adequate supplementary feedings must be given.
- Solid foods are usually introduced when the child is developmentally ready to chew and when the need for formula exceeds 1 quart per day.
- Although weight gain is the best method to determine whether food intake meets energy and nutrient needs, examining what and when the child is eating can help determine any changes needed in food intake.

- Breast-fed babies do not consume as much food and tend to gain weight more slowly than their bottle-fed counterparts.
- Use of foods, eating utensils, and the eating situation as educational tools should begin during infancy.
- Iron-deficiency anemia, lactose intolerance, food allergies, constipation, diarrhea, and nursing bottle caries are nutrition-related problems facing parents during their child's infancy.
- Exercise and fitness routines for infants are looked upon as activities that most mothers have done naturally for centuries.
- Policies should be written and communicated to parents by care providers.

DISCUSSION QUESTIONS

1. Do breast-fed infants and bottle-fed infants grow at the same rate?
2. What are some questions to ask the mother of the child who is below the 5th percentile height for weight?
3. Why should a mother be encouraged to breast-feed her child?
4. Name several ways you could encourage the mother to breast-feed. What resources should be available to the mother at the center and in the community?
5. How does a mother's health and diet during pregnancy and lactation affect the infant?
6. What are the consequences of introducing solid foods before 4 months of age?
7. What are sources of iron after 6 months of age?
8. Consider two nutrition-related problems of infancy. How might these problems be managed?
9. What can care providers do to stimulate movement activities for infants?
10. What role does the physical environment of an infant center play in infant fitness?

REFERENCES

1. Black, J., Puckett, M., and Bell, M.: The young child: development from prebirth through age eight, Columbus, OH, 1992, Merrill Publishing Co.
2. National Center for Health Statistics: NCHS growth charts, monthly vital statistics report 25, Suppl. 3 (HRA) 76–1120, Rockville, MD, 1976, Health Resource Administration.
3. Hammill, P. V. V., and Moore, W. M.: Contemporary growth charts: needs, construction, and application, Public Health Currents (Ross Laboratory), 1976.
4. Dewey, K., Heinig, M.J., Nommsen, L. A., and Lonnerdal, B.: Adequacy of energy intake among breast-fed infants in the Darling study: relationships to growth velocity, morbidity and activity levels, Pediatrics 119:538–547, 1991.
5. Guo, S., Roche A. F., Fomon, S. J., et al.: Reference data on gains in weight and length dur-

ing the first two years of life, J. Pediatr. 119:355–362, 1991.

6. Frisancho, A. R.: Triceps skinfold and upper arm muscle size norms for assessment of nutritional status, Am. J. Clin. Nutr. 27:1052–1058, 1974.

7. U.S. Public Law 94–105, Oct. 7, 1975.

8. Institute of Medicine: Nutrition during pregnancy: weight gain and nutrient supplements. Report of the Subcommittee on Nutritional Status and Weight Gain during Pregnancy, Subcommittee on Dietary Intake and Nutrient Supplements during Pregnancy, Committee on Nutritional Status during Pregnancy and Lactation, Food and Nutrition Board, Washington, DC, 1990, National Academy Press p. 468.

9. Institute of Medicine: Nutrition during lactation. Report of the Subcommittee on Nutrition during Lactation, Committee on Nutrition Status during Pregnancy and Lactation, Food and Nutrition Board, Washington, DC, 1991, National Academy Press.

10. Lucas, A., Morley, R., Cole, T. J., Lister, G., and Leeson-Payne, C.: Breast milk and subsequent IQ in preterm children, The Lancet 339:261–264, 1992.

11. Lawrence, R.: Breastfeeding: a guide for the medicalprofessional, St. Louis, 1989, The C. V. Mosby Co.

12. Lewis, P., et al.: The resumption of ovulation and menstruation in a well-nourished population of women breastfeeding for an extended period of time, Fertil. Steril. 55(3):529–536, 1991.

13. Layde, P.: The independent associations of parity, age at first full term pregnancy and duration of breast feeding with the risk of breast cancer, J. Clin. Epidemiol. 42:963–973, 1989.

14. Ryan, A. S., Rush, D., Krieger, F.W., and Lewandowski, G.E.: Recent declines in breastfeeding in the U.S., 1984 through 1989, Pediatrics 88:719–727,1991

15. U.S. Department of Health and Human Services: Healthy people 2000: national health promotion and disease prevention objectives, DHHS Publication No. (DHS) 91–50213, Washington, DC, 1990, U.S. Government Printing Office.

16. LaLeche League International: A mother's guide to milk expression and breast pumps, 9615 Minneapolis Ave. Box 1209, Franklin Park, IL, 1991, LaLeche League Int.

17. Schoensiegel, B. B.: The expanded role of the dietitian as lactation educator or consultant, Top. Clin. Nutr. 2:21–30, 1987.

18. Dusdieker, L., et al.: Prolonged maternal fluid supplementation in breastfeeding, Pediatrics 86(5):737–740, 1990.

19. Lovelady, C., Lonnerdal B., and Dewey, K.: Lactation performance of exercising women, Am. J. Clin. Nutr. 52:103–109, 1990.

20. National Research Council: Recommended dietary allowances, ed. 10, Washington, DC, 1989, National Academy Press.

21. van Raaij, J., et al.: Energy cost of lactation, and energy balances of well-nourished Dutch lactating women reappraisal of the extra energy requirements of lactation, Am. J. Clin. Nutr. 53(3):612–619, 1991.

22. Endres, J., and Rockwell, R.: Food nutrition and young child, Columbus, OH, 1990, Macmillan Pub. Co.

23. American Academy of Pediatrics, Committee on Nutrition: The use of whole cow's milk in infancy, Pediatrics 72:253–255, 1983.

24. Shannon, M., and Graef, J.: Hazard of lead in infant formula, N. Eng. J. Med. 326:137, 1992.

25. Puczynski, M., Rademaker, D., and Gatson, R.L.: Burn injury related to the improper use of a microwave oven, Pediatrics 72:714–715, 1983.

26. American Academy of Pediatrics, Committee on Nutrition: Vitamin and mineral supplement needs, Pediatrics 66:1015–1020, 1980.

27. American Academy of Pediatrics, Committee on Nutrition: Pediatric nutrition handbook, ed. 2, Chicago, 1985, American Academy of Pediatrics.

28. Paige, D. M., and Bayless, T. M.: Lactose digestion, Baltimore, 1981, The Johns Hopkins University Press.

29. Johns, S. B.: Allergy guide to brand name foods and food additives, New York, 1988, Nal Penguim Inc.

30. Scipien, G. M., Barnard, M. U., Chard, M. A., et al.: Comprehensive pediatric nursing, New York, 1979, McGraw-Hill Book Co.

31. Marino, R.V., Bomze, K., Scholl, T.O., and Anhalt, H.: Nursing bottle caries: characteristics of children at risk, Clin. Pediatr. 28:129–131, 1989.

32. Johnsen, D., and Nowjack-Raymer, R.: Baby bottle tooth decay (BBTD): issues, assessment for the nutritionist, J. Am. Dietet. Assoc. 89:1112–1116, 1989.

33. Ideas that work with young children: what is curriculum for infants in family day care (or elsewhere)? Young Children 42(5):59, 1987.

34. Interviews and observation: Lessie Bates Davis Neighborhood House, East St. Louis, IL, March 29, 1988.

APPENDIX 3–A   Resources for Lactating Mothers

EDUCATIONAL MATERIALS

Health Education Associates, Inc.
211 S. Easton Rd.
Glendale, PA 19038
(215) 659-1149

La Leche League International
9615 Minneapolis Ave.
Franklin Park, IL 60131-8209
(312) 451-1891

Childbirth Graphic, Ltd.
1210 Culver Rd.
Rochester, NY 14609-5454
(716) 482-7940

ICEA Bookstore
P.O. Box 20048
Minneapolis, MN 55420-0048
(800) 328-4815

Lactation Institute and Breastfeeding Clinic
16161 Ventura Blvd., Suite 223
Encino, CA 91436
(818) 995-1913

Healthy Mother Coalition
Directory of Educational Materials
U.S. Dept. of Health and Human Services
200 Independence Ave. SW
Room 740-G
Washington, DC 20201

WIC Supplemental Food Section
Dept. of Health Services
WIC Warehouse
1103 N. B St., Suite E
Sacramento, CA 95814
(916) 324-6352

BOOKS FOR PROFESSIONALS

Areango, J.: Promoting breastfeeding: a guide for health professionals working in the WIC and CSF programs, Washington, DC, 1984, USDA Food and Nurition Services, National Health Information Clearinghouse.

Lawrence, R. A.: Breastfeeding: a guide for the medical professional, St. Louis, 1985, Times Mirror/Mosby Co.

Olson, C., Psiaki, D., and Kaplowitz, D.: Current knowledge on breastfeeding, Ithaca, NY, 1982, Cooperative Extension Distribution Center.

Riordan, J.: A practical guide to breastfeeding, St. Louis, 1983, Mosby Company.

Worthington-Roberts, B. S., Veremeersch, J., and Williams, S. R.: Nutrition in pregnancy and lactation, St. Louis, 1985, Times Mirror/Mosby Co.

BOOKS FOR CONSUMERS

La Leche League International: The womanly art of breastfeeding, ed. 3, Frankling Park, Il, 1981.

McDonald, L.: The joy of breastfeeding, Pasadena, CA, 1978, Oaklawn Press.

Pryor, K.: Nursing your baby, New York, 1973, Pocket Books.

Satter, E.: Child of mine: feeding with love and good sense, Palo Alto, CA, 1983, Bull Publishing.

Sears, W.: Creative parenting, New York, 1982, Dodd Mead.

White, A.: The total nutrition guide for mother and baby: from pregnancy through the first three years, New York, 1983, Ballantine Books.

APPENDIX 3–B Special Supplemental Food Program for Women, Infants and Children

In 1972 Congress authorized the Special Supplemental Food Program for Women, Infants and Children (WIC)*. WIC provides participants with specific nutritious supplemental foods and nutrition education, at no cost. WIC participants are eligible low-income persons who are determined by health professionals (physicians, nutritionists, nurses, and other officials) to be a "nutritional risk" because of inadequate nutrition, health care, or both. Federal funds are available to participating state health departments or comparable state agencies. Indian tribes, bands, groups, or their authorized representatives who are recognized by the Bureau of Indian Affairs (U.S. Department of Interior) or the appropriate area office of the Indian Health Service (U.S. Department of Health and Human Services) may also act as state agencies. These agencies distribute funds to the participating local agencies. The funds pay for supplemental foods for participants and pay specified administrative costs, including those of nutrition education.

ELIGIBILITY FOR THE PROGRAM

Pregnant, postpartum, and breast-feeding women and infants and children up to 5 years of age are eligible if they (1) meet the income standards (a state agency may either set a statewide income standard or allow local agencies to set their own); (2) are individually determined to be at nutritional risk and in need of the supplemental foods the program offers; and (3) live in an approved project area (if the state has a residency requirement) or belong to special population groups, such as migrant farm workers, Native Americans (Indians), or refugees.

*U.S. Public Law 94–105, Oct. 7, 1975.

FOODS INCLUDED IN THE WIC PROGRAM

The program allows infants up to 3 months of age to receive iron-fortified formula. Older infants (4 through 12 months) receive formula, iron-fortified infant cereal, and fruit juices high in vitamin C. An infant may receive non-iron-fortified or special therapeutic formula when it is prescribed by a physician for a specified medical condition. Participating women and children receive fortified milk and/or cheese; eggs; hot or cold cereals high in iron; fruit and vegetable juices high in vitamin C; and either peanut butter or dried beans or peas. WIC provides breast-feeding women with a food package to meet their extra nutritional needs. Women and children with special dietary needs may receive a package containing cereal, juice, and special therapeutic formulas. For a participant to receive this package, a physician must determine that the participant has a medical condition that precludes or restricts the use of conventional foods.

The state agency administering the program may use one or all of the following food delivery systems: (1) retail purchase, where participants use vouchers or checks to buy foods at local retail stores authorized by the state agency to accept WIC vouchers or checks; (2) home delivery, where the food is delivered to participants' homes; and (3) direct distribution, where participants pick up the food from the warehouse.

NUTRITION EDUCATION IN WIC

Nutrition education is available to parents or care givers of infant and child participants, and whenever possible, to the child who participates. This nutrition education is designed to have a practical relationship to participants' nutritional needs, household situations, and cultural preferences and includes information on how participants can select food for themselves and their families. The goals of WIC nutrition education are to teach the relationship between proper nutritional risk to develop better food habits, and to prevent nutrition-related problems by showing participants how to best use their supplemental and other foods. The WIC program also encourages breast-feeding and counsels pregnant women on its nutritional advantages.

4

The Toddler (1 to 3 Years)

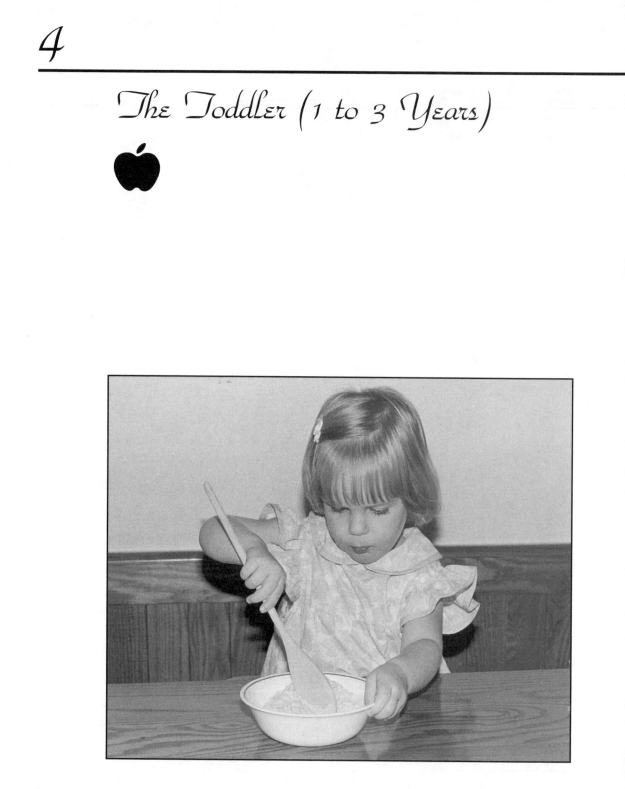

LEARNING OBJECTIVES

Students will be able to
- State the physical and psychosocial characteristics of the toddler that may affect eating habits.
- State the nutrient, energy, and food needs of the toddler.
- Describe the care provider's activities related to foods and the eating environment.
- Describe the management of nutrition-related problems.

If you could look back to your own development, you would realize that the toddler stage was a time when you became your own person. During the years from 1 to 3, you began to take on a unique personality with individual characteristics. This, coupled with a newfound ability to move about freely, gave your care provider some anxious moments. But, in turn, you provided those around you with a delightful array of surprises as you mastered one new task after another. Many of the new tasks you learned were associated with food and eating. If you and your family enjoyed consuming a wide variety of foods, today you probably select a nutritionally adequate diet (Figure 4–1).

GROWTH AND DEVELOPMENT

This section reviews the growth and development of the toddler; however, for more detailed information, see additional references [1, 2]. During the toddler years, the rate of growth declines compared with infancy. Never again after the first year should the child triple its weight in 12 months. The infant takes on the appearance of a young child, with the increase in height or length often exceeding the weight gain. It is estimated that at 18 to 24 months for girls and 24 to 30 months for boys, about 50% of adult height has been achieved. However, increase in weight is only beginning. The median weights and heights of children from 1 to 3 years are shown in Table 4–1; the gain in weight is approximately 5 pounds (2.25 kg) per year.

As discussed in Chapter 3, height and weight recorded over time are two of the best indicators of the child's growth pattern. Charts used to record the monthly height and weight for infants shown in Chapter 3 can be used during the toddler years. If the child remains in the center through the preschool years, you could switch to the charts used for prepubertal girls and boys (found in Appendix VI at the back of this book). However, we recommend that you continue to use the charts labeled "Birth to 36 months" for the most accurate assessment of toddler growth.

Figure 4–1 The toddler eats a variety of foods.
Photo by Robert M. Wagner.

The National Center for Health Statistics charts for children to 36 months are based on recumbent length and require that the toddler be lying down on a surface with an immovable head piece and a movable foot piece (Chapter 3). In practice, however, the child of 2 years will want to stand for measurements. For the charts marked for prepubertal boys and girls, the measurements are properly taken with the child in a standing position.

Table 4–1 Weights and Lengths of girls and boys 1 to 3 years old.

Age (years)	*Girls*		*Boys*	
	Weight (pounds)	Stature (inches)	Weight (pounds)	Stature (inches)
1	21.0	29.3	22.3	30.0
2	26.0	34.2	27.1	34.2
3	32.2	37.4	31.0	37.0

Source: National Center for Health Statistics, Health Resource Administration, Department of Health, Education and Welfare, Hyattsville, MD. Data from the Fels Research Institute, Yellow Springs, OH, 1977.

Standing height is best measured by a fixed rather than a free-standing measuring device. The child is positioned with the back against the measuring device and the feet close together and touching the device. The back should show as little curvature as possible. The whole body should be carefully centered and the head held erect with the gaze straight forward. The movable board should contact the top of the head (Figure 4–2). Three measurements should be taken and averaged, when possible.

Weight is best measured using a beam-balanced scale with nondetachable weights. Remove outer clothing. For serial measurements, the same amount of clothing should be worn at each measuring.

What do the measurements, height (length) and weight, mean? In referring to the weight and length areas of the chart, single measurements at the 5th or 95th percentile should arouse some concern. Weight for height, or stature, is the most meaningful measure. Using the prepubertal weight-for-height chart (ages 2 to 10), Figure 4–3 plots the growth of three toddler girls.

Note that one child represented in Figure 4–3 weighs 35.5 pounds (16 kg) and is 40.5 inches (101 cm) tall. These measurements correspond with the 50th percentile. Two additional measurements have been plotted using heights and weights that indicate possible problems. The one denoted with a circle between the 90th and 95th percentile indicates that with a height of 40.5 inches and a weight of 41 pounds (18.5 kg), the child may weigh too much. Likewise, the

**Figure 4–2
Technique for measuring standing height.**
Source: Reprinted with permission from *Maternal and Child Health Program Manual*, Maternal and Child Health Branch, North Carolina Division of Health Services, Raleigh, NC, 1978.

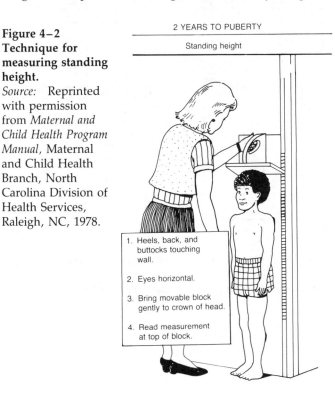

2 YEARS TO PUBERTY

Standing height

1. Heels, back, and buttocks touching wall.

2. Eyes horizontal.

3. Bring movable block gently to crown of head.

4. Read measurement at top of block.

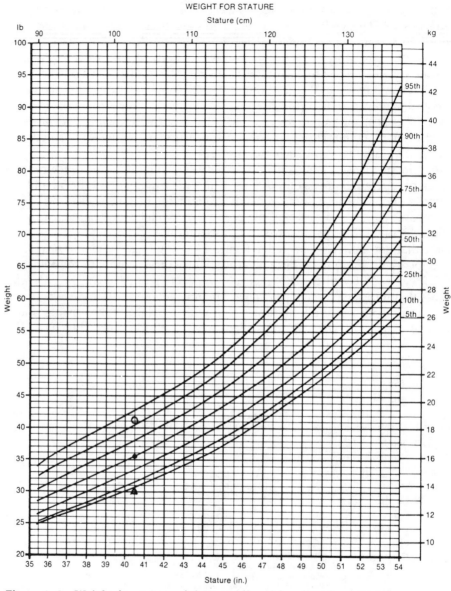

Figure 4–3   Weight for stature of three toddler girls, plotted on chart for 2- to 10-year-olds.
Source: U.S. Department of Health, Education and Welfare, National Center for Health Statistics, 1979.

triangle shows a child of similar stature with weight less than 30 pounds (13.5 kg). This, too, could present a problem, because the weight for stature is less than the 5th percentile.

Before referring the child to a health agency for further evaluation, the following factors must be taken into consideration: (1) birth weight, (2) nationality, and (3) heights and weights of biological parents. The premature or low birth weight child may take several years to catch up with the child who was in the normal range for height and weight at birth. Likewise, height and weight may be strongly influenced by the biological parents [3, 4], and attention to parental body structure may help determine if the pattern of growth is actually abnormal for the child. Nationality of the child may also play a role; certain groups have longer legs and a shorter body structure, whereas others have shorter legs and a longer body structure.

If none of the above factors apply, a child's weight may still vary from month to month because of:

- Faulty measuring equipment.
- Error in measurement.
- Recent over- or underconsumption of food.
- Frequent or recent acute illness (for example, upper respiratory infection or diarrhea).
- Chronic illnesses.

If none of these conditions exist and losses or gains fall a pound or more above or below expected ranges, seek a more thorough examination from a health professional. The pediatrician or dietitian can help the care provider and parents plan any modification in diet and exercise patterns.

Along with the toddler's decrease in rate of growth comes a decreased interest in and need for food. This phenomenon may be interpreted by the parent as illness or a sign to begin supplementing the diet with vitamins and minerals. It is merely a natural development of this period.

DEVELOPMENTAL SKILLS

The toddler is gaining control of the body by practicing large muscle movements over and over [5]. Fine muscle control also is developing, allowing the child to master such tasks as drinking through a straw, eating with a spoon, and attempting to eat an ice-cream cone (Figure 4–4).

Developmental scales provide a quick reference for parents who want to ensure that their child is feeding and eating according to developmental readiness. Table 4–2 lists developmental abilities that can be expected during the toddler years.

Having mastered hand-to-mouth coordination, the child can eat independently. Toddlers are still curious babies, and every new object must be handled

**Figure 4–4
Toddlers learn to
drink through
straws.**
Photo by Kevin
French.

and explored, probably with the mouth as well as the hands. Any solid or liquid, including poisons, becomes an item for exploration and a potential safety hazard.

To further help with the process of eating, teeth erupt; the front teeth begin erupting at about 6 months of age, and the molars at about 1 year. All 20 primary (baby) teeth have usually erupted by 2½ to 3 years of age. Often it is believed that children can be given foods to chew only after the teeth have erupted; however, most chewing can be done with the gums. We have observed that, if given proper stimulation, children can chew many foods although they do not have a large number of teeth.

Developmentally, the child is ready for a wide range of foods from the family table. However, these are new food tastes for the child. The commercially prepared ground or chopped foods probably eaten until now taste and feel quite different from the same foods served at the family table. The toddler may need time to adjust to new flavors and textures.

PSYCHOLOGICAL AND SOCIAL CHARACTERISTICS

Another characteristic of this period is sudden changes in mood, from the cooperative child who is a helper to the child who responds with only "no, no, no." Any question beginning with "do you want" may be answered "no," including questions regarding food and eating. Care providers often avoid confrontation by offering the child a choice between two equally acceptable alternatives.

Table 4–2 Stages of development for toddler years.*

Stage	Physical	Nutrition	Intellectual
Toddler I: 1 year	Loses subcutaneous fat. Mild lordosis and protuberant abdomen appear. Eight more teeth erupt.	Growth continues at a rapid pace (physical and brain). Appetite good with bitesize foods tolerated.	More words appear; words combined into phrases and short sentences. Thought can sometimes be substituted for action.
Toddler II: 2 years	Slow but steady gain in height and weight.	Tolerates regular foods well. Growth begins to slow with some decrease in appetite.	Perception of self as distinct from others very prominent; child very assertive.

Stage	Gross Motor	Fine Motor	Oral/Motor
Toddler I: 1 year	Climbs on and off furniture. Sits in a small chair with no lateral support. Walks well and rises to standing without assistance.	Opposition or thumb/forefinger grasp. Wrist extended and deviated to ulnar side for accurate prehension (12–14 months).	More refined cup-drinking (Stage II, Stage III). Chewing. Refined spoonfeeding by 2 years.
Toddler II: 2 years	Runs. Ascends and descends stairs independently. Backs self into a small chair for sitting. Squats in play. Rides and steers a tricycle well.	Gradual progression of three jaw chuck position occurs.	By 3 years sucking through straw.

Stage	Speech and Language	Social/Behavioral	
Toddler I: 1 year	13–18 months: Rapid receptive growth. Slow expressive development. 18–24 months: The naming stage. Holophrases. Jargoning. Echolalia. Two and three-word phrases.	Eats at table with family. More social and verbal. Negativism emerges.	
Toddler II: 2 years	By 2 years, uses 40% sentences. Rapid syntactic development. Early-developing consonants emerge.	Temper tantrums and refusal of food common. Toilet training in process if not already completed.	

*This chart provides the health professional with a standard tool for assessing feeding levels.

Source: Modified from Harvey-Smith, M., et al.: Feeding management of a child with a handicap: a guide for professionals, Memphis, 1982, University of Tennessee Center for the Health Sciences.

The child wants and needs to become independent and must demonstrate the need for autonomy by doing things alone. Erikson [6] described the situation as autonomy versus shame. Attempting to accomplish tasks beyond the toddler's ability causes frustration and feelings of shame and doubt. The child's skill may outrun judgment, and the child must be restrained from certain activities that can be harmful [5]. Wanting to help the care provider chop vegetables with a knife instead of breaking them, to pour water from the large rather than small container, and to mix the fruit salad or bread dough with a large spoon in a large bowl are examples of how the child's curiosity and enthusiasm must be channeled into productive, but safe, activities (Figure 4–5).

Just at the time when the child is mastering the eating process and when almost all foods can be given directly from the family table, the toddler may experience a less than enthusiastic desire for food. This may be a result of physical, psychological, or social conditions. As previously stated, the child's rate of growth is slower during this period; the child gains less than ½ pound

Figure 4–5   A young boy shapes small portions of bread dough.
Photo by Kevin French.

Figure 4–6
Toddlers may
become
unenthusiastic
about food.

(0.22 kg) per month as compared to 1 pound (0.45 kg) or more per month during the first 6 months of life. In addition, the child may be too busy exploring the new environment, now viewed from an upright position, to be concerned about food. (See Figure 4–6.) In any case, the care provider must be concerned that the nutritional needs of the toddler are met and be prepared to assure parents that the child is progressing at a normal rate of growth or, if necessary, to seek help from the health professional.

NUTRITIONAL NEEDS

Calories must count! Although the rate of growth slows and the child's appetite may decline, the needs brought about by continued growth and development remain. The toddler's additional activity will increase energy needs. The infant and toddler have similar needs for nutrients but in different amounts (Table 4–3).

In many cases, the toddler will need more of each nutrient than the infant. The RDA may be used in planning diets for the toddler. However, it can be used only as a guide when looking at individual diets, because the nutritional status of a toddler whose diet is less than 100% of the RDA [7] may still be good.

Certain nutrients are of predominant concern in caring for the toddler and need special consideration when menus are planned for children. These include protein, calcium, ascorbic acid, and iron.

Table 4–3   RDA for toddler compared with that of infant.

Nutrient	Infant 6–12 Months (20 lb, 28 in. [9 kg, 70 cm])	Toddler 1 to 3 Years (29 lb, 35 in. [13 kg, 87.5 cm])
Resting Energy	kg × 98	kg × 102
Equivalent	(lb × 44.5)	(lb × 46.4)
Protein (g)	kg × 1.6	kg × 1.1
(g/day)	14	16
Vitamin A (μg RE)	375	400
Vitamin D (μg)	10	10
Vitamin E (mg -TE)	4	6
Vitamin K (μg)	10	15
Ascorbic acid (mg)	35	40
Folate (μg)	35	50
Niacin (mg NE)	6	9
Riboflavin (mg)	0.5	0.8
Thiamin (mg)	0.4	0.7
Vitamin B_6 (mg)	0.6	1.0
Vitamin B_{12} (μg)	0.5	0.7
Calcium (mg)	600	800
Phosphorus (mg)	500	800
Iodine (μg)	50	70
Iron (mg)	10	10
Magnesium (mg)	60	80
Zinc (mg)	5	10

Source: Based on Food and Nutrition Board, National Academy of Sciences—National Research Council: Recommend dietary allowances, revised 1989.

Energy

As shown in Table 4–3, the caloric recommendation (RDA) for the toddler is 1300 kcal (approximately 46 kcal per pound of body weight). This amount is greater per pound than between the 6- to 12-month period (44.5 kcal per pound). Any child's recommended allowance for energy can be calculated, given the weight and assuming moderate activity. (The toddler's energy needs may be viewed as about two-thirds of what is recommended [RDA] for a woman 25 to 50 years of age [2200 kcal].) Remember, the energy allowance is only an estimate. Intake may range from 900 to 1800 kcal, and many children may eat more or less without a loss or gain in weight. The data obtained from taking heights and weights each month should be used as the best indicator of caloric needs.

Calculating Calories. If the child's eating pattern is determined to be typical and the weight in relation to height is within acceptable ranges, there is little need to recommend a change in energy allowance. However, the care provider should have some knowledge of the energy needs of the young child.

Three methods are used to determine energy needs:

Method 1:   Start with a base of 1000 calories and add 100 calories for each year of age.
1100 calories for a 1-year-old
1200 calories for a 2-year-old
1300 calories for a 3-year-old

Method 2:   When energy needs are presented in this text, the recommended amount is calculated based on body weight.

6–12 months	98 kcal/kg (44.5 kcal/lb)
1–3 years	102 kcal/kg (46.6 kcal/lb)
4–6 years	90 kcal/kg (40.9 kcal/lb)

A 2-year-old weighing 27 pounds will need 1258 calories (27 lb × 46.6 kcal/lb).

Method 3:   Use the RDA for energy based upon height:

1–3 years	37.1 kcal/in. (14.4 kcal/cm)
4–6 years	40.9 kcal/in. (16.1 kcal/cm)

A 3-year-old 37.5 in. (95.3 cm) tall will need 1391 calories (37.5 × 37.1 kcal/cm).

With the latter method, energy needs increase as the child grows taller, thus taking into consideration individual growth patterns.

Protein

The recommended amount of protein is 1.2 g per kilogram or 0.6 g per pound of body weight (Table 4–3). A 29-pound (13 kg) child will need only about 16 g protein—less than that found in three glasses (24 ounces) of milk (8 ounces = 8 g protein) and 2 ounces of meat (1 ounce = 7 g protein). This is excluding the protein in vegetables and bread. Protein intake is perhaps overemphasized; national studies [8] have shown that few children consume less than the recommended levels. However, additional servings of milk and meat are rich sources of other nutrients.

Minerals

Calcium.   With the development of bones and teeth, calcium becomes crucial. A glass of milk contains approximately 300 mg calcium. Two to three glasses of milk per day along with other foods will supply the amount of calcium necessary to meet the needs of the 1- to 3-year-old child.

Milk and milk products are the main sources of calcium, but other sources include dried beans and dark green vegetables. Table 4–4 provides calcium equivalents. It becomes obvious that milk is by far the best source of calcium. Children who do not drink milk should have the diet supplemented with other calcium-containing foods. A wide variety of dairy foods can be used in the center to encourage adequate milk intake, and supplements are rarely indicated.

Table 4–4 Calcium values (mg) in common foods.

Dairy products		Legumes	
Buttermilk, 1 C	296	Pork and beans, in sauce, 1 C	138
Cheese, American, paseturized, process, 1 oz	198	Garbanzo beans, cooked, 1 C	150
		Soybeans, cooked, 1 C	131
Cheese, cheddar, 1 oz	204	Tofu, processed with calcium sulfate, 4 oz	145
Cheese, cottage, creamed and low fat 2%, ½ C	77		
Cheese, ricotta, part skim, ½ C	337	Fruits and vegetables	
Cheese, Swiss, 1 oz	272	Bok choy, ½ C	126
Cheese food, American, 1 oz	163	Collards, raw, ½ C	179
Sour cream, 1 tbsp	14	Kale, raw, ½ C	103
Ice cream, vanilla, ½ C	88	Spinach, ½ C	84
Milk, chocolate, 1 C	284	Broccoli, stalk, ½ C	68
Milk, evaporated, 1 C	635	Turnip greens, raw, ½ C	126
Milk, evaporated, 1 part to 1 of water, 1 C	318	Orange, 1 medium	54
Milkshake, vanilla, 11 fl. oz	457	Grains	
Milk, low fat, 2%, 1 C	297	Bread enriched white, 1 slice	19
Milk, skim, 1 C	302	Bread, whole wheat, 1 slice	22
Yogurt, plain, low fat, 1 C	415	Corn bread, 2½" square	94
Pudding, chocolate, ½ C	133	Pancakes, 4" diameter (2)	116
Meat, fish, eggs, and nuts		Tortilla, corn, 6" diameter	60
		Waffle, 7" diameter	179
Almonds, ¼ C	83	Combination foods	
Brazil nuts, ¼ C	65		
Egg, scrambled, 1 large	47	Spaghetti, meatballs, and tomato sauce, 1 C	124
Meat loaf, 3 oz	68	Macaroni and cheese, ½ C	181
Oysters, raw, 7–9	113	Pizza, cheese, ¼ of 14" pie	332
Salmon, red, with bones, 3 oz	167	Taco, beef, 1	174
Sardines, with bones, 3 oz	372	Other	
Shrimp, canned, 3 oz	99		
		Cake, devil's food, ¹⁄₁₆ of 9" cake	41
		Chocolate bar, milk, 1 oz	65
		Molasses, blackstrap, 1 tbsp	137
		Sherbet, orange, ½ C	52

Source: Ohio State University Data Base, NDDA Laboratory, Southern Illinois University at Carbondale, 1984.

Iron.   The baby uses iron stored during the first months of life. However, stores may be low by the age of 1 year, particularly if the child was given whole milk and table foods by 6 months of age. For this reason, breast milk or iron-fortified formula is often recommended for the child to 1 year of age and iron-fortified infant cereal to 18 months of age.

In practice, breast-feeding, iron-fortified formula, and infant cereal are often terminated by the toddler stage. Thus, it is especially important that the child be given other good sources, such as meat, green vegetables, and enriched or whole-grain cereal products.

The amount of iron available to the body depends on the body's need for iron, the form of iron, the composition of the meal, and bulk in the diet. A child in need of iron will absorb more iron than a child who has normal levels in the body. The absorption of iron is greatest from meat (for example, beef or pork) and poorest from grains and vegetables. If meat, fish, or poultry is eaten with vegetables, the absorption of iron from the vegetables is enhanced. Consumption of foods high in vitamin C along with iron-rich foods will also help the body absorb iron. Excessive bulk in the diet, especially bran, may interfere with iron absorption.

It is often difficult to provide the recommended 10 mg of iron for the toddler. Table 4–5 indicates the quantities of certain foods that a youngster would have to eat to obtain from 1 to 5 mg of iron. Note that only small quantities of formula and infant cereal are required to supply 1 and 5 mg of iron.

Fluoride.   Children younger than 3 years of age do not need supplemental fluoride if (1) they brush their teeth (as they should in the center) and (2) fluoride is present in the drinking water. If fluoride is not present in the water at home or in the center, the child's parents should consult the pediatrician or dentist for recommendations on supplementation. Children are prone to swallow much of the toothpaste used in brushing their teeth. If they brush more than twice a day, this may be at least 1 to 3 mg.

Other Nutrients

A balance of all nutrients is important, and a daily source of vitamin C (ascorbic acid) is recommended, with sources of vitamin A every other day. The recommended amount of vitamin C, 40 mg, is supplied by less than 4 ounces (½ cup) orange or grapefruit juice or foods rich in vitamin C. Likewise, 400 µg RE of vitamin A is relatively easy to acquire if the child eats a wide variety of foods including green and yellow vegetables such as carrots or spinach, fortified margarine, butter, and other fortified dairy products.

Supplementation

The toddler's decreased interest in food may be interpreted by the parent as illness or a sign to begin supplementing the diet with vitamins and minerals. In reality, it is a natural development of this period. By the time the child reaches 1 year of age, an adequate diet can be obtained using a variety of foods. It is generally believed that if the child receives sufficient nourishment from foods, vitamin and mineral supplementation are unnecessary. No particular benefit is seen from a multivitamin and mineral preparation. For a complete discussion of supplementation, see Chapter 5.

Table 4–5 Approximate iron equivalents of selected foods.

Foods	Iron (1 mg)	Iron (5 mg)
Meat and Meat Alternatives		
Beans, dry (cooked)	>3 tbsp	1 C
Beef round steak	1.0 oz	5.0 oz
Black walnuts	>¼ C	1⅓ C
Cashews	>3 tbsp	1 C
Egg yolk, medium	1¼ egg yolks	6¼ egg yolks
Lentils, dry (cooked)	¼ C	1¼ C
Liver, beef	<½ oz	2 oz
Liver, pork	<¼ oz	<1 oz
Osyters (raw)	1 medium	5 medium
Peanuts, roasted	⅓ C	1½ C
Peas, dry (cooked)	5 tbsp	>1½ C
Pecans	⅓ C	1½ C
Pork loin chops	1.0 oz	5.0 oz
Bread and Cereals		
Enriched cream of wheat, cooked*	1 tbsp	⅓ C
Enriched bread	1½ slices	7½ slices
Infant cereal (dry)	¾ to 1 tbsp	4 to 5 tbsp
Iron-rich formula	⅓ C	1½ C
Oatmeal (cooked)	⅔ C	3½ C
Ready-to-eat cereal, iron enriched (100% U.S. RDA)	>2½ tsp†	4½ tbsp†
Wheat germ	2 tbsp	½ C + 2 tbsp
Whole wheat bread	1¼ slices	6¼ slices
Fruits and Vegetables		
Asparagus (canned)	2½ spears	13 spears
Dried apricots	5 medium halves	25 medium halves
Dried prunes	3	15
Oranges, small	2	10
Raisins	3 tbsp	1 C
Spinach (cooked)	¼ C	1¼ C

*40% U.S. RDA.

†Serving sized indicated on box. If the serving size is 1 C (16 tbsp), the amount provided would be 18 mg/C or more than 1 mg/tbsp.

Source: NDDA Laboratory, Southern Illinois University at Carbondale, 1984.

FOOD GUIDE FOR THE TODDLER

The Food Guide (Chapter 2) is the practical guide for planning food needs of adults as well as children. Table 4–6 specifies the recommended food intake in each food group with average serving sizes for the toddler years. These serving sizes have been derived from the authors' observing children eating in day-care and preschool centers.

Table 4-6 Recommended food intake according to food group and average serving sizes (ages 1 up to 3 years).

Food Group	Servings/Day	Average Serving‖	
		Ages 1 up to 2	Ages 2 up to 3
Vegetables	3–5		
Green vegetables	1*	1–2 tbsp	2–3 tbsp
Other vegetables (potato and other green or yellow vegetables)	2	1–2 tbsp	2–3 tbsp
Fruits	2–4		
Vitamin C source (citrus fruits, berries, melons)		¼ C	¼ C
Breads and Cereals (Whole Grain)	6–11		
Bread*		½ slice	½ slice
Ready-to-eat cereals, whole grain, iron-fortified		¼ C or ⅓ oz	¼ C or ⅓ oz
Cooked cereal including macaroni, spaghetti, rice, etc. (whole grain, enriched)		¼ C	¼ C
Milk and Milk Products	At least 4		
Whole or 2% milk (1.5 oz cheese = 1 C milk) (C = 8 oz or 240 g)		¾ C	¾
Meat and Alternates	3–4 including:		
Lean meat, fish, poultry, and eggs†	2	1 oz	1 oz
Nutbutters (peanut, soynut)‡		2 tbsp§	2 tbsp§
Cooked dried beans or peas	1–2	1 oz = ¼ C	1 oz = ¼ C
Nuts			½ oz
Fats and Oils	3		
Butter, margarine, mayonnaise, oils		1 tsp	1 tsp

*Allow a minimum service of 1 tbsp/year of age for cooked fruits, vegetables, cereals, and pasta until the child reaches 8 years or ½ C portion size.

†To enhance overall nutrient content of diet include eggs (two to three times a week) and liver occasionally.

§As recommended by Illinois State Board of Education, Department of Child Nutrition: Child Care Food Program—required meal patterns, Springfield, IL, June 1986, The Board.

‡Include nutbutters, dried (cooked) beans, or peas at least once a day to meet nutrient recommendations and decrease the fat content of the diet. Use additional servings of meats when legumes, beans, and nuts are omitted.

‖Additional servings of food may be needed to meet energy requirements.

Figure 4–7 Nutrient analysis of toddler's diet using the minimum servings derived from Table 4–6

Percent Energy Distribution:

Fat   30%
Carbohydrate   51%
Protein   21%

```
TOTAL            NUTRIENT      %RDA   0%        20%  33% 40%       60% 66%    80%        100%
                                      I----I----I----I----I----I----I----I----I----I----I
998.6 KCAL       ENERGY         76%   XXXXXXXXXXXXXXXXXXXXXXXXXXXXXXXXXXXXXX
 52.7 GM         PROTEIN       329%   XXXXXXXXXXXXXXXXXXXXXXXXXXXXXXXXXXXXXXXXXXXXXXXXXXX
4526.9 IU        VITAMIN A     226%   XXXXXXXXXXXXXXXXXXXXXXXXXXXXXXXXXXXXXXXXXXXXXXXXXXX
273.2 IU         VITAMIN D      68%   XXXXXXXXXXXXXXXXXXXXXXXXXXXXXXXXXXX
  3.6 IU         VITAMIN E      60%   XXXXXXXXXXXXXXXXXXXXXXXXXXXXXX
 70.6 MG         VITAMIN C     176%   XXXXXXXXXXXXXXXXXXXXXXXXXXXXXXXXXXXXXXXXXXXXXXXXXXX
138.3 MCG        FOLACIN       276%   XXXXXXXXXXXXXXXXXXXXXXXXXXXXXXXXXXXXXXXXXXXXXXXXXXX
  7.6 MG         NIACIN         84%   XXXXXXXXXXXXXXXXXXXXXXXXXXXXXXXXXXXXXXXXXX
  1.6 MG         RIBOFLAVIN    205%   XXXXXXXXXXXXXXXXXXXXXXXXXXXXXXXXXXXXXXXXXXXXXXXXXXX
  0.8 MG         THIAMIN       112%   XXXXXXXXXXXXXXXXXXXXXXXXXXXXXXXXXXXXXXXXXXXXXXXXXXX
  0.9 MG         VITAMIN B6     91%   XXXXXXXXXXXXXXXXXXXXXXXXXXXXXXXXXXXXXXXXXXXXXX
  3.0 MCG        VITAMIN B12   423%   XXXXXXXXXXXXXXXXXXXXXXXXXXXXXXXXXXXXXXXXXXXXXXXXXXX
1066.4 MG        CALCIUM       133%   XXXXXXXXXXXXXXXXXXXXXXXXXXXXXXXXXXXXXXXXXXXXXXXXXXX
1116.0 MG        PHOSPHOROUS   139%   XXXXXXXXXXXXXXXXXXXXXXXXXXXXXXXXXXXXXXXXXXXXXXXXXXX
  6.3 MG         IRON           63%   XXXXXXXXXXXXXXXXXXXXXXXXXXXXXXX
213.1 MG         MAGNESIUM     266%   XXXXXXXXXXXXXXXXXXXXXXXXXXXXXXXXXXXXXXXXXXXXXXXXXXX
  6.5 MG         ZINC           65%   XXXXXXXXXXXXXXXXXXXXXXXXXXXXXX
                                      I----I----I----I----I----I----I----I----I----I----I
105.4 MG CHOLESTEROL           1120.0 MG SODIUM
```

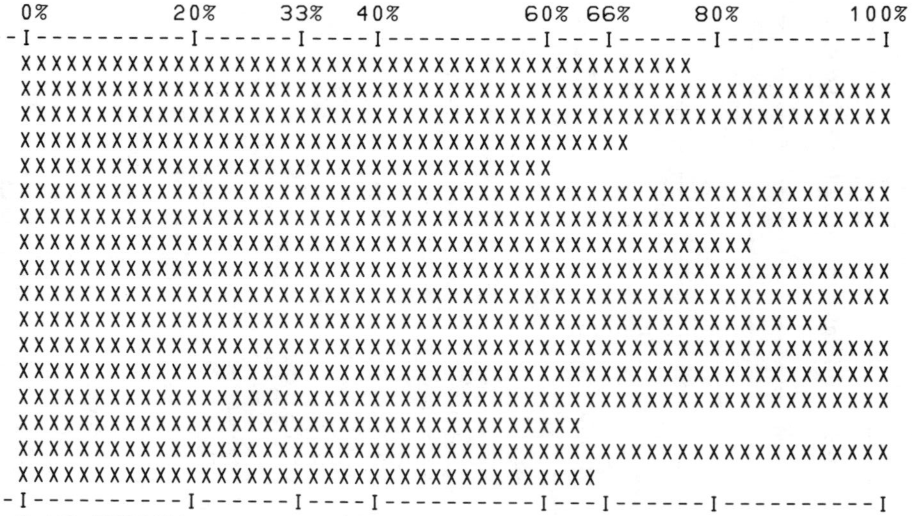

Source: NDDA Laboratory, Southern Illinois University at Carbondale.

Using this guide and the Child Care Food Program guidelines (Chapter 7), care providers and parents can plan nutritious meals that meet RDA standards. Figure 4–7 shows the nutrient analysis of a diet planned from Table 4–6. The minimum servings from each food group were used.

It is difficult to plan diets that meet 100% of the RDA without including fortified cereals. Although the RDAs are not requirements, they serve as a nutrient guide in planning diets. The recommended daily Food Guide in Table 4–6 will help in choosing foods needed by the toddler, but additional foods should be included to meet energy needs. Select fortified cereals or choose foods with high values for iron, zinc, and vitamin E.

Fruits and Vegetables

Five servings of fresh fruits and vegetables are the minimum recommended each day. Fruits and vegetables should provide the major sources of vitamin C in the diet. This group also contributes significant amounts of vitamin A, magnesium, and fiber to the diet. Children may have poor acceptance of this group because parents or care providers may eat as few as 1 or 2 servings of fruits and vegetables a day [8]. Preparation methods used by care providers may also contribute to a child's rejection of certain foods.

Unfamiliar vegetables should be introduced when the child is hungry. Offer vegetables first, while the other foods are being prepared for the toddler's tray. The hungry toddler will explore with interest a small serving of cooked vegetables (for instance, 1 inch of asparagus, one flowerette of broccoli, one green bean, one slice of carrot, or 1 tablespoon of cabbage).

Chopped or sliced foods are preferred for this age group because they require less chewing and may be used as finger foods. This does not mean that toddlers should be given only chopped or peeled foods. Toddlers approaching the age of 2 can hold a piece of fruit or a cooked vegetable. Softer raw foods (such as bananas or ripe pears) may be safer cut in large pieces than small chunks because the child can hold and chew the larger piece. Children should always be closely supervised when eating (Figure 4–8).

Preparation time presents a good opportunity to let children try a new food—perhaps cooked broccoli, green beans, or greens. Fresh foods rather than canned, especially fruits and vegetables, have more appeal. A good rule to follow is never prepare frozen when you can buy fresh, and never prepare canned if you can buy frozen. Because overcooked vegetables are likely to lose nutritional value and be less accepted by children, food service personnel and teachers should keep cooking times brief. Vegetables should be slightly crunchy when served (Chapter 7).

The Food Guide recommends five different servings of fruits and vegetables each day. Care should be taken to include a vitamin C source daily, a vitamin A source three to four times per week, and a dark green vegetable daily, if possible. Vitamin A and C sources were reviewed in Chapter 1.

Figure 4-8   Toddlers eat raw vegetables and fruit.
Photo by Kevin French.

Meat and Meat Alternates

Most parents encourage the consumption of meats and meat products. How-ever, meat alternates, beans, peas, and nutbutters can also provide a good protein source, especially when taken with a small amount of meat, milk, and cheese or when combined with grain (such as rice or wheat). Peas and beans should be included in the diet at an early age: When cooked in a soup, these foods are generally well accepted. Use caution when serving nuts, which could become lodged in a child's throat.

Beans should be cooked until they can be mashed with a fork. Flatulence seems to be less of a problem if beans are served on a regular basis (two to three times per week). It appears that there is a change in the intestinal flora with frequent use of the product. A general rule to follow is ¼ cup of cooked beans in exchange for 1 ounce of meat.

Meat alternates, beans, peas, and nutbutters help to provide magnesium, zinc, folacin, iron, and B_6 (Chapter 1) to the young child's diet and should be eaten each day. Include a serving of these foods along with 2 ounces of meat.

Meats and fish should be cooked until tender and prepared for finger- or spoon-feeding. Cooked meat may be cut into meat sticks, which are easy to chew and to manipulate with fingers. Generally, gravies and sauces are too high in fat and low in nutritional value to be included in the child's diet, except low-fat "milk gravies," cheese sauces, or the newer low-fat gravy mixes.

Luncheon meats, hot dogs, and other processed meats used to be off-limits because all were prepared with excessive fat and salt. Newer varieties fit into a nutritious diet and are generally well liked by children. Chicken and fish sticks (breaded) prepared in the oven may be an attractive item for children, but check to be sure that the meat makes up more than 50% of the item. Most care providers choose processed meats because of their quick preparation, but read the labels carefully.

The debate over the relationship of diet—including the effect of sodium, saturated fat, and cholesterol—to heart disease continues. Excessive use of saturated fat, cholesterol, and/or sodium may or may not affect the health of the child later in life. However, regardless of the possible consequences, most convenience foods (luncheon meats, hot dogs, and packaged dinners) are used in the home. The preschool or toddler center should provide the child with new learning experiences involving foods. Convenience foods, although a necessity in some centers, limit the child's involvement in food and nutrition activities.

Breads and Cereals

The easiest foods to chew and the easiest to abuse may be from the bread and cereal group. High-fat cookies have soothed many tears and have replaced foods served at regular mealtime. Although children need diets high in carbohydrates, grain products often come with 50% of energy from fat. Check the labels!

Most commercially prepared breads and cereals are enriched or whole grain. Enriched flour has had the wheat bran and germ removed and some of the nutrients added after the flour has been milled. The enrichment process adds iron and several B vitamins, but other nutrients (vitamin E, vitamin B_6, folacin, and magnesium) are lost. Whole-grain cereals have retained the nutrients originally found in the grains of flour. Certain specialty cereal products need not be enriched, and local bakeries need not use enriched flour. However, any bread sold across state lines must be enriched.

Labels from bread and cereal products (bread, crackers, pastas, and so on) should always be checked to determine whether the product is prepared with enriched or whole-grain flours. If high-iron cereal becomes the only food eaten by a child there is a chance of excessive iron intake. A 1 ounce serving of ready-to-eat iron-fortified cereal may contain as much as 18 mg of iron. This amount exceeds the iron recommendation of 10 mg for toddlers.

Unlike fruits and vegetables, breads and cereals retain nutrients during preparation; because little preparation is necessary for many of the products, this food group should be popular in the American diet and form the foundation of the low-fat diet. However, many bread and cereal products consumed by children (for example, cakes, sweet rolls, some cookies, and sugar-coated cereals) are prepared with a high sugar and fat content and cannot be counted as part of the bread and cereal servings. It is difficult for a care provider to justify high fat/sugar grain products for the child-care center menu. Table 4–7 shows the sugar content, cost, and iron content of commonly eaten cereals.

Table 4–7 Sugar content, iron content, and cost of popular cereals.

Cereal	Cost* (cents/serving)	Iron (mg/serving)	Sugar (g/serving)
Smacks	.22	1.8	15
Apple Jacks	.26	4.5	14
Super Golden Crisp	.17	2.7	14
Cookie Crisp	.28	4.5	13
Fruit Loops	.24	4.5	13
Cocoa Pebbles	.24	1.8	13
Trix	.27	4.5	12
Cap'n Crunch	.20	4.5	12
Sugar Corn Pops	.25	1.8	12
Cocoa Puffs	.26	4.5	11
Lucky Charms	.27	4.5	11
Alpha Bits	.20	2.7	11
Honeycomb	.27	2.7	11
Cocoa Krispies	.24	1.8	11
Frosted Flakes	.17	1.8	11
Raisin Bran	.17	18.0	10
Crispy Wheats 'n Raisins	.22	4.5	10
Golden Grahams	.22	4.5	9
King Vitamin	.23	8.1	6
Life	.18	8.1	6
100% Bran	.17	2.7	6
Frosted Mini Wheats	.24	1.8	6
Bran Chex	.26	4.5	5
Product 19	.25	18.0	3
Total	.30	18.0	3
Corn Chex	.24	8.1	3
Kix	.29	8.1	3
Special K	.26	4.5	3
Grape-nuts	.16	2.7	3
Rice Krispies	.16	1.8	3
Rice Chex	.24	8.1	2
Corn Flakes†	.15	1.8	2
Cheerios	.24	8.1	1
Cream of Wheat	.12	8.1	0
Puffed Wheat	.22	0.3	0

*Costs are based on prices listed at retail stores in Carbondale, IL, Spring 1992.

†Some brands include higher amounts of iron.

A toddler needs a minimum of six servings per day from the bread and cereal group according to the to Food Guide. One-half slice of bread can be considered a serving for the young toddler, and approximately 3 tablespoons of cooked cereal or ¼ to ⅓ cup (½ oz) of dry cereal equals one bread or cereal serving. To meet 100% of the RDA for iron, approximately ½ cup dry, fortified infant cereal must be eaten.

Milk and Milk Products

If the toddler is using the bottle, milk consumption may be excessive (over 3 cups per day); if recently weaned, the child may need a reminder to drink milk or eat foods with more calcium. The milk group contributes excellent sources of most nutrients, but it contains small quantities of iron and vitamin C (Chapter 1).

Milk is often consumed in large quantities at the expense of other foods, especially if a bottle is taken between meals. Milk intake should be curtailed if more than 24 ounces (3 cups or 720 mL) are consumed per day, unless all foods are readily eaten and the child is not overweight. It is easy for an 18–month-old to drink a lot of milk and then be unwilling to eat other foods. On the other hand, a child who drinks only scant amounts of milk may need to begin the meal with milk and be offered milk for snacks. Dairy products such as American cheese, cottage cheese, and yogurt are substitutes for milk (for calcium values see Table 4–4). If dairy products are not eaten, large quantities of other foods must be included in the diet to ensure adequate amounts of calcium.

Dairy foods with added sugar are not recommended unless additional energy is needed. Some ice creams and puddings have small amounts of calcium compared with caloric value and, thus, have limited use in the preschool menu. Yogurt may be sweetened and still provide more calcium per ounce than milk. Cream cheese, butter, and margarine cannot be used as milk substitutes. Three cups of milk meet the calcium allowance of 800 mg for the toddler.

EATING AND CARE PROVIDER'S ROLE

Beginning in infancy and continuing through the toddler stage, the development of good food habits is crucial. If given only a few selected food items, the child will have a limited range of food experiences as well as a limited number of foods from which to receive the necessary nutrients (Figure 4–9).

The care provider's role is supportive. You do not feed the toddler; the toddler eats! Messy as it may be, this is the time to allow the toddler to be an independent person. Food is put on the spoon with fingers, or fingers are used in place of a spoon, even for such foods as applesauce and scalloped potatoes. Sometimes foods are just squashed or crumbled to see how they feel. Care providers can cover the floor with newspapers, an old shower curtain, or a vinyl tablecloth, which can be discarded or cleaned.

Figure 4–9   The toddler learns to eat a variety of foods. Photo by Robert M. Wagner.

   Mealtime should not be rushed in order to "put the toddler down for a nap." If facilities and resources permit, it is ideal for the care provider to eat with the toddler while carrying on a conversation about the food and eating situation. Encouraging a toddler to try broccoli is much easier if the care provider is eating broccoli.

Bottle or Cup

You would be hard pressed to find research that supports a particular time when toddlers must abandon bottle or breast. For most toddlers, weaning occurs as a natural part of development when the child begins to rely on a cup and more regular feeding periods. However, there is support for the strong recommendation that the child not be allowed to fall asleep at the breast or bottle or to drink more than 24 ounces (720 mL) of milk or formula when other essential foods are omitted.

   The bottle presents a dilemma for many parents. It is easy to lull the baby to sleep with the bottle, and the baby can usually hold the bottle while drifting off to sleep at nap time. If you give a bottle, you should hold the toddler and not allow the child to fall asleep until drinking is completed (see the discussion of dental caries).

Commercial Toddler Foods

Although commercially prepared toddler foods are available and convenient, these are not practical from an economic viewpoint, especially in a group-care setting. However, they are now prepared without additional salt and are nutritionally acceptable when plain vegetables and meats are used.

Many of the commercially prepared foods called "junior" or "toddler" foods, like the "strained" infant foods, are really combinations of foods. Spaghetti and meat sauce and vegetables with meat are examples of these products. It is tempting to buy the combination foods, and they may serve a useful purpose for parents at home or when traveling, but they are generally more expensive compared with the nutrient density of plain meats, vegetables, and cereals. During the toddler stage, child-care centers should encourage all children (1 year or older) to consume a wide variety of table foods prepared with limited quantities of salt, fat, and sugar.

Serving Food to the Toddler

Foods should be served in small portions, and less desired foods may be offered first while other foods cool or are being prepared; 1 tablespoon per year of age is the general rule for the serving size for cooked foods. This means 1 to 3 measuring tablespoons (15 mg), not "serving" tablespoons (Figure 4–10).

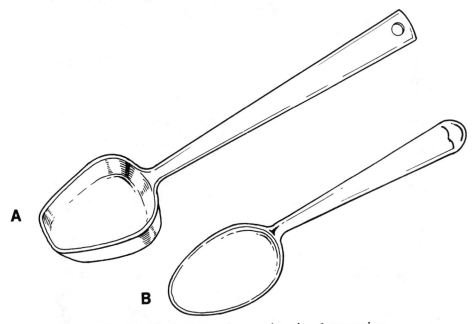

Figure 4–10   General guide for measuring serving size: 1 measuring tablespoon (A), not serving spoon (B), per year of age.

Serving small quantities permits the child to ask for additional servings. Milk should be given in a small cup (4 to 6 ounces) filled one-quarter to one-half full (2 to 3 ounces). Keep the servings small as shown in Figure 4–11.

Food should be given at five to six intervals throughout the day with at least 2 to 2½ hours between eating periods. The number of feeding periods may vary, depending on the appetite of the child and length of stay in the center; however, calorie and nutrient consumption tends to increase when the frequency of eating increases. Food and energy intake are positively affected by allowing the toddler to eat more than three times per day.

Serving family style at an early age helps develop the child's capacity to make choices. However, for the very young toddler the plate may need to be prepared in the kitchen because the child's ability to wait for other children to serve themselves is too limited. On the other hand, the young toddler may come to the serving area after food has been served onto the plate. By 18 to 24 months the child can definitely begin participating in the meal service at least by watching older children serve themselves.

Time and schedules usually run child-care centers, especially centers in which children spend only part of the day. However, the meal service should be expected to take at least 30 minutes if the care provider is using the environment as an educational tool. Discussing the eating process and the foods the child eats

Figure 4–11
Small servings of food work best for the toddler.

is important. This time is also needed to practice the use of a fork and spoon (Figure 4–12). All activities surrounding food can be used to stimulate language development (Chapter 8).

Equipment

High chairs are useful for the very young, but the child can quickly graduate to small tables and chairs. Some states prohibit the use of high chairs in child-care facilities, so alternate equipment suitable for the very young child should be used. The child's feet should touch the floor, or a wooden box can be provided on the floor so that the child's feet do not dangle. Papers may be spread on the floor to prevent excessive cleanup.

Small flatware—spoons, knives, and forks—can be introduced by the toddler stage. The plate or bowl for the young toddler should have a curved edge so that the child can push the food against the edge in filling the spoon. In case you think this is unnecessary, we suggest you try eating peas from a flat plate, left-handed (if you are right-handed). Glasses or cups with heavy bottoms help to prevent spills. Filling a glass only partially full not only gives the child the opportunity to ask for more, but also limits the amount you need to clean up if accidents occur. Clear glasses (plastic) allow the care provider and the child to judge how much milk has been poured.

Eating Behavior

By the time the toddler stage is reached, the child may show strong preferences for particular foods. Although you may have taken care to give the infant a

Figure 4–12   Mealtime gives toddlers a chance to practice using a fork and spoon.
Photos by Kevin French.

variety of nourishing foods without the addition of sugar or salt, the toddler may, even with limited exposure, demand these foods over other foods when available. Food may be refused at mealtime because children may not be hungry, may be exerting their independence, may be too busy exploring the environment, or may simply be tired and need to rest.

When a child does not eat at mealtime, especially the very young child, many care providers become anxious and supplement with snacks between meals. There is nothing wrong with snacks chosen from the Food Guide, but many times the snacks do not match up nutritionally to the meal or they replace important nutrients provided by the meal. Often energy needs are met with foods containing a high proportion of carbohydrate or fat or both with few other nutrients.

What if the child does not eat? The first word of caution is not to punish the child for refusing foods; on the other hand, center activities can be managed so that the child will learn to readily accept most, if not all, foods. Through positive experiences with food, the child can learn to like most foods. Research is explicit in stating that children dislike foods unfamiliar to them and those that their parents dislike [9]. Clearly, the responsibility for providing opportunities in which a variety of foods will be introduced to the child over and over rests with the care provider and food service personnel. The child becomes familiar with new foods only after frequent experiences with such foods.

The effectiveness of various methods of encouraging the child to eat or try new foods has been reviewed by Satter [10]. The frequency of exposure has been shown to be important at least during the toddler stage [11]. The more a child is exposed to a food, the more likely it is that the child will try the food. However, quality of exposure can also affect food preferences. Preschoolers who are enticed with a reward to try new foods were less likely to go back to that food than those who were simply exposed to it and allowed to try it on their own [12]. Foods that are presented in a positive situation or along with a rewarding situation (for example, a birthday or holiday) tend to be preferred [13]. Once the care provider has offered the foods and presented a positive and encouraging environment, the child should be allowed to enjoy the mealtime along with the care providers [14].

When the care provider is faced with a child who will not eat, there may be little the center can do but discuss the child's behavior with the family or, if available, a social service professional. The parent-child relationship at home may affect the food intake and preferences. The following list of concerns may help the care provider understand why the child won't eat. Is the child

- Developmentally ready for the foods and equipment presented?
- Hungry?
- Exerting some independence?
- Too busy "on the go" exploring the environment?
- Tired and in need of sleep more than food?
- Expected to eat foods not eaten by other family members or care providers?
- Using utensils, chair, and table of right size?

- Served portions that are an appropriate size?
- Eating enough?
- Becoming ill or recovering from an illness?
- Emotionally distressed from interactions at home?

Teachers use many techniques to encourage children to try new foods after they are sure none of the concerns listed above apply to the child. Imitation is still one of the best means by which children learn. Children like to imitate adults as well as other siblings. Placing the picky eater at the table next to a child who has learned to enjoy all foods often helps encourage the child to try a variety of foods. Offering the new food first, while the child is hungry, also encourages the child to become acquainted with a new food.

If schedules and policies permit, allow the toddler to prepare food or watch you or the food service personnel prepare foods. The child will want to explore by tasting each ingredient (for example, vegetables for the soup). Involving the food service staff in educational activities often improves the acceptance of food by children and teacher and may improve the quality of food service.

Another technique often used when a child refuses to eat is ignoring the behavior by walking away from the "whiny" child, especially if the child is using food to get attention. A frustrated and fatigued child should be allowed to rest before eating; you then avoid a tug-of-war over food.

NUTRITION-RELATED HEALTH CONCERNS

The major health problems that are nutrition-related and may be affected by diet during childhood are anemia, obesity, dental caries, cardiovascular disease, and lactose intolerance. Food allergies usually occur earlier and were discussed in Chapter 3.

Anemia

"Reduce iron deficiency to less than 3 percent among children 1 through 4—" is the objective stated in *Healthy People 2000* [15]. The baseline data for children aged 1 to 2 was 9%; however, from low income families, aged 1 to 2, the incidence was 21% in 1976–80. The target for the year 2000 is 10% for this population.

The transition from infant feeding regimens, which often include fortified formulas and infant cereals, to whole milk and family foods can affect the iron content of the diet and subsequently the iron status of the child. Anemia is a condition in which the concentration of hemoglobin (measurement of the color of the red blood cells) and the hematocrit (measurement of the quantity of red cells) are below a certain standard. One of the most common causes of anemia is an iron deficiency in the diet.

Recent reports indicate an improvement of nutritional status related to iron among infants and children of high- and low-risk backgrounds [16, 17]. The

Women, Infants and Children (WIC) Supplemental Food Program has helped lower the prevalence of anemia in low-income families, and researchers also note a decline in prevalence of anemia among middle income children seen in private practices. This is considered a pediatric success story!

Children in the WIC program (Chapter 3, Appendix 3–B) receive iron-rich formulas instead of whole milk. Toddlers also can receive iron-rich infant cereals until 18 months or longer followed by iron-fortified cereals through the WIC program.

Although the incidence of anemia appears to be declining with the use of iron-rich foods and medical attention, certain groups are still at high risk for anemia [18]. Children in these groups are characterized by:

1. Low socioeconomic background.
2. Regular use of cow's milk started before 6 months.
3. Use of formula without iron.
4. Low birth weight.

Unfortunately, discontinuing iron-fortified formulas at 6 months and inappropriately applying adult dietary guidelines to diets of very young children may reverse the decrease in anemia seen recently. Although low-fat, high-fiber foods are beneficial for the whole family, overuse of these foods is not best for very young children. As mentioned earlier, too much fiber may inhibit iron absorption. Also, while legumes, breads, iron-fortified cereals, and certain vegetables and fruits are good sources of iron, iron from "red" meats—which some families may be avoiding—is more readily available to the body than that supplied from plant products. Serve a diet with some readily available sources of iron, such as red meat, and a vitamin C source along with the high-fiber grains and legumes for optimal benefit.

In summary, nutrition guidelines to prevent iron deficiency include:

1. Prolong breast-feeding to 6 months or more.
2. Use iron-fortified formula after weaning and for infants not breast-fed.
3. Delay starting regular cow's milk until 12 months.
4. Use infant cereals fortified with iron and ascorbic acid as one of the first solid foods introduced after 4 to 6 months.
5. Combine iron-rich and ascorbic acid-rich foods when meals of solid foods are given. For example, iron-fortified cereals, beans, and peas should be given with orange juice.
6. Give the young child some meat, fish, or poultry along with whole grains, legumes, beans, and peanut butters.
7. Limit intake of whole cow's milk to no more than 32 ounces per day.

Obesity

Data [19, 20] show that 25 to 29% of 6- to 11-year-olds are obese. Assessing a child's weight-for-height status is discussed in detail in previous chapters. Measurements greater than 95th percentile, using the height-for-weight grids, usually indicate obesity. However, these measurements are best confirmed by the health professional using a family history, dietary habit survey, and skinfold techniques.

Recommending dietary restrictions for the young child based only on height and weight grids is not advisable. These measurements do not take into consideration the family history of obesity, environment, and physical activity patterns. The Committee on Nutrition of the American Academy of Pediatrics [21] estimates that for most obese children, unlike adults, lean body mass accounts for as much as 50% of the obese child's excess weight. The committee states that the weight-for-height grids will indicate false positives with heavy muscular children and false negatives with lighter children who have a relative excess of body fat. The grids also tend to underestimate adiposity (fatness) in children less than 3 years old.

Although techniques are available to assess and help prevent obesity, success has not been easy to achieve. In fact, research indicates that childhood family environment alone as seen in adoptive homes has little if any apparent influence on fatness in adults. There is, however, a clear relationship between the body mass of the biological parents and the weight class of their children. Although children favor the weight of their biological parents, not their adoptive parents, fatness is not necessarily determined at conception. The genetic tendency toward fatness can be fully expressed or repressed depending on environmental factors such as food supply and emphasis on exercise [3, 4].

What should be done? "Prevention" is the obvious quick and easy response given to parents concerned that their child may be becoming obese. Peck and Ullrich [22] have addressed the current attitudes and practices involved with actual and potential weight-related problems of children and have detailed several recommendations for action. Their recommendations, based on the child's age and the severity of the weight problem, are given in Table 4–8.

A conservative approach to treating overweight children is recommended because no one has enough information to predict which children will spontaneously lose their excess fat, which will do so with some treatment, and which will always be fat.

No action should be taken unless you assess the problem and plan for intervention:

1. A family history for obesity should be assessed. Is there a genetic component?
2. Assess whether the attitude of the parents toward the child's obesity is a high priority. Is the child's obesity a concern for the parents at this time?
3. Record the eating behavior of the child in the center and the home, asking the parents to keep a dietary record (Appendix IV).
4. Record the activity patterns of the child in the center and the home, asking the parents to note the kind of exercise or activity and the time spent in exercise or activities.

Table 4–8   Recommended actions for weight problems by degree of severity and age.

		Degree of Overweight*		
		Mild†	Moderate†	Severe
Weight for Height Percentile		75–89	90–94	95 and above
Developmental Stage	*Age Range*	*Levels of Activities*		
Infant	0–12 mo	Action 1	Action 1	Action 1
Toddler	1–2 yrs	Action 1	Action 1	Action 2
Preschool	3–5 yrs	Action 1	Action 2	Action 2
Schoolage	6–9 yrs	Action 1	Action 2	Action 3
		Mild	Moderate	Servere
Percent overweight for height, age, sex		120–139	140–159	160 and above
Preadolescent	varies	Action 1	Action 2	Action 3
Adolescent	15–18	Action 1	Action 2	Action 3
Levels of Activity Related to Prevention and Treatment				

Action 1

A. Ascertain history of the child's physical growth by use of National Center for Health Statistics growth charts if possible. If there is a marked change from the child's usual pattern of growth, move to Action 2.

*Based on NCHS growth charts.

†Mild and moderate may actually be heaviness due to factors other than fat, i.e., muscularity and/or heavy body frame. Skinfold measurements can substantiate fatness.

Source: Peck, E. B., and Ullrich, H. D.: Children and weight: a changing perspective, Berkeley, CA, 1985, Nutrition Communications Associates. Used by permission.

5. Parents and care provider with dietitian or nutritionist can:
   a. Evaluate eating and activity patterns.
   b. Develop alternate weight management programs to discuss with those at home and center to control excessive weight gain.
   c. Determine how the child's progress will be assessed.
   d. Take and record accurate measurements of length and weight and plot on growth charts.

Weight Gain History.   The history of one child's weight gain is superimposed on Figure 4–13. Note that the goal in working with an overweight child is slowing down the weight gain process or curtailing weight gain, not reducing weight. As the child continued to grow taller (Figure 4–13), his weight remained the same for 6 months. During the next year he gained only 4 pounds (1.8 kg). At 30 months the boy weighed 36 pounds (16.2 kg) and was 36 inches (90 cm)

Table 4–8   (Continued)

B. Ascertain family history of obesity: Neither parent obese—low risk of child becoming more obese; may need to explore other causes of obesity; one parent obese—moderate risk of child becoming more obese; Two parents obese—high risk of child becoming more obese. If moderate or high risk automatically move to Action 2.

C. Ascertain caretakers' or individual's knowledge, attitudes, and practices related to the following items and provide education where needed: Normal growth patterns; Body size and shape; Nutrient and food needs; Normal psychosocial development, especially in relation to food intake, discipline and control; Physical activity.

Action 2

A. A thorough assessment of the problem by a health practitioner who has an understanding of the many aspects of the problem and is capable of recognizing when referral is required, i.e., dietitian-nutritionist, pediatrician or other M.D. or nurse with special expertise in this practice.

B. Intervention program based on individual need for a period of time (6–12 months) to bring about change in behavior of caretaker and or child. If unsuccessful move to Action 3.

Action 3

A health assessment and the development of an intervention program by a multidisciplinary team at a specialized clinic. This program could then be carried out by a team of local professionals if the clinic is a distance from the home community.

tall. The child was above the 95th percentile (weight for stature) as seen in Figure 4–14. By 36 months the child had grown to 37 inches (92.5 cm), but held his weight constant. This was accomplished primarily by changing his activity patterns and following a plan agreed on by the care provider and the parents. At age 3½ years (40 mo) he was 39 inches (97.5 cm) and weighed 37.5 pounds (16.9 kg). As the child reached 4 years, his height was 40.5 inches (101.3 cm), and he weighed 40 pounds (18 kg), but his weight for height was now below the 90th percentile.

Parents and the Health Professional.   Finally, these activities must be coordinated with parents and pediatrician. Care providers must cooperatively plan the best strategy for the child. The child's nutrition, food intake, exercise, and eating behavior should be assessed as described above by a registered dietitian or one trained specifically to conduct nutrition assessments on children. This information can be provided to the family's pediatrician to verify that modifications in exercise and diet will not interfere with any other medical treatment.

Action Plan.   If the child has been evaluated and parents and care providers both recognize the need to address the problem, the center's consulting dietitian or nutritionist should be asked to assist. Planning and implementation of center activities may include the following:

1. Each week the child should be weighed and measured, and these weight and height measurements recorded and given to the parents along with information on the child's educational progress.

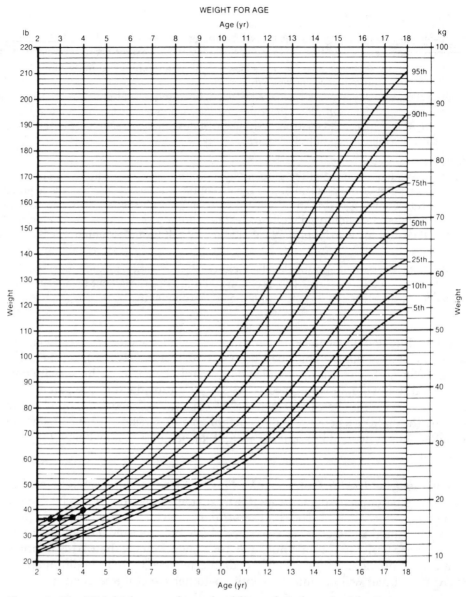

WEIGHT FOR AGE

Figure 4–13. Weight for age of preschool boy, plotted on chart for 2- to 18-year-olds.

Source: U.S. Department of Health, Education and Welfare, National Center for Health Statistics, 1979.

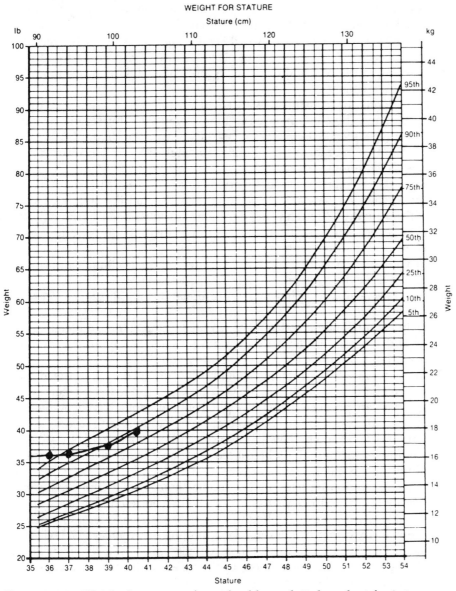

Figure 4–14.   Weight for stature of preschool boy, plotted on chart for 2- to 11½-year-olds.
Source: U.S. Department of Health, Education and Welfare, National Center for Health Statistics, 1979.

2. A child's activity pattern can be modified by planning more gross motor activities and remembering that the child must be successful at these activities, especially the overweight child. The obese, nonactive child may stay obese because gross motor activities have not been particularly rewarding in the past and even young preschool children learn to ridicule the obese child.

3. If all foods are consumed with equal gusto, then portion size can be limited and the child diverted to low-calorie foods for second helpings. Encourage second helpings of vegetables with fat-reduced low-calorie dips and grain products. If the child is a "milk drinker," milk can be given in smaller amounts.

4. Keep the child busy with table serving or cleanup activities or running to the kitchen for flatware, or napkins, and slow all the children in their eating activities through your educational activities and by asking them to chew every bite completely, to put down their spoon or fork between bites, and to describe the taste.

5. Providing a snack (low-calorie) 30 minutes before mealtime may also help curtail the child's appetite.

6. Don't serve food that has a low nutritional density in proportion to the caloric value.

7. Help parents understand what constitutes sound eating and feeding habits and the need to develop them during infancy, because a pattern of overfeeding in infancy may persist into adult life.

8. In the infant center, mothers should be encouraged to breast-feed for at least 6 months. Nevertheless, if every cry is interpreted as hunger, breast-feeding can produce an overweight baby. A mother who bottle-feeds should not pressure the baby to empty the bottle during feedings.

9. Care providers and parents should not use food as a reward or pacifier for any form of distress. Both breast-fed and bottle-fed babies have used the nipple as a pacifier.

10. Time spent viewing television is one of the most powerful predictors of obesity for the 6- to 11-year-olds even when controlling for other known variables associated with childhood obesity [23]. Therefore, one definite action every care provider can take is limiting the number of television or video viewing hours. True, other activities may have to substitute for sitting in front of the television, but these activities may be more educational for the child.

The treatment goal, generally, is the slowing of the rate of weight gain in proportion to linear growth, not an actual loss in weight. Dietary restrictions that are too severe may reduce fat-free tissue, inhibit growth, and deplete energy reserves needed for periods of stress.

Dental Caries

Conditions that affect the incidence of dental caries begin during the toddler years. Dental caries consist of localized, progressive decay of teeth, initiated by demineralization of the outer surface of the tooth. This process is caused by organic acids produced locally by bacteria that ferment deposits of dietary carbohydrates; sucrose, or table sugar, is the primary carbohydrate. While many common foods can be cariogenic, some foods, such as aged cheddar cheese, can help decrease acid conditions and prevent caries formation.

After the toddler eats, care providers can clean the teeth as soon as practical by wiping the mouth with fine gauze wrapped around the finger. You can introduce a toothbrush by 12 to 15 months when the teeth have erupted, and by 18 months the routine can be well established. Toothpaste may be used, but it is not necessary.

Nursing bottle caries, or nursing bottle syndrome (Chapter 3), refers to the destruction of the anterior (front) teeth as a result of contact with carbohydrate-containing solutions fed through the bottle. When the child is allowed to take a bottle to bed at nap time or in the evening, sucking and swallowing are infrequent, saliva flow is minimal, and sugar remains in contact with the teeth for a long time. This is especially true if the child is taking liquids with sucrose or glucose.

Bottles at bedtime should not be allowed in the center. If the child is drinking from a bottle, it should be given when the child is fully awake and upright. All sweetened fluids, including formula, should be given by cup and teeth should be brushed after the feedings, if possible.

Although frequent eating periods are advocated for the toddler, these feedings should not include calorie-dense foods that are cavity-producing (see Chapter 6 for a list of acceptable foods). Snacks, as well as meals, should include selections from the basic food groups—fruits, vegetables, breads and crackers, meats and dairy products, with margarine or peanut butter, cheeses, milk, and meats.

Fluoride has a beneficial effect in decreasing the incidence and severity of dental caries. However, excessive intake of fluoride may cause mottled discoloration of teeth. Child-care centers located in areas where water is unfluoridated should alert parents whose children remain in the center all day to the need for supplementing the child's intake of fluoride.

Cardiovascular Disease

There is controversy over whether older children should be given a diet that is limited in total fat, saturated fat, and cholesterol [24, 25]. Although at home the child will likely be consuming a diet similar to the parents, the center should not aim to restrict the very young child's intake of red meats, dairy products, and eggs. These foods provide high-quality protein, iron, calcium, and other nutrients necessary for the growth of children. A complete discussion of diet and cardiovascular disease for children after 2 years of age is included in Chapter 6.

Lactose Intolerance

Lactose, the disaccharide or carbohydrate found in milk and milk products, is broadly consumed in its natural form and in a variety of manufactured and processed products. The adequacy of lactose digestion and absorption has important implications for care providers in centers that have a predominantly nonwhite population. Throughout the world, lactose intolerance—a lack of sufficient quantities of the digestive enzyme lactase—is far more common than tolerance. Tolerance of lactose and large quantities of milk is peculiar to northern European and white American ethnic groups; most adults in the world cannot ingest large quantities of milk because of lactose intolerance [26, 27].

Studies of black children in the United States show a progressive decrease in lactose absorption with age. Most infants at birth can tolerate the high percentage of lactose found in breast milk or can tolerate formulas that contain lactose. However, at 1 or 2 years of age, 27% of black children have evidence of lactose malabsorption, and at ages 5 to 6 years, 33% may be malabsorbers [26]. This progressive increase in the prevalence of malabsorption with age has been noted for black children in both high and low socioeconomic groups.

It is important to recognize that lactose intolerance is not an all-or-none phenomenon. Rather, the availability of the enzyme lactase slowly declines, and this decline can be influenced by transit time (how fast the food moves through the intestinal tract), the food (cheese, milk, yogurt) in which the lactose is consumed, and intake of additional foods.

A child may not be able to tolerate a glass of milk upon arrival at the center, but after or when eating other foods, tolerates milk well. Likewise, cheese may be tolerated when cow's milk causes gastric distress. Although a child may have been given a test that involves a tolerance dosage of lactose, there is a difference between an individual's ability to tolerate a large challenge dose of lactose and the ability to use the lesser amounts of lactose found in commonly consumed amounts of milk.

Because milk is an important food source for many vitamins, minerals, and protein, lactase can be purchased under various trade names and added to dairy products to predigest the milk sugar. Milk with lactaid is now available in some grocery stores. In addition, the care provider and parents can try cured cheese and yogurt, in which much of the lactose is broken down in the fermentation process. Finally, one can substitute other foods for the calcium in milk by referring to Table 4–4 for alternate calcium sources. Supplementation with calcium may be necessary in some cases.

EXERCISE AND PHYSICAL FITNESS

Concerned parents often begin pressuring care providers to provide more energy expenditure through exercise for children in this age span. This is the result of a constant barrage of fitness survey reports that are reported over and over on television and in magazines and newspapers. National studies of youth fitness over a period of 29 years have revealed that children in the United States are underexercised [28]. Interestingly, these surveys were conducted with children aged 6 years to 17 years. Still, the message is loud and clear. Our kids are overweight and out of shape.

There is a mounting concern among young parents that something needs to be done and it needs to be done early. Many parents of toddlers are beginning to react by seeking out early childhood programs that offer fitness as part of their curriculums. Some national child-care chains are offering "muscle rooms"— large rooms with balance beams, tumbling mats, climbing cubes, and an obstacle course that children can travel [29].

Home programs are also on the market. Matchbox Toys manufactures a do-it-yourself kiddie exercise kit called Baby-Cise. The kit costs $100 plus for an instructional video, plastic barbells, a baby balance beam, and a clutch ball for developing hand-eye coordination [30].

Over the past 17 years, a number of fitness programs targeted specifically for children aged 3 months through 4 years have begun. One such program, Gymboree, began with one center in 1976 and has expanded to over 300 franchises located in 34 states, as well as the countries of France, Israel, Canada, Australia, Mexico, and Taiwan. Gymboree has also expanded to offer a retail line of fitness equipment designed for movement and growth [31].

Figure 4–15   A toddler enjoys playing with balls. Photo by Robert E. Rockwell.

The hallmarks of the majority of the franchise programs are songs and games and stretching and climbing exercises in which the children participate with one or both parents. Activities are designed to foster the development of both gross and fine motor skills. Classes are priced $8 to $12 a week for 12 weekly sessions.

The concerns of these parents are valid; however, again we refer you to the cautions regarding exercise programs that were given in Chapter 3.

The early childhood environment should be well stocked with climbers, large cardboard boxes, slides, barrels, large blocks, large balls, puzzles, four-wheeled toys, and push-and-pull play materials (Figure 4–15) [32].

Exercise will occur naturally as the toddlers climb, crawl, pull, walk, bend, and jump. These movements will provide an abundance of exercise for all muscles. Since toddlers are excited and happy about these new movement skills, they will spend much time practicing them over and over both indoors and out of doors. There is no need for a structured exercise program.

SUMMARY

- The toddler, age 12 to 36 months, is growing proportionately more slowly than the infant; however, continued attention to the child's height and weight, developmental skills, and dietary intake is important.
- Although the toddler's demand for energy is higher, 46.4 kcal per pound compared with 44.5 for a 6- to 12-month-old infant, the need for essential nutrients is still great. The food eaten must contain essential nutrients without excessive energy or calories.
- The care provider's task is to interest the child in food and eating when the child is hungry and to acquaint the child with a wide variety of food experiences.
- Foods from the daily Food Guide should be carefully chosen to encourage the child to self-feed using fingers and small-sized flatware. A variety of new and interesting combinations of foods along with familiar foods should be offered.
- Some nutrition-related problems develop during the toddler stage. Iron-deficiency anemia may become acute if the infant was not breast-fed exclusively or given iron supplements or a diet high in iron-containing foods during the 6- to 12-month period.
- Obesity may persist or become evident in the toddler years, although prevention more than treatment is emphasized. Dental caries may develop as a result of frequent consumption of foods that contain large quantities of sticky carbohydrates, nursing bottle syndrome, or consumption of an unfluoridated water supply without the addition of fluoride supplements.
- A few toddlers who could tolerate milk during infancy may develop an intolerance to milk during the toddler and preschool years as a result of the condition known as lactose intolerance.

- Exercise for children during the toddler years should be considered, and as the family participates in exercise, children can be encouraged to go along with the family.

DISCUSSION QUESTIONS

1. List preparation methods that could be used with specific foods to stimulate a toddler to use fingers, spoon, and fork.
2. What are some of the reasons a child will not eat?
3. A child is anemic. How would you help the mother choose foods that would increase the iron supply in the child's diet? Suppose the child's mother requested that the child consume a vegetarian diet.
4. A toddler's height for weight is above the 95th percentile. Which factors would you take into consideration before discussing the perceived problem with the parents and health professionals?
5. A toddler drinks 4 cups of whole milk and consumes very little other food but is not overweight. Do you need to consider modifying the diet?
6. Will the toddler be able to eat the foods from the daily Food Guide or should you provide a special diet for this age group?
7. What are the energy and nutrient needs of the toddler compared with those of the infant?
8. What type of exercises occur naturally during the toddler period?
9. What are the dangers presented by structured exercise programs for toddlers?
10. What roles can care providers play in providing toddlers with an environment that fosters natural movement and growth experiences?

REFERENCES

1. Black J., Puckett, M., and Bell, M.: The young child: development from prebirth through age eight, Columbus, OH, 1992, Merrill Publishing Co.
2. Grand, R. J., Sutphen, J. L., and Dietz, W. H.: Pediatric nutrition theory and practice, Boston, 1987, Butterworth Publishers.
3. Stunkard, A. J., Sorensen, T. I. A., Hanis, C., et al.: An adoption study on human obesity, N. Engl. J. Med. 314:193–198, 1986.
4. Stanzo, P.R., and Schiffman, S.S.: Thinness—not obesity—has a genetic component, Neuroscience and Biobehavioral Reviews, 13:55–58, 1989.
5. Anselmo, S.: Early childhood development: prenatal through age eight, Columbus, OH, 1987, Merrill Publishing Co.
6. Erikson, E. H.: Childhood and society, ed. 2, New York, 1963, W. W. Norton & Co., Inc.
7. National Research Council, Food and Nutrition Board: Recommended dietary allowance, ed. 10, Washington, DC, 1989, National Academy of Science.
8. U.S. Department of Agriculture Nationwide Food Consumption Survey: Continuing Survey of Food Intakes of Individuals. Women 19–50 years and their children 1–5 years, 1 day, 1986, Report No. 86-1 Nutrition Monitor-

ing Division, Human Nutrition Information Service, USDA.

9. Burt, J. V., and Hertzler, A. A.: Parental influence on the child's food preference, J. Nutr. Educ. 10:127–128, 1978.

10. Satter, E. M.: The feeding relationship, J. Am. Diet. Assoc., 86:352–356, 1986.

11. Birch, L. L., and Marlin, D. W.: I don't like it: I never tried it: effects of exposure on two-year-old children's food preferences, Appetite: J. for Intake Research 3:353–360, 1982.

12. Birch, L. L., Marlin, D. W., and Rotter, J.: Eating as the "means" activity in a contingency: effects on young children's food preference, Child Dev. 55:431–439, 1984.

13. Birch, L. L., Zimmerman, S. I., and Hind, H.: The influence of social- affective context on the formation of children's food preferences, Child Dev., 51:856–861, 1980.

14. Satter, E. M.: Child of mine: feeding with love and good sense, Palo Alto, CA, 1986, Bull Publishing Co.

15. U.S. Department of Health and Human Services, Public Health Service: Healthy people 2000: health promotion and disease prevention objectives, Washington, DC, 1990, U.S. Government Printing Office.

16. Yip, R., Walsh, K. M., Goldfarb, M. G., and Blinkin, N. J.: Declining prevalence of anemia in childhood in middle class children: a pediatric success story? Pediatrics 80:330, 1987.

17. Yip, R., Blinkin, N. J., Fleshood, L., and Trowbridge, F. L.: Declining prevalence of anemia among low-income children in the United States, J.A.M.A. 258:1619–1623, 1987.

18. Dallman, P. R.: Has routine screening of infants for anemia become obsolete in the United States? Pediatrics 80:439, 1987.

19. Gortmaker, S. L., Dietz, W. H., Sobol, A. M., and Wehler, C. A.: Increasing pediatric obesity in the United States, Am. J. Dis. Child. 141:535–540, 1987.

20. Ginsberg-Fellner, F., Jagendorf, L. A., Carmel, H., et al.: Overweight and obesity in pre-school children in New York City, Am. J. Clin. Nutr. 34:2236–2241, 1981.

21. American Academy of Pediatrics, Committee on Nutrition: Nutritional aspects of obesity in infancy and childhood, Pediatrics 68:880–883, 1981.

22. Peck, E. B., and Ullrich, H. D.: Children and weight: a changing perspective, Berkeley, CA, 1985, Nutrition Communications Associates.

23. Dietz, W. H., and Gortmaker, S. L.: Do we fatten our children at the television set? Obesity and television viewing in children and adolescents, Pediatrics 75:807–812, 1985.

24. National Cholesterol Education Program: Report of the Expert Panel on Blood Cholesterol Levels in Children and Adolescents, Pub No. 91–2732, U.S. Department of Health and Human Services, 1991, National Institutes of Health.

25. American Academy of Pediatrics, Committee on Nutrition: Prudent lifestyle for children: dietary fat and cholesterol, Pediatrics 78:521, 1986.

26. Paige, D. M., and Bayless, T. M.: Lactose digestion, Baltimore, MD, 1981, The Johns Hopkins University Press.

27. Dobbler, M.L.: Lactose intolerance, Chicago, IL., 1991, Am. Dietet. Assn.

28. The President's Council on Physical Fitness and Sports: National School Population Fitness Survey, HHS-Office of the Assistant Secretary for Health Research Project No. 282-84-0086, 1986, University of Michigan Press.

29. Ward, A.: Born to jog: exercise programs for preschoolers, The Physician and Sports Medicine 14:163, 1986.

30. Kantrowitz, B., and Joseph, N.: Building baby biceps, Newsweek 107:79, May 26, 1986.

31. Gymboree Gazette, Hillman, D., ed.: 13(3), Burlingame, CA, 1991, Gymboree Corporation.

32. Mena, J. G.: Toddlers: what to expect, Young Children 42:50, 1986.

5

The Preschooler (3 to 5 Years)

LEARNING OBJECTIVES

Students will be able to:
- State the physiological characteristics of the preschooler that may affect eating habits.
- State the nutrient and energy needs of the preschool child.
- Evaluate the diet using the Food Guide.
- List acceptable snack foods from each food group.
- Describe the vegetarian diet and its use in the preschool center.
- Describe appropriate exercise for this age group.

The preschool child is often called the "runabout." However, the run for the table is not simply to practice running, but for a specific purpose—to join friends at lunch. The child between 3 and 5 years of age is usually a physical child, and although the toddler moved around excessively, the preschooler often surpasses the toddler in activity. As new skills develop, those learned during the toddler stage become refined, and the preschooler gains sophistication in motion control. Long gone are the days when the child practiced gaining head control, the upright posture, and the basic abilities.

The beauty of this particular age is that the child no longer has to struggle with learning to suck, swallow, chew, and use a spoon, fork, and knife. If the parents or care providers have regularly eaten with the child and the child has practiced using utensils, only the use of a knife for cutting and spreading may need some refinement. Thus, this is the first real opportunity for the care provider and child to actively participate together in the food and nutrition program (Figure 5–1).

Up to now the challenges for the teacher have been to acquaint the child with a wide variety of food tastes and choices and to teach the basic use of utensils. If this is done successfully before 3 years of age, any food can be used as an educational experience. However, if the child has been encouraged to eat only a small number of foods and many foods of poor nutritional quality, the task of introducing a wide variety of foods into the child's diet will be added to the responsibilities of the nutrition program at the child-care center.

Physically, though, the child will want to participate in most activities in the center. This means that preparing food, setting the table, serving the food, cleaning up, and occasionally going to the market can become a regular part of the child's activities. The child at this point can use scissors to cut out and color pictures. These skills can be used to make placemats for the tables and can be incorporated into other activities that will make meals a special learning time. Psychosocially, the child struggles to develop a sense of initiative and takes an eager and inquisitive approach to the surroundings. Size, form, color, shape,

Figure 5–1 Care giver and preschoolers participate in use of food as a learning experience.

time, and space take on a new meaning and can be related to foods and meal-time.

WEIGHT AND STATURE

The child's relative state of health influences growth. Ordinary illnesses such as upper respiratory tract infections or the childhood diseases usually are not severe or prolonged enough to interfere with growth. Chronic, repeated, or severe illness, however, may cause the body to conserve resources, and the rate of growth may slow.

Watching the stature and weight charts can be important, and any prolonged slowdown in growth should be noted. Stature and weight of the preschool child should be taken on a monthly basis and recorded on charts for boys and girls ages 2 to 18 years (Appendix V). The physical growth of the preschooler can be

Table 5–1 Weights and stature by sex and age for 3– to 5–year-olds.

Age (years)	Girls		Boys	
	Weight (pounds)	Stature (inches)	Weight (pounds)	Stature (inches)
3	31.0	37.0	32.2	37.4
4	35.0	40.0	36.7	40.5
5	38.9	42.7	41.1	43.3

Source: Modified from charts showing smoothed percentiles of weight and stature by sex and age developed by National Center for Health Statistics, U.S. Department of Health, Education and Welfare, PHS, Hyattsville, MD, 1977, The Center.

monitored through the use of a scale and measuring stick as described in Chapter 4.

The preschooler's height and weight do not increase as rapidly as they did during the first 12 months. The 4-year-old probably will weigh five times as much as at birth. Therefore, the 7.5 pound (3.8 kg) baby can now be expected to weigh about 37 pounds (16.7 kg). This is a general rule, and individual weights will vary. Between 3 and 5 years of age, the child will probably not gain more than 4 pounds (1.8 kg) per year or approximately ⅓ pound (0.15 kg) each month (Table 5–1).

If the child has gained a pound or two in less than a month, look for the reasons. Weight gain or loss may be a result of chronic illness, overeating, error in measurement, faulty equipment, or stress in the home environment. Losses or gains of a pound or two each month over a 2- or 3-month period without a change in height should cause concern. After ensuring proper use of measuring equipment, take time to talk with the parents about any changes in the child's physical or eating behavior. Then, if necessary, check with the physician or dietitian/nutritionist who will review height, weight, skinfold, dietary, and health history.

CHILD DEVELOPMENT SKILLS

The child is now ready for verbal exchange during the eating period. The child is eager to help the care provider and parents with preparation, service, and cleanup of food. However, it should be remembered that the child's quickness in movement and occasional inattentiveness may result in spills or broken dishes. Mishaps are inevitable, but generally these are not intentional. The child simply misjudges situations, and these miscalculations, combined with the haste of a preschooler to accomplish a task, cause accidents. During the preschool period the rate of growth stabilizes and appetite is regular. The child still needs both meals and several snacks.

The child likes to be included in food-related activities (Table 5–2) and is generally a welcomed helper.

Table 5–2   Stages of development for preschooler and elementary years.*

Stage	Physical	Nutritional	Intellectual
Preschool: 3 to 4 years	Slowed steady height-weight gain; lordosis and prominent abdomen disappear; face grows faster than cranial cavity; jaw widens	Assertion of independence increases; appetite declines with picky food habits	Concept of "conservation" begins (i.e., some features of objects remain the same despite changes in other features)
Elementary I: 5 to 6 years	Steady average weight gain 3 to 3.5 kg/yr and height gain of 6 cm/yr; growth of head slows	Rate of growth stabilizes, accompanied by more regular appetite; likes to be included in food-related activities	Child can begin to take others' viewpoints; school begins

Stage	Gross Motor	Fine Motor	Speech and Language
Preschool: 3 to 4 years	Stands and hops on one foot; jumps heights and distances	Minute degrees of flexion and extension of interphalangeal joints in three jaw chuck position	Sentence length and complexity increase; uses language for a variety of purposes (to satisfy needs, pretend, argue, etc.); other consonants emerge
Elementary I: 5 to 6 years	Rides a bicycle; begins organized play activities and perfects game skills	Refinement of individual finger coordination (i.e., piano playing); ability to use one upper extremity for one task, one for a different task	Receptive and expressive language develops in relation to cognitive growth

Stage	Social/Behavioral
Preschool: 3 to 4 years	Moves from parallel to cooperative play; able to conform
Elementary I: 5 to 6 years	Acceptable table manners; peers becoming more important

*This chart provides the health of professional with a standard tool for assessing feeding levels.

Source: Modified from Harvey-Smith, M., et al.: Feeding management of a child with a handicap: a guide for professionals, Memphis, 1982, University of Tennessee Center for the Health Sciences.

ENERGY AND NUTRIENT NEEDS

Energy

The energy needs of children of the same age, sex, and size can vary as a result of differences in physical activity or the efficiency with which children utilize energy. The RDA is only a guide for energy needs for the 4- to 6-year-old. Table 5–3 shows that the energy requirements per pound or per kilogram of body weight have decreased since the toddler years.

At birth the child required about 49 kcal per pound; between 1 and 3 years approximately 46 kcal per pound; and by 4 years the child requires only about 41 kcal per pound. Total calories will increase as the child grows taller and gains weight. For this age group it may be easier to base energy needs on an individual basis and consider allowing 41 calories per inch (Chapter 4). A very active child requires additional energy.

Given an energy allowance (RDA) of approximately 1600–1800 kcal (for 4- to 6-year-olds) and a need for a wide variety of nutrients, the diet should contain foods of high nutrient density. Foods that supply few nutrients in addition to

Table 5–3 RDA for ages 1–3 and 4–6.

NUTRIENT	1 to 3 Years (29 lb, 35 in. [20 kg, 112 cm])	4 to 6 Years (44 lb, 44 in. [28 kg, 132 cm])
Resting Energy Equivalent	$kg \times 102$ ($lb \times 46.4$)	$kg \times 90$ ($lb \times 40.9$)
Protein (g/day)	$kg \times 1.2$	$kg \times 1.1$
Vitamin A (μg RE)	400	500
Vitamin D (μg)	10	10
Vitamin E (mg α-TE)	6	7
Vitamin K (μg)	15	20
Ascorbic acid (mg)	40	45
Folate (μg)	50	75
Niacin (mg NE)	9	12
Riboflavin (mg)	0.8	1.1
Thiamin (mg)	0.7	0.9
Vitamin B_6 (mg)	1.0	1.1
Vitamin B_{12} (μg)	0.7	1.0
Calcium (mg)	800	800
Phosphorus (mg)	800	800
Iodine (μg)	70	90
Iron (mg)	10	10
Magnesium (mg)	80	120
Zinc (mg)	10	10

Source: Based on Food and Nutrition Board, National Academy of Sciences—National Research Council: Recommended Dietary Allowances, revised 1989.

energy should not be included in the diet. Children often prefer sweet grain products; however, adding foods such as cakes and pies adds fat and calories without adding other necessary nutrients. The energy needs are not fixed for the child and depend on whether the child is maintaining a reasonable height for weight gain.

Protein

The recommended amount of protein is 1.1 g per kilogram (RDA for the 4- to 6-year-old). Therefore, for a 45-pound (20 kg) 4-year-old child, 22 g of protein is recommended. You are reminded that this is the recommended amount, not the amount actually required by the child. To meet the protein recommendation, the child should drink between 2 and 3 cups (16 to 24 ounces) of milk (16 to 24 g of protein). This quantity not only supplies protein, but also helps to meet the child's calcium, riboflavin, and other vitamin and mineral needs. Two cups of milk supply 16 g of protein (more than half the RDA). Two ounces of meat (7 g of protein per ounce of meat) will supply 14 g of protein, making a total of 30 grams of protein, more than the RDA. This amount excludes the protein in vegetables and grain products, which would increase the total protein intake. Studies have indicated that the average intake of protein for the 1- to 5-year-old child from both high- and low-income families meets or exceeds the standards [1].

Recipes using high protein foods such as nuts, legumes, and beans as ingredients also provide the much-needed magnesium, zinc, folacin, and vitamin B_6. These nutrients are difficult to obtain without a wide variety of high-protein sources including nuts, legumes, and beans.

Fat

By 2 years of age, care providers are urged to begin use of a diet with lower fat. There is no RDA for fat but the Dietary Guidelines for Americans (Chapter 2) recommend no more than 30% of calories as fat. Increasing grain products in the diet to at least 6 servings and fruits and vegetables to 5 servings will decrease the fat intake so long as fat is not added in preparation of these foods. Children who are under desirable weight will probably need more fat in the diet as a concentrated form of energy. A complete discussion of limiting fat and calculating a diet with 30% of calories from fat is found in Chapter 6.

Minerals/Vitamins

Calcium. Calcium is one of the nutrients found in less than recommended amounts in some diets. Three cups of milk readily provide the necessary 800 mg (Table 5–3) of calcium (1 cup supplies approximately 280 mg calcium). If the child likes milk, calcium will probably be taken in sufficient quantities for building bones and teeth. However, obtaining enough calcium without consuming dairy products is difficult (Chapter 4 includes a list of calcium-rich foods). Dried beans and green vegetables are sources of calcium, but the quantity of these foods necessary to meet the child's calcium needs is large and not a practical option during the growing years. If the child cannot drink fresh, fluid milk, then canned (processed) milk, dry milk, yogurt, and cheese (excluding cream cheese) could be eaten. These products contain comparable quantities of calcium and may be more easily tolerated.

Iron.   Table 5–3 shows the RDA for iron at 10 mg. As the child eats more food, the iron intake will increase. About 4% of all children 3 to 4 years of age have iron-deficiency anemia while almost 95% of preschoolers are believed to have intakes below the standard [2]. *Healthy People 2000* [3] has addressed this issue by proposing that anemia in this age group be reduced from 4% to less than 3%. However, 10% of low-income children have iron-deficiency, with the target of 5% by the year 2000. Centers serving low-income children may need to consider serving diets with many high-iron foods.

Milk is a poor source of iron, and consuming it in large quantities (more than 3 to 4 cups) may replace foods with higher iron content, especially iron-rich cereals. Discontinuing fortified infant cereals and iron-rich formula also contributes to iron-deficiency anemia in the toddler years. In some cases, the toddler may still be eating cooked iron-fortified cereal or iron-fortified infant cereal. But by the preschool years the cooked cereals (for example, Cream of Wheat, Malt-O-Meal) have given way to more dry cereals. Check the labels and keep iron-fortified cereals available.

The 3- to 5-year-old child is able to chew most meat products, which tend to provide an available source of iron. Grains, legumes, and fruits and vegetables can provide some iron. Some of the iron from plant sources, however, may not be readily available because of the phytate and fiber components that naturally occur in plants. It has been reported that phytate and fiber bind some of the iron into a complex that the body cannot use [4]. However, the evidence is not conclusive and does not warrant the discontinuation of the use of plant foods as a source of iron.

It is difficult to consume enough food with iron if the energy intake is "wasted" on food with low nutrient density. Good sources of iron with a high nutrient density are meat, greens, and enriched or iron-fortified whole-grain cereal products (see Chapter 4). Egg yolk, beans, nuts, molasses, and dried fruits are good sources of iron, but some of these products are seldom eaten.

Liver is often cited as one of the best sources of iron, and indeed it is but the high cholesterol value of liver has discouraged its use. One ounce of beef liver supplies almost 2 mg of iron, whereas 1 ounce of ground beef supplies only 1 mg. Likewise, 2 tablespoons of wheat germ, ¾ cup of oatmeal or rolled oats, two rye wafers, or 3 tablespoons of cooked spinach supply 1 mg of iron. See Chapter 7 for ways to include iron in the menu.

Vitamin C.   A balance of all nutrients is as important for the 3- to 5-year-old as it is for the younger child. A daily source of vitamin C is important, since there is evidence that vitamin C enhances iron absorption.

The question of whether to add vitamin C to the child's diet to prevent the common cold is often raised. Studies have indicated that vitamin C does not reduce the number of colds, but it can make one or more cold symptoms less severe. The greatest effect seems to be to reduce total sick days rather than to actually prevent the common cold [5–7]. See Chapters 1 and 7 for further discussion of vitamin C and foods that contain vitamin C.

Zinc.   Zinc, like iron, is needed in small amounts. The RDA is 10 mg for the preschooler. Zinc is part of the insulin molecule and is necessary for the passage of glucose from the blood into many body cells. The energy of glucose cannot be released until this passage is accomplished.

Zinc is an essential nutrient found in many food sources, including organ meats, oysters, egg yolk, beans, and nuts. Milk, meats, legumes, beans, whole-grain cereals, and wheat germ supply more than 1 mg per serving. Many of these foods are also good protein sources. If the Food Guide's recommendation of 6 servings of grains and more use of legumes and beans is followed, the zinc RDA can be met.

Many other nutrients must be included in the diet. We have singled out those nutrients that have been found to be consumed in less than recommended amounts or are often presented on child-care centers' menus in less than recommended quantities. These nutrients are difficult to supply without careful planning of menus.

FOOD NEEDS

The preschooler needs to eat frequently throughout the day. Assessing the child's nutritional needs includes determining a child's acceptance of food. You can use the dietary history along with physical measurements of growth and development. You may use the 24–hour dietary recall method described in Chapter 2 or a dietary questionnaire listing frequency of foods eaten (Appendix IV). Because many preschoolers are on the go constantly and are now more self-sufficient than during the toddler stage, they can open refrigerator doors, climb onto kitchen cabinets, and open jars to find their favorite foods. This means, for example, that cookies may be stuffed into little pockets when the child enters the center at 7:00 A.M. The care provider should realize that the parents may not be able to provide complete information on the kinds and amounts of food the child has eaten.

A good dietary history taken by the care provider may reveal that the child is consuming less than recommend amounts of food. Looking further into the family's food intake will reveal numerous occasions when the child may have acquired food without the parents' knowledge.

Parents and care providers should expose children to a variety of foods without rewards or punishments [8, 9]. If only a limited diet is served, the child learns to enjoy only a few foods. Given the dietary record, the Food Guide is used to evaluate the nutrient intake (Table 5–4).

Table 5–4　Recommended food intake according to food group and average serving sizes (ages 3 up to 6 years).

Food Group	Servings/Day	Average Serving (ages 3 up to 6)
Vegetables	3–5	
Green vegetables	1*	4–6 tbsp (⅓ C)
Other vegetables (potato and other green or yellow vegetables)	2	4–6 tbsp (⅓ C)
Fruits	2–4	
Vitamin C source (citrus fruits, berries, melons)		¼–½ C
Breads and Cereals (Whole Grain)	6–11	
Bread*		¾–1 slice
Ready-to-eat cereals, whole grain, iron-fortified		½ oz
Cooked cereal including macaroni, spaghetti, rice, etc. (whole grain, enriched)		¼ C
Milk and Milk Products	At least 4	
Whole or 2% milk (1.5 oz cheese = 1 C milk) (C = 8 oz or 240 g)		¾ C
Meat and Alternates	3–4 including:	
Lean meat, fish, poultry, and eggs†	2	2 oz
Nutbutters (peanut, soynut)*		3 tbsp§
Cooked dried beans or peas	1–2‡	⅜ C
Nuts		¾ oz
Fats and Oils	3	
Butter, margarine, mayonnaise, oils		1 tsp

*Allow a minimum service of 1 tbsp/year of age for cooked fruits, vegetables, cereals, and pasta until the child reaches 8 years or ½ C portion size.

†To enhance overall nutrient content of diet include eggs two to three times a week and liver occasionally.

§As recommended by Illinois State Board of Education, Department of Child Nutrition: Child Care Food Program—required meal patterns, Springfield, IL, June 1986, The Board.

‡Include nutbutters, dried (cooked) beans, or peas at least once a day to meet nutrient recommendations and decrease the fat content of the diet. Use additional servings of meats when legumes, beans, and nuts are omitted.

A preschooler would need to consume only ½ to ¾ of a slice of whole-grain bread; however, one slice has been allowed in the example. The general rule for minimum serving size is 1 tablespoon (measuring) per year of age. The diet emphasizes use of beans as a substitute for part of the protein, whole-grain cereals and breads, fruits and vegetables, specifically the dark green varieties and those with a high vitamin C content, and milk and milk products (Table 5–5).

Table 5–5   Preschooler diet compared with Food Guide and RDA.

Food (amounts)	Milk	Protein	Vegetables	Fruit	Whole-Grain Products	Fats/ Oils
7 A.M.						
Orange juice, ½ C				1		
Cereal, iron-fortified, ¾ oz					1	
Milk, 2%, ⅜ C	½					
Whole wheat toast, 1 slice					1	
Margarine, 1 tsp						1
10 A.M						
Bagel, ½					1	
Jelly, 1 tsp						
Low-fat cheese, ½ oz		⅓				
Milk 2%, ⅜	½					
12:30 P.M.						
Hamburger, 1 oz		⅔				
Whole wheat bun, 1					2	
Cooked beans, 2 tbsp		⅓				
Mayonnaise, 1 tsp						1
Broccoli, ½ C			2			
Milk 2%, ¾ C	1					
5:30 P.M.						
Broiled fish, 2 oz		1⅓				
New potatoes, ⅓ C			1			
Carrots, ⅓ C			1			
Whole wheat roll, 1					1	
Margarine, 1 tsp						1
Milk, 2%, ¾ C	1					
8 P.M.						
Milk, 2%, ¾ C	1					
Finger jello with banana, ½ C				1		
TOTAL	4	3	4	2	6	3
RECOMMENDED SERVINGS	2–3	2–3	3–5	2–4	6–11	

This meal provides: 1400 cal, 76 g pro, 46 g fat, 180 g car, 154 mg sod, 11 g iron. Caloric distribution = 22% pro, 29% fat, 49% car

*Iron-fortified cereal may be included to meet recommended needs. Add additional servings to meet energy needs.

The preschooler's diet in Table 5–5 meets or exceeds the Recommended Dietary Allowance [10] for most essential vitamins and minerals. However, the diet provides fewer than the recommended calories for a child weighing 40 pounds (energy needs are approximately 1600 kcal, 41 kcal per pound). Additional energy or calories may be needed for some children.

A child needs the same foods as an adult but in smaller portions, and the care giver should serve some of the food as between-meal snacks. Note at the bottom of Table 5–5 that this child consumed at least the minimum number of servings from the food groups.

Fruits and Vegetables

You will remember that the care provider perhaps had more success at introducing a new food when the child was still a toddler. You were urged to present new foods, especially vegetables, when the child was hungry, while other foods were in preparation. However, the care provider has less control over the eating environment of the preschooler, who eats with the other children at the table and who selects foods from serving bowls.

Many preschoolers do not readily consume vegetables and some fruits. Fruits and vegetables introduced in the child-care center may be strange to the child, and vegetables may not be properly prepared. Both situations can easily be remedied if the menus are part of the educational curriculum (Chapters 7 and 8). Obviously, you will have to pay particular attention to introducing vegetables and fruits with high nutritional content, especially the dark green and yellow vegetables and those with high vitamin C content (Table 5–6).

To help the child become familiar with new foods, the picky eater should be encouraged and allowed to participate in preparing and serving vegetables and fruits. During service, small pieces of broccoli and cauliflower should be placed in the serving bowls so a child takes only one flower of broccoli, one asparagus spear, or one brussels sprout. Cooked cabbage is often served to the preschooler in large chunks and spinach greens served with a large spoon instead of tongs; therefore, the child cannot take a small serving. Sometimes the greens are overcooked and mushy. Chopped greens or spinach, not overcooked, may be easier to serve. A child should be allowed to serve only a teaspoonful of a particular item. This gives the child an opportunity to successfully taste the food without being responsible for a large portion.

Meats and Meat Alternates

Most preschoolers accept some meat products readily. For example, hamburgers and hot dogs seem to be favorites. Meats and meat alternates are an important part of the preschool center menu, because they are the best source of iron as well as protein. However, meat alternates or protein foods including lentils and legumes (such as peas, beans, and nuts) also provide iron as well as folacin, magnesium, vitamin E, vitamin B_6, and zinc and should be included frequently.

Table 5–6   Contributions of vitamin C and iron made by fruits and vegetables.

Item	Serving	Energy (kcal)	Vitamin C (mg)	Iron (mg)
*Fruits**				
Apricots	2 halves (dried or cooked)	18	>1	0.4
Blackberries	½ C	42	15	0.3
Cantaloupe	¼ fruit	48	54	0.6
Grapefruit	½ C	36	34	0.4
Grapes	1 oz	19	1	0.1
Mango	½ C	55	29	0.3
Orange	1 small fruit	64	66	0.5
Papaya	½ C	28	39	0.2
Peaches	½ C	39	7	0.5
Pineapple	½ C	45	13	0.4
Plums	5 small fruits	33	0	0.3
Prunes	⅛ C	52	1	1.6
Raisins	1 oz	82	>1	0.8
Raspberries, black	½ C	49	11	0.6
Raspberries, red	½ C	38	16	0.6
Strawberries	½ C	28	44	0.8
Tangerine	1	34	27	0.4
Vegetables				
Acorn squash	½ C, mashed	57	14	1.2
Asparagus	½ C, cooked	22	25	1.0
Broccoli	½ C, cooked	24	70	0.6
Brussels sprouts	½ C, cooked	24	63	0.6
Cabbage	½ C, shredded	15	75	0.2
Cauliflower	½ C, cooked	28	35	0.5
Collards	½ C, cooked	32	49	0.7
Green beans	½ C, cooked	16	8	0.4
Green peppers	½ C, raw	8	51	0.3
Kale	½ C, cooked	22	51	0.9
Lima beans	½ C, cooked	111	11	2.4
Mustard greens	½ C, cooked	16	34	1.3
Potatoes, white	½ C, no skin	51	13	0.4
Pumpkin	½ C, canned	40	6	0.5
Spinach	½ C, cooked	21	25	2.0
Sweet potatoes	½ C, mashed	146	22	0.9
Swiss chard	½ C, leaves	16	14	1.6
Tomato, raw	1 small	19	20	0.4
Tomatoes	½ C, canned	26	21	0.6
Turnip greens	½ C, cooked	15	50	0.8
Turnips	½ C, cubed	18	17	0.3
Zucchini	½ C, cubed	13	10	0.4

*Fresh unless specified.

Meat alternates emphasized along with meats in the diet raise the nutrient content of the diet.

Meats and meat alternates should be cooked until tender and prepared so that the children can easily serve themselves from bowls on the table. This means that one-half of a hamburger, a small pork chop, or a piece of roast beef will be on the serving plate. Meat does not have to be chopped fine or legumes cooked until they appear as puree, but meats should be soft and moist enough to cut with table knives or to allow the child to eat them as finger foods. Gravies and sauces should be evaluated for their nutritional quality when included in the preschool diet. However, cheese sauces and milk gravy made with meats, low-fat milk, and vegetable purees are nutritious and acceptable in the preschool menu. Low-fat gravies and sauces are being develped by industries and can be incorporated into children's diets.

Should you serve luncheon meats, hot dogs, and sausages, which are salty and high in fat, but are generally well-liked by children and care providers? The nutritional content of the food as well as the potential for providing educational experiences must be taken into account. For example, when a wiener roast is planned as part of the curriculum, hot dogs can be an appropriate part of the child-care menu. Luncheon meats can be on a "make your own sandwich" menu, and today, these luncheon meats can be low-fat. The final decision regarding food choices may rest with the center food service supervisor who plans the menus. We recommend those foods with lower salt and fat content. They are becoming available, reasonably priced, and good tasting.

Breads and Cereals

The Food Guide recommends a minimum of 6 servings of grain products. Items from the bread and cereal group are probably the easiest for the preschooler to ingest. Cookies are easy for the preschooler who wants to "eat and run." They satisfy the child's hunger and may not be as messy as fresh vegetables and fruit, milk, or some meat products, but they can also be high in fat and sugar.

Either whole-grain or iron-fortified "breakfast cereals" can be served in the child-care center. Because the nutrient density of whole-grain cereals is higher than that of some fortified cereals, whole-grain cereals should be encouraged. However, check the labels! Some cereals advertised as whole grain may also include a high sugar and fat content along with fortification with iron and other nutrients.

Wheat germ adds iron and other nutrients to cereal products. One teaspoon of toasted wheat germ can replace a teaspoon of cereal before it is cooked, e.g., oatmeal. Preschoolers accept wheat germ when it is substituted for part of the cooked cereal.

The center can serve pastas and rice, flavored with herbs and spices. Cooked grains with steamed vegetables or fruits, served hot or cold, can increase servings of grains. More than one grain product per meal must be served in the centers if the Food Guide is followed.

Birthdays without birthday cake are sometimes difficult to justify to parents. However, many parents welcome more nourishing substitutes in their children's diets. Watermelon or cantaloupe, hollowed out and filled with fruit, with candles around the edge, can substitute for birthday cake. Infrequently providing foods that have a low nutrient density (such as birthday cakes) will not harm the child; however, a center with 15 to 30 children could conceivably have many birthday celebrations.

Milk and Milk Products

During the toddler years, drinking from the bottle may have caused an overconsumption of milk; however, the preschool child who is no longer taking milk from the bottle may still be drinking more than 3 cups of milk a day. More than 3 cups of milk is too much if it replaces other foods and nutrients in the diet.

Imitation milk is a nondairy product, usually fortified with vitamins and calcium, but it is not approved by the USDA Child Care Food Program, where reimbursement is allowed for milk and for meals served to children (Chapter 7). Whole milk, skim milk, or 2% milk can be served in the preschool center, either plain or chocolate-flavored.

In line with the National Cholesterol Education Program [11], after 2 years of age low-fat products are recommended. However, if the child is underweight the use of high-fat products such as whole milk may still be recommended.

The caloric contribution of skim milk is one-half that of whole milk. Most whole milk contains 3.2% to 3.5% butterfat, whereas skim milk has less than 1% butterfat. Two-percent milk contains 2% butterfat. The difference in energy between a half cup of 2% and a half cup of whole milk equals about 15 to 16 kcal, making 2% milk an acceptable product for children.

To review, milk and milk products are primary sources of riboflavin, vitamin A, vitamin D, calcium, and protein. During the preschool period, milk may replace other nutrients in the diet, or the child may not be consuming enough milk.

Ice cream, puddings, and sweetened yogurt may be used on the menu of the child-care center but the contribution of fat and calories to the diet may be unnecessary. There are many good low-fat products that can provide extra calcium and protein to the diet. A small serving of frozen yogurt served with fruit may increase the fruit intake. Plain yogurt (unsweetened) or yogurt sweetened with fresh fruit can be a substitute for fluid milk according to the Food Guide, but current regulations by USDA (Chapter 7) require use of yogurt as a supplement only. Cream cheese, butter, and margarine cannot be used as milk substitutes.

SUPPLEMENTATION

A question frequently asked by the center staff is whether to supplement the diet of the preschooler with medicinal supplements such as vitamin or mineral pills. Supplementation is a real concern, and if a nutritionist or dietitian is available, a group meeting to discuss this issue is often helpful for parents. If a vitamin or mineral—including fluoride—must be added to the diet, it should be prescribed by the physician or public health clinic. This is especially true in the case of iron. Anemia is not always caused by iron deficiency; it may also be caused by lack of folacin or may be secondary to other disease states and should be further investigated by a health professional.

The strict vegetarian diet will need supplementation with vitamin B_{12} if animal products (milk, eggs, meat, and fish) are not included in the diet or the child is not consuming a fortified soy product. Further discussion of the diet is included in the section, "Special Concerns Related to Dietary Intake."

Too many vitamins, especially the fat-soluble vitamins A and D, may prove harmful. Because scientists do not completely understand the interaction between certain vitamins and minerals and the effect of megadoses, a word of caution is advised in providing vitamin and mineral supplementation.

Poor growth records are not a signal to start supplementation; instead they should signal the care provider to advise parents to seek a more thorough examination from a physician or other health professional. The supplement could mask a more serious medical condition.

EATING BEHAVIOR

At least 2½ hours should elapse between snacks and meals. Many preschool centers that operate half-day programs try to supply a snack and a meal or two meals. Care providers often rush to serve breakfast and then a snack or lunch before the children go home. If children are not in the center for more than 3½ hours, it is difficult or impossible to serve more than one meal unless children come to the center hungry and are given a snack immediately.

During the toddler stage, the care provider is probably placing most of the food on the child's plate. However, the 2½-year-old enjoys being able to serve food. The care provider should fill the spoon for the child and be ready to assist, but the young preschooler should put the food on the plate (Figure 5–2). A child who is progressing normally will be capable of serving independently by 3½ years of age. This activity may seem like a small accomplishment to the care provider or parents; however, the child is given the opportunity to make a decision about a very important activity: How much food will I eat?

The child should be expected to try each food that is served; however, the child may take only a small portion. Eating at least one green bean, one flower of broccoli, or one-half spear of asparagus is appropriate when becoming familiar with a new food. The child should taste all the food prepared and served. Having the opportunity to serve from the bowls of food or pour from the pitcher allows the child, not the teacher, to decide how much the child is going to eat. When the teacher decides how much food to serve onto the child's plate and then insists that the food be consumed, the battle has begun. The teacher is really telling the child, "I want you to eat the food that I have decided you

Figure 5–2
Preschooler places
food onto plate.
Photo courtesy of
USDA.

should eat." If the situation is reversed, the teacher can give the responsibility to the child by asking the child to eat the food taken from the serving bowl. You cannot expect perfection during the child's first, second, or even third week in the center. However, after a month or two the child should begin to be able to make decisions regarding how much food to serve and to take responsibility for eating the food. There are exceptions, and some children overestimate portion sizes and must be monitored by the care provider.

As discussed in Chapter 7, utensils should be used at mealtime. These may include a spoon, fork, and knife for spreading (Figure 5–3). Foods for the spoon include those that stick to the spoon (for example, fruit, plain yogurt). Foods that can be used with a fork include mashed potatoes and small pieces of meat and vegetables; margarine can be served to give the child an opportunity to use a knife for spreading. Allow the child to spread margarine onto one-half slice of bread and then cut the bread. These activities stimulate fine motor coordination. In addition, the child should be able to begin to cut pieces of vegetables and

Figure 5–3 Preschooler learns to spread margarine.
Photo by Kevin French.

tender meat with a table knife (not a sharp knife). Serving foods, spreading margarine, and making sandwiches can be done more easily by the food service personnel in the kitchen, but if we are to use mealtime as a learning experience, the child should be allowed to fully participate in these activities.

Equipment

Equipment should be the proper size for young children. Eating utensils should be small. The chairs should be of child's proportion, allowing feet to be placed squarely on the floor. Buy sturdy chairs, because adults should sit on the children's chairs rather than having the children sit on adult chairs.

Avoid spilled milk and the accompanying frustration by checking the glass design and noting that a small glass (not larger than 4 to 6 ounces) is filled with only 2 to 4 ounces of milk. The glass should have a weighted bottom, making it less likely to tip. Use clear glasses so that the child can see how much milk is being poured into the glass. The child can refill the glass from a small pitcher of milk on the table (Figure 5–4).

Table arrangements for young children are important. The table should be attractive and the chairs comfortable. Active or easily excitable children should

Figure 5–4   Child learns to pour from small pitcher.
Photo by Kevin French.

be seated between quiet, calm children, and children who enjoy eating should sit next to children who tend to be picky eaters.

Six and possibly eight children may sit at one table with a care provider. It is important to allow enough room for children to pass the bowls of food from one child to another. Small groups of children allow for a small quantity of food to be placed in each bowl. If there are three or four items served at each meal, at least half of the children can begin serving themselves when food service starts. For example, one child can be pouring milk, one serving broccoli, one serving mashed potatoes, one serving meat, one serving the fruit dish, and one taking a slice of bread. Allowing children to serve food at the center takes 4 to 5 minutes after 4 to 6 weeks of practice. Do not attempt to encourage a child to serve all the foods during the first week at the child-care center. Begin with carrot and celery sticks, and let the child serve these foods onto the plate. If your center has not begun this experience, start with only one serving bowl per table and progress slowly until children are serving all foods onto their plates.

Location

In some cases the gymnasium is the only location for food service; however, if at all possible carts should be purchased and food should be transported to the classroom or center or a place that is relatively quiet. Generally, children and care providers can converse about food and food service with less confusion if they are in the center or in a room where they participate in other activities during the day. They may then relate food on the table to pictures of menu items discussed before the meal. They may also decorate tables for meal service or set tables and serve food.

SPECIAL CONCERNS RELATED TO DIETARY INTAKE

It is not the intention of this book to cover all the diet-related concerns of the preschool period. Diet-related health concerns discussed in Chapters 3 and 4 include obesity, lactose intolerance, and food allergies. Chapter 6 includes cardiovascular disease and dental caries, which also affect the preschooler. There may also be children in the center who require diabetic diets, or who have other conditions that require special dietary treatment. The administrator should have specific written instructions from the physician or nutritionist explaining how the diet can be implemented in the center.

Snack Foods

Snack foods with low nutrient density may include snack cakes, soft drinks, or even breakfast cereals, as well as some foods sold in fast food restaurants. These foods may provide little nutritional value, although they may now be modified to meet the preschooler's needs.

How do you combat the child's intake of foods with low nutrient density? Withholding these foods may be easier at the center than at home. Feeding only foods that appear in the Food Guide is perhaps idealistic. Grandparents, friends, and neighbors supply children with high-fat cake, cookies, candies, and snack chips, especially during holiday seasons.

Some of the snack foods currently on the market provide relatively few nutrients in relation to calories. However, more low-fat products are becoming available. Judging whether a food should be served as a snack depends on whether the food:

1. Can be classified as part of the Food Guide (Table 5–4).
2. Contains sufficient nutrients to justify the caloric value.
3. Will enhance the educational objectives of the food program at the center.

The USDA Child and Adult Care Food Program has guidelines (Chapter 7) for which foods are permissible in the food program and offer an excellent source for determining whether a food is an acceptable part of the program. If all the required foods are consumed in addition to high-calorie snacks, and the child is not overweight, the child may simply need the extra energy for growth and physical activity.

Snack foods from the cereal group are presented in Table 5–7. It includes the energy and iron values for high and low nutrient density cereal products. The

Table 5–7 Energy and iron value for snacks from bread and cereal group.

Food Quantities	Iron (mg)	Energy (kcal)
Bread, 1 slice (25 g)	0.7	70
Cereals, ready-to-serve (1 oz)		
Special K, 1 C	4.5	108
Rice Krispies, 1 C	1.8	93
Sugar Frosted Flakes, 1 C	1.8	114
Total, 1 C	18.0	110
Buc Wheats, 1 C	8.1	110
Crackers		
Round, 1⅞ in., 4	0.08	60
Cheese, 1 in. square, 10	0.1	45
Saltines, 4	0.1	50
Oyster, 10	0.1	35
Graham, 2½ in., 2	0.2	60
Rye wafers, 2	0.5	45
Wheat rye thins, 2	0.6	71
Danish pastry, 4 in.	0.6	270
Muffin, 2½ to 3 in.	0.6	100–130
Rolls		
Brown and serve, white flour, enriched, 1	0.5	90
Hamburger or hot dog, white flour, enriched, 1	0.7	120
Cake, plain, 3 × 3 × 2 in., ⅑ of a cake	0.3	313
Fruitcake, ⅟₁₅ of a 1 lb loaf	0.4–0.8	120
Angel food, ⅟₁₆ of 9 in. tube pan	0.1	120
Devil's food, 2 × 2 × 4 in.	0.7	160
+ White icing	(trace)	280
Gingerbread, 3 in. square	1.14	200
Coffee cake, ⅙ of a cake	1.2	230
Pretzel		
Dutch, twisted, 1	0.2	60
Thins, twisted, 1	0.09	25
Sticks, 10	0.1	25
Pie, ⅙ of 9 in.		
Banana custard	0.8	336
Custard	0.9	331
Pumpkin	0.8	321
Apple	0.5	404
Chocolate meringue	1.1	383
Lemon meringue	0.7	357
Butterscotch	1.4	406
Peach	0.8	403
Raisin	1.4	427
Pecan	3.9	577

Source: Information as interpreted from manufacturers' labels by the NDDA Laboratory, Southern Illinois University at Carbondale, 1983.

bread and cereal choices presented provide the foundation for the diet. They present the easiest opportunity for selecting foods that are high in nutrients needed in the child's diet. As can be seen from Table 5–7, the choice of whole wheat crackers over saltines can increase the iron content by at least five times.

Dairy products used as snack foods are included in Table 5–8. Using products with added sugar raises the energy value without providing extra calcium, the nutrient supplied most readily from milk or dairy products.

Table 5–9 provides a general list of snack foods primarily from the fruit and vegetable group. The list includes opportunities for pouring (and drinking), for using fingers, and for practicing spreading with a knife. Care providers can use snack time as well as mealtime to practice some of the fine motor skills of the eating activity.

Table 5–8 Nutritional values for snacks from milk group (with common additions).

Food	Energy (kcal)	Calcium (mg)
Milk, whole, 1 C	160	300
+Chocolate syrup, 2 tbsp	+90	—
Buttermilk, 1 C	90	300
Half-and-half, 1 tbsp	15	16
Ice cream, school lunch, 3 oz	98	80
Ice cream, regular, ½ C	130	100
+Fudge sauce, 2 tbsp	+120	—
+Whipping cream, ¼ C	+220	+50
+Coconut, ¼ C	+110	—
Ice milk, soft serve, 1 C	270	250
Yogurt, plain, 1 C		
Made from whole milk	150	250
Made from skim milk	120	300
+Preserves or jam, 1 tbsp	+60	—
Cheese		
Cheddar, 1 oz (on pie)	110	200
Parmesan (on spaghetti), 2 tbsp	45	130
American, 1 oz	110	200
Pudding, ½ C		
Mix made with whole milk	160	135
Vanilla, home recipe	140	150
Chocolate, home recipe	195	125
Tapioca	110	85
Cottage cheese, ½ C		
Creamed	130	115
Uncreamed	85	90

Source: Approximate values from Agricultural Research Service, United States Department of Agriculture: Nutritive value of American foods in common units, Agriculture Handbook No. 456, Washington, DC, Nov. 1975.

Table 5–9 Snacks that provide educational opportunities for children.

Activity	Snack
To pour and drink	Natural fruit juices, milk, protein shake (½ C milk, ½ C orange juice, ¼ C powdered milk), water
For fingers	Fruit:* Orange, grapefruit, tangerine, banana slices, apple, pear, peach slices, pineapple wedges, dried apricots, dates, raisins, grapes, plums, berries
	Ice pop made from fruit juice or pureed fruit, fruit puree, pudding (made with fluid milk), plain yogurt
	Vegetables: Cherry tomatoes and other vegetables, raw or cooked crunchy—cucumber, zucchini, potato, turnip, green beans, cauliflower, green pepper strips or wedges, asparagus, broccoli, brussels sprouts, peas (for older children), lima beans
To spread on	Peanut butter, yogurt dips, flavored margarine (make your own)
To use spoon, fork	Yogurt,† cottage cheese, cold meat cubes, whole-grain crackers and cookies (limit sugar and fat), whole-grain bread, whole-grain or fortified cereals with milk

*Most fresh or canned fruit (e.g., bananas cut in disks or pieces, oranges, grapefruit, pineapple) can be frozen on a tray, brought out 10 minutes before snack time, and enjoyed as a crunchy snack.

†Plain yogurt may be sweetened by adding fresh fruit.

Fast Food

The question of whether to eat at fast food establishments is often asked of nutritionists, especially when the preschool center wishes to take the children "down the street" for a hamburger and french fries. Table 5–10 provides a listing of several items from fast food establishments and their relative nutrient composition. Other complete listings of the nutritional analysis of fast foods are available from other sources [12]. Low-fat items are now available for easier selection of a low-fat diet. Certainly an occasional meal from a fast food establishment is not objectionable, but a diet composed primarily of these foods would be nutritionally limited.

Sweeteners

A question that you will be asked is, "Should I serve artificial sweeteners or sugar to preschoolers?" Nutritionists are often tempted to answer with a question, "Is either really necessary?" It is difficult to find extensive scientific literature indicating that consumption of table sugar per se is detrimental to health for the preschooler. However, reduction of simple sugars may be advisable for treatment of diabetes, treatment and prevention of obesity, and prevention of dental caries. The Dietary Guidelines for Americans suggest sugar should be used in moderation.

Sorbitol and xylitol are also sweeteners with approximately the same caloric value as table sugar. Many "sugar-free" candies and gums that contain sorbitol and xylitol can cause diarrhea, especially in young children. Therefore, although candy or gum may be labeled sugar-free, it may still contain calories and in some cases cause the preschooler gastric distress and diarrhea. Read the labels!

The iron content of natural sweeteners such as molasses is often discussed. Blackstrap molasses (first extraction) contains iron and calcium (1 tablespoon is equal to calcium in ½ cup milk and iron in 3 ounces of meat). Because iron is one of the nutrients that is apparently in short supply in the child's diet, the use of a sweetener other than granulated sugar may increase this nutrient to provide more iron in the diet. However, the flavor of molasses is not generally acceptable to the child and care provider. Cooked with cereal products and baked beans, it may become an acceptable product on the child-care menu. Light molasses with the less pungent taste may be better accepted, but it has less iron.

Brown sugar might be the next choice. The amount of iron found in 1 tablespoon of packed brown sugar is equal to about ½ slice whole wheat bread (0.4 mg). However, ½ slice of bread in addition to supplying other nutrients has approximately 30 to 35 kcal, whereas 1 tablespoon of brown sugar supplies 51 kcal.

Aspartame.   A low-calorie nutritive sweetener, aspartame is commonly known as NutraSweet. This sugar replacement available as an ingredient in the table-top sweetener called Equal is 200 times sweeter than sugar. Composed of two amino acids, it is used by the body as are other amino acids found in food. Research to date has shown that use of aspartame presents no risk of toxicity [13]. The use of any sugar replacement or table sugar should be limited in the child-care center, thus allowing parents to decide when and how much of any sweetener the child can consume.

Acesulfame-K.   Acesulfame-K (the K stands for potassium) is a chemical substance similar in structure to saccharin. The body absorbs Acesulfame-K but does not metabolize it. The kidneys excrete it unchanged. It is known as Sunette or as a table-top sweetener, Sweet One. It is a white, odorless, crystalline sweetener that is approximately 200 times sweeter than sucrose. High concentrations can produce a bitter taste.

It is stable in liquids and during baking or cooking. Like other sweeteners, it does not provide the functional or structural qualities that you need in baking.

Saccharin.   Saccharin is a chemical substance and the oldest sugar substitute. It is not metabolized by the body and is excreted unchanged. Saccharin is 300 times sweeter than sugar and when used in large quantities has a bitter after-taste.

Table 5–10 Nutrient composition of fast foods.*

	Weight (g)	Energy (kcal)	Protein (g)	Carbohydrate (g)
Arby's†				
Roast Beef	147	353	22	32
Light Roast Beef Deluxe	182	296	18	33
Burger King‡				
Hamburger	103	260	14	28
Cheeseburger	115	300	16	28
Dairy Queen§				
DQ cone, small	85	140	4	22
DQ chocolate sundae, regular	177	300	6	54
Jack in the Box‖				
Hamburger	96	267	13	28
French fries, small	68	219	3	28
Onion rings	103	380	5	38
Kentucky Fried Chicken#				
Original Recipe breast	115	283	28	9
Kentucky Nuggets (6 pieces), french fries, chocolate pudding	266	676	22	64
*Long John Silver's***				
Batter dipped Fish (2 pieces)	176	360	24	24
Light Portion Fish w/lemon crumb (with rice and salad, without dressing)	277	270	23	37
McDonald's††				
McLean Deluxe	206	320	22	35
Egg McMuffin	135	280	18	28
Chunky chicken salad	255	150	25	7
Wendy's‡‡				
Plain single hamburger (white bun)	133	350	25	31
Grilled Chicken salad	338	200	25	9
Grilled Chicken sandwich	130	260	24	31

Dashes indicate no data available or trace amounts.

*Edible portion.

†Arby's Inc, Atlanta, Georgia. Analyses by Arby's Laboratory and other independent testing laboratories.

‡Pillsbury Company. Analyses by Hazelton Laboratory Inc., Madison, Wisconsin, Silliker Laboratories, ABC Research Corp., and USDA.

§International Dairy Queen Inc., Minneapolis, Minnesota, Analyses by Commercial Testing Laboratory, Inc., Medallion Laboratory, and A&L Laboratory. Representative values from our Suppliers and USDA were also used.

Table 5–10 (Continued)

Fat (g)	Saturated Fat (g)	Cholesterol (mg)	C (mg)	Ca (mg)	Fe (mg)	Na (mg)
15	7	39	—	4	2.0	588
10	—	42	1.2	—	3.6	826
10	4	37	3.0	20	2.7	500
14	6	45	3.0	100	2.7	660
4	3	15	—	100	0.4	60
7	5	20	—	150	1.1	140
11	4	26	—	15	10	556
11	3	—	27	—	4	121
23	5.5	—	5	3	12	451
15	4	93	—	40	0.9	672
37	13	75	15.6	70	1.8	1106
22	5.4	60	—	—	.7	980
5	0.8	75	12	—	2.4	680
10	4	60	6	120	3.6	670
11	4	235	—	250	2.7	710
4	1	78	27	40	1.1	230
15	6	70	—	100	5.4	500
8	1	55	27	200	2.7	690
2	2	55	—	100	1.8	620

‖Jack in the Box Restaurants, Foodmaker, Inc, San Diego, California. Analyses by Hazelton Laboratory (formerly Raltech Scientific Services Inc), Madison, Wisconsin.

#Kentucky Fried Chicken Corp. Analyses by Hazelton Laboratory of America (formerly Raltech Scientific Services Inc), Madison, Wisconsin.

**Long John Silver's Inc, Lexington, Kentucky. Nutrient Analyses by Department of Nutrition and Food Science, University of Kentucky.

††McDonald's Corp, Oak Brook, Illinois. Nutrient Analyses by Hazelton Laboratory of America (formerly Raltech Scientific Services Inc), Madison, Wisconsin.

‡‡Wendy's International Inc, Dublin, Ohio. Nutrient Analyses: entree items, Hazelton Laboratory of America (formerly Raltech Scientific Services Inc), Madison, Wisconsin.

The safety of saccharin has been questioned; however, the American Academy of Pediatrics Committee on Nutrition [14] indicates that saccharin use by children should be limited pending further review. Saccharin is stable when heated and is used primarily in table-top sweeteners and fountain drinks. With other sweeteners on the market, the use of saccharin has decreased.

VEGETARIAN DIET

With an apparently increasing interest in the vegetarian diet and requests by some child-care centers to serve vegetarian meals, a discussion of the types and nutrient composition of each seems appropriate. Diets differ in the extent to which they avoid animal products. Diets are classified as follows:

- *Veganism,* or total vegetarainism avoids meat, fish, fowl, eggs, and dairy products.
- *Lactoism* avoids meat, fish, fowl, and eggs.
- *Ovolactoism* avoids meat, fish, and fowl.
- *Semivegetarianism* patterns allow limited amounts of most animal foods [15].

According to the American Dietetic Association [16, 17], when planning a diet one should choose a wide variety of foods from the major food groups. The foods may include fresh fruits, vegetables, whole-grain breads and cereals, nuts and seeds, legumes, low-fat dairy products or fortified soy substitutes, and a limited number of eggs, if desired. Vegetarians are advised to limit their intake of foods with low nutrient density. Consuming a good food source of ascorbic acid with meals will further enhance absorption of available iron. Grains, vegetables, legumes, seeds, and nuts eaten over the course of the day complement one another in their amino acid profiles to form complete proteins, and precise planning and complementation of proteins within each meal, as urged by the recently popular "combined proteins theory," is unnecessary.

With the help of a registered dietitian or public health nutritionist, care providers should discuss the diets of children with parents. Growth charts, especially heights for age, should be used to record and monitor height and weight in the center for children on modified diets as well as for all children.

Children's diets that are restricted in animal products should contain fortified soy milk through the preschool years. Another good protein alternate is tofu, the curd produced from clotting soy milk (soybean product). A good protein and calcium source, this custard-like product can be used in a variety of ways, and it appeals to many children.

The U.S. Department of Agriculture allows reimbursement for meals served to vegetarian children if a suitable protein substitute is included in the meal (for example, eggs, cheese, legumes, soy protein) in the amounts required. Combination dishes with complementary proteins or which include milk and eggs are included in Figure 5–5.

Figure 5–5
Food combinations
that supply
complete protein.
(See Chapter 7 for
combinations and
quantities of foods
that qualify for
Child Care Food
Program
reimbursement.)

Baked beans and brown bread
Lentil soup with rice
Hopping John (beans and rice)
Split pea soup with bread
Cereal, hot or cold, with milk
Cereal cooked with milk
Pizza, cheese, with whole wheat crust
Cheese sandwich
Peanut butter sandwich
Tamale pie with beans and cheese
Toast and eggs
Granola with cereal, nuts, and seeds

Is the Vegetarian Diet Safe for Children?

Many care providers are concerned whether the diet will retard growth and development of children. Use of a vegetarian diet that allows ample energy and adequate supplies of dairy products and eggs is safe for children. Researchers have found that preschool children raised in families using lacto-ovo-vegetarian diets compare favorably for most nutrients [18].

On the other hand, multiple nutritional deficiencies have been found in infants raised in a strict vegetarian community without the use of fortified soy milk products [19]. Some vegetarian groups who describe their diets as "macrobiotic" do not include any egg and dairy products in their diets. The growth curves, especially for height, for one group of macrobiotic vegetarian children were more depressed than those of other vegetarian children. Growth patterns among vegetarians vary; when diets were more restricted to animal foods, children's growth was consistently more affected. Obtaining enough energy in the diet appears difficult for some vegetarian children. Although protein intake may fall within the normal range, energy levels for some vegetarian children may be below recommended levels.

Nutrients that are most difficult to acquire on a vegan or strict vegetarian diet are listed in Table 5–11 along with the animal and plant sources for the nutrients. The nutrients include protein, vitamin A, riboflavin, vitamin B_{12}, vitamin D, calcium, and iron. We concur with the American Dietetic Association, which states that vegetarian diets are adequate if "planned according to established scientific nutritional principles" [15, 16].

Natural? Organic?

Natural and organic foods are discussed frequently, and more and more centers are asked if they provide only "natural" foods. Words such as *processed, natural, organic,* and *refined* provide little solid nutrition information, unless they are defined in a quantitative framework. Today this is not possible. In the super-

Table 5–11   Nutrients often limited in vegan or strict vegetarian diets.

| Nutrient | Food Sources | |
	Animal	Plant
Protein-amino acids	Meat, poultry	Legumes
	Fish	Nuts, seeds
	Eggs	Soy milk
	Milk, cheese	Meat analogs
	Yogurt	
Vitamin A value	Liver	Orange vegetables and fruits
	Butter	Greens
	Whole milk	Fortified margarine
	Cheese	
	Fortified low-fat milk	
Riboflavin (B$_2$)	Liver	Fortified cereals
	Milk products	Fortified soy milk
	Red meat	
Vitamin B$_{12}$	Liver, meat	Fortified soy milk, cereals,
	Poultry, fish	and meat analogs
	Milk products	
	Eggs	
Vitamin D	Fortified milk	Fortified soy milk
	Fish oils	
Calcium	Milk, cheese	Calcium-fortified soy milk
	Yogurt	Greens
	Sardines and salmon	Almonds, filberts
	with bones	
Iron	Liver	Fortified grain products
	Red meat	Dried beans and lentils
		Whole wheat bulgar

Source: Modified from Vegetarian nutrition, Rosemont, IL, 1979, National Dairy Council.

market, "natural" may mean absence of artificial colors, flavors, and additives in one food product and the absence of processing or refinement in another.

Although there is no clear definition, natural foods may also mean those products grown without use of chemical fertilizers and pesticides, but the term *organic* rather than *natural* has generally been applied to these foods. The plant cannot tell the difference between nitrogen, phosphorus, and potassium coming from organic (containing carbon), or "natural," fertilizers and inorganic forms (chemical fertilizers). One serves equally as well as the other for converting the nutrients in the soil to "plant nutrients."

Everyone would agree that a fresh apple is a natural food, although perhaps not organically grown. What about cheese and yogurt, which are processed and prepared in the factory? The rennin used to make over 60% of the cheese is produced in the laboratory through the process of biotechnology (recombinant

DNA). Sugar derived from beets or sugar cane goes through processes to become *refined*, and molasses, which undergoes a variety of processes and is derived from sorghum, is often called *natural*. It is wise to keep these thoughts in mind when considering whether to use all "natural" or "unprocessed" products.

Additives

The question of additives is often bothersome for the care provider, and parents may question the use of food with additives. Table 5–12 provides a list of some of the additives and their functions. Because of the use of additives, mainly preservatives, the marketplace is filled with a variety of products that would otherwise not be marketable. Without additives, the shelf life of a loaf of bread, including whole wheat bread, would be a day or two instead of more than a week. The cost of such a product would be at least doubled or tripled, making bread an unobtainable product to the lower-income family that depends on it for many nutrients.

On the other hand, many of the products in which additives are used could be eliminated from the child's diet if the calories are not required for weight gain (for example, gelatin, cake mixes, jams, jellies, or foods that have a low nutrient density).

Diet and Hyperactivity

In the 1970s the Feingold diet [20] became popular for the treatment of hyperactivity. The diet is based on the idea that much of the hyperactivity associated with learning disabilities that occurs in school-aged children can be attributed to ingestion of food additives and salicylates (an ingredient commonly found in aspirin). Feingold asserted that hyperactivity could be treated effectively through dietary changes in up to two-thirds of the children. Claims of the diet's success have had an impact on care providers and parents who have children with hyperkinesis (severe hyperactivity) in their care.

Since that time, the scientific community, the National Institutes of Health, the Food and Drug Administration, and the National Education Association have studied the issues and diet. Recommendations have been published, and those that are relevant to the care giver and parents are as follows:

1. There is no evidence to recommend a ban on foods containing artificial food colorings in federally supported food programs such as those served by care givers.
2. Because the diet has no apparent harmful effects and because the nonspecific effects of this dietary treatment are frequently beneficial to families, there is no reason to discourage families that wish to use the diet as long as other therapy is continued and the child's nutritional status is monitored [21].

Table 5–12   Role of some common additives in food.

Additive	Function
Tocopherols	Inhibit rancidity in fatty foods, though not as effectively as BHA/BHT. One of the tocopherols is vitamin E, which prevents cell membranes from breaking down.
Benzoate of soda	Controls mold in syrups, margarine, soft drinks, and fruit products. Remains stable under the high temperatures used in canning.
BHA (butylated hydroxyanisole)	Prevents fats, oils, and dried meats from turning rancid; keeps baked goods fresh. Extends storage life of breakfast cereals. Stable even under high temperatures.
BHT (butylated hydroxytoluene)	Prevents rancidity in potato flakes, enriched rice, and shortenings containing animal fats. Stable even under high temperatures.
Diglycerides	Most common emulsifiers, derived primarily from vegetable oils. Prevent ice cream from separating while melting, and keep oil in peanut butter from separating. Make baked goods soft.
Disodium guanylate	Brings out flavor of meat and meat-based products.
EDTA (ethylene-diaminetetraacetic acid)	Prevents unappealing color changes in salad dressings, sauces, and canned vegetables. Stable under the high temperatures used in canning.
Guar gum	One of the most common vegetable gums, which, in some foods, are much more effective than starches as thickeners. Used in gravies, sauces, pet foods.

Studies of hyperactivity and sucrose and aspartame use show that sucrose does not adversely affect behavior of children [22]. There was no significant effect on behavior when sucrose was consumed. Parents of hyperactive children often attempt to control sugar intake but are unsuccessful. Attempting to impose restrictions may exacerbate already strained parent-child interactions [23]. A review of the research can be found in a paper published by the Hershey Foods Corporation [24].

EXERCISE AND PHYSICAL FITNESS

Three-, 4-, and 5-year-olds are beginning to gain control of fine muscles while the large muscles are still growing. They love to run, jump, throw, and catch,

Table 5–12   (Continued)

Additive	Function
Modified food starches	Special starches with desired characteristics (heat-stable, freeze-thaw stable) "built-in." Give body to pie fillings, gravies, and sauces. Derived from cereal grains and potato.
Pectin	Jelling substance extracted from citrus rind; provides consistency of body in all jams, jellies, and preserves.
Potassium sorbate	Controls surface molds on cheese, syrups, margarine, mayonnaise.
Sulfur dioxide	Inhibits browning in fresh and dried fruits. Prevents undesirable color changes when wine is exposed to air.
Acetic acid	Commonly used to give tartness to dressing, sauces, relishes. The key ingredient in vinegar.
Ascorbic acid (vitamin C, sodium ascorbate)	Keeps fruit slices from darkening, inhibits rancidity in fatty foods. Enhances nutrition value of beverages, beverage mixes.
Carrageenan	Improves consistency and texture of chocolate milk, frozen desserts, puddings, syrups. The most common stabilizer used in ice creams. Derived from seaweed.
Vitamin B_6	Needed to help body use protein, carbohydrate, and fat. Added to cereals, other foods.
Vitamin B_{12}	Helps all body cells function normally. Added to cereals, other foods.
Zinc	Mineral added to cereals to promote proper growth. Deficiency can cause dwarfism.

and need little encouragement for active movement. However, the care giver needs to be acutely aware of the necessity to include motor fitness into the total curriculum (Figure 5–6).

Javernick reports that "although most preschool programs purport to encourage gross motor development, we teachers often neglect this area of development and emphasize instead fine motor, cognitive and social development" [25]. Javernick also cites Broadhead and Church [26], who wrote, "Without enriching experiences, children are often thought to be at risk educationally. Typically, intervention programs aimed at compensating for existing or expected problems are cognitively and socially oriented. There is little emphasis upon motor development."

In their position statement on Good Teaching Practices for 4- and 5-year-olds, the National Association for the Education of Young Children recommends that

Figure 5–6   A preschooler exercises naturally.
Photo by Robert M. Wagner.

"children have daily opportunities to use large muscles, including running, jumping, and balancing. Outdoor activity is planned daily so children can develop large muscle skills, learn about outdoor environments and express themselves freely. Children have daily opportunities to develop small muscle skills through play activities such as pegboards, puzzles, painting, cutting, and other similar activities" [27].

Gallahue categorizes fundamental movement abilities developed through play as locomotor, manipulative, and stability abilities [28]. He feels that teachers should integrate into their daily program opportunities for movement activities that reflect preschoolers' needs, interests, and levels of ability (Figure 5–7).

Vannier and Gallahue [29] classify the fundamental abilities into three groups: locomotor, manipulative, and nonlocomotor. They define locomotor movement abilities (LMA) as those by which the body is transported in a horizontal or vertical direction from one point in space to another. Activities that are considered to be fundamental LMA are running, jumping (vertical or horizontal), leaping, galloping, skipping, hopping, sliding, and climbing.

Manipulative movement abilities (MMA) are those that involve giving force to objects or receiving force from objects. Activities are overhand throwing, catching, kicking, striking, dribbling, ball rolling, trapping, and volleying.

Nonlocomotor movement abilities (NLMA) are those where the body remains in place but moves around on its horizontal or vertical axis. Nonlocomotor

Figure 5–7 A preschooler makes the most of a movement opportunity.

movements place a premium on gaining and maintaining equilibrium in relation to the force of gravity. Axial movements such as reaching, twisting, turning, bending, stretching, lifting, carrying, pushing, and pulling are fundamental nonlocomotor abilities.

The following suggestions will help you offer a better balanced fitness program:

1. Be aware that preschoolers are involved in developing and refining fundamental movement patterns in the three categories of movement. These movements are developed and refined through exploration and discovery. Plan your environment to facilitate such.
2. Follow the NAEYC's "Good Teaching Practices for 4 to 5-Year-Olds" [27] to provide a program that daily encompasses all areas of child development including physical development.
3. Get into the act. The teacher/care giver needs to participate enthusiastically but not to dominate or control motor activities. It will help you to become physically fit also.
4. Be aware that during ages 3 to 5 there should be no reason to provide formal periods of exercise. Under "normal" conditions (that is, in a balanced program), preschoolers will acquire movement skills through everyday activity.*
5. Beware of unusual-sounding movement activity programs that make extravagant but untested claims. (See Appendix 5–A for a listing of appropriate play materials for 3-, 4- and 5-year-olds.)

* In special situations with the handicapped child more structured motor experience may be necessary. See Cook, Ruth E., Tessier, Annette, and Armbruster, Virginia B.: Adapting early childhood curricula for children with special needs, Columbus, OH, 1987, Merrill Publishing Co.

SUMMARY

- The preschool child should interact with other children and the teacher regarding food, food preparation, food service, and cleanup.
- Mealtime should be related to other educational activities in the center (for example, those fostering language development skills).
- Energy needs per pound of body weight are decreasing during the preschool years, although the actual amount of energy required has been increasing over the previous 3 years.
- Dietary intakes of the preschooler may be less than recommended for iron, calcium, vitamin C, and vitamin A.
- The care provider, along with the dietitian or nutritionist, can assess growth patterns and dietary intake patterns to ensure that growth is progressing within normal limits and that the dietary intake contains enough of the energy and nutrients known to be essential for the preschooler.
- Snacks should be offered from the basic food groups. They should contribute nutrients without supplying excessive energy to the diet.
- Children consuming diets can be well nourished if their diets contain all the essential amino acids.
- When considering the use of sweeteners, care providers and food service personnel must take responsibility for preparing foods with a high nutrient density and without excessive calories from fat and sugar.
- Studies of the Feingold diet for hyperactivity have shown no evidence to recommend banning all additives, nor evidence that the diet is harmful. Therefore, there is no reason to discourage families from continuing its use.
- The early childhood environment provides numerous opportunities for both fine and gross motor development, yet teachers often neglect the gross motor, which results in an unbalanced program.

DISCUSSION QUESTIONS

1. List the reasons you may record a gain of 2 pounds or more per month for a 4-year-old.
2. How do the nutrient and energy needs of the preschooler compare with those of the toddler?
3. State how the food needs of the preschooler differ from and are similar to your own.
4. What special considerations should be given to the arrangements of the eating situation?
5. Describe the diet and its use in the preschool center.
6. Should foods containing additives be eliminated from the preschool diet to control hyperactivity?
7. Should low-fat foods with a sugar substitute ever be used in the center?
8. What do you feel can be done to ensure a balanced program that will include opportunities for total motor fitness?

REFERENCES

1. U.S. Department of Agriculture Nationwide Food Consumption Survey: Continuing Survey of Food Intakes of Individuals. Women 19–50 years and their children 1–5 years, 1 day, 1986. Report No. 86–1 Nutrition Monitoring Division, Human Nutrition Information Service, Hyattsville, MD, 1987, U.S Government Printing Office.

2. Robinson, C. H., Lawler, M. R., Chenoweth, W. L., et al.: Normal and therapeutic nutrition, ed. 17, New York, 1990, Macmillan Publishing Co.

3. U.S. Department of Health and Human Services, Public Health Service: Healthy people 2000: health promotion and disease prevention objectives, Washington, DC, 1990, U.S. Government Printing Office.

4. Gillooly, M., Bothwell, T. H., Torrance, A. P., et al.: The effects of organic acids, phytates, and polyphenols on the absorption of iron from vegetables, Brit. J. Nutr. 49:331, 1983.

5. Counsell, J. N., and Hornig, D. H.(eds.): Vitamin C (ascorbic acid), Englewood, NJ, 1982, Applied Science Publishers, Inc.

6. Karlowski, T. R., Chalmers, T. C., Frenkel, L. D., et al.: Ascorbic acid for the common cold: a prophylactic and therapeutic trial, J.A.M.A. 231:1038–1042, 1975.

7. Hodges, R. E.: Ascorbic acid, New York, 1976, The Nutrition Foundation, Inc.

8. Burt, J. V., and Hertzler, A. A.: Parental influences on the child's food preferences, J. Nutr. Educ. 10:127–128, 1978.

9. Birch, L. L., Marlin, D. W., and Rotter, J.: Eating as the "means" activity in a contingency: effects on young children's food preference, Child Dev. 55:431–439, 1984.

10. Food and Nutrition Board, National Research Council: Recommended dietary allowances, ed. 10, Washington, DC, 1989, National Academy of Science.

11. U.S. Department of Health and Human Services: National Cholesterol Education Program: Report of the Expert Panel on Blood Cholesterol Levels in Children and Adolescents. NIH Publication No. 91–2732, Washington, DC, 1991, U. S. Government Printing Office.

12. Jacobson, M. F., and Fritschner, S.: The completely revised and updated fast-food guide, ed. 2, New York, 1991, Workman Publishing Company.

13. Horwitz, D. L., and Bauer-Nehrling, J. K.: Can aspartame meet our expectations? J. Am. Diet. Assoc. 83:142–146, 1983.

14. American Academy of Pediatrics Report of the Committee on Nutrition: Nutritional management of children and adolescents with insulin dependent diabetes. FDA publ. no 223-82-2393, Washington, DC, 1985, U.S. Government Printing Office.

15. American Dietetic Association: Position paper on the vegetarian approach to eating, J. Am. Diet. Assoc. 77:61–69, 1980.

16. American Dietetic Association: Position of the American Dietetic Association: Vegetarian diets—technical support paper, J. Am. Dietet. Assoc. 88:352–355, 1988.

17. American Dietetic Association: Position of the American Dietetic Association: Vegetarian diets, J. Am. Diet. Assoc. 88:351, 1988.

18. Tayter, M., and Kaye, L.S.: Anthropometric and dietary assessment of omnivore and lacto-ovo- children, Am. Diet. Assoc. 89:1661–1663, 1989.

19. Zmora, E., Gorodischer, R., and Bar-Ziv, J.: Multiple nutritional deficiencies in infants from a strict vegetarian community, Am. J. Dis. Child. 133:141, 1979.

20. Feingold, B. F.: Why your child is hyperactive, New York, 1975, Random House, Inc.

21. Lipton, M. A., and Mayo, J. P.: Diet and hyperkinesis—an update, J. Am. Diet. Assoc. 83:132–134, 1983.

22. Wender, E.H., and Solanto, M.V.: Effects of sugar on aggressive and inattentive behavior in children with attention-deficit disorder with hyperactivity and normal children, Pediatrics 88:960, 1991.

23. Wolraich, M., Stumbo, P. J., and Milich, R., et al.: Dietary characteristics of hyperactive and control boys, J. Am. Diet. Assoc. 86:500–504, 1986.

24. Krummel, D.: Hyperactivity: is candy causal? in Topics in Nutrition and Food Safety, Her-

shey, PA, Summer 1992, Hershey Foods Corporation.

25. Javernick, E.: Johnny's not jumping: can we help obese children? Young Children 43:21, 1988.

26. Broadhead, G., and Church, G.: Motor characteristics of preschool children, Research Quarterly for Exercise and Sport 56:208–214, 1985.

27. Good teaching practices for 4 and 5 year olds—a position for the National Association for the Education of Young Children, Washington, DC, 1986, National Association for the Education of Young Children.

28. Gallahue, D.: Understanding motor development in children, New York, 1982, John Wiley & Sons.

29. Vannier, M. H., and Gallahue, D.: Teaching physical education in elementary schools, Philadelphia, 1978, W. B. Saunders Co.

APPENDIX 5–A   Equipment and Play Materials for Preschoolers

Equipment must be available in needed quantity and it must be varied according to children's needs. The following items* are suggested.

Balance boards

Balls   of various sizes and materials.

Barrels   for creeping through, for rolling in, and for imaginative play.

Bars   Firmly fixed and at varied heights for hanging, swinging, turning.

Bats   paddles, mallets.

Batting tees   these should be adjustable; they may be made of galvanized pipe and pieces of old garden hose.

Bean bags

Benches   these must be sturdy but light enough for children to carry; they can be used for jumping, as inclined planes, and for vaulting.

Blocks, bricks, stones, and boards   for building and for carrying, lifting, pushing, and pulling.

Boards   these should be well-cured, smooth, and 6 to 8 inches wide; cleats underneath or hooks on the ends allow various attachments.

Bounce board   this may be purchased or constructed.

Boxes   sturdy wooden boxes and large corrugated cardboard boxes such as those refrigerators come in.

Cargo nets (climbing nets)   these may be obtained as Army-Navy surplus or from regular supply sources; they are useful for a variety of climbing activities.

Climbing structures   sturdy arrangements of metal tubing sometimes called towers, jungle gyms, etc. The larger ones are permanent fixtures; smaller structures are portable but also must be very sturdy.

Flip-It Bowling Set   a useful device easily cared for; it may be purchased or constructed.

Hoops

*Source: Sinclair, C.B.: Movement of the young child age two to six, Columbus, OH, 1973, Merrill Publishing Co.

Jumping standards   these may be easily constructed and are now commercially available in suitable sizes.

Ladders   to be used vertically, horizontally, and inclined at various angles; hooks on the end provide stable fixation.

Logs   short and long; poles with smooth surfaces.

Mats   small and washable for individual use; larger mats for small group activities; pads of foam rubber may be used temporarily.

Obstacle course   a wide variety of materials may be used to involve jumping, running, climbing, going over, under, and through.

Old bathtub   when appropriately set up is fine for water play.

Padded sawhorses, tables, and benches   may be used for vaulting and many tumbling activities instead of more expensive apparatus.

Parachute   may be obtained as Army-Navy surplus.

Pitchback net   may be purchased or constructed; enables one child to play throw and catch.

Pool   portable plastic pool for wading and shallow water play.

Portable metal stands   these are light enough for children to carry but well constructed; they may be utilized with boards and ladders to make ever-changing apparatus.

Reach and jump target   strips of plastic graduated in length and suspended from a bar so that children may jump and reach to touch them.

Record player and records   readily available from many sources. Records selected should allow for creativity in movement.

Rhythm instruments   a sturdy drum is a must and should be used often by the teacher; rattles, drums, triangles, and many other instruments may be purchased or constructed.

Roller skates   these are not usual in nursery schools but may be used if facilities and space permit.

Rope ladder   one or more of these offer an interesting challenge and they are easily stored.

Ropes   long ropes are useful for turning and as climbing equiment; they may be used on the ground to mark off areas to jump over, to define floor patterns, etc. Short ropes for individual use may be used in countless ways.

Rugs   for outdoor use a blanket or sheet of foam rubber may be used as a rug. Small woven rugs may be used as substitutes for mats.

Slides and swings   these should be selected, located, and erected with professional advice.

Spades, rakes, shovels   these are available in small sizes and should be of strong construction.

Spools   large wooden spools are often discarded after utility construction; they should be weatherproofed and used for jumping, climbing, and building. They may also be rolled about the area.

Stairways   five to seven steps should be provided for a realistic experience. Many children do not use stairways at home or school.

Stall bars   ladder-like bars erected close to a wall; these take up little space and are excellent for indoor use.

Suspended balls   good for hitting practice; require adequate space; should be pulled up after use.

Stools and tables   if strongly constructed these may be used for many purposes, and old ones may be substituted for more expensive equipment.

Swinging bridge   made of rope and boards and suspended about head height.

Targets   fixed or portable; these may vary widely in type—an open frame, concentric circles painted on cloth or plastic, flags or traffic cones for markers, and many others.

Tires   bicycle, car, and truck; tubes and casings.

Traffic cones   these may be available without cost or can be easily constructed. They are useful as markers and goals and may also be used a supports for light objects.

Tree trunks and stumps   wonderful for climinb, valutling, jumping; they may be used as or converted into ships, horses, trucks, houses, etc.

Trestles and sawbenches   these may be used as supports for boards, ladders, and bridges. When constructed of wood the tops can be padded and used for vaulting and tumbling.

Tricycles and bicycles

Tunnels   fabric and collapsible, concrete or ceramic.

Wagons, sleds, and wheelbarrows

Walking beam

Wands   smooth wooden sticks, also may be made of metal; the wooden ones are strong and inexpensive.

6

The 6- to 8-Year-Old

Students will be able to:
- State the characteristics of the young child that may affect food intake.
- State food needs related to nutrient and energy recommendations.
- Describe acceptable foods for after-school snacks.
- List steps in managing the low-fat diet to prevent cardiovascular disease.
- State the concern for dental caries at this age.
- Describe physical activities that can facilitate energy balance.

Middle childhood is generally defined as beginning at 6 years of age and ending at the onset of puberty. Whereas the young girl at 7 to 8 years may already have accelerated growth, rapid growth rate will not be seen in the young boy until 9 or 10 years at the earliest. For both girls and boys, the period from 6 to 8 years is a relatively stable growth period and may even be called latent compared to the preschool years or what is still to come during adolescence.

The influence of school and extracurricular activities becomes more important during middle childhood. The significance of body image, especially for young girls, may be seen in what clothing is worn and what foods are eaten. School and community activities allow children to use their increased physical ability. Attendance at school for a full day provides regularity for activities, including food service. Foods are generally accepted and appetite improves as the child participates in activities that increase energy expenditure. The routines and activities of full-day school seem to encourage systematic snacks and meals.

WEIGHT AND STATURE

Before 6 years, boys may be taller and heavier than most girls, but by 8 to 9 years the girls are catching up and many weigh almost as much as the average boy in the same class. The 7- to 8-year-old girls are beginning to admire their older peers, and "dieting" can occur at this early age.

From infancy to 6 years, the percentage of body fat for both boys and girls decreases, while lean body mass increases. However, at about 6 years girls again begin to have a higher proportion of their weight as fat. Girls will continue into adolescence and adult years to have a higher proportion of their weight as fat. Children at this age gain approximately 2 to 3 inches in height and 4.5 to 6.5 pounds per year (Table 6–1).

Table 6–1   Weight and stature for 6- to 8-year-olds.

Age	Girls		Boys	
(years)	Weight (pounds)	Stature (inches)	Weight (pounds)	Stature (inches)
6	42.9	45.1	45.5	45.7
7	48.0	47.5	50.3	47.9
8	54.6	49.8	55.7	50.0

Source: Modified from charts showing smoothed percentiles of weight and stature by sex and age developed by National Center for Health Statistics, U.S. Department of Health, Education and Welfare, PHS, Hyattsville, MD, 1977, The Center.

ENERGY AND NUTRIENT NEEDS

Dietary recommendations for the 6- to 8-year-old are found in two RDA groupings (Table 6–2). Decreased amounts of protein and energy are required per pound of body weight as growth slows, but wide ranges in recommendations reflect the variation in individual growth and physical activity of children at this age.

The 6-year-old's energy need, according to the RDA, is 39 calories per inch or 41 per pound; by 10 years it will be 46 calories per inch or 32 per pound. In addition, the energy allowance per inch is greater for the child who begins an early growth spurt. A child's height and weight should be plotted on the growth charts (Appendix V) at regular intervals. Changes will alert the care provider to any abnormalities and the need to refer the child to a dietitian or other health professional for further evaluation.

Nutrients

The nutrient needs are increasing in proportion to the need for energy. Diets of children during this period have been found to supply sufficient amounts of most nutrients. Parents who have been concerned about their child's appetite earlier in life often find the child willing to eat more foods now.

Fat. The fat intake from food served outside the home becomes an increasing concern as the 6- to 10-year-old spends more time away from parents and in school activities.

By 6 years of age, the child can benefit from moderate dietary modifications of a low-fat diet. Take care to ensure that the child is consuming enough energy for growth and physical activities, but the height and weight charts can be used to monitor how well the child is growing.

Table 6–2   RDA for ages 4–6 and 7–10 years.

Nutrient	4 to 6 Years (44 lb, 44 in. [20 kg, 112 cm])	7 to 10 Years (62 lb, 52 in. [28 kg, 132 cm])
Resting Energy	kg × 90	kg × 70
Equivalent	(lb × 40.9)	(lb × 32.3)
Protein (g)	kg × 1.1	kg × 1.0
(g/day)	24	28
Vitamin A (μg RE)	500	700
Vitamin D (μg)	10	10
Vitamin E (mg α-TE)	7	7
Vitamin K (μg)	20	30
Ascorbic acid (mg)	45	45
Folate (μg)	75	100
Niacin (mg NE)	12	13
Riboflavin (mg)	1.1	1.2
Thiamin (mg)	0.9	1.0
Vitamin B_6 (mg)	1.1	1.4
Vitamin B_{12} (μg)	1.0	1.4
Calcium (mg)	800	800
Phosphorus (mg)	800	800
Iodine (μg)	90	120
Iron (mg)	10	10
Magnesium (mg)	120	170
Zinc (mg)	10	10

Source: Based on Food and Nutrition Board, National Academy of Sciences—National Research Council: Recommend dietary allowances, revised 1989.

Calculating the Low-Fat Diet.   Care providers may wish to determine how to plan a diet with 30% of calories from fat. What foods should be selected for the elementary school child to restrict fat intake? Figure 6–1 shows how to calculate a low-fat diet.

Dietary Supplementation

According to the American Academy of Pediatrics [1], national dietary and health surveys have shown little evidence of vitamin or mineral inadequacies, with the exception of iron, for this age group. There is little basis for routine vitamin and mineral supplementation in healthy children, especially as the growth rate decreases after infancy. However, supplements may be indicated for some children, including those:

- From deprived families, especially children who suffer from parental neglect or abuse.
- With anorexia, poor and capricious appetites, or poor eating habits.

Steps
1. Find energy level (kcal) of diet (total calories needed).
2. Multiply energy (kcal) by percent fat allowed (kcal × 0.30 = fat kcal).
3. Divide fat kcal by 9 (Step 2 divided by 9 kcal/g fat) to get total grams of fat allowed in diet.
4. Find the serving of food you plan to eat using food tables (Appendix I) or food labels.
5. Note the number of grams of fat for a food and subtract from total grams of fat allowed in the diet (Step 3).

Example
Step 1. 2000 kcal (estimated total energy needs)
Step 2. 0.30 × 2000 = 600 kcal from fat
Step 3. 600 ÷ 9 = 66–67 g fat
Step 4. 6 oz hamburger = 19 g fat
Step 5. 67 − 19 = 48 g of fat remain from allowance

Figure 6–1   Calculation of diet with 30% of calories from fat.

- On dietary regimens to manage obesity.
- Consuming vegetarian diets without adequate dairy products (vitamin B_{12} is absent from vegetable foods)

FOOD NEEDS

Meeting the food needs of middle childhood requires consumption of food in slightly greater quantities than at earlier years. Because energy needs for these children vary widely, monthly heights and weights should serve as a guide to the need for additional energy. Serving portions will be similar to, and in some cases larger than, the adult serving size. Table 6–3 shows a recommended food pattern that meets the RDA for nutrients for the child 6 to 10 years of age.

Energy allowances average 2000 calories or 32 calories per pound. More food can be included to meet additional energy needs without large amounts of fat if the Food Guide is used. The number of calories that would be supplied by fat in diets of various caloric levels is shown in Table 6–4.

The menu in Table 6–5 was developed from interviewing 7-year-old children. The difficulty in meeting an actual child's energy needs and still keeping fat within 30% of calories without changing current eating patterns becomes evident. Assuming the child needs 2000 kcal, the fat would be limited to 66 to 67 grams (30% of total calories from fat).

The child still preferred french fries and cookies (not graham crackers) for a snack. The snack crackers with peanut butter were acceptable, but chips and dip were preferred. The food pattern in Table 6–3 is a guide from which to choose foods for a nutritionally adequate, low-fat diet. Table 6–6 gives additional suggestions for planning low-fat meals.

Table 6–3 Recommended food intake according to food group and average serving sizes (ages 6 up to 10 years).

Food Group	Servings/Day*	Average Serving (ages 6 up to 10)
Vegetables	3–5	
Emphasize green or yellow vegetables		½ C*
Fruits	2–4	
Vitamin C source (citrus fruits, berries, melons)		½ C
Breads and Cereals (Whole Grain)	6–11	
Bread		1 slice
Ready-to-eat cereals, whole grain, iron-fortified		1 oz
Cooked cereal including macaroni, spaghetti, rice, etc. (whole grain, enriched)		½ C
Milk and Milk Products	3–4	
Whole or 2% milk (1.5 oz cheese = 1 C milk) (C = 8 oz or 240 g)		1 C
Meat and Alternates	3–4 including:	
Lean meat, fish, poultry, eggs†	2	3 oz
Nutbutters (peanut, soynut)	1–2§	4 tbsp‡
Cooked dried beans or peas		½ C
Nuts		1 oz
Fats and Oils	3	
Butter, margarine, mayonnaise, oils		1 tsp

*Allow a minimum service of 1 tbsp/year of age for cooked fruits, vegetables, cereals, and pasta until the child reaches 8 years or ½ C portion size.

†To enhance overall nutrient content of diet, include eggs (two to three times a week) and liver occasionally.

‡Serving size recommended by Illinois State Board of Education, Department of Child Nutrition: Child Care Food Program—required meal patterns, Springfield, IL, June 1986, The Board.

§Include nutbutters, dried (cooked) beans, or peas as often as possible to meet nutrient recommendations and use additional servings of meats when legumes, beans, and nuts are omitted.

Table 6–4   Fat as 30% of calories in various diets

Total Calories	Fat (kcal)	Fat (g)
1500	450	50
1600	480	53
1800	540	60
2000	600	67
2200	660	73
2400	720	80

Table 6–5   Grams of fat in menu pattern for 6- to 8-year-old.

Foods	Fat (g)	Kcal (approx.)
½ C broccoli	trace	25
1 large baked potato	trace	150
1 C whole kernel corn	1	150
½ C peaches	trace	35
1 small orange	0	50
3 slices whole wheat bread	3	225
½ C spaghetti	trace	110
1 oz American cheese	9	110
1 C whole milk* (at school)	9	160
1 C 2% milk (at restaurant)	5	120
1 C skim milk (at home)	trace	90
6 oz hamburger (lean)	19	400
1½ oz peanut butter snack crackers	11	250
1 tbsp catsup/mustard	0	45
½ tbsp margarine (served w/ vegetables)	6	53
TOTAL	63	1975

*Note difference in fat content between whole and skim milk.

Table 6–6   Specific recommendations to lower fat intake.

Use	Include Less Often
Skim milk	Whole milk
Yogurt, skim cottage cheese, low-fat sour cream and dips*	Dairy dips with sour cream
Fruit ices, sorbets, and sherbets	Ice cream, prepared pudding
Low-fat meats	High-fat meats
Margarine (sparingly), low-fat margarine	Butter, palm and coconut oil
Low-fat cheese*	High-fat cheese
Low-fat dressings	Regular oil- or fat-based dressings
Legumes, beans, and peas	High-fat nuts, high-fat meats
Fruits and vegetables, fresh, or frozen, steamed	Deep-fried vegetables and fruits
Crackers or low-fat snack chips	Snack chips

*Check labels for fat content.

WHAT INFLUENCES EATING PATTERNS?

Media

Eating patterns can be influenced when specific foods are promoted by the media, especially by television. The child in elementary school spends more time in front of a television set each year, and television competes with the classroom activities. In after-school care it is often used as the care provider and is accompanied by abundant snacks that may be high in fat.

Hours of television viewing for the school-age child have increased and have been related to increases in obesity and decreases in physical ability. Television shows directed toward children advertise foods that are usually expensive in relation to the nutrient composition of the food. Children are fascinated with the characters portrayed in cartoons and then displayed on food packages offered for sale.

Family

Some studies show that preteens are influenced more by peer pressure than by parental actions [2]. However, family income and economic status do influence the types and amounts of food that can be purchased and where foods will be eaten (restaurants or in the home). Family structure and employment patterns of parents may make preparing meals with a wide variety of foods difficult. For example, single-parent families may use convenience foods and visit fast food restaurants more often than the general public [3].

Six- to 8-year-olds increasingly select their own meals, especially breakfast, from what is available in the kitchen. They alone can be responsible for choosing from 15% to 20% of their foods every day. With widespread use of microwaves and prepackaged frozen microwave items, children have a wider variety of foods from which to choose and can learn at an earlier age to prepare nutritious meals for themselves (Figure 6–2).

Providers should educate parents on choices for quick, nutritious food service at home. The varied diet that began in the preschool years should be continued with only minor modifications; larger portion sizes will provide the required energy and nutrient needs.

School

Parents are now less in control of what the child eats. Responsibility rests with the school system to provide at least one-third of recommended nutrients for the child participating in school lunches, and at least one-half if breakfast is eaten at school. An after-school care provider may provide another 150 to 300 calories (for example, with crackers or cookies and milk), 10% to 15% of energy and nutrients. Parents, therefore, may be responsible for less than 40% of total energy needs, serving the child only one meal per day.

Figure 6–2 A child should be able to read before using a microwave.
Photo by Janet K. Kniepkamp.

As after-school providers, you have a challenge to select carefully what foods will be available to help the child maintain a desirable body weight and contribute to the child's growth and development. Teachers', coaches', and after-school providers' advice on what to eat and their eating behavior influence the child's food choices. An educator who eats a wide variety of foods, gets involved in the food programs at school, and demonstrates a positive attitude toward nutritious foods served at school will encourage children to become interested in eating an array of nutritious foods. Teachers or food service supervisors who complain about food service negatively influence children. Teachers should support the food service, or if changes are needed, they should get involved in helping make changes.

Snack Foods

As with younger children, sugary and especially high-fat snacks should be avoided when possible. By the time the child reaches 6 years, the diet should contain no more than 30% of the calories from fat; thus, foods in the diet that are high in fat must be complemented with low-fat fruits, vegetables, and grains (Figure 6–3).

Table 6–7 shows the fat and sugar content of snacks consumed by one group of children during a weekend period.

Fat contributed more than 30% of the calories for 9 of 11 items chosen by the youngsters. Soda, fruit pastries and pudding treats, were lower in fat than most of the other snacks but have a high quantity of simple sugars. "Sugars," mono- and disaccharides such as table sugar and corn syrups, provided 100% of the calories from soda and 50–60% of the calories from several other items.

Some snack foods that seem to be low in fat are just the opposite. Popcorn cooked in oil and potato chips get more than 30% of their calories from fat while plain popcorn and potatoes are high in carbohydrate. Restricting fat generally means avoiding calorie-rich foods that are often low in other nutrients. As new food products are being developed, care providers will need to carefully read the labels. No longer can we say all "chip" snacks are high fat. Fat-free dips are also being developed.

The recommended snack foods may be those in which complex carbohydrates, not fat, are the largest single source of energy.

As children get older, they get more calories from snack foods that tend to be higher in fat than at the earlier age. High-fat foods are often not balanced with

Figure 6–3   Low-fat fruits and diary products should replace high-fat snack foods.

Table 6–7   Energy from fat for snack foods.

Food (serving size)	Total Kcal*	Fat	
		Kcal	%Kcal
Favorite Snacks			
Milk chocolate with almonds (1 oz)	151	91	60
Chocolate-covered peanut butter chips (1 pkg.)	240	90	38
Chocolate-covered peanuts (1 pkg.)	240	108	45
Chocolate chip cookie (1)	52	21	40
Chocolate creme sandwich cookie (1)	51	20	40
Toaster pastry, blueberry, frosted (1)	200	45	23
Ice cream, 10% fat (1 C)	273	131	48
Soda (12 oz)	144	0	0
Potato chips (1 oz)	161	102	63
Cheese-flavored puffs (1 oz)	155	87	56
Popcorn/oil (1 oz)	128	56	44
Recommended Snacks			
Apple (1 medium)	81	4	5
Apple with ½ tbsp peanut butter	128	41	32
Banana (1 medium)	105	5	5
Grapes (1 C)	107	5	5
Orange (1)	64	3	5
Bagel with 2 tsp jelly	201	13	6
Whole wheat bread with fruit butter (2 tsp)	87	11	13
Saltine crackers (6)	78	19	24
Graham cracker (3 squares)	81	18	22
Wheat cracker (4 small)	64	20	31
Apple butter (2 tsp)	26	1	4
Yogurt, plain, low fat (1 C)	144	32	22

*Kilocalories from protein, fat, and carbohydrates.

Source: Data from

U.S. Department of Agriculture: Nutritive value of American foods in common units. Agriculture handbook No. 456, November 1975.

NDDA Laboratory, Southern Illinois University at Carbondale, 1988.

low-fat fruits, vegetables, and grains. However, no single food should be judged "too high in fat." The fat contained in the total diet should be considered.

Much of the carbohydrate is complex and is "packaged" along with other nutrients. Even though peanut butters and nuts are a rich source of many nutrients not readily available in other foods, the high fat content and the risk of dental caries from excessive sticky peanut butter snacks should be taken into consideration. Choosing fruit and vegetables with high calcium (dairy) dips along with whole grain crackers or low-fat grain products with a salsa or bean dip could be low-fat alternatives.

NUTRITION-RELATED HEALTH CONCERNS

Lactose intolerance, dental caries, cardiovascular disease, and persistent weight problems are directly related to nutrition. Lactose intolerance, discussed in detail earlier, may be seen in as many as 30% of children in this age group. Many children have learned that they can drink milk with meals but not alone for the afternoon milk break. Some children can tolerate flavored milk better than regular whole or skim milk. Once children reach this age, parents and teachers must include them in decisions regarding foods that can be tolerated. The importance of continuing a supply of calcium to this age group is essential. Bone density is established during the early years of life. Prevention of osteoporosis during early years by establishing a pattern of eating dairy products high in calcium is crucial.

Dental Health

Dental caries in the 6- to 8-year-old is recognized as a serious problem and *Healthy People 2000* [4] objectives for oral health include:

> Reduce dental caries (cavities) so that the proportion of children with one or more caries (in permanent or primary teeth) is no more than 35% among children aged 6 through 8—.

In 1986–87 53% of children 6 through 8 had one or more caries. The prevalence of dental caries is greatest among special population groups which include: children from homes where parents do not have a high school education, American Indian/Alaska Native children, and black children aged 6 through 8.

A second national objective states:

> Reduce untreated dental caries so that the proportion of children with untreated caries (in permanent or primary teeth) is no more than 20% among children aged 6 through 8.

Baseline data indicate untreated caries in certain segments of this age group to be as high as 64%.

In order to be sure caries are reduced or if present, treated, the objectives suggest that we

> Increase to at least 90% the proportion of all children entering school programs for the first time who have received an oral health screening, referral and follow-up for necessary diagnostic preventive and treatment services.

Centers caring for children can encourage oral health screening as well as promote sound dental health through (1) provision of nutritious but less sticky foods, (2) follow-up on dental screenings, and (3) promoting good oral health practices.

The "stickiness" of snack foods and the length of time taken for the saliva to remove the snack from the teeth should be considered when providing nutritious snacks. Of the following foods studied by dental researchers [5] some barely stick to the teeth while others are rated stickiest.

Barely sticky: apples, bananas, hot fudge sundaes, milk chocolate bar
Moderately sticky: chocolate caramel bars, white bread, caramels, creme-filled sponge cake
Stickier: dried figs, jelly beans, plain doughnuts, chocolate-caramel-peanut bars, raisins
Stickiest: granola bars, oatmeal cookies, sugared cereal flakes, potato chips, salted crackers, puffed oat cereal, creme sandwich cookies, peanut butter crackers.

The longer particles remain on the teeth, the more likely they will be attacked by enamel-eroding acids produced by bacteria. It seems foods we recommend as snacks–cereals, crackers, and cookies (even plain, low-fat/sugar)—are considered stickiest. According to research, sugary foods such as jelly beans, although they appear sticky, are washed out of the mouth more easily than other foods.

Emphasizing snacks that are less sticky may help to reduce the dental problems seen in this group. A discussion of snacks that do not stick to the teeth for long periods of time are included under the section on *Snack Foods*. Any snack can be eaten if the teeth are cleaned after eating.

The school personnel should reinforce the parents' and child's efforts to maintain good dental health by following up on dental screenings and treatment. Children should have a regular routine established for care of teeth and gums at home and brush after meals at school. They should be familiar with the dentist, participating in regular visits at least once a year. Many dentists apply sealants as new permanent teeth emerge to deter the development of caries.

Cardiovascular Diseases

The child 6 to 8 years old is generally healthy and at low risk for many of the nutrition-related problems occurring at earlier ages. As a result of increasing media coverage of the risk factors associated with cardiovascular disease, care providers and parents want diets for their very young children that will protect the heart. There is general agreement that coronary heart disease may begin in youth and undergo progression through young adulthood, even though clinical manifestations usually do not appear until middle age or later.

Whether to recommend diet restrictions for young children and at what age is still being debated. There appears to be agreement that lowering dietary fat during the primary school years is a good preventive measure without undue effects on growth and development. However, modification of diets in healthy children after 2 years of age has recently been advocated as a means of influencing plasma cholesterol levels [6]. The American Academy of Pediatrics takes a more moderate approach, providing the following recommendations for planning children's diets:

Current dietary trends in the United States toward a decreased consumption of saturated fats, cholesterol, and salt should be followed with moderation.

DIETS THAT AVOID EXTREMES ARE SAFE FOR CHILDREN. THE SAFETY OF DIETS DESIGNED TO DECREASE CALORIC INTAKE, INCREASE CONSUMPTION OF COMPLEX CARBOHYDRATES, DECREASE INTAKE OF REFINED SUGARS, DECREASE CONSUMPTION OF FAT AND CHOLESTEROL, AND LIMIT SODIUM INTAKE HAS NOT BEEN ESTABLISHED IN GROWING CHILDREN AND PREGNANT WOMEN [7].

If cereal grains with high fiber content are chosen in place of animal protein, the intake of vitamins and minerals that have protective value—for example, iron—may decrease. The loss of these nutrients might pose health risks to children. Animal products are rich in protein and have many essential nutrients difficult to obtain from other foods.

More attention is now being focused on identifying risk factors for coronary heart disease (CHD) in very young children so that preventive measures can be introduced early. CHD risk factors in children are primarily hypertension and elevated plasma cholesterol. High-risk children, those whose parents have been identified as having one or more of the risk factors such as elevated cholesterol, should be screened by 7 years of age. Modifying diets in these children seems appropriate as long as sufficient calories and nutrients are available for adequate growth.

The recommendations for lowering the risk of coronary heart disease include cutting fat intake to 30% of calories and cholesterol to 100 mg/1000 kcal. Considering that one egg has approximately 300 mg cholesterol and a 2- to 4-year-old needs less than 1500 kcal per day, this means that eggs and whole milk would be almost totally excluded from the diet. Care providers must first consider meeting the energy needs of the child. This may be best accomplished by using whole milk and/or egg products that are nutrient-dense.

Other dietary measures that have been shown to be effective in promoting good health habits include those from the Dietary Guidelines for Americans:

Eat a variety of foods.
Maintain healthy weight.
Choose a diet low in fat, saturated fat, and cholesterol.
Choose a diet with plenty of vegetables, fruits, and grain products.
Use sugars only in moderation.
Use salt and sodium only in moderation [8].

Measures to limit fat in the diet have been included earlier in this chapter and in Chapters 1 and 2.

Other Concerns.   Problems requiring attention to energy and perhaps protein content of the diet include AIDS and allergies.

Some of the medications used for both of these conditions may cause a decrease in appetite. The allergic child may even be required to stay away from certain areas and engage in less physical activity than the other children. Therefore, more attention to nutritious snacks will be necessary.

Acquired Immune Deficiency Syndrome (AIDS) may have little effect on the child who is infected. However, those children attending the center should be monitored and parents alerted if the child does not eat or has lost weight. It is important for children infected with the AIDS virus to maintain good nutritional status. Malnutrition increases the likelihood of compromised immune status [9].

Obesity

The treatment for childhood obesity has been reviewed by Peck and Ullrich [10] and included in Chapter 4. The persistence of adolescent obesity into adulthood and its resistance to current successful treatment programs provide valid reasons for developing school programs that focus on prevention and treatment [11]. Some successful programs have included behavior modification, nutrition education, and physical activity. In one 10-week school-based program for 5- to 12-year-olds, 95% of the children lost weight and reversed a trend to steady weight gain [12]. School food service programs can be an asset in prevention of obesity [13].

EXERCISE AND PHYSICAL FITNESS

Children 6 to 8 years old have gained better control of small muscles and can coordinate hand and eye to an increasing degree. This is a time when children become immersed in games and physical activities. To continually develop and refine locomotor and non-locomotor skills, they must have many opportunities to test and retest their abilities [14]. It is during this age span that the green light is given to begin more structured physical fitness activities both at home and at school.

Components of Fitness

The American Academy of Pediatrics Committee on Sports Medicine and School Health defines the components of fitness to include muscle strength and endurance, flexibility, body fat composition, and cardiorespiratory endurance [15].

Frequency of Physical Education Classes

In their position statement regarding integrated components of appropriate and inappropriate practice in the primary grades, the National Association for the Education of Young Children recommends that physical education be integrated into the curriculum each day [16]. The American Academy of Pediatrics stresses that physical education classes be held at least three times weekly in the primary grades and that such classes are critical to developing and maintaining physical fitness in young children [17].

Parents often feel that their children get plenty of exercise in their school's gym classes and at recess. The fact is that many students get as little as one hour of physical education a week. In addition, schools have traditionally emphasized sports that promote agility and specialized skills (baseball, basketball, football) rather than cardiovascular fitness (bicycling, swimming, running, fast walking, aerobic exercise, tennis). Most of a typical primary child's physical activity occurs outside of physical education classes (Figure 6–4) [18].

In light of these facts, in 1987 the American Academy of Pediatrics issued a policy statement urging parents and pediatricians to appeal to their local school boards to maintain, if not increase, physical education programs [17].

As indicated in Chapter 2, numerous fitness surveys have indicated that children in the United States are underexercised. Society's current emphasis on academics has resulted in an unbalanced curriculum that lacks opportunities for children to develop and refine motor skills. Nevertheless, the United States has more physical educators, more gyms, more swimming pools, and more recreational opportunities than any country in the world. Some would say we also have the best medical science system in the world, yet we lead the world in degenerative diseases [18]. Regularly scheduled physical education classes, in-

Figure 6–4
Physical activity of the 6- to 8-year-old takes many forms.
Photo by Robert E. Rockwell.

corporating lifelong cardiovascular fitness skills, rather than those that promote game skills which are often not carried into adulthood, must be provided. Without such programs the risk of latent disorders such as obesity, elevated blood pressure, and high cholesterol level, all of which can lead to coronary heart disease, will continue to threaten our children.

The President's Council on Fitness and Sports recommends that the cardiovascular system be stressed for at least 30 minutes a day through vigorous activity. Without this activity, children can progressively decondition with the final result being alarmingly poor cardiac condition [18].

Parent's Role

As with all societal problems, the schools can't do it all. Parents can do much to instill awareness of fitness in the primary-aged child. We caution, however, that parents must remember that if it is not fun, children won't do it. The American Academy of Pediatrics suggests that parents:

1. Incorporate fitness activities into the family lifestyle.
2. Introduce children to a variety of athletic activities; they are easily bored.
3. Become involved with your children's activities by either playing a sport with them or coaching a team.
4. If safe, encourage your child to walk to school or take a shorter bus ride and walk part way.
5. Encourage after-school activities and limit TV viewing during this time.
6. Set a good example [15].

The 6- to 8-year-old has everything to gain by being physically fit. Exercise boosts self-image and improves physical strength and stamina as well as scholastic performance.

SUMMARY

- The young child's eating habits during the 6- to 8-year period are influenced by the school setting, coaches, and teachers.
- Girls will continue into adolescence having a higher proportion of their weight as fat.
- Supplementation with vitamins and minerals is needed only in children at high risk for poor dietary intake.
- No attempt should be made to restrict the young child's intake of a variety of nutrient-dense foods on the basis of fat, sodium, or cholesterol. By age 2, the diet can conform to the Dietary Guidelines for Americans and include no more than 30% of total calories as fat.
- To limit fat to 30%, substitutions should be found for high-fat snacks.
- Dental caries appear to be a problem with some high-risk groups and have been targeted by *Healthy People 2000* [4] as requiring special attention by care providers.

- Children of parents who are at high risk for coronary heart disease should be screened for elevated cholesterol by 7 years of age [8].
- Parents as well as the school play a critical role in providing opportunities for 6- to 8-year-olds to participate in both structured and unstructured physical fitness activities.

DISCUSSION QUESTIONS

1. How does the 7-year-old differ from the 4-year-old in eating habits?
2. Compared to the younger child, would you expect to see more or less anemia?
3. How do the nutrient and energy needs of the school-aged child compare to those of the preschooler?
4. Calculate the energy you need each day and list foods usually eaten. How can your diet be modified to include only 30% calories from fat?
5. Can snack foods with more than 30% fat be included in the diet?
6. Which foods are most cariogenic? Why is there special concern for foods that cause caries at this age?
7. Discuss the need to both modify and increase physical education activities.

REFERENCES

1. American Academy of Pediatrics, Committee on Nutrition: Pediatric nutrition handbook, ed. 2, Chicago, 1985, American Academy of Pediatrics.
2. Baskett, L. M.: Ordinal position differences in child's family interactions, Developmental Psychology 20:1026–1031, 1984.
3. Sheridan, M. J., and McPherrin, G.: Fast food and the American diet, Summit, NJ, 1981, American Council on Science and Health.
4. U.S. Department of Health and Human Services, Public Health Service: Healthy people 2000: health promotion and disease prevention objectives, Washington, DC, 1990, U.S. Government Printing Office.
5. Kashket, S.: Lack of correlation between food retention in the human dentition and consumer perception of food stickiness, Journal of Dental Research 42:1314–1319, 1991.
6. U. S. Department of Health and Human Services: National Cholesterol Education Program: Report of the Expert Panel on Blood Cholesterol Levels in Children and Adolescents. NIH Publication No. 91–2732, Wash-

ington, DC, 1991, U. S. Government Printing Office.
7. American Academy of Pediatrics, Committee on Nutrition: Toward a prudent diet for children, Pediatrics 71:78, 1983.
8. U.S. Department of Agriculture and U.S. Department of Health and Human Services: Nutrition and your health: dietary guidelines for Americans, Washington, DC, 1990, U.S. Government Printing Office.
9. Bentler, M., and Stanish, M.: Nutrition support of the pediatric patient with AIDS, J. Am. Diet. Assn. 87:488–491, 1987.
10. Peck, E. B., and Ullrich, H. D.: Children and weight: a changing perspective, Berkeley, CA, 1985, Nutrition Communications Associates.
11. Summer, S. K.: Obesity in the school age child, School Food Service Review 10(2), 1986.
12. Brownell, K. D., and Kaye, F. S.: A school-based behavior modification, nutrition education and physical activity program for obese children, Am. J. Clin. Nutr. 35:277, 1982.
13. Stitt, K. R.: Weight control and school food service, School Food Serv. Res. Rev. 3:5, 1979.

14. Arnheim, D. D., and Sinclair, W. A.: The clumsy child: a program of motor therapy, St. Louis, 1979, C. V. Mosby Co., p. 21.

15. Fitness: the myths and the facts, American Academy of Pediatrics Fact Sheet, Elk Grove Village, IL, 1987.

16. National Association for the Education of Young Children: Position statement on developmentally appropriate practice in the primary grades, serving 5- through 8-year-olds, Young Children, 43, January 1988, pp. 64–68.

17. Policy statement from American Academy of Pediatrics, Physical fitness and the schools, Pediatrics 80(3):449–450, September 1987.

18. The President's Council on Physical Fitness and Sports, National School Population Fitness Survey, HHS-Office of the Assistant Secretary of Health, Research Project 282–84–0086, 1986, University of Michigan Press, p. 2.

7

The Menu

LEARNING OBJECTIVES

Students will be able to:
- List the daily food plans for infants, toddlers, and preschoolers.
- Discuss acceptable foods as part of the Child and Adult Food Care Program (CACFP).
- Define cycle menus and describe the roles of the food service supervisor and teacher.
- Describe how food service personnel and teachers may participate in making the menu a focal point of the curriculum.
- State the parents' contributions to the menu.
- State the Seven Steps to Successful Ethnic Meals
- Define how the community dietitian could facilitate the care provider's objectives for quality child care.

Food service for the child cared for away from home can occur in a variety of settings. Some of the settings, especially those receiving public funds, must follow regulations outlined by such federal agencies as the U.S. Department of Agriculture and the Department of Health and Human Services, as well as various other state and local agencies.

In addition to providing nourishment, the foods served can be used to teach nutritional practices that will lead to a life of good nutrition. To provide nourishment and nutrition education in the classroom, the principles of food service must first be understood and practiced. The menu can be the tool used to help coordinate the nutrition and food needs of children with learning activities in the various settings.

When teachers and food service personnel work together to select foods and plan the style in which they are served, both professional groups feel committed to making food and nutrition work in the classroom. Although you as a care provider may not take direct responsibility for writing the menus or preparing foods, you are an important component of the process if the menu, food preparation, foods, and food service are to be used in the curriculum or learning activities of the children. Without center food service there can be no nourishment. Likewise, without curriculum planning involving food service activities there can be few educational activities around mealtime. The food service system described in this chapter is planned jointly by the preschool teacher and food service supervisor or "cook." An outcome of this joint planning may be seen when teachers do not have to "beg the cook" for a fresh pineapple or have to purchase one themselves for the classroom. Instead, the teacher and food service personnel plan "menus for learning" from which educational experiences naturally evolve.

Table 7–1   A pattern for daily food choices.

Food Group	Suggested Daily Servings	What Counts as a Serving?
Breads, cereals, and other grain products Whole-grain Enriched	6–11 servings from entire group (Include serveral servings of whole-grain products daily)	• 1 slice of bread • ½ hamburger bun or English muffin • a small roll, biscuit, or muffin • 3 to 4 small or 2 large crackers • ½ C cooked cereal, rice, or pasta • 1 oz of ready-to-eat breakfast cereal
Fruits citrus, melon, berries other fruits	2–4 servings from entire group	• a whole fruit such as medium apple, banana, or orange • a grapefruit half • a melon wedge • ¾ C of juice • ½ C of berries • ½ C cooked or canned fruit • ¼ C dried fruit
Vegetables dark-green leafy deep-yellow dried beans and peas (legumes) starchy other vegetables	3–5 servings from entire group (Include all types regularly; use dark-green leafy vegetables and dried beans and peas several times a week.)	• ½ C of cooked vegetables • ½ C of chopped raw vegetables • 1 C of leafy raw vegetables, such as lettuce or spinach
Meat, poultry, fish, and alternates (eggs, dried beans and peas, nuts, and seeds)	2–3 servings from entire group	Amounts should total 5 to 7 oz of cooked lean meat, poultry, or fish a day. Count 1 egg, ½ C cooked beans, or 2 tablespoons peanut butter as 1 ounce of meat
Milk, cheese, and yogurt	2 servings from entire group (3 servings for women who are pregnant or breastfeeding and for teens; 4 servings for teens who are pregnant or breastfeeding)	• 1 C of milk • 8 oz of yogurt • 1½ oz of natural cheese • 2 oz of process cheese
Fats, sweets, and alcoholic beverages	Avoid too many fats and sweets. If you drink alcoholic beverages, do so in moderation.	

Source: USDA Human Nutrition Information Service: Nutrition and your health: dietary guidelines for Americans, Home and Garden Bull. N. 232-8, Washington, DC, 1989, U.S. Government Printing Office.

WHAT FOOD TO SERVE CHILDREN

Before one begins to plan menus or to discuss the planning of the curriculum around the menu, it is necessary to review the Food Guides [1].

To receive funding for food served, the Child and Adult Food Program Patterns [2] must be met. The Guides you should use in planning are:

1. Dietary Guidelines for Americans (see Chapter 2).
2. A Pattern for Daily Food Choices [1] (Table 7–1).
3. USDA Infant and Child Meal Patterns [2] (Tables 7–2 and 7–3).

A recent publication, *Nutrition Guidance for the Child Nutrition Programs* [3], offers advice on how to use the tools listed above.

The Infant

Table 7–2 provides an infant meal pattern that allows for the optional introduction of infant cereals, fruits, and vegetables by 4 months. Children should not take solid foods until after 4 to 6 months of age. In practice, however, many parents are providing their children with solid foods earlier.

Schedule.   Depending on the age of the infant, a feeding schedule may be established before the child enters the center. This should be carefully recorded from the interview with the mother or father and discussed with the food service personnel. Taking a dietary history, including a 24-hour recall, when the infant enters the center is important in determining the child's schedule. A master feeding schedule for infants is advisable to help communicate with all staff as well as parents. Centers often set 4-hour feeding schedules, but our experiences show that some babies, both breast- and bottle-fed, demand nourishment every 2 to 3 hours. Food is one of the primary means whereby the very young child can interact with the care provider. This opportunity may be lost if the child is either hungry and irritable or fed too often and disinterested.

Formula Preparation.   It is best for the center to purchase or have parents bring in unopened cans of formula and prepare infant formulas on-site for children who will remain in the center all day. The preparation methods and correct sanitation procedures were discussed in Chapter 3. If the formula is prepared in the center, there can be no question as to its freshness or the extent to which proper methods have been used during preparation. The date on the label of the container of formula should be checked by the food service personnel before purchasing and after formula has been stored for some time. Although past-dated formula may not be injurious to the child's health, the taste is often affected by prolonged storage. In most cases powdered formulas are available and can be stored in freezer or refrigerator to retain freshness longer than concentrated or ready-to-feed formulas, which may separate on freezing. A partially used bottle of formula should be discarded at the end of the day. When parents

Table 7–2 Child-care infant meal pattern.

Birth Through 3 Months	4 Through 7 Months	8 Through 11 Months
	Breakfast	
4–6 fl. oz. formula*	4–8 fl. oz. formula* or breast milk	6–8 fl. oz. formula*, breast milk, or whole milk
	0–3 tbsp infant cereal† (optional)	2–4 tbsp infant cereal†
		1–4 tbsp fruit and/or vegetable
	Lunch or Supper	
4–6 fl. oz. formula*	4–8 fl. oz. formula* or breast milk	6–8 fl. oz. formula*, breast milk, or whole milk
	0–3 tbsp infant cereal† (optional)	2–4 tbsp infant cereal† and/or
	0–3 tbsp fruit and/or vegetable (optional)	1–4 tbsp meat, fish, poultry, egg yolk, or cooked dry beans or peas, or ½–2 oz cheese or
		1–4 oz cottage cheese, cheese food, or cheese spread
		1–4 tbsp fruit and/or vegetable
	Supplement	
4–6 fl. oz. formula*	4–6 fl. oz. formula* or breast milk	2–4 fl. oz. formula,* breast milk, whole milk, or juice‡
		0–½ bread slice or
		0–2 crackers (optional)§

*Iron-fortified infant formula.
†Iron-fortified dry infant cereal.
‡Full-strength fruit juice.
§From whole-grain or enriched meal or flour.
Source: Data from Federal Register 53(129):25309, July 6, 1988.

bring formula in bottles to the center, bottles should be refrigerated immediately by care providers, or a policy should be established to allow parents to place bottles in the refrigerator. Each bottle should be clearly labeled with the individual child's name.

Strained or Solid Foods.   The recommended practices for feeding infants were reviewed in Chapter 3. The basic requirements of the infant until 6 months and even longer can be met with iron-fortified formulas. Therefore, there appears to be no advantage in introducing solid foods during the first 6 months of life. In fact the substitution of cow's milk, especially skim milk, causes an excess of protein in the diet. The end products of protein metabolism must be excreted by the infant's kidneys. Social customs favor earlier introduction of solid foods, and each center must establish guidelines and policies that consider these practices. Whenever solid foods are introduced, do not overfeed. A 6-month-old's persistent refusal of the spoon with food previously accepted is saying "stop!" to the care provider—discard the last 2 teaspoons of food (Figure 7–1).

Figure 7–1   Child turns head as a signal to stop feeding.
Photo by Kevin French.

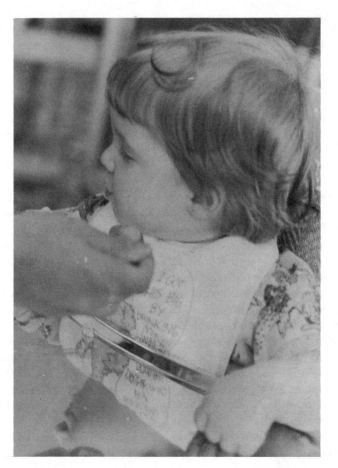

Our recommended sequence for introduction of strained foods is:

1. Infant cereal—iron-fortified, single-grain
2. Vegetables
3. Fruits and fruit juices
4. Meats

It appears that a taste for salt may be acquired by the preschool years and is not predetermined. Some infants given home-prepared strained foods or table foods receive more sodium than would be found in commercial baby foods [4]. Care providers who prepare food for infants should add no salt or seasoning with sodium.

Commercially Prepared Foods.   Purchasing commercially prepared foods may be advisable for infants at child-care centers with fewer than four to six children. To obtain the best nutrition for the least cost for the infant who is beginning to accept solid foods, the following guidelines should be followed.

Recommended	*Not Recommended*
Strained vegetables	Creamed vegetables
Strained meats	Vegetable and meat dinners
Single-grain infant cereal	Custards
Yogurt	Fruit puddings and desserts
Fruits without added sugar	with added starch
or starch	Cereal and fruit
	Fruit-flavored yogurt
	(flavored with preserves)
	Fruits with sugar and starch
	Cream cheese, cheese spread

Center-prepared Infant Foods.   Serve fresh or frozen foods that have been properly prepared in the kitchen of the infant center. They can be pureed or ground from fresh or frozen vegetables (no salt added) and fruits that have not been overcooked ("crunchy cooked"). These may be the same as those prepared for the preschool center. A crunchy cooked vegetable or fruit is one that requires chewing and cannot be mashed with the tongue.

Leftovers that have been prepared for older children and allowed to stand in cooking water or on the table are not acceptable. Extra portions of freshly cooked food can be prepared (ground or pureed), placed in ice cube trays, and immediately frozen. One or two cubes per feeding will be sufficient for the young infant. Frozen cubes kept in a covered container can be thawed in the refrigerator overnight or cooked in the microwave oven before serving. Always stir foods taken from the microwave and test to be sure the food is not too hot.

By 6 to 7 months, the infant will be ready to accept center-prepared foods with a texture other than pureed. The infants are developmentally ready to chew and will do so with their gums, even though teeth have not erupted. Any chopped or mashed bite-sized pieces of table foods, crunchy cooked, are acceptable.

These foods should not contain seasonings or additional sugar and salt. Foods that are hard and can become lodged in the throat (such as raw celery, nuts, and popcorn) should be avoided.

The Toddler and Preschooler

Food service for the toddler and the preschooler is different. Interaction among children is limited at the toddler stage; however, this does not preclude the use of conversation about foods and eating. The amount of food is generally smaller for the toddler and served more frequently when compared with the preschooler. Young children, 12 to 20 months, may still be fed individually, but shortly after age 2 years, they like and can learn from other children in the center.

By 30 months, they can be using tablespoons to take food from serving bowls. Chapters 4 and 5 include the recommended food patterns to meet children's daily nutritional needs. Frequent use of legumes and green vegetables contributes significantly to specific nutrients often difficult to acquire in the diet. Whole-grain cereals have been included, while "dessert" (something sweet at the end of the meal) is fruit or a component of the meal. Children are allowed to take a serving of all the menu items at the start of the meal. No food is withheld at the beginning of a meal.

The food pattern requirements established by the CACFP for children 1 to 12 years old are included in Table 7–3. Programs that qualify can receive reimbursement for serving meals that follow the approved USDA patterns. See Appendix VI for instructions on how to apply for the USDA CACFP.

CACFP Food Requirements

There is often confusion about which foods are included under the Child and Adult Food Program guidelines. Table 7–4 presents specific foods for the older child that do not meet the Child and Adult Food Program requirements.

CACFP Questions Frequently Asked

The following are selected questions and answers supplied by the Illinois State Board of Education, Department of Child Nutrition, regarding the CACFP program requirements.

Milk Component

1. Which types of milk can be served to meet the Child and Adult Food Program regulations?
   The milk must be a pasteurized fresh fluid product that is served as a beverage, poured over cereal, or used partly for each purpose. Reconsti-

Table 7–3 Child Care Food Program required meal pattern.

Foods	Ages 1 up to 3*	Ages 3 up to 6	Ages 6 up to 12
Breakfast			
Milk, fluid†	½ C	¾ C	1 C
Juice/vegetable(s) and/or fruits	¼ C	½ C	½ C
Bread/bread alternates‡			
Bread, cornbread, biscuits, rolls or	½ slice	½ slice	1 slice
Cereal:			
Cold, dry, or	¼ C or ⅓ oz	⅓ C or ½ oz	¾ C or 1 oz
Hot, cooked, or	¼ C	¼ C	½ C
Cooked pasta, noodle products, or rice	¼ C	¼ C	½ C
Snack *(Select 2 out of 4 components)*			
Milk, fluid†	½ C	½ C	1 C
Meat/meat alternates§			
Lean meat, poultry, fish‖ or	½ oz	½ oz	1 oz
Cheese or	½ oz	½ oz	1 oz
Egg, large, or	½ egg	½ egg	1 egg
Cooked dried beans or peas or	⅛ C	⅛ C	¼ C
Peanut butter, soynut butter, other nut or seed butters or	1 tbsp	1 tbsp	2 tbsp
Peanuts, soynuts, tree nuts, or seeds	½ oz	½ oz	1 oz
Juice/vegetable(s) and/or fruit#	½ C	½ C	¾ C

*For required serving amounts for infants up to age 1 year, refer to program regulations.
†Fluid milk should be used as a beverage, on cereal, or in part for each purpose.
‡Or an equivalent serving of an acceptable bread, pasta, or noodle product. Cereals must be whole grain, enriched, or fortified.
§Or an equivalent quantity of any combination of foods listed under meat/meat alternates.
‖Cooked lean meat without bone, breading, or skin.
#Juice may not be served when milk is served as the only other component.

tuted milk from a dry powder or canned milk cannot be used to meet the milk requirement. Likewise, a cocoa mix made from dried milk powder or canned milk products will not count toward the milk requirement. At breakfast milk may be used on cereal, as a beverage, or as a beverage and on cereal. At lunch and supper you must serve milk as a beverage.

2. Can the milk used in preparation of custards, puddings, and ice cream be counted toward the milk requirement?
   No. The milk must be served as a beverage, poured over cereal, or used partly for each purpose.
3. Can yogurt be used to meet the milk or meat requirement?
   Under current Child and Adult Food Program regulations, yogurt is an

Table 7–3   (Continued)

Foods	Ages 1 up to 3*	Ages 3 up to 6	Ages 6 up to 12
Bread/bread alternates‡			
Bread, cornbread, biscuits, rolls or	½ slice	½ slice	1 slice
Cereal:			
Cold, dry, or	¼ C or ⅓ oz	⅓ C or ½ oz	¾ C or 1 oz
Hot, cooked, or	¼ C	¼ C	½ C
Cooked pasta, noodle products, or rice	¼ C	¼ C	½ C
Lunch/Supper			
Milk, fluid, served as beverage	½ C	¾ C	1 C
Meat/meat alternates§			
Meat, poultry, fish‖ or	1 oz	1½ oz	2 oz
Cheese or	1 oz	1½ oz	2 oz
Egg, large, or	1	1	1
Cooked dry beans or peas or	¼ C	⅜ C	½ C
Peanut butter, soynut butter, other nut or seed butters or	2 tbsp	3 tbsp	4 tbsp
Peanuts, soynuts, tree nuts, or seeds**	½ oz = 50%	¾ oz = 50%	1 oz = 50%
Juice/vegetable(s) and/or fruits‡‡	¼ C total	½ C total	¾ C total
Bread/bread alternates‡			
Bread, cornbread, biscuits, rolls or	½ slice	½ slice	1 slice
Cooked pasta, noodle products, or rice	¼ C	¼ C	½ C

**Tree nuts and seeds, except acorns, chestnuts, and coconuts, may be used as meat alternates. Nuts and seeds may supply no more than half of the meat alternate requirement at lunch/supper. Nuts and seeds must be combined with another meat/meat alternate. For purposes of determining combinations, 1 ounce of nuts or seeds is equal to 1 ounce of cooked lean meat, poultry, or fish.

‡‡Serve two or more kinds of vegetable(s) and/or fruits(s) or a combination of both. Full-strength vegetable or fruit juice may be counted to meet not more than one-half of this requirement.

     extra food and cannot be used to meet basic meal pattern requirements, but it can be used as a meat alternate for a supplement only.

4. Can imitation milk products be used to meet the milk requirement?
   No. Imitation milk products do not meet the definition of fluid milk and cannot receive credit toward the meal pattern requirement. Imitation milk products are made from the following ingredients: whey, corn syrup solids, coconut oil, sodium caseinate, and nonfat milk. In addition, there may be added artificial colors, sugar, and gum.
5. Can a milkshake be served to meet the milk requirement?
   Yes, if it contains 8 fluid ounces of milk for 6- to 12-year-olds; 6 fluid ounces for 3- to 6-year-olds; and 4 fluid ounces for 1- to 3-year-olds.
6. Is fluid milk mixed with grape juice, orange juice, and other juices creditable?

Table 7–4 Foods that do not meet Child Care Food Program requirements.

Milk Components	Jellies	Imitation cheese
Evaporated milk	Dried vegetables for seasoning	Nut or seed meal or flour
Nonfat dry milk	Fruit breads (pumpkin, banana, carrot, and zucchini)	Commercial packaged macaroni and cheese*
Cocoa mix (added to water)		Pot pies (store bought)*
Pudding, custard		Canned ravioli*
Ice cream, sherbet	Cranberry juice cocktail	Canned spaghetti*
Yogurt	Coconut	*Miscellaneous Foods*
Half and half	*Bread Component*	Soda pop
Sour cream	Hominy	Tea
Whipping cream	Popcorn, caramel corn	Marshmallows
Cream cheese	Cake, snack cakes	Catsup
Eggnog	Dessert pie crust	Pickle relish
Powdered drinks	Hard pretzels	Mustard
Fruit/Vegetable Component	Shaped snack chips	Gelatin
Fruit nectar	Brownies	Candy
Fruit drinks or punch	Shoestring potatoes	Honey
Garnishes, e.g., pickles, parsley, that amount to less than ⅛ C	*Meat/Meat Alternate Component*	Sour cream
	Bacon	Syrup
Potato chips, corn chips, and similar packaged snacks	Cream cheese	Butter
	Tofu	Margarine
Pickle relish	Parmesan cheese, if used as garnish	Salad dressing
Lemonade		Yeast
Jams		

*These foods cannot be used unless the label obtained by the center indicates Child Nutrition (CN) or it includes a manufacturer's statement of composition.

Yes. The milk-juice mixture is creditable in both the milk and fruit/vegetable categories when served for breakfast, lunch, or supper if the required amount of milk plus the required amount of fruit juice is served.
7. If I use fluid milk, can hot chocolate or cocoa be served to meet the milk requirement?
Yes. When made with fluid milk, this beverage is creditable. Flavored hot chocolate mixes reconstituted with water are not creditable.

Bread and Bread Alternate Component. The following criteria must be met for food items to be creditable as bread or bread alternates, whether purchased or prepared in the home or center:

• The item must contain whole-grain and/or enriched flour and/or meal as the primary ingredient(s) by weight as specified on the label or according to the recipe, or must be enriched in preparation or processing and labeled "enriched." If a cereal is fortified, the label must indicate it is fortified.

1. Can cake, cookies, and snack-type foods be used at lunch?
   No. Desserts or snack-type foods such as cakes, cookies, and pie cannot be used for the bread requirement at lunch and supper.
2. Can glorified rice and bread or rice pudding be credited as a bread or bread alternate?
   At lunch or supper, bread or rice pudding cannot be used to meet the bread requirements, because it is not served as an accompaniment or integral part of the main dish. However, for supplements, bread or rice pudding can be used to meet the bread component if there is at least ¼ cup cooked rice or approximately ½ slice of bread per serving.
3. Can Rice Krispies bars or similar cereal bar products be credited toward the bread or bread alternate supplement?
   Rice Krispies bars or similar bars made from a cereal product may be credited as an acceptable bread/bread alternate for breakfast and snacks if the cereal is whole grain or enriched and if the amount of cereal can be measured to ⅓ cup (volume) or ½ ounce (weight), whichever is less per one-half serving. Because these have a high sugar content, they should be served no more than twice per week.
4. Can cinnamon rolls and quick breads be credited as a bread alternate?
   Yes. Center-made or homemade cinnamon rolls prepared with whole-grain or enriched flour as the predominant ingredient by weight can meet the requirements for breakfast, snack, lunch, and supper, since these rolls are traditionally served as bread.
5. Can Danish pastries, Long Johns, and rich sweet rolls be used at breakfast or as supplements?
   No. Because the predominant ingredient by weight is generally not enriched flour, they cannot be used as a bread item.
6. Can cookies and animal crackers be used as a snack to meet the bread alternate?
   Yes. Cookies may be used as an acceptable bread alternate when the following criteria have been met:
   a. Whole-grain or enriched meal or flour must be the predominant ingredient(s) as specified on the label or according to the recipe.
   b. The total weight of a serving must be a minimum of 35 g. This quantity represents a serving equivalent to one slice of bread. Cookies should not be served more than twice a week. Cookies can only be used as the bread alternate for supplements.
7. Can items such as potato sticks, popcorn, corn chips, potato chips, hard thin pretzels, and so on, be used to meet the bread requirement?
   No. Extruded grain products and snack-type foods such as these cannot be used for the bread requirement. These foods are counted as extras.
8. Can corn tortillas and other corn products be credited as a bread alternate?
   Corn tortillas and other corn products can be credited if the main ingredient is one of the following: whole-grain corn, whole-ground corn, whole-germed corn, cornmeal, corn flour, enriched cornmeal, enriched

corn flour, or enriched corn grits. However, if the main ingredient is listed as corn grits, degerminated corn flour, or degerminated cornmeal, the corn products cannot be credited.

Fruit/Vegetable Component.   The fruit/vegetable component must be two different servings. Menu items such as fruit cocktail and mixed vegetables are considered as only one item. Large combination vegetable or fruit salad entrees, containing at least ½ cup (for 3- to 6-year-old) of two or more vegetables and/or fruits in combination with meat or meat alternates (such as chef's salad or fruit plate with cottage cheese), are considered two or more servings and will meet the full requirement.

1. Which types of juice can be used?
   Any product, either liquid or frozen, that is labeled "juice," "full-strength juice," "single-strength juice," or "reconstituted juice" is considered full-strength juice. Examples of full-strength juice are apple, grape, grapefruit, grapefruit-orange, lemon, lime, orange, pear-apple, pineapple, prune, tomato, and vegetable juice.

   "Juice drinks" and other combination products such as a frozen juice bar may contain only a small amount of full-strength juice. The product label may indicate the percentage of full-strength juice in the product. To be used in meeting a part of the fruit/vegetable requirement, the product must contain a minimum of 50% full-strength juice. Only the full-strength juice portion may be counted to meet the fruit/vegetable requirement.

   Products labeled as "-ade," "juice cocktail drink," or "drink" cannot be used. Nectars, lemonade, and cranberry juice cocktail contain less than 50% full-strength juice and cannot be used to meet the fruit/vegetable requirement.

Meat/Meat Alternate Component

1. Must all the protein foods be in the main dish?
   The meat/meat alternate must be served in the main dish or the main dish and one other menu item. This means that two menu items are the maximum number that may be used to meet the meat/meat alternate requirement.
2. Do cooked beans count as meat or vegetable?
   Cooked dried beans or peas may be used to meet the meat/meat alternate requirement or the fruit/vegetable requirement but not both in the same meal.
3. Do nuts count as a meat alternate?
   Yes. Peanuts, soynuts, and tree nuts such as walnuts and seeds, which are nutritionally comparable to meat or other meat alternates, may be used.

Because of their extremely low protein content and iron values, nuts that cannot be used as a meat alternate are acorns, chestnuts, and coconuts. Nuts and seeds may fulfill all the meat alternate requirements for snacks, but not more than one-half of the meat/meat alternate requirement for lunch/supper.

4. Can vegetable-protein products be used?

Hydrated vegetable-protein products (such as those made from soy) may be used to meet no more than 30% of the meat/meat alternate requirement or a maximum ratio of 30 parts hydrated vegetable protein to 70 parts uncooked meat, poultry, or fish.

Coordinating Center and Home Food Intake

Is the child getting enough food? Meals following the CACFP pattern are required to provide only one-third of the child's RDA. If the lunch provides only one-third of the recommended amount of the nutrients, the parents at home must supply an additional two-thirds of the recommended allowances through the other meals. In many cases the child must leave home early, possibly without a morning meal, and return late in the evening. Staff of centers may need to evaluate what foods are eaten at home compared to those eaten in the center in order to help parents provide all the nutrition necessary for growth and development.

Figure 7–2 shows the actual foods eaten by a 4-year-old during the day, including foods eaten at the center. The bar graph shows the nutrient composition of the foods for the entire day. The child attended a half-day program, and the menu is like that served in many centers.

Seventy-five percent of the iron allowance was met by serving fortified cereal, bread, meat, and beans. The energy values are somewhat higher than the 30% recommended after 2 years of age (37%). Although the child ate a large quantity of food, no fresh vegetables or fruits were eaten and potato chips do not count as a vegetable under current guidelines. As low-fat snack products become available, we may be able to serve snack chips with all the taste of a chip and the nutrition of fruits and vegetables. The vitamin C came primarily from gelatin and Kool-Aid, which were fortified.

How well did the diet meet the Food Guide? The following summarizes the recommended servings compared to the actual servings. More grains, fruits, and vegetables are needed.

	Recommended Minimum Servings (Food Guide)	*Child's Diet*
Meat	2 serv	2 serv
Grains	6 serv	5 serv
Fruits	2 serv	0 serv
Vegetables	3 serv	2 serv

Dietary Intake

Amount Consumed	*Food*	*Amount Consumed*	*Food*
2 C	*Whole milk (1¼ C served at home)	1 oz	*Cornbread
¼ C	*White beans, cooked	4	Graham crackers
2 oz	Bologna	1 C	Wheat puffs, w/sugar coating
1½ oz	*Frankfurter	2 C	Kool-Aid fortified with vitamin C
½ C	Fried potato	½ C	Sweetened gelatin, plain
1 oz	Potato chips	—	*Carrot/celery chips
1 slice	White bread		

*Denotes foods served during center meal service.

Percent Energy Distribution:

Fat	37%
Carbohydrate	51%
Protein	12%

```
TOTAL         NUTRIENT       RDA    0%        20%    33%  40%        60% 66%    80%       100%
-------------------------------------I----------I------I----I----------I---I------I----------I
 1636.5 KCAL  ENERGY            91%  XXXXXXXXXXXXXXXXXXXXXXXXXXXXXXXXXXXXXXXXXXXXXXXXXXXXX
   47.7 GM    PROTEIN          199%  XXXXXXXXXXXXXXXXXXXXXXXXXXXXXXXXXXXXXXXXXXXXXXXXXXXXXXXXX
 3811.3 IU    VITAMIN A        152%  XXXXXXXXXXXXXXXXXXXXXXXXXXXXXXXXXXXXXXXXXXXXXXXXXXXXXXXXX
  252.0 IU    VITAMIN D         63%  XXXXXXXXXXXXXXXXXXXXXXXXXXXXXXXXXXXX
    4.9 IU    VITAMIN E         70%  XXXXXXXXXXXXXXXXXXXXXXXXXXXXXXXXXXXXXXXX
   94.9 MG    VITAMIN C        211%  XXXXXXXXXXXXXXXXXXXXXXXXXXXXXXXXXXXXXXXXXXXXXXXXXXXXXXXXX
  189.5 MCG   FOLACIN          253%  XXXXXXXXXXXXXXXXXXXXXXXXXXXXXXXXXXXXXXXXXXXXXXXXXXXXXXXXX
   14.6 MG    NIACIN           122%  XXXXXXXXXXXXXXXXXXXXXXXXXXXXXXXXXXXXXXXXXXXXXXXXXXXXXXXXX
    1.7 MG    RIBOFLAVIN       151%  XXXXXXXXXXXXXXXXXXXXXXXXXXXXXXXXXXXXXXXXXXXXXXXXXXXXXXXXX
    1.2 MG    THIAMIN          138%  XXXXXXXXXXXXXXXXXXXXXXXXXXXXXXXXXXXXXXXXXXXXXXXXXXXXXXXXX
    1.0 MG    VITAMIN B6        93%  XXXXXXXXXXXXXXXXXXXXXXXXXXXXXXXXXXXXXXXXXXXXXXXXXXXXXX
    3.0 MCG   VITAMIN B12      295%  XXXXXXXXXXXXXXXXXXXXXXXXXXXXXXXXXXXXXXXXXXXXXXXXXXXXXXXXX
  707.4 MG    CALCIUM           88%  XXXXXXXXXXXXXXXXXXXXXXXXXXXXXXXXXXXXXXXXXXXXXXXXX
  940.9 MG    PHOSPHOROUS      118%  XXXXXXXXXXXXXXXXXXXXXXXXXXXXXXXXXXXXXXXXXXXXXXXXXXXXXXXXX
    7.5 MG    IRON              75%  XXXXXXXXXXXXXXXXXXXXXXXXXXXXXXXXXXXXXXXXXXX
  111.1 MG    MAGNESIUM         93%  XXXXXXXXXXXXXXXXXXXXXXXXXXXXXXXXXXXXXXXXXXXXXXXXXXXXXX
    6.9 MG    ZINC              69%  XXXXXXXXXXXXXXXXXXXXXXXXXXXXXXXXXXXXXXXX
-------------------------------------I----------I------I----I----------I---I------I----------I
```

Figure 7–2 Dietary intake of preschool child with nutrient analysis
Source: NDDA Laboratory, Southern Illinois University at Carbondale.

PLANNING MENUS WITH STAFF

Menus are often planned to include foods that children like and will eat. This process seems logical because it reduces food waste and appears to be most cost-effective. However, this approach is based on the fact that food service personnel are in charge of planning as well as serving foods, and the teacher or care provider has little, if any, responsibility for these activities. We believe the meal service and foods served should be both educational and nutritional.

Children eat the foods they know, but new or less familiar foods may be viewed with suspicion or rejected. The menu-planning system that involves teachers and food service personnel can accomplish the goal of good nutrition while introducing the child to a wide variety of foods.

Menus are usually viewed as the foundation of food service operation. The process of using an educational approach to develop a center's menu requires the food service personnel and the teacher to coordinate activities. The menus still must contain the basic foods and consider the constraints of the food service facility, but, in addition, the menu will be used as a tool for learning (Figure 7–3). The day's menu should be a written translation of the CACFP patterns, the Food Guide, and the teacher's learning objective.

The proper menu has foods with the appropriate combinations of taste, texture, and color. Producing a menu that (1) meets the child's requirements and (2) meets the constraints of the food service facility and is part of the educational curriculum takes careful planning.

Food Service Supervisor's Contribution

As indicated in Figure 7–3 the nutrition or dietetic consultant and food service personnel come to the menu-planning session with a set of nutritional guidelines or needs of children. They have knowledge of the guides, standards, and food production. The equipment and personnel may limit the number and kinds of food items. Baked potatoes and meat loaf may not be served together, since the oven may not be large enough to prepare both at the same time. Likewise, the number of products to be prepared in the preschool kitchen may be limited by personnel. Some foods may need to be prepared from mixes. Most food service personnel can solve these problems if freezer and refrigerator space are available.

Preparing mashed potatoes for 30 to 50 children requires special equipment, and instant potatoes may be the only solution. Baked ham, baked sweet potatoes, and hot rolls require excessive oven space. Fruited gelatin (gelatin prepared with fruit juice), tossed salad, and cold meat and cheese platters may require too much refrigerator space. Fruited gelatin is impractical to serve on Monday in a Monday-to-Friday center, because it must be prepared on Friday and allowed to stand over the 2–day weekend.

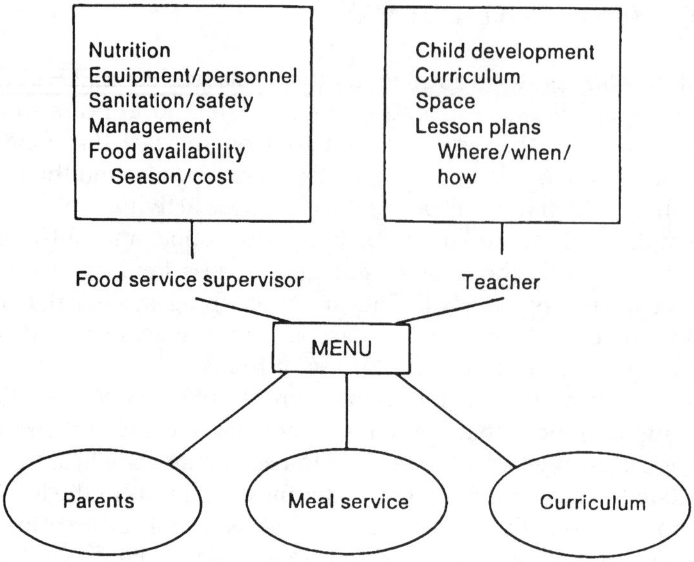

Figure 7–3
Components for the
successful
implementation of
a menu.

| Nutrition |
| Equipment/personnel |
| Sanitation/safety |
| Management |
| Food availability |
| Season/cost |

| Child development |
| Curriculum |
| Space |
| Lesson plans |
| Where/when/ |
| how |

Food service supervisor   Teacher

MENU

Parents   Meal service   Curriculum

Availability of Foods

Availability depends on locality, season, budget, and inventory (which foods are on hand). Most of these factors are interrelated. The foods in season are usually available in your locality and fit within the budgetary constraints. However, in some areas many fresh foods, especially fruits and vegetables, are available all year.

Some programs serve food prepared in one site and transported to another. Some foods cannot maintain their quality with this treatment, no matter how they are handled. The use of various types of meal services may also be limited by equipment and personnel. Large numbers of bag lunches may be difficult to prepare. If the center has not purchased serving equipment for family-style meal service, this service may be impossible. However, to use the concepts discussed in this text and to ensure the child's participation, family-style meal service is recommended.

Teacher's Contribution

The teacher brings to the menu-planning session knowledge of the educational needs of children (Figure 7–4). Available space, equipment, and location will limit some activities; for example, inner-city schools find it difficult to pick apples from nearby orchards, whereas rural preschoolers cannot walk to the grocery or nearby parks.

The food service personnel can suggest various options for involving children in food preparation, service, and cleanup, but the teacher or care provider is the

Figure 7–4   **The teacher and the food service supervisor plan meals together.**

director of the learning activities. Without the teacher's cooperation the food service will not be used effectively to help children learn about food.

The teacher may use the menu as a tool to learning through a specific food service style, for example, family (formal, informal), buffet, cafeteria, bag lunch, and picnic. A particular food item may also be used in conjunction with a learning resource center in the classroom. A new food or preparation method with which the child is becoming familiar may be used along with a science activity (see Chapter 8).

When food service personnel are planning menus, a list of foods and preparation methods can be made available to the teacher (Table 7–5). The teachers can circle or indicate which food items or preparation methods are new for the child and should be introduced. A checklist of various foods, preparation methods and good sources of vitamins A and C are included in Table 7–5.

Table 7–5   Checklist of foods and preparation methods for menu planning.

Vegetables

Beans
  Fresh lima beans
    Raw
    Buttered
    Cooked with bacon or
      ham
    With tomatoes
  Snap beans
    Raw
    With bacon or salt pork
    With crisp bacon chips
    With cream sauce
    With new potatoes
    With tomatoes
    With carrot circles
    Salad
Beets
  Buttered
  Harvard
  Cold sliced
  And lettuce salad
Broccoli*†
  Raw
  Buttered
  With lemon sauce
  With cheese sauce
  With cream sauce
Cabbage§
  With carrots, cooked
  Buttered
  Cole slaw
  Creamed
  In gelatin
  Raw wedge
  Salad with fruit or other
    vegetables
  With corned beef
  Sauerkraut
Carrots*
  Raw sticks, curls,
    wheels

Baked
Cooked with celery
Cooked with peas
Creamed
Glazed
In gelatin (with fruit juice)
Mashed
Scalloped
And cabbage slaw
And raisin salad
Cauliflower†
  Raw
  With cheese sauce
  Buttered
  Cream sauce
  With peas
Celery
  Raw sticks
  Braised
  Buttered
  With carrots, cooked
Corn
  On ear
  Buttered
  Creamed
  With lima beans
  Popped
Cucumber
  Raw slices
  In salads
Eggplant
  Baked
  Scalloped
  With tomatoes
Green peas
  Buttered
  Creamed
  Scalloped
  With onion
  With bacon or ham
  Raw

Green pea pods (snow peas)
  Raw
  Sauteed
  Buttered
Lettuce
  Raw
  Shredded
  Wilted
  Combination salad
  Wedges
  Cooked
  Fried
  Creamed
Okra§
  Raw
  Boiled
  Buttered
  Stewed with tomato
Onions, green, yellow, white,
    dry
  Fried
  Raw
  Boiled with peas
  Salad
Parsnips
  Buttered
  Browned
  Raw strips
Potatoes (white)§
  Raw
  With cheese sauce
  Baked
  Boiled and sprinkled with
    parsley and butter
  Browned in oven
  Creamed
  Pancakes
  Mashed
  Salad
  Scalloped
  Peeled baked

*Rich in Vitamin A.
†Rich in Vitamin C.
‡Fair source of Vitamin A.
§Fair source of Vitamin C.

Table 7–5 (Continued)

Hash browns	Squash (summer)	Tomatoes†‡
French fries	Raw	Baked
Pumpkin*	Buttered	Broiled
Baked	With tomato	Raw wedge
Mashed	Seasoned with bacon and/	Juice
Cooked whole—cut lid	or onion	Scalloped
and remove seeds and	Baked	Stewed
roast	Squash (winter)	Cold canned
Rutabagas§	Raw sticks, curls, wheels	Sliced
Raw	Baked	And okra
Cubes	Mashed	And cucumber salad
Mashed	Cooked in shell	And lettuce salad
Raw strips	Roast seeds	Aspic
Spinach/other greens*†	Sweet Potato*†	Turnips
Buttered	Baked	Buttered
Creamed	Mashed	Mashed
Raw leaf	Scalloped with apple	Scalloped
With celery	With marshmallows (rarely)	Raw strips
With hard-cooked eggs	Fried	
With cheese sauce	Buttered	
With onions and bacon		

Fruits

Apple	In orange juice	Grapes (seedless)
Applesauce	Pudding	In gelatin
Applesauce with cinnamon	Sliced	Plain
hearts or raisins	Snow	Melons§
Baked	Whole or half	Balls
Brown Betty	With milk	Cubes
Fresh Wedge	Fried	Fruit cup
Pudding	Berries	Sliced
Snow	Plain	Oranges†
Tapioca	With milk	Betty
And raisin salad	Cantaloupe*†	Custard
Fried	Balls	Juice
Apricot*	In fruit cup	Sections
In fruit cup	Sliced	Wedges
Plain	Cherries‡	Wheel
Stewed dry fruit	Plain	Peach‡
Whip	Pudding	In gelatin
With cheese	Grapefruit†	Plain—sliced, half
Banana	Juice	Salad
In fruit cup	Salad	Sauce
In gelatin	Sections	Snow

*Rich in Vitamin A.
†Rich in Vitamin C.
‡Fair source of Vitamin A.
§Fair source of Vitamin C.

Table 7–5 **(Continued)**

Stewed dry fruit
Tapioca
Pear
  Plain
  Stewed dry fruit
  Whip
  With cheese
  Sauce
  With other fruit
  Fried

Pineapple
  Crushed
  Cubes, plain
  In gelatin (cooked)‖
  With cabbage or carrot
Plum*
  Plain
Prunes‡
  Custard
  Snow

Stewed
Whipped
With applesauce
Pumpkin*
  See vegetables
Raisins
  In bread or rice pudding
  Plain
  Stewed
  In salad

Meat

Beef
  American chop suey
  Beef-noodle casserole
  Beef and liver loaf*
  Ground beef patty
  Roast
  Hot beef sandwich with
    gravy
  Beef stew with vegetables
  Cold sliced beef
  Meat balls and spaghetti
  Meat balls and vegetable
    casserole
  Beef hash

Ground beef and macaroni
  casserole
Cold sliced beef sandwich
Meat sauce and spaghetti
Corned beef with cabbage
Beef stew with brown
  gravy over rice
Beef stew with red gravy
  over noodles
Sloppy Joe
Meat loaf with tomato
  gravy
Pork
  Chop suey

Creamed ham and peas on
  toast
Ham salad
Ham and sweet potato*
  casserole
Lean pork steak
Scalloped ham and potato
Sliced baked ham
Ham sandwich
Pork roast
Lamb
  Lamb patty
  Lamb meat loaf
  Lamb stew
  Roast leg of lamb
  Scalloped lamb

Poultry and Fish

Poultry
  Stewed chicken with rice
  Chicken and dumplings
  Chicken with noodles
  Chicken with vegetables
  Creamed chicken
  Smothered chicken
  Baked chicken
  Fried chicken
  Chicken salad

Baked turkey
Turkey hash
Hot turkey sandwich with
  gravy
Cold sliced turkey sand-
  wich
Turkey salad
Fish
  Baked fish fillet with creole

Creamed fish with celery
  and peas
Salmon loaf
Tuna fish salad
Tuna-noodle casserole
Tuna boats
Salmon patty
Baked fish sticks
Fish flake balls

Other Meats

Strips
With gravy

Liver with onions

Rice dressing with giblets

Meat Alternates

Cheese
  American cheese cubes or
    wedges

Cheese and noodle or mac-
  aroni

Cheese, tomato, and maca-
  roni

‖Gelatin will not become firm if fresh rather than cooked is used.
*Rich in Vitamin A.
†Rich in Vitamin C.
‡Fair source of Vitamin A.
§Fair source of Vitamin C.

Table 7–5 (Continued)

Cheeseburger
Cheese toast
Cheese and vegetables
Cottage cheese with fruit
American cheese sandwich
Beans
  Dried beans, peas, and
    peanut butter
  Baked beans with ham sea-
    soning
  Bean, rice, tomato, and
    cheese casserole

Bean soup with ham
Red beans with ham
Lima beans with cheese
Lima beans and cheese
  casserole
Lima beans with tomatoes,
  celery, and wieners
Pinto beans and wiener
  rings
Black-eyed peas with ham
Eggs**
  Baked egg and cheese

Baked egg and vegetable
Creamed egg and spinach
Egg à la king
Goldenrod eggs
Hard-cooked eggs in
  tomato sauce
Scrambled eggs
Scrambled eggs with
  cheese
Stuffed deviled eggs
Tofu††

Breads, Sandwiches, and Cereals

Bread
  Plain
    Whole wheat
    Raisin
    Rye
    Biscuit
    Corn bread (pan or
      sticks)
    Corn spoon bread
  Hot
    Biscuits
    Corn bread
    Muffins
    Rolls
  Shapes
    Strips
    Squares
    Triangles
    Circles
    Animals

Sandwiches
  Butter
  Cheese
  Meat
  Peanut butter
  Vegetable*‡
    Grated carrots and cab-
      bage
    Sliced tomato/green
      pepper
    Cream cheese
Macaroni
  Buttered
  Bouillon
  Plain
  Salad
  With cheese
  With tomato sauce
  See beef list
Noodles
  Buttered

Plain
With sauce
See meats
Rice (brown)
  Buttered
  Bouillon
  Pudding
  With raisins
  With cheese
  With chicken
Grits
  Buttered
  With ham
  With cheese
  Baked
Crackers
  Graham
  Whole grain
  With peanut butter
  With cheese
  With cream cheese

Other Foods (Use Occasionally)

Cake (using whole-grain
    flour)
  Gingerbread
  Plain cake with fruits
Cookie (with whole-grain
    cereal)
  Gingersnap
  Oatmeal/raisin
  Peanut butter

Plain vanilla
Molasses
Gelatin (unsweetened)
  Plain, add fruit juice
  Whipped, add fruit juice
  With fruit
Pudding
  Cornstarch

Vanilla with fruit
Squash or pumpkin
Custard
  Bread pudding with raisins
  Egg
  Rice
Tapioca
  With raisins

††Not a replacement for protein source in the Child and Adult Care Food Program.
*Rich in Vitamin A.
‡Fair source of Vitamin A.
§Fair source of Vitamin C.
**Egg yolk fair source of Vitamin A.

STYLES OF FOOD SERVICE

Children love variety. Therefore, weather permitting, teachers may plan some meals outside, picnic style. Inside, a variety of settings are available (for instance, a Christmas buffet for older preschoolers). Food service styles include family, buffet, cafeteria, picnic, and bag lunch.

In *family style* food service, all children sit at a table, which has been prepared with individual plates and flatware. Food is placed on the table in serving bowls and is passed. Children help themselves from serving bowls with the assistance of the teacher.

A *modified family style* may be used with a group of children new to the center. Only one or two items would be placed in serving bowls, and the teacher would place other foods on the plates. This method is used only until the children are familiar with this style of meal service.

Food, flatware, and plates are placed on the serving table in a *buffet style* presentation. The child takes a plate, flatware, and food from the table with or without assistance from adults, but foods are not "dished up" for the child. This style may be used with an experienced group of preschoolers to add variety. The younger children's flatware may be placed at the table, and the child takes only a plate on which food is placed from the buffet table.

In *cafeteria style* service, food, flatware, and plates are placed on a serving tray. An adult places foods on the child's plate or tray. The child may select one or more items. Portion sizes are usually set by the server. However, children may be asked how much they can eat. This service is not recommended for preschoolers.

No formal definition exists for *picnic style* meal service, except that the meal is usually eaten at a picnic table or on the ground out-of-doors. This style has been used indoors where playgrounds or parks have not been available or where the weather has not cooperated. Children love picnics! Foods should be easy to prepare and carry. One or more of the foods may be prepared outside over an open fire; however, outdoor cooking is not necessary for a successful picnic. Paper plates, cups, and plastic utensils may be used. Remember, infants as well as preschoolers like to eat outside.

For the *bag lunch*, easy-to-prepare foods are packed in a bag. A spoon may be added for eating some foods, but most foods should be finger foods. Bag lunches can be used for field trips. All the nutrients in a regular lunch can be supplied through the bag lunch—candy bars, potato chips, and sweet cakes do not have to be included. A menu may include peanut butter or cheese sandwich on whole-wheat bread, raw vegetables and fruit, and milk. Remember, providing liquids for children in hot weather is important.

Planning Cycle Menus

Planning menus well in advance is a key to good management. Cycle menus are a series of carefully planned menus, used for a definite period of time and then repeated. They can be planned for an odd number of days not divisible by five, such as 11, 13, 21, or 29 days, to ensure that a menu is not repeated on the same day in consecutive weeks.

Using cycle menus reduces the time required for menu planning. After the initial cycle has been completed, the menu can be changed to account for special occasions such as holidays and vacations. To make a cycle menu successful, at least three to four new menu items should be added in the subsequent cycle. This ensures that meals do not become monotonous or boring. In addition, with a cycle menu, food preparation procedures can be standardized and costs can be identified and controlled.

Teacher activities can be easily varied from the first 3- or 4-week cycle to the second time the cycle is used. A menu can be thought of as a road map, always allowing opportunities to change direction. The menu should be flexible for side trips, but the food service supervisor and teacher should be conscientious enough not to get seriously sidetracked into a poor nutritional program.

Several forms will assist the food service manager and the teacher in the preparation of menus to meet CACFP guidelines. Figure 7–5 was taken from materials supplied to home day-care providers who may have children at their homes for breakfast, lunch, dinner and snacks.

USE WHEN PREPARING YOUR MENU—WRITE IN EVERYTHING SERVED		
BREAKFAST: (Time)	**LUNCH: (Time)**	**SUPPER: (Time)**
1. Juice or fruit or vegetable AND 2. Cereal or bread or pasta or rice (enriched or whole grain) AND 3. Fluid milk	1. Meat or meat alternative (cheese, eggs, legumes, peanut butter, other nuts or seed butters, fish, or poultry) (nuts, seeds—no more than 50%) AND 2. Bread or cooked grains, pasta (enriched or whole grain) or rice. 3. (a) and (b) Vegetables and/or fruits: AND 2 fruits or 2 vegetables or 1 fruit and 1 vegetable 4. Fluid milk	
1. Ju/Fr/Veg	1. Protein	1. Protein
	2. Grain	2. Grain
2. Grain	3a. Fr/Veg	3a. Fr/Veg
	b. Fr/Veg	b. Fr/Veg
3. Milk	4. Milk	4. Milk

Figure 7–5 Menu planning worksheet.
Source: A portion of worksheet record illustrating use of the Child Care Food Program requirements prepared by Association for Child Development, Lansing, Michigan, a home day-care sponsor in Illinois and Michigan.

Table 7–6 Winter cycle menus for preschooler

Day 1	Day 2	Day 3	Day 4
Beef and vegetable stew 1½ oz beef	Chicken livers, 1½ oz	Fish, baked, 1½ oz	Roast pork, 1½ oz
¼ C carrots and potatoes	Green beans, ¼ C	Seasoned brown rice, ¼ C	Sweet potato, ¼ C
Molded salad (orange sections, ¼ C)	Cooked tomatoes or tomato wedges, ¼ C	Asparagus spears, ¼ C	Baby lima beans, ¼ C
Whole wheat bread, ½ slice	Whole wheat bread, ½ slice	Plums, 2	Carrot sticks, 4 (6 in. long)
Margarine, 1 tsp	Margarine, 1 tsp	Margarine, 1 tsp	Whole wheat bread, ½ slice
2% milk, ¾ C	2% milk, ¾ C	Whole wheat muffin, 1	Margarine, 1 tsp
SNACKS:	*SNACKS:*	2% milk, ¾ C	2% milk, ¾ C
Deviled egg, ½	Pineapple chunks, ½ C	*SNACKS:*	*SNACKS:*
2% milk, ½ C	2% milk, ½ C	Mandarin oranges, ½ C	Grapefruit sections, ½ C
		2% milk, ½ C	2% milk, ½ C

Day 5	Day 6	Day 7	Day 8
Baked chicken, 1½ oz	White beans and ham	Beef cubes, 1½ oz	Fried chicken, 1½ oz
Cooked zucchini, ½ C	½ C beans	Brown rice, ¼ C	Mashed potatoes, ¼ C
Tossed salad, ½ C	1 oz ham	Broccoli, ¼ C	Cranberry sauce, ⅛ C
Whole wheat bread, ½ slice	Coleslaw, ¼ C	Applesauce, ¼ C	Brussels sprouts, ¼ C
Margarine, 1 tsp	Tomato, ¼ C	Whole wheat bread, ½ slice	Whole wheat bread, ½ slice
2% milk, ¾ C	Corn bread, 1 to 2 in. square	Margarine, 1 tsp	Margarine, 1 tsp
SNACKS:	Margarine, 1 tsp	2% milk, ¾ C	2% milk, ¾ C
Dried fruits—peach slice, apricot slice, dates, approximately 8 slices	2% milk, ¾ C	*SNACKS:*	*SNACKS:*
2% milk, ½ C	*SNACKS:*	Floating banana (½ banana and ¼ C orange juice)	Pineapple, ½ C
	Grapes (green), 18	2% milk, ½ C	2% milk, ½ C
	2% milk, ½ C		

Day 9	Day 10	Day 11	Day 12
Broiled fish, 1½ oz	Chili, ½ C	Omelet	Meat loaf (1½ oz hamburger)
Scalloped corn, ½ C	1 oz. hamburger	1 large egg	Mashed potatoes, ¼ C
Cooked greens, ¼ C	¼ C beans	½ oz cheddar cheese	Cooked cabbage with carrots, ¼ C
Whole wheat bread, ½ slice	2 tbsp tomato sauce	Oven browned potato, ¼ C	Whole wheat bread, ½ slice
Margarine, 1 tsp	Vegetable salad, ½ C	Broccoli, ¼ C	Margarine, 1 tsp
2% milk, ¾ C	Grapefruit, ¼ C	Whole wheat bread, ½ slice	2% milk, ¾ C
SNACKS:	Whole wheat crackers, 3	Margarine, 1 tsp	*SNACKS:*
Cooked prunes, ½ C	Margarine, 1 tsp	2% milk, ¾ C	Pear halves, 2, with raisins and sunflower seeds
2% milk, ½ C	2% milk, ¾ C	*SNACKS:*	2% milk, ½ C
	SNACKS:	Bread sticks, 2	
	Sliced peaches, ½ C	Peanut butter, 1 tbsp	
	2% milk, ½ C	Tomato juice, ½ C	

Day 13	Day 14	Day 15	Day 16
Roast turkey, 1½ oz	Beef liver, 1½ oz	Pizza	Baked breaded fish sticks, 3 (1½ oz fish)
Sweet potatoes, ¼ C	Beets, ¼ C	5⅛ in. arc whole wheat crust with	Au gratin potatoes, ¼ C
Cranberry salad, ¼ C	Buttered noodles, ¼ C	1 oz beef	Spinach salad
Whole wheat bread, ½ slice	Lettuce salad, ½ C	Carrot sticks, 2	¼ C spinach
Margarine, 1 tsp	Whole wheat bread, ¼ slice	Green pepper rings, 2	2 tbsp chopped egg
2% milk, ¾ C	Margarine, 1 tsp	Sweet cherries, ¼ C	1½ tsp salad dressing
	2% milk, ¾ C	2% milk, ¾ C	Pineapple slice
SNACKS:			2% milk, ¾ C
	SNACKS:	*SNACKS:*	
Citrus cup, ½ C			*SNACKS:*
Toasted wheat germ, 1 tsp	Waldorf salad: ½ C apple, 1 tsp raisins, ½ tsp walnuts, 1 tsp mayonnaise	Orange sections, ¼ C	
2% milk, ½ C		Banana chunks, ¼ banana	Bread pudding (bread, ½ slice)
	2% milk, ½ C	2% milk, ½ C	Orange juice, ½ C

Day 17	Day 18	Day 19	
Ham and cheese sandwich	Spaghetti dinner	Seafood or chicken chop suey	
1 oz ham	¼ C spaghetti	1½ oz meat	
½ oz cheese	2 tbsp sauce	Bean sprouts, bamboo shoots, water chestnuts, and green pepper, ½ C	
Baked beans in tomato sauce, ¼ C	1½ oz meat		
Apricots, ¼ C	Tossed salad	Brown rice, ¼ C	
Whole wheat bread, 1 slice	¼ C lettuce	Whole wheat bread, ½ slice	
Margarine, 1 tsp	¼ C greens	Margarine, ½ tsp	
2% milk, ¾ C	¼ tomato	2% milk, ¾ C	
	Whole wheat roll, ½		
SNACKS:	Margarine, 1 tsp	*SNACKS*	
	2% milk, ¾ C		
Apple and peanut butter snacks		Strawberries, ½ C	
2 crosscut slices apple, ¼ in.	*SNACKS:*	2% milk, ½ C	
1 tbsp peanut butter			
2% milk, ½ C	Whole wheat crackers, 4		
	Tomato juice, ½ C		

Note: Appreciation is extended to Maureen Conley, R.D., Supervisor, Food and Nutrition Programs, Illinois State Board of Education.

Table 7–6 (Continued) Nutrient analysis of preceding cycle menus

Percent Energy Distribution:

Fat	32%
Carbohydrate	50%
Protein	18%

TOTAL		NUTRIENT	%RDA
663.0	KCAL	ENERGY	37%
30.8	GM	PROTEIN	128%
1596.6	IU	VITAMIN A	63%
108.8	IU	VITAMIN D	27%
5.3	IU	VITAMIN E	75%
21.6	MG	VITAMIN C	48%
58.7	MCG	FOLACIN	78%
5.6	MG	NIACIN	46%
0.7	MG	RIBOFLAVIN	66%
0.5	MG	THIAMIN	54%
0.4	MG	VITAMIN B6	39%
1.1	MCG	VITAMIN B12	110%
463.8	MG	CALCIUM	58%
539.3	MG	PHOSPHOROUS	67%
3.9	MG	IRON	39%
88.9	MG	MAGNESIUM	74%
2.9	MG	ZINC	29%

Bar chart scale: 0% 20% 33% 40% 60% 66% 80% 100%

Source: NDDA Laboratory, Southern Illinois University at Carbondale.

Although no rule dictates how the menu should be planned, food service planners usually start with the meat, meat alternate, or protein foods and add other components in order to get a wide variety. You could begin with any food component. Table 7–5 gives a variety of foods and preparation methods to assist in planning. At least one fruit and vegetable for lunch and dinner (main meals) should be chosen. Vegetables, fruits, and grains are now the foundation of the diet and provide many vitamins and minerals as well as fiber. A minimum of *11 SERVINGS* a day should be included in the menus, two from fruits, three from vegetables, and six from the grain products.

A set of menus for 19 days is included in this chapter (Table 7–6). These menus have been planned for one meal and a snack, meeting approximately the one-third of the RDA for the 4-year-old in the center for one-half day. With additional servings from the foods listed on the menus, more energy can be added to the diets and these menus will easily meet 50% of the RDA. The energy allotment has been set at 1500 kcal for the 4- to 5-year-old. The two nutrients that are difficult to meet are zinc and vitamin D as can be seen from the nutrient analysis included with Table 7–6. Vitamin D can be obtained from the sun. Children should have an opportunity to be in the sun as much as possible but for short periods of time.

Some states require that if children are in the center 8 hours or more they should receive one-third and preferably one-half of the RDA. However, in at least one study if the children are given breakfast, lunch, and two snacks they still could not meet 75% of the standard for energy, iron, zinc, magnesium, vitamin A, and folic acid [5]. Looking at both the home and the day-care food intake, children did not eat foods with nutrients meeting the RDA for folic acid and iron [6].

Child Nutrition Labeling

To assist in purchasing foods that meet meal pattern requirements, some foods are identified with a Child Nutrition (CN) label. Child Nutrition labeling is a voluntary federal labeling program that provides a warranty for CN-labeled products. A CN label allows manufacturers to clearly state the contribution of a product toward the meal pattern requirements while protecting the consumer from exaggerated claims about a product. However, it does not provide any assurance of product quality.

Products eligible for CN labels include main dish products that contribute significantly to the meat/meat alternate component of the meal pattern requirements and juice and juice drink products that contain at least 50% full-strength juice by volume.

A facsimile of a CN label is presented in Figure 7–6. Note the distinct border of the CN logo, the meal pattern contribution statement, the 6-digit product identification number, the USDA/FNS authorization, and the month and year of approval.

Figure 7–6   Facsimile Child Nutrition label.

CULTURAL FOOD PATTERNS

Knowledge of cultural food patterns helps the care provider establish rapport with the child and family. Serving foods that represent different cultural food patterns can be a nourishing and educational experience for children. What people eat depends on ethnic, social, and economic factors. Children who were born in this country generally like and will eat foods that are readily available.

Table 7–7 illustrates the similarities among traditional foods of six ethnic groups—black, Hispanic-American, Japanese, Chinese, Vietnamese, and American Indian. Using these common foods, menu planners will find it relatively easy to accommodate diverse tastes. However, preparation methods vary greatly from one ethnic group to another.

Although there are many similarities, the teacher should capitalize on the diverse ethnic cuisines found in this country and make an effort to incorporate as many of the foods as possible into the child-care menu and curriculum.

Table 7–7   Foods common to most ethnic food patterns.

Meat and Alternates	Milk and Milk Products	Grain Products	Vegetables	Fruits	Others
Pork*	Milk, fluid	Rice	Carrots	Apples	Fruit juices
Beef	Ice cream	White bread	Cabbage	Bananas	
Chicken		Noodles, macaroni, spaghetti	Green beans	Oranges	
Eggs		Dry cereal	Greens (especially spinach)	Peaches	
			Sweet potatoes or yams	Pears	
			Tomatoes	Tangerines	

*May be restricted because of religious custom.

The following guidelines were developed by the authors when working with preschool centers to foster ethnic meal preparation.

Seven Steps to Successful Ethnic Meals

1. Obtain information. Acquire material; cookbooks and articles from the library, book store, or CACFP program. Include standardized recipes among the resource materials.
2. Get a commitment. Involve all teachers, food service personnel, dietitians, and those responsible for menus and food preparation in planning
   a. the number of ethnic meals to serve.
   b. the kind of ethnic meals.
   c. the lesson plans and educational use of menus.
   d. a list of parents as resources.
3. Meet with parents. Serve ethnic foods suggested by parents from different ethnic backgrounds. Have them write down their favorite menu or recipes and try to match the foods they like with standardized recipes in ethnic cook books. Your objective is to have as many complete ethnic menus and corresponding recipes planned as possible.
4. Consultation. Consult with dietitian/nutritionist to be sure the CACFP guidelines are met. Low-fat products can make traditional menus lower in fat.
5. Pilot test menus/recipes. Unless the food service supervisor is familiar with the ethnic food, prepare samples of food at least a week in advance and have parents, teachers, and children sample just a little taste of the new food. Build anticipation!
6. Publicize ethnic day. If staff and parents are involved, let other parents and the community know through newsletters, newspapers, and other media.
7. Evaluate and modify. Make changes as necessary for the next cycle of menus.

MENU CHECKLIST

The following questions will serve as a convenient checklist in your menu planning.

1. Do the lunches meet the minimum requirements for the group served?
2. Is a raw vegetable or fruit included daily for preschoolers and finger foods for toddlers?
3. Is a carotene-rich fruit or vegetable included daily or at least twice a week? Is a dark green vegetable included almost every day?
4. Is a vitamin C-rich fruit or vegetable included each day?
5. Are foods that are good sources of iron included daily (5 mg)?
6. Are sugar and salt used in limited quantities (for example, potato chips not served with ham or lunch meats, no sweet desserts)?

7. Do the lunches include a good balance of color, texture, shape, flavor, and temperature?
8. Are the foods varied from day to day and week to week from cycle to cycle?
9. Is at least one new food or preparation method introduced each week?
10. Are new foods introduced in combination with popular foods?
11. Are the instructor's objectives integrated into the menus?
12. Can the lunches be prepared successfully within the time available?
13. Can the lunches be prepared with the staff, facilities, and equipment available?
14. Can food be purchased with money budgeted?
15. Do cycle menus reflect both the children's own culture and that of unfamiliar cultures?
16. Do the menus give opportunities for the child to develop motor skills (foods for spoon, knife, and fork for the preschooler; finger foods and foods for the spoon for the toddler)?

GOOD MANAGEMENT PRINCIPLES

We strongly encourage the directors of early childhood education programs as well as directors of food service facilities to obtain a good food service textbook [7] as well as *Food for Fifty* [8], a frequently used reference for quantity recipes if your center has 25 or more children.

The teacher or care provider and food service personnel must work jointly to decide on the foods purchased, prepared, stored, and eaten. Menu planning is not the same as that carried out by the family at home. In the home day-care situation the food service person is of course the teacher. Certain controls must be established on ordering and purchasing foods, scheduling, preparation, and recording costs.

Quantity food service principles and procedures are applied through planning the menu, ordering and purchasing food, controlling supplies, preparing food, and analyzing costs. The following highlights each area:

Planning the Menu

1. Plan preferably a month or more in advance.
2. Maintain up-to-the-minute inventories on which menus can be based.
3. Use locally abundant foods.
4. Order and use donated commodities, if available.
5. Evaluate menus for adequacy, appearance, acceptance, and workload.

Ordering and Purchasing Food

1. Develop purchase orders or grocery lists in advance.
2. Order by the case or in quantities that are least expensive. (Small centers

may purchase with other nearby child-care centers, senior citizen programs, or schools.)
3. Obtain competitive quotations each time purchases are authorized.
4. Check deliveries for quantity, quality, weight, and conformity to all specifications.

Controlling Supplies

1. Record correctly all merchandise issued from storage.
2. Refrigerate food that needs to be kept cold, and keep frozen foods in a freezer.
3. Prevent loss from the kitchen and warehouse by keeping records and making regular checks. (Keep freezers locked.)
4. Allow no leftover food to be taken from the kitchen.

Preparing Food

1. Follow tested recipes. This assures a uniform product, prevents waste, and makes it easier to provide portions of the correct size. (Recipes for child-care services are available from USDA [9].)
2. Avoid providing too much or too little food by keeping accurate records of participation. If all the food is used, the extra handling and storage of leftover food is avoided. If there is too little food, nutrition and educational programs will suffer.
3. In estimating the number to be served, consider the weather, center activities, and other factors.
4. Simplify preparation and serving.
5. Maintain food production records.

Analyzing Costs

1. Keep accurate daily cost records.
2. Do not repeat expensive menu items unless they can be balanced by inexpensive items or unless funds are available. Food service personnel should be encouraged to attend School Food Service Certification Workshops as well as to receive the Certification for Food Service Managers in states where such services are available. Contact the regional or state agency that administers the USDA Child and Adult Food Program for more information and the specific requirements of each state.

SANITARY PRACTICES

The topic of sanitation deserves special attention, especially in preparation of foods for vulnerable, "high-risk" groups such as infants and young children. Some states now require a food handler's certificate. Food service textbooks can provide additional information, and consumer brochures are available from the American Dietetic Association [10–12] on safe cooking, eating, storage, and foodborne illness in the home.

Organisms

Bacteria, which cause food-borne illnesses, are so tiny they can be seen only with a microscope. They are found everywhere on everything, in the air we breathe, on the things we touch—we even carry them on our skin, hair, and clothing. Food, moisture, and moderate temperatures promote life and growth of these organisms. When all these conditions are present, they grow and multiply at a rapid rate. About every 20 minutes the organism may split, grow, and divide again and again. In 24 hours, one may grow and divide into 281 trillion organisms.

Three common types of organisms are *Staphylococcus*, *Salmonella*, and *Clostridium*. Knowing their sources and how they are spread, the food service worker can protect food from these organisms. *Staphylococcus* or "staph" organisms come in contact with food through someone who has an infected sore, cut, or burn. Coughing and sneezing can also bring *Staphylococcus* organisms in contact with dirty equipment. They grow most rapidly in custards, cream fillings, egg, tuna and potato salads, and most of the high-protein foods. As the *Staphylococcus* organisms quickly multiply, they produce a poisonous substance called a toxin. The toxin is the cause of sickness. If food is left at room temperature, these organisms grow and produce toxin, but if food is kept refrigerated or hot— above 140° F—after preparation, *Staphylococcus* organisms will not grow and produce toxin. Once a food is exposed to *Staphylococcus*, cooking will kill the organism, but the poisonous toxin will remain.

It is possible that food may enter the kitchen with the *Salmonella* organism already in it; these organisms may be spread by someone who has handled the infected food and then handled other foods. *Salmonella* organisms may also be spread by someone who has been ill and still carries the organism. The foods that are most often involved in this type of food poisoning are eggs, poultry, meat pies, and unpasteurized milk products. *Salmonella* organisms from uncooked meats may get onto your cutting board and be spread to any cooked meats prepared on the same board. To prevent this, you should use separate boards for uncooked and cooked meats and wash the cutting boards frequently. Proper refrigeration, 40° F and under, will stop the growth of *Salmonella* organisms. Thorough cooking will kill this organism and prevent food-borne illness.

Two types of *Clostridium* organisms can affect food. The first of these is *Clostridium perfringens*. Its major source is meat. This organism originally comes from soil. It infects animals that are used for meat products, so it is possible that freshly delivered meat may be infected. *Clostridium perfringens* multiplies rapidly, not only in meat products, but in broths and gravies as well. These bacteria are heat resistant, so they cannot be destroyed by cooking. To prevent further bacteria growth, broths, gravies, and meats that are not to be served immediately should be placed in shallow pans and refrigerated promptly.

The second *Clostridium* organism, *Clostridium botulinum,* causes botulism, which is a rare but deadly form of food poisoning. It occurs mainly in foods that are canned, perhaps developing when a can is damaged. Therefore, cans that are dented, bulging, or leaking or have contents that foam, smell bad, or have an off color or milky appearance should not be used. Also, botulism may occur in home canning when foods that have a low acid content—green beans and beets—are canned either in an "open kettle" or "water bath." It may also occur when some low-acid fruits are home canned without the use of a pressure cooker. Therefore, child-care centers should not accept home-canned foods from well-meaning parents. You, the care provider or administrator, could be held responsible for a child who becomes ill from contaminated food.

Dangerous organisms may get into your kitchen through several ways:

1. Food service personnel may bring in disease-causing organisms and, because of careless personal hygiene, pass these on to food.
   Therefore, it is important that those in food service maintain a high degree of personal hygiene.
2. Disease-ridden insects and rodents will carry organisms in with them.
   It is the responsibility of the kitchen employee to be on the lookout for signs of pest infestation, such as droppings and food damage, and report any findings to the supervisor so that proper steps for extermination may be taken.
3. The organisms may be carried into the child-care center already on the food.
   Remember, living organisms need food, moisture, and moderate temperature to grow. After preparation, keep foods in a cold refrigerator, 40° F and under, or hot, over 140° F. Do not leave food out in warm kitchen temperatures. All refrigerators and freezers should contain thermometers (Figure 7–7).

Commonly asked questions and answers about food safety are listed in Figure 7–8.

Personnel Sanitation

Personal hygiene means more than just a clean face and hands. It means a clean body, clean clothes, and clean habits. Everyone's skin harbors organisms.

Food service personnel should wear clean uniforms or aprons each day. An apron should be changed when it gets soiled. It is necessary that a kitchen cap, chef's cap, or hairnet be worn, since organisms are on hair. Also, caps or nets prevent hair from falling onto the food. The hands of a food service worker should be kept clean, with short, clean nails and no jewelry other than a watch or wedding ring. Hands frequently harbor organisms that can be transferred to food. Because of this, it is essential that hands be washed before working, each time they become dirty, after smoking (organisms from your mouth get onto cigarettes and then onto fingers), and after using the toilet. To effectively wash hands use soap and hot water. The mechanical scrub of hand against hand gets

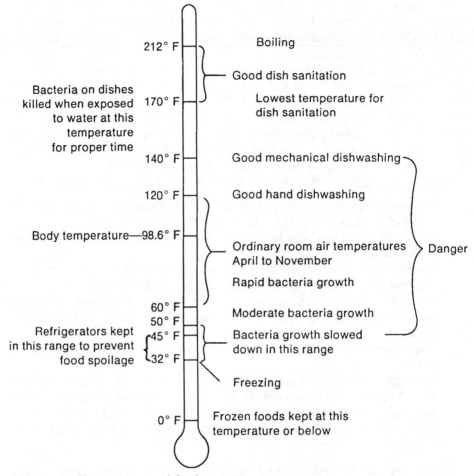

Figure 7-7   Temperature and food sanitation.

the trapped dirt and grime out. Take time to do a thorough job. Do not lean against the basin; organisms outside the basin will get on your uniform and then onto the work counter and work area. Rinse and dry hands thoroughly with a fresh paper towel. Do not use your clean hands to turn off water. Use a paper towel. This will keep the clean hands from touching the unsanitary water faucet. Food service personnel should not handle the food if they have boils, running sores, skin eruptions, or infected cuts, since these conditions may be sources of infection. It is possible to work in a non-food-handling part of the kitchen until the skin condition has disappeared.

Food should not be handled by anyone with an illness. Turn away from food to sneeze or cough, and cover mouth and nose with a disposable tissue. (A sneeze alone will explode millions of organisms into the air and contaminate not only food but also work areas, equipment, and coworkers.) Because organisms

Figure 7–8   General food safety questions.

1. **Are fruits and vegetables safe to eat?**
   Yes. In fact, health authorities such as the National Cancer Institute, the National Academy of Sciences and The American Dietetic Association recommend that we eat more fruits and vegetables—at least five servings a day—to reduce the risk of cancer and other chronic diseases and for better health.

2. **How can I be sure that foods grown using pesticides are safe to eat?**
   Pesticides, like pharmaceuticals, are extensively tested and regulated. The U.S. Environmental Protection Agency and state regulatory agencies review the test data and grant a registration, or license to sell, only if the product meets its standards. A single pesticide is subjected to more than 120 tests. It takes eight to 10 years and $35 to $50 million to develop and register a pesticide product. On average, only one in 20,000 chemicals makes it from the laboratory to the farmer's field.

3. **Who ensures that the food is safe?**
   Our government sets strict standards and monitors food safety very closely. The U.S. Food and Drug Administration, U.S. Environmental Protection Agency, U.S. Department of Agriculture and individual states all play important roles in protecting the safety of our food supply. In addition, agricultural chemical companies work closely with these government regulatory agencies and continuously assess the safety and efficacy of their products to be sure they meet today's high standards and satisfy the needs of both growers and consumers.

4. **How much pesticide residue remains on food? How can I tell if residues are there? Can I taste residues?**
   Very little, if any, pesticide residue remains on the foods we buy. According to the U.S. Food and Drug Administration's Residue Monitoring Program, the majority of foods on the market have no detectable residues. If residues do exist, they are at levels so small that special laboratory equipment is necessary to detect them. These small amounts are described as parts per million (ppm). One ppm is equivalent to one cent in $10,000. You cannot taste or smell them.

5. **Should I wash produce before serving?**
   Washing produce is always recommended for sanitary reasons. However, do not wash foods in soapy water because the soap can leave residues of its own.

6. **Who should I look to about the safety of our food?**
   The scientific and regulatory communities, including the Food and Drug Administration, the U.S. Public Health Service and the Environmental Protection Agency, agree that any risk to humans of all ages from pesticide residue is negligible—so small that there should not be cause for concern. Heatlh experts, including the former U.S. Surgeon General C. Everett Koop, believe that dietary exposure to pesticides is not a source of danger to children or adults.

(Continued on p. 238)

Source: Taken from The Children's Food Safety Kit, developed by the National Center for Nutrition and Dietetics of the American Dietetic Association and made possible by an educational grant from the Du Pont Company.

Figure 7–8   (Continued)

7. **Are there pesticide residues in processed foods?** Processed foods must meet the same rigorous standards for safety as fresh foods. Any residue remaining in processed foods must not exceed the amount established to be safe by the Environmental Protection Agency. 8. **Should I be concerned about the waxy coating on some fruits and vegetables?**	The thin, waxy coat on some produce (such as apples and cucumbers) is not a cause for concern. This practice helps maintain the quality of the produce by retaining the moisture, protecting the food from bruising and preventing spoilage. Waxed produce should also be washed (in water only). There is no need to peel waxed produce.

from a sneeze or cough can penetrate the tissue used and get onto the hands, dispose of the tissue after use and wash hands.

The warmth of a kitchen often causes one to perspire. When wiping perspiration from the face, use a paper towel, not a kitchen towel. After using, dispose of the paper towel and wash hands. Always comb hair in the lavatory, not in the kitchen. Try not to touch hair or skin while working, for the hand could then serve as a carrier of organisms to the food.

Food Handling

The guidelines shown in Figure 7–9 for food handling must be followed by centers, parents, and children:

Figure 7–9   **Safe food handling tips for parents and children.**

Food-borne illness (food poisoning) can strike anyone, but kids are especially susceptible. Here are ten basic food-handling tips that you should know: 1. Wash your hands thoroughly with soap before and after handling food. 2. Wash all work surfaces, cutting boards, utensils and your hands immediately after they have come into contact with any raw meat, raw fish, raw poultry or raw eggs. Never let any raw juices from these foods touch any other food.	3. Use acrylic, not wooden, cutting boards. Wooden surfaces harbor bacteria. Acrylic boards can be scrubbed with hot soapy water or cleaned in the dishwasher. 4. Don't serve raw fish (i.e., sushi, oysters, clams) or dishes made with raw eggs that could contain harmful bacteria, viruses or parasites. If cookie, bread or cake dough contains raw eggs, don't lick the bowl or spoon. Homemade ice cream is often made with raw egg *(Continued on p. 239)*

Source: Taken from The Children' Food Safety Kit, developed by the National Center for Nutrition and Dietetics of the American Dietetic Association and made possible by an educational grant from the Du Pont Company.

Figure 7-9   (Continued)

yolks. Instead, use an egg substitute which has been pasteurized or follow a recipe that calls for cooking the ice cream mixture before freezing.

5. Freeze foods at 0°F or below. Refrigerate foods at 40°F or below. Buy a freezer/refrigerator thermometer at the supermarket and check temperatures regularly.

6. Thaw meats and poultry in your refrigerator overnight or in a microwave oven. If thawed in the microwave, cook immediately. Never thaw meats on the counter at room temperature.

7. Refrigeration and freezing slows bacterial growth, but does not kill the bacteria. Once frozen foods thaw to room temperature, bacteria continue to thrive. Only heating foods to a high enough internal temperature can kill bacteria, so cook foods thoroughly. Use a meat thermometer to check the internal temperature of food.

Beef	Internal temperature of at least 160°F
Pork	Internal temperature of at least 170°F
Lamb and poultry	Internal temperature of at least 180°

Foods cooked in the microwave may heat unevenly, resulting in some parts of the food not being heated to safe temperatures. Be sure

to follow microwave directions, rotating dishes and allowing standing time if required. Check internal food temperature in a variety of areas.

8. Keep hot foods above 140°F and cold foods below 40°F. Don't allow foods to sit at room temperature for more than two hours. The "danger zone," when bacteria multiply the fastest, is between 40°F and 140°F.

9. If canned food is not completely consumed when opened, either cover the can securely or transfer food to another container. Store leftovers in the refrigerator.

10. Cool leftovers quickly in a refrigerator or freezer. Large batches should be divided into small portions in shallow containers so food can cool more quickly. Do not stack items during cooling or freezing in order to allow air to circulate. Reheat leftovers to at least 165°F.

11. Do not save raw or cooked food too long. A complete chart of holding times is available (ask your doctor or dietitian). However, a simple rule of thumb applies: *"When in doubt, throw it out!"* Food harboring harmful bacteria does not necessarily have a foul odor or spoiled appearance.

12. Be sure to separate diapering from food handling and preparation activities. Always wash hands well after diapering.

Microwave Ovens

Microwave ovens have become popular for child-care centers that have foods prepared in locations other than the centers or if special diets are required that have been frozen. Some basic rules should be applied when using the microwave.

- Always use containers designed for microwave. Plastic butter cartons are not designed for microwaves and may produce undesirable oders and tastes when the plastic heats.
- When covering a container with plastic wrap, be sure to turn back a corner to allow heat to escape. Do not put closed plastic bottles in the microwave— they may explode from the heat and steam.
- Containers designed for microwave may remain cool while foods are hot enough to burn a child.
- Never warm a baby bottle in the microwave.
- Children who are too young to read are too young to use microwaves.
- Always check temperature of food removed from microwaves because "hot spots" develop; stir foods if possible.

Care Providers and Food Service

In many cases it is necessary and even advantageous for child-care workers to assist the food service personnel. In some centers unions may forbid this activity. However, where permitted, the care provider should follow the same procedures to ensure maintenance of sanitary conditions in the food service facility.

Personal hygiene principles should be followed. (Hands should be washed before personnel come into the kitchen area.) Likewise, providing a clean apron and wearing a hairnet or cap are essential during food preparation and cleanup.

Eating and drinking of food by staff should be permitted only outside the kitchen or food preparation area. It is disruptive for care providers to take "tastes" from the containers of food while food service personnel are preparing and serving it.

PARENT PARTICIPATION

Most centers assume the large task of educating parents as well as children about nutrition. Menus and basic nutrition education programs are shared with parents. Because food idiosyncrasies and poor eating habits may be a result of relatively few foods being served or offered in the home, preventing possible nutritional deficiencies and maintaining the child in the best possible nutritional status involves the parents' continuation of sound principles at home. Parents can be participants in the food programs by helping plan menus and by participating in food preparation and service. Many preschool centers require parents to serve on advisory or policy boards, which approve cycle menus before they are used. However, too often this means "rubber stamping" a menu or set of menus without being provided with proper information on which to judge the quality of the menus. If possible, a parent should serve along with teacher and food service personnel in the total planning process. At minimum, the parents should receive a copy of the menus, which should explain how foods will be used in the center to help the child learn about new foods and accept a wide variety. In some states the licensing regulations require that menus be posted at least 2 weeks in advance and must be kept on file for up to 6 months. Many centers arrange group sessions conducted by a nutritionist on the food and nutrition needs of children. These sessions include the nutritional needs of children as related to the specific menus of the center. The nutritionist, along with the food service personnel and care provider, must be accountable to parents for the food served, how foods are used in the child-care center, and for the education of the child's parents so that the efforts begun in the center will be continued at home.

COMMUNITY DIETITIAN

Both child-care workers and food service personnel find it helpful to consult with a community dietitian or public health nutritionist.

The center director should expect that the dietitian can

1. Use the tools of nutrition assessment, planning, and evaluation to help teachers, food service workers and parents solve children's food- and nutrition-related problems.
2. Manage chronic conditions such as overweight, underweight, diabetes, heart disease, allergies, bottle mouth caries, or anemia.
3. Negotiate with food service supervisors and teachers in planning menus.
4. Have the ability to verify and interpret the nutrient content of the menus ensuring compliance with established state and federal guidelines
5. Negotiate with regulatory agencies during their visit with the program.
6. Train food service personnel in sanitary requirements and use of safe practices when handling food.

Qualifications Expected

The public health nutritionist has had courses in public health and community nutrition from an accredited college or university and an approved dietetic internship or equivalent training and experience in a health care program that meets requirements for the registered dietitian (R.D.). The community dietitian, also an R.D., is experienced in working with food and nutrition programs for mothers and children in a variety of settings such as day care, supplemental feeding programs, and institutions. The local Dietetic Association, Home Economics Association, Society for Nutrition Education, or National Dairy Council may be contacted to help your center locate professionals with experience in the areas of child feeding.

Training

Some training for the food service personnel is required. In no other facility where food is prepared do we expect the extent of involvement of the teacher and food service personnel. The Child and Adult Care Food Program often provides workshops (usually free or at a small cost) on food service and nutrition for food service personnel as well as teachers. The School Lunch Program, usually operated by the state educational agency, conducts workshops for food service personnel that the center staff may attend. These are generally geared to specific aspects of food service. In addition, in-service training should be requested of nutritionists consulting for the program.

SUMMARY

- The daily food plans for toddlers and preschoolers may differ in texture and amounts served; however, table foods can be used for all groups.
- If the menu is to become a tool for the educational curriculum, the food service personnel and teachers must participate together in menu planning.
- Cycle menus, which are flexible enough to be changed frequently, not only help meet the nutritional needs of the individual child but also assist the food service personnel and teacher in planning food service and the curriculum.
- Without the use of good management principles, foods will not provide the quality necessary to encourage children to actively participate in the educational process.
- The Child and Adult Food Program provides reimbursement for meals that meet USDA specifications. These guidelines can be followed in helping provide infants, toddlers, and preschoolers with the RDA.

DISCUSSION QUESTIONS

1. How are the food patterns for the various age groups different?
2. How might the teacher and food service personnel participate in planning?
3. Are there foods or combinations of foods that meet the Child and Adult Food Program requirements but might be questioned for the child given the principles outlined in Chapters 4, 5, and 6?
4. Have you observed the good management principles outlined in this chapter in preschool or day-care facilities?
5. List possible constraints from the food service management viewpoint of preparing the following menu: meat loaf, baked potato, cooked broccoli, tossed salad, freshly baked whole wheat rolls, baked apple, and milk.
6. Which factors must be considered in food storage, preparation, and cleanup in order to follow good sanitary practices?
7. Evaluate the menu of ham salad sandwich, gelatin with orange and apple pieces, carrot sticks, chocolate pudding, and graham crackers and milk. Does this menu meet the CACFP guidelines?

8. Does the menu above pose any problems for the food service personnel? The teacher?
9. Are pesticide residues a threat to the child's food supply?
10. List three ways the parents could be involved in the food service.
11. When would the director of a center use a dietitian?

REFERENCES

1. USDA Human Nutrition Information Service: Nutrition and your health: dietary guidelines for Americans, Home and Garden Bull. N. 232–8, Washington, DC, 1989, U.S. Government Printing Office.
2. The Federal Register 53 (129):25309, July 6, 1988.
3. Food and Nutrition Service, U.S. Department of Agriculture: Building for the future: nutrition guidance for the child nutrition programs, Washington, DC, 1992, USDA, Nutrition and Technical Services Division.
4. Endres, J., Poon, S. W., Welch, P., et al.: Dietary sodium intake of infants fed commercially prepared baby food and table food, J. Am. Diet. Assoc. 87:750–753, 1987.
5. Drake, M.A.: Menu evaluation, nutrient intake of young children, and nutrition knowledge of menu planners in child care centers in Missouri, J. Nutr. Educ. 24(3):145–147, 1992.
6. Drake, M.A.: Anthropometry, biochemical iron indexes, and energy and nutrient intake of preschool children: comparison of intake at day care center and at home, J. Am. Diet. Assn. 91:1587–1588, 1991.
7. West, B. W., Wood, L. W., revised by Harger, V. F., Shugart, G. S., and Payne-Palacio, J.: Food service in institutions, ed. 6, 1988, The Macmillan Publishing Co.
8. Shugart, G., and Molt, M.: Food for fifty, ed. 8, 1989, The Macmillan Publishing Co.
9. U.S. Department of Agriculture, Food and Nutrition Services: Quantity recipes for child care centers, FNS-86, Washington, DC, 1986, U.S. Government Printing Office.
10. American Dietetic Association: Safe cooking for safe eating: tips on proper food preparation, Chicago, 1988, ADA.
11. American Dietetic Association, Food borne illness in the home: how and why what you eat can make you sick, Chicago, 1988, ADA.
12. American Dietetic Association, Safe keeping for safe eating: tips on proper food storage, Chicago, 1988, ADA.

Integrating Food and Nutrition Concepts into the Early Childhood Curriculum

LEARNING OBJECTIVES

Students will be able to:

- List and describe the four major curriculum approaches used in early childhood education programs.
- List the characteristics of the cognitive-interactionist approach.
- List six programmatic insights to be gained in using any approach to learning.
- State the goals and objectives for teaching nutrition directly to young children (3 to 5 years).
- Using one food from each of the food groups, describe how the food can be used according to Blank's model [1].
- Write nutrition education objectives and list activities to teach the young child (birth to 3 years) good nutrition principles.
- Discuss the use of the menu as a key resource for nutrition education in early childhood programs.
- Write a lesson plan for at least one curriculum area, incorporating food or nutrition in the activities.
- List the four developmental areas used to integrate food and nutrition activities in the learning environment.
- Develop written lesson plans using nutrition activities related to the four developmental skills.
- List some precautions to be observed when cooking in the classroom.

In compiling information for this chapter, we considered the following questions: How do children develop intellectually? Which concepts do they acquire? At which age do they begin to develop these concepts? How can we as teachers of young children teach concepts using foods as one of the primary teaching tools? Can food and nutrition concepts be integrated into the curriculum? Is cooking in the classroom feasible? Are there classroom recipes that young children can prepare? How can recipes be followed by nonreaders? We have attempted to answer these questions through the use of one approach or model, while presenting additional common teaching approaches that are practical in early childhood settings. All these approaches can be adapted to the nutrition curriculum.

PROGRAMMATIC APPROACHES TO LEARNING

As we examine the development of thought and the many implications it has for teaching, it becomes evident that the environment and the kind of stimulation and interaction with adults to which a child is exposed in the early years will have a significant impact on the child's capabilities.

The child learns through interaction and encounters with objects and persons in the environment. Food, the eating situation, and those persons who provide the food and food service are components of the environment. Thus, the child learns through observing and interacting with foods and the eating situation, manipulating foods, and modeling or imitating those significant adults who participate with the child in the eating situation. The child's perception of the world becomes stabilized, and concepts about the world develop into usable entities. How much and how well this is learned and the kinds of things learned depend on the child's exposure to examples of foods and the eating experiences. The nutrition education curriculum in early childhood settings should provide the appropriate kinds of experiences, materials, and opportunities to explore and interact for each child's complete development.

It is generally agreed that the early years in a child's life are critical to development and that appropriate early childhood programs can have a positive influence [2]. There is less agreement on which kind of educational program is appropriate, and this, too, has a significant relationship to nutrition education for the young child. The Head Start planned variation studies [3] and numerous educational laboratories and universities have been and are involved in trying to answer that question.

There are at least four major types of approaches to early childhood education: the cognitive-interactionist, traditional nursery school, perceptual motor, and the academic skills [4]. We have chosen the cognitive-interactionist approach to express ways of teaching nutrition education concepts to children. This does not mean that the other approaches are not appropriate for helping children select the proper foods. Any of the methods can be used with success.

Cognitive-interactionist Approach

Cognition refers to mental growth and activity. It defines most of the processes of thinking and knowing that children employ daily—planning what to do in the morning, learning the rules of a game, or making up an excuse for not going to bed early. Cognition includes thinking, remembering, problem solving, understanding, planning, imagining, judging, and deciding. These processes develop in a predictable way according to Piaget [5]. Cognitive ability, which makes understanding possible, develops in three major stages: sensorimotor (birth to 24 months), preoperational (24 months to 6 years), concrete operational (7 years to 11 years).

Sensorimotor Stage.   This stage covers the period of growth from birth through 24 months. During this period the child depends on inborn sensorimotor reflexes for interaction with the environment. The environment does not just turn on and off those tools provided by heredity. The infant profits from experience and actively modifies the reflex schemes. For example, the child learns to recognize the nipple and to search for it [5]. The smell or sight of food can cause the older infant to crawl to the kitchen in pursuit of it.

Preoperational Stage.   This stage of development extends from 2 to 6 years of age. During this period, the child starts to play symbolically and to explore the world in a more able way than the random exploration of an infant. The child has gained more control over the body and thus has freer movement within the environment. Socializing and interacting with others has started. The child's powers of thought are still at a primitive stage, and the sense organs, which have further developed from the sensorimotor period, are still the primary tools for learning. The child needs to look, feel, taste, smell, and even listen to food before, during, and after preparation and to experience this involvement over and over until different experiences (that is, eating a variety of foods) make sense and are internalized.

Concrete Operations Stage.   During this stage of development, which extends from age 7 to 11 years, the child continues to develop in ability to handle concepts both in terms of forming them and in manipulating them in a thought process. Actually concrete operations are an internalized set of actions that allow the child to do in the head what was previously done with the hands. The child still isn't able to think abstractly but can solve problems with concrete content. As a result, overt trial and error is reduced. At this stage, the child can deal with more than one concrete aspect at once yet can only consider one abstraction at a time. The child is now able to substitute thought for actual performance. Development of mental process can be encouraged and facilitated during this stage through the use of concrete or real objects as opposed to hypothetical situations and places. The child needs to be involved in a learning setting that promotes experiences with real objects, things, and people; i.e., cooking in the classroom, using real utensils, recipes, and ingredients [5].

Concepts.   Concepts play an important role in cognitive development. Understanding is based on concepts, which in turn determine what one knows and believes and, to a large extent, what one does. Flavell [6] states that "once a concept develops, it serves as an experimental filter through which impinging events are screened, gauged, and evaluated, a process that determines in large part what responses can and will occur."

As you work with children, you will find that they frequently possess a number of misconceptions. These misconceptions are often caused by incorrect information, limited experience, gullibility, faulty reasoning, vivid imagination, unrealistic thinking, and misunderstanding of words. For example, a child might say, "Milk comes from the grocery store, not from cows." Once a misconception is formed, it is difficult to change. This is where the care provider plays an important role, since it is the care provider's responsibility to present experiences that teach children about food, thus minimizing the development of nutritional misconceptions.

The cognitive development approach, also referred to as verbal cognitive or interactionist, includes a variety of diverse types of programs. These approaches share a common emphasis on the development of cognitive skills and abilities such as understanding and using language; concept formation, association, and discrimination; problem solving; and memory. The amount of structure and teaching vis-à-vis child-directed activity varies among programs.

The Perry Preschool High/Scope Curriculum exemplifies the cognitive-interactionist approach [7]. This program follows the Piagetian sequence of content areas with respect to motor and verbal levels of operation. The daily routine is one in which teachers carry out their goals and objectives. When teaching nutrition to children, the care provider takes on a directing role. The routine involving food, food service, and nutrition principles is made as tangible and concrete for the child as possible. The approach is similar to the traditional nursery school, or child development model (discussed later), in the number and kinds of materials used and in the prearranged activity areas.

Morrison identified four recurring themes that are present in programs which implement curricula based on Piaget's ideas:

1. Children's thinking is substantially different from that of adults, and adults must not try to impose their way of thinking on children. The educational environment should enable children to think of their own ideas and construct their own models of the world.
2. Children must be actively involved in learning.
3. Learning should involve concrete objects and experiences with both children and adults particularly at the sensorimotor and preoperational stages.
4. Children learn best by being continually exposed to quality learning experiences. Their comprehension of any event is greatly dependent upon the proximity of the event to concepts involved. If the children have nothing to associate an experience to, it will be meaningless assimilation (fitting or adding new knowledge into already existing knowledge) and accommodation (changing one's ideas of reality to fit the new knowledge one is trying to assimilate) cannot function unless experiences closely parallel each other [8].

Other Approaches

Three additional approaches to early childhood education described by Mayer [4] are the academic skills, traditional nursery school, and perceptual-motor approaches. The academic skills approach teaches the preschool child the academic skills usually learned in the first years of elementary school through a program of planned, sequenced, highly structured activities. The best known example is the Bereiter-Englemann academically oriented preschool program. Children receive direct instruction in language, arithmetic, and reading, with some time for music and semistructured play. Each teacher takes responsibility for one of the subject areas, and the children in small ability groups rotate from one subject area and teacher to the next. The method of instruction is intense oral drill. Sentence patterns are taught as didactic repetitive formulas, and they increase in complexity as children master them. Concepts such as number and volume, for example, are presented as rules and learned by rote memorization. Children may be expected to memorize examples of the concepts "fruit" or "vegetable."

Another common approach is often termed the traditional nursery school. This type stresses the social and emotional development of the child through free play and organized group activities, such as making placemats for mealtime table settings, reading stories about food, and singing songs about food. Also referred to as the child development model [4], this curricular approach has been the pattern for most preschools serving middle-class populations. It is based on the physiological belief that effective development fosters cognitive development. This approach ranks highest in child-child interaction, providing opportunities for children to participate together without teaching intervention. The care giver's role is subtle. By planning and arranging the eating environment, children learn about foods. Observations of each child's readiness to profit from a food experience determine the use of that experience.

The perceptual-motor approach, or sensory-cognitive model, is best illustrated in the Montessori preschool program. This type of program emphasizes self-corrective sensorimotor activities with specially designed materials. The approach ranks high in child-material interaction but lowest of the four approaches in teacher-child interaction [4]. Learning occurs through "doing," with emphasis on concrete nonverbal experiences. The child is free to choose the activity and to move from task to task, and the teaching materials are planned in a carefully prescribed sequence. The importance of the child's having contact with the natural environment is stressed. Specific experiences with food are planned and encouraged.

Programmatic Insights

Much is yet to be learned from educational philosophies and practices inherent in various early child development curriculum approaches. Each has been carefully and meticulously thought through, tested over a considerable period, and critically evaluated in terms of later school achievement and the personal adequacies of the children involved. From the many models and approaches we can glean important information about children and their learning. Important programmatic insights can be summarized as follows [9]:

1. There is no absolute or preferred approach to learning for all children.
2. Educational goals are determined by an emphasis on child growth or child learning. Where growth objectives dominate, curricular items are introduced when the child can integrate them. Where learning is emphasized, a systematic planned sequence of events is in order.
3. The recognition of individual differences is vital in effective preschool training.
4. A child should experience a continuity in education with curriculum introduced at the developmentally appropriate time and reinforced until the behavior indicates the desired achievement.

5. The teacher's commitment to imparting new social and intellectual skills is necessary for a positive educational experience.
6. Stimulating child-centered environments that provide numerous opportunities for exploration and experimentation are crucial for normal personality and intellectual development.

Early childhood programs cannot be homogeneous in a pluralistic society [10]. There is no single "best" approach or system. Each program should reflect the particular orientation, background, and aspirations of the children's community in the educational setting. This provides us the opportunity to maximize the development of each group rather than attempting to equalize the development of all groups in our society.

GOALS AND OBJECTIVES FOR NUTRITION EDUCATION

The goal of the nutrition education program, whether using a direct or indirect method, may be stated as follows:

Children will eat a well-balanced diet daily to establish and protect their nutritional health for life.

Ideally, after a sound and effective nutrition education program, it should be expected of preschool children that the following would occur:

Given a choice of foods, the child will select those foods with a high nutrient density (quality) as frequently or more frequently than those with a low nutrient density.

The implication of this objective can be far-reaching. If the nutrition education program is successful, children when confronted with candy or soda should be willing to choose vegetables, fruit, fruit juices, or foods high in nutrient density. Because it is perhaps not practical to expect to change the total environment of the child and the eating habits of all persons coming in contact with the child at home, in the community, and at the marketplace, an alternate overall objective would be the following:

Given a variety of foods through a well-planned, prepared, and served menu, the child will accept (taste) all foods provided.

This objective is based on the belief that young children with a sufficient number of positive experiences with many high-quality foods will learn to eat a wide variety of foods.

At the close of their preschool experiences children should be able to:

1. State names of all foods served.
2. Identify foods by taste, odor, or touch.
3. Classify foods into food groups, such as vegetables, fruits, meats/meat alternates (nuts, legumes, lentils), cereals/grains, milk and milk products,

fats (butter, margarine, oil), and other foods (low nutrient density foods or "empty calories").

4. Match foods served at mealtime with the basic food groups.
5. Match foods served at home with the basic food groups.
6. State number of times each day a child should eat foods from each food group (optional).
7. Name major nutrients in each food group (optional).

Although it is our belief that the last two objectives are too advanced for the preschooler, some centers find that their children can progress to this stage. Objectives 1 through 5 should be accomplished before progressing to objectives 6 and 7.

TEACHING CHILDREN TO EAT NOURISHING FOOD

The food groups provide the basis for teaching children to eat a wide variety of nourishing foods. The menu provides the substance for the nutrition education activities that ultimately lead to the child's acceptance of these foods.

Food Group Reference

A visual aid provides a concrete reference point to help young children (3 to 8 years) understand the food groups. One such aid can be constructed with six or more boxes. The boxes can be large enough to hold empty food containers brought from home, or they can be used as a receptacle for food models and pictures of foods. Children can help prepare each box as you progress through the food groups, teaching them the concepts of grains and cereals, vegetables, fruits, milk and milk products, meat and meat alternates, and fats, oils, and sweets (Figure 8–1).

| Bread, cereal, rice, and pasta | Vegetables | Fruits | Milk, yogurt, and cheese | Meat and meat alternates | Fats, oils, and sweets |

Figure 8–1 Boxes representing food groups.

You may choose to combine the food groups into only six categories:

Group 1: bread, cereal, rice, and pasta
Group 2: vegetables
Group 3: fruits
Group 4: milk, yogurt, and cheese
Group 5: meat, poultry, fish, dry beans, eggs, and nuts
Group 6: fats, oils, and sweets

The preparation can include gathering boxes of various sizes. Because the bread, cereal, rice, and pasta and vegetable and fruit groups should contain the most variety, these boxes may be largest, followed by those for the milk and milk products and the meat and the meat alternates. The fat, oils, and sweets group would be the smallest. The boxes can be sprayed white or color coded, and children can cut out pictures of food from magazines to paste onto the boxes. The meat and meat alternates box may need to be divided to emphasize the importance of including nuts, legumes, and lentils in the diet (Figure 8–2).

Each food box should be prepared separately, and the foods should be matched with foods served on the menu (objective 4).

The tasting of food items before, during, and after preparation is exciting and educational for children. For example, select a day when white beans appear on the menu. Although children cannot chew a hard, dry bean, they can identify it by touch (objective 2).

Materials for this activity include:

Menu with beans	Pictures of beans in food boxes
Food boxes	Pictures or models of other
Uncooked beans	meats and meat alternates
Partially cooked beans	Covered can

Let the child feel beans placed in a covered can. Pictures of beans can then be placed in the meat and meat alternates food group box (objective 3), and children can note other pictures in the meat alternates box that look similar and that look different. Pinto beans and red beans are similar to white beans, but ham-

**Figure 8–2
Divided box
emphasizing both
meats and meat
alternatives.**

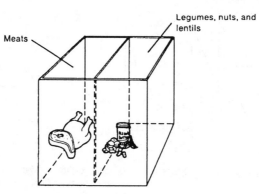

burger and eggs are much different from beans, although they all fall into the meat and meat alternate group.

When planning this event with the cook or food service personnel, you will ask for some partially cooked beans, still crunchy, to taste (objective 1), to feel, to smell, and to note how they have become soft. (In addition, beans may be soaked overnight to allow the children an opportunity to see how they have expanded and become softer.) It is best to teach nutrition education concepts before a meal or snack, since the interest in food and food-related activities will be stronger. At mealtime children can compare the fully cooked beans with the uncooked and partially cooked product as well as with the basic food group "meat and meat alternates" (objective 4).

We have presented the nutrition concept of beans informally. However, if lesson plans were to be written and one needed a model to follow, the following is another illustration using a six-stage model.

Teaching a Nutrition Concept

Objectives 1 through 5 can be taught directly to the child, and each involves teaching a concept. The food and nutrition concepts may be taught through a modified hierarchical sequence of six steps. This is especially true for the 2- through 4-year-old. The six stages as described by Blank [1] are (1) a clear instance, (2) a clear definition of the function or attribute of the instance, (3) extension of the concept to similar instances, (4) extension of the concept to less obvious positive instances, (5) consideration of negative instances, and (6) extension of category.

In giving a preschooler a clear instance, we are in fact giving an example. We associate a word with an object. The following presents a modified version of the hierarchical sequence and examples of the use of this scheme. Whenever possible, let the child taste the example presented—regardless of how small the portion is.

MATERIALS: The food group boxes; menu with apples; red and yellow apples, preferably with stems; fresh samples or pictures of dissimilar fruits; other red fruits and vegetables (e.g., onion, red grape); pictures or models of apples and apple pie; covered can. (Figure 8–3).

Steps	Example—The Red Apple
1. Give an example.	"This is an apple; watch the apple roll; this is a big apple."
2. Give a clear definition of the function or attribute of the instance characteristic of the concept. Actions must accompany the verbal dialogue to make the concept clear to the child.	"This apple is round; it has a stem; its skin is smooth. Apples are from the fruit group." ACTIONS: Have the child feel, taste, smell, and listen to the crunchy sound of the apple. Use covered can (Figure 8–3).

3. To extend the concept to similar instances, use contrast. Choose items that are definitely dissimilar.

Use nonfood items or dissimilar food items. An apple may be compared with all the food groups other than fruit. Once again, review the characteristics of the apple.

4. To extend the concept to less obvious instances, present foods with confusing characteristics. These most often will be within food groups but may also be across groups.

Given bananas, grapes, pineapples, lemons, and a yellow apple, ask the child to find another apple. Let the child taste as many fruits as possible.

5. Consider subtle negative instances meaning that the characteristics of the food are primarily present, yet the food is different.

"Let's find something that is red and round and not an apple." Display red grapes, a red plum, red onion, or a red-orange nectarine. Let child taste even the onion.

6. Extend the category to relate to activities using the apple either at mealtime or during a special activity.

When baked or fried apples are served, the children can be asked, "How can we prepare (cook) apples?" Note that the question "What can we make with apples?" will be answered undoubtedly with "apple pie." When this happens, be prepared. Pictures of low-density foods are readily available. Have children place the picture of apple pie in the "other food group" box, thus emphasizing the low nutrient quality.

**Figure 8–3
Identifying item in
covered can by
touch.**

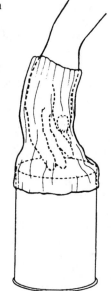

Because we have provided an example of a meat alternate (beans) and a fruit (apple), vegetables cannot be forgotten. Choose a vegetable high in nutrient quality to provide the child not only with a learning experience but also with a chance to become more familiar with a food that has a high nutrient density. Beans were chosen over other meat products because they have many nutrients that the American diet appears to need in greater quantity. In addition, dietary intake studies show that consumption of meat protein generally is adequate to high. Most homes provide children with meat products. (See preceding chapters for discussion of nutrition and foods.)

Because greens and broccoli have a high vitamin C (ascorbic acid), vitamin A, and iron content, they should be included in the educational curriculum of the preschool center. Because greens are usually less expensive than broccoli, this food has been chosen for illustration.

MATERIALS: The food group boxes; menu with greens; facilities to stir-fry greens in center*; fresh (if possible) or frozen greens, fresh broccoli, lettuce, cabbage, and celery leaves, or pictures of these foods.

Steps	Example—Greens
1. Give a clear example.	Each child is given a fresh leaf of spinach, turnip, beet, or mustard. "This food is called greens—beet greens, mustard greens, turnip greens, spinach greens."
2. Give a clear definition of the function or attribute.	"Greens are colored green; they are crisp to taste; greens are from the vegetable food group." ACTIONS: Have the children feel, taste, smell, and listen to the crispy sound of the green when they taste it raw.
3. Extend the concept to similar instances.	Use food items from other food groups (e.g., breads, milk, or meat). Compare the greens to at least one item from each of the other food group boxes. Children may select the picture from the boxes of meat, cereals, milk, and fruit. Using the vegetable box with pictures of greens and other vegetables, find a picture of greens.
4. Extend the concept to less obvious positive instances.	In a group of items having the same color or texture (e.g., lettuce, celery leaves), have the child notice the difference between beet greens, spinach greens, and turnip greens.

*The stir-fry method can be used with a frying pan in the classroom. Just use ½ tablespoon of margarine for a pound of greens, and stir in frying pan to the "crunchy cooked" stage (takes less than 5 minutes).

5. Consider negative instances.

Using broccoli, lettuce, and cabbage leaves (or models or pictures), discuss the differences between these green vegetables.

6. Extend the category.

"Let's eat these greens, raw, cooked with salad dressing, cream sauce, or margarine." Be sure greens are on the menu. Do not be concerned if the cooked (remember, crunchy cooked) greens are not hot; children prefer foods that are not hot and will eat many cooked vegetables cold.

Teaching about Nutrients

Those care providers who wish to stress nutrient content of specific foods (such as protein in meats, iron in meats, vitamins A and C in fruits and vegetables) can follow the same format. Appendix I provides the nutrient composition of most foods. A discussion of protein, fat, and carbohydrate can be found in Chapter 1 and in basic nutrition textbooks.

The Very Young Child.   With a child of 4 to 6 months (when food is first introduced) or one of 12 to 16 months (when language becomes useful), the preceding objectives are inappropriate. The child is not expected to indicate wants by pointing until approximately 15 to 18 months. Many children can, however, indicate desire for food before this time and can identify the foods they are eating by repeating or imitating care givers and the names given to the food. Therefore, with the 1-year-old child, begin with objective 1, "State names of all foods served." The child at 12 months can look at pictures of foods and hear the sound of their names, can begin to imitate words, and can and generally will follow simple instructions such as "Please eat the carrots."

Children may first need to become familiar with the food and like it before they actually eat it. With foods high in nutritive value we may have to allow the child to practice getting acquainted with the texture and flavors by frequently serving and having the child taste the food item. Infants will refuse some new foods, but given continual exposure they will accept them. This is perhaps best illustrated in breast-fed infants. When breast-fed infants are suddenly switched to infant formula, they often do not like the formula and refuse to drink it. Likewise, infants who are milk intolerant dislike being switched to soy formulas, but parents and care providers persist, since the health and well-being of the child are at stake. Eventually they "learn" to like the new formula, as older infants and toddlers learn to like a variety of foods.

Specific activities for the very young child from birth to 12 months include the following:

1. Hold the very young infant while bottle-feeding. When several infants are being cared for at the center, their feeding schedules may need to be adjusted, with parents' cooperation, so that each child can be held, just as infants who are breast-fed are held.
2. Talk to the infant and young toddler about the food in a pleasant voice while looking at the child, although the child cannot respond with verbal communication.
3. State the names of all foods and eating utensils you are using or that you let the child use; for example, "Would you like a drink of milk? Here is your blue cup. Can you take the handle of the cup? See the milk in the cup. You're drinking the milk by yourself. Good! I only put a small amount of milk into the cup, but I will give you more milk. Would you like more milk? I'll give you just a little more milk from this carton to see if you would like more milk. See, I'm pouring the milk from the carton into the blue cup. Now, I'll give you the blue cup. Can you take the blue cup? [Baby does not take the cup.] Okay, I think you've had enough milk and you don't seem to want any more milk. Perhaps later you'd like some more milk." The child needs to hear your voice and the names of food and eating utensils. Note that after the child has taken at least a taste of the food, any signal from the nonverbal child that additional food or drink is not desired should cause you to stop feeding at once.

When the toddler or older infant is accepting table foods and is fed individually, the care provider must provide a model for the child to imitate by eating the same foods.

1. Make the eating experience pleasant by allowing the child to eat the quantity desired of a variety of foods. Praise the child for trying new, less favorite foods, but expect the child to taste all foods. Refusing a food one day should signal that this food must be reintroduced in small quantities on another day.
2. Give the child finger foods as soon as the child can manipulate the foods in the hand. It is important for the child to experience the touch of the food as well as the taste. This also encourages hand-to-mouth coordination and strengthens finger manipulation. Ideas for finger-feeding have been given in previous chapters. Be sure food is appropriate (for example, cubes of cheese, crunchy cooked vegetables, dry whole-grain toast).
3. Encourage the child to share finger foods with you.
4. Be sure infant seats are fastened to table when feeding small infants, or strap the infant into the high chair securely.
5. Use dishes with sides that facilitate filling by spoon. Use spoons and forks sized for the young child.
6. Tolerate spills and learn to plan for them. Have equipment for spilled milk ready for the cleanup job. As soon as children are capable, have them participate in the cleanup activity.

The Young Toddler (12 to 24 Months)

1. Initiate objective 1. Name all foods served.
2. Let the child begin to put cup, plate, spoon, and fork on table setting.
3. Allow the child to develop self-help skills at mealtime.
4. Allow the child to help you prepare food. Children this age can mix several ingredients with spoons, and they like to taste as they explore.
5. Introduce all foods by this period, except those that may become lodged in the throat (popcorn, nuts).

The Older Toddler (24 to 36 Months)

1. Continue with objective 1. Name all foods served.
2. Begin with objectives 2 and 3. Classify and match foods eaten with the food groups.
3. The child should be able to set the table with minimal assistance.
4. The child should be able to use spoon and fork and begin using knife for spreading.
5. Provide a low cabinet drawer or shelf for unbreakable cooking utensils to use in play to imitate food preparation activities.
6. Provide a table and table-setting equipment—cups, plates, flatware—to practice table setting.
7. The child should be able to serve self from serving bowls.
8. Provide opportunity to prepare food and practice objectives 1 to 3. Prepare fresh green beans, make tossed salad, mix ingredients for fruit breads, etc.

Strategies for Incorporating Nutrition Education

Although feeding or eating times are excellent settings for nutrition education, the staff must be cautious not to make them the only setting, since nutrition education can be incorporated in the total early childhood curriculum. Careful consideration should be given to a method of curriculum construction, and a plan should be developed for implementation.

It is not unusual to see children as young as 2 years old serving themselves at mealtime in early childhood centers across the nation. They set the table and pass dishes filled with fresh vegetables and meat. They butter bread that they have baked themselves. They pour their own milk (Figure 8–4). They are joined at the table by their teachers and other staff members who engage in conversation. The children eat, giggle, and talk about their favorite foods, often discussing important nutrition concepts in the process.

Through this process, positive attitudes toward food can be developed in early childhood settings. However, only through planning based on assessment of needs of individual children and calculations of future status can you be sure that you are helping the child.

Figure 8–4   A preschooler pours milk.
Photo by Janet K. Kniepkamp.

THE MENU

The menu can be considered the major raw material in planning and implementing nutrition learning activities in early childhood education. Chapter 7 discussed use of the menu as a process for planning with the food service personnel. In this chapter, we have indicated that menu items can be used to teach basic nutrition concepts. Figure 8–5 shows the menu at the hub of many of the curriculum areas, including nutrition education.

Care providers may integrate the menu into the early childhood curriculum in a variety of ways; two approaches are presented in this chapter. In the first approach, the care provider uses a single food (in our example a raisin) to develop instruction in various curriculum areas—language, science, art, math, social studies, music, and physical education (motor development). Next, the behavioral-objective approach is used to teach skills related to personal-social, sensorimotor, language, and perceptual-cognitive areas.

Figure 8–5 The
menu as a source
for activities in all
curriculum areas.

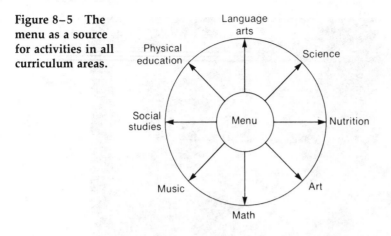

Use of Food from the Menu

When you are selecting a food for use in the curriculum, the first consideration should be its nutritional quality. To encourage the intake of nourishing foods, exposure to these foods is important. Raisins are used as the first example [11].

Class Introduction to Raisin (Pre-kindergarten)

Nutrition

> ½ cup approximate measure
> 230 kcal energy (15% of energy allowance, based on 1500 kcal)
> 2 g protein
> Trace fat
> 60 g carbohydrate
> 45 g calcium
> 3 mg iron (30% of iron allowance)

General Introduction.   Raisins can be introduced in the following way:

ACTIVITY: Let's solve a mystery.

MATERIALS: Menu with raisins, opaque container with holes, raisins, clear glass or plastic container with water, and clear glass or plastic container (empty).

PROCEDURE: Have each member of the class smell raisins that have been placed in an opaque container with holes in the lid. Ask them not to guess what is in the container until everyone has smelled the raisins. Then ask those who think they know to raise their hands but not to name the mystery item. (About half of some 4-year-old groups will have no idea what they have smelled.) Then have the class members close their eyes. Hand each child a few raisins and have them describe the mystery item. Such observations may be "small," "squishy," "soft," "round," and even "square": one child squished the raisin into a perfect cube after hearing classmates agree that raisins were round. After much discussion, ask the children to open their eyes to check their identification. Discuss such additional questions as: "What color is a raisin? How big is it? Is it smooth? What do you do with it?" Finally, ask, "What does it taste like?" Following the discussion, the children again can close their eyes and count as several raisins are dropped into water ("plop") and then into an empty cup, noting the difference in sound. Talk about how the raisins look in the water; they do not float, but they fall more slowly than when dropped into an empty cup. At the end of the day, compare the raisins in the two cups. What happened? Are they the same color? Are they the same size? Do they float? How do they taste? Note that the raisins in water have absorbed liquid, diluting the concentration of natural sugar and making them taste less sweet than the dried product. At mealtime be sure to review and ask the children to identify raisins in other foods such as salads (menu) or raisin bread or cereal. Discuss how to prepare grapes to make raisins. Grapes may be covered with cheesecloth and set to dry in the sun. Let the children observe the changes in the grapes and try to guess what will happen next. A warm oven turned off, door ajar, may be used for drying overnight (see Science Activity).

Language Arts.   Let children discuss a variety of sensory experiences with raisins. How do they smell? (Put in opaque container with holes in lid.) How do they feel? Squishy, small, round, soft. How do they look? Black, little, bumpy, sort of shaped like an egg. How do they sound? Drop raisins in water, empty cups, on paper, and so on. How do they taste? Do different kinds have different tastes?

ACTIVITY: Mr. Raisin pictures

PROCEDURE: Have each child draw a picture of Mr. Raisin and tell you what he is doing. Write dialogue on the picture: "He's going to punch a hole through the raisin box so he can get out!" Have them make other pictures and combine these into their own Mr. Raisin book. A class may talk about iron helping to keep them strong and healthy. Mr. Raisin may be endowed with bionic powers. Ask each child to draw a series of pictures showing how a grape turns into a raisin. Let them cut these out, back them with flannel (or Velcro), and use them for their own flannel board story. How does Mr. Grape feel? What does Mr. Raisin think about when he's sitting out in the sun? For the older pre-schooler, you may use the letters in the word *raisin*. Find the same letters in the children's names on the name chart or in signs around the room. See how many words, silly or real, you can rhyme with raisin. Then write a poem or song using those words. Find words that start with the same sound and other foods, animals, and things in school that start with the same sound.

Science.   What is a raisin? A raisin is a dehydrated grape. What does dehydrated mean? It means "dried." How do you remove the water? Most commercially processed raisins are dried in the vineyard in bunches on wooden or paper trays.

ACTIVITY: Making raisins

MATERIALS: Fresh, ripe, firm seedless Thompson grapes; scales; large pan or bowl of water; plastic-coated trays or paper plates; pieces of clean cheesecloth, mosquito netting, or wire screen, large enough to cover the trays; and glass container with tight-fitting lid.

PROCEDURE: Weigh the grapes and record the weight. (Measuring weight of grapes will only be meaningful for older preschooler.) Handle carefully, as grapes bruise easily. Save a few for comparison later or be prepared to purchase grapes 4 to 5 days later for children to compare to dried grapes. Place grapes in a container of water, and wash them thoroughly. Lift the grapes from the water, and blot with a towel. Remove the grapes from the stem, and spread one layer of grapes evenly on the tray. Cover the tray with the cloth or screen to keep insects and dust from getting on the grapes. Fasten the cloth so it will not blow off. Place the tray in direct sunlight to dry, away from dirt and dust and where air can circulate freely over and under the tray. Temperatures under 80° F are not recommended. Rotate the grapes daily to help in the drying process. After 4 days test the grapes for dryness by squeezing them in your hand. If there is no moisture left in your hand and the grape springs apart when the hand is opened, they are dry enough. They should be pliable and leathery to touch. If they are not dry enough, test them again the next day. When the grapes are dry, remove them from the tray and weigh. Record the weight and compare with the first weight. Compare raisins' qualities to those of the grapes you set aside (or a fresh bunch of grapes).

Comparisons

Color	Green to brown
Form	Sphere to flat
Texture	Smooth to wrinkled
Taste	Sweet and mild to sweeter and rich

Put several raisins in a cup of water. Do they sink or float? What happens after they soak for an hour or two? Are they the same color? Size? Texture?

How long will raisins keep? In tight containers in a cool, dry place they will keep for 6 months. How long will grapes keep? In the refrigerator they will keep for 3 to 5 days.

Experiment! Try observing the effect of different locations on raisins: What happens to them in the sun, the dark, the refrigerator, the oven, and so on?

If you have pets in the classroom, find out which ones can eat raisins. One teacher reported, "For several days we had a young guinea pig in the class. The children fed him raisins and other bits of fresh fruit and vegetables. Then one day the baby went home, and papa was brought in for a day. The children were very excited and decided the raisins, with all that iron, had made him grow fast."

Art.   Raisins can be used for art projects.

ACTIVITY: Edible artwork

MATERIALS: Give the children graham crackers or large cookies, softened peanut butter or cream cheese as paste, and light and dark raisins, and let them make their own pictures—for example, funny faces. You might add nuts, cereal, coconut, or other small edibles for interest.

PROCEDURE: Use raisins for features on gingerbread men or as faces on peanut butter sandwiches. Put them on a table with a bunch of toothpicks, and let the children make raisin critters. Children can make a grapevine by drawing green scribbles and pasting on leaves and raisins (for the grapes). Or they can draw pictures of Mr. Raisin in various moods. (See suggestions in Language Arts.)

Math.   Let the children pass out and divide the completed food. Passing out the food is an excellent one-to-one math activity for very young children, and older children can work out how to share a loaf of raisin bread or 31 raisin cookies with 11 children.

Some of the best math work done with foods is in actual cooking. To follow a recipe, you must practice numeral recognition, one-to-one counting, adding and subtracting, measuring, fractions, weights and volume, and time intervals. As the children are cooking, ask them questions that will help them work out how to follow the recipe accurately. How many cups of flour have we used? How many more do we need? Of course, the answers will depend on age level.

Give the children a small cup filled with raisins and nuts. Let them sort and count. How many nuts? How many raisins? Which do you have more of? How can you make them the same? What can you do so you will have more raisins? Children enjoy eating their way through these math problems.

Give each child several raisins. Have the child find and eat the smallest and the largest. Sort the rest by size, and eat the middle one. You may have to use grapes and raisins for comparison, since often young children cannot determine small differences in size.

Have the child close his eyes and count as you drop raisins into a cup of water.

Social Studies.   The following are questions from which to develop your plans:

Which kinds.of grapes are used to make raisins? Thompson seedless, Muscat, and Black Corinth are used. (Unless you are an expert on grape varieties, buy several kinds, if available, or cut out pictures of grapes.)

What growing conditions do they require? Hot, dry summer climate at harvest time is needed. Could we grow them here?

How are grapes grown? Who grows them?

Are machines used to pick grapes?

How are grapes prepared to be dried? How are they dried? How long does it take?

Who packages them? Do they use a machine?

How are they stored?

What can they be used for?

What are the advantages of drying fruit? Where might we use dried fruits? They may be eaten during camping trips, eaten as snacks, cooked in bread, mixed in salads.

Music.   After a number of experiences with raisins, a care provider asked her preschool children to make up a song about raisins, as follows:

Kelly: Five little raisins sitting on a bench. Along came a witch and ate them.
Sarah: Started setting it to music to the tune of "Five Little Ducks Went Out to Play."

> Three little raisins sitting on a bench,
> Sitting there as quiet as could be.
> Along came a witch and ate one.
> Two little raisins sitting on a bench.
> Along came a witch and ate one.
> One little raisin sitting on a bench.
> He jumped off so the witch couldn't get him.
> Zero little raisins sitting on a bench.

If you are a 4-year-old, and you made it up yourself, that's a great song! You may write the music for the song using raisins as the musical notes.

Physical Education

Fine motor development. Any of the math or art activities requiring the picking up of individual raisins aids in fine motor development. Stabbing raisins with toothpicks for construction materials or stick people requires a good deal of coordination.

Gross motor development (raisin treasure hunt). Make a treasure map leading to a treasure of individual boxes or containers of raisins. Children can be required to crawl under tables, hop around chairs, and climb over gross motor equipment or appropriate furniture to find the treasure. You can substitute raisins for the "candy" associated with Easter, along with hard-cooked eggs.

Developmental Areas

The cognitive-interactionist approach and most other approaches to learning feature commonly emphasized areas or skills around which the objectives for a curriculum can be constructed. These areas are personal and social, sensori-motor, language, and perceptual-cognitive.

It is crucial to remember that some children are able to demonstrate all or most of the following behaviors as measured by teacher observation or objective-referenced instruments. Some children attain even higher levels of achievement, whereas others continue to progress toward mastery of some of these objectives during their primary school experience.

Personal and Social Development.   Personal and social development involves becoming aware of the environment. Children identify themselves in relation to peers and others in their surroundings. Young children depend on adults to meet their needs, and this dependence motivates children to obey parents' rules and demands. Between the ages of about 2 and 3 years, children go through a transitional period where they are seeking independence and resisting adults. This is a time when the young child attempts to make independent decisions. Personal growth is evidenced by the child's ability to be independent.

In the next stage of development, from ages 3 to 5 years, the child tries to win the approval and acceptance of peers and is becoming more sensitive to the opinions of adults. Children in this age group are friendly and cooperative. They begin to express emotions and seek solutions to problems. By seeking solutions, children learn to control their behavior.

Children need to be loved, enjoyed, and needed. Preparing food helps children to feel both useful and needed and allows direct interaction with adults. Being able to complete a task and having others enjoy the finished product contribute to the child's self-worth and provide convenient avenues for meeting basic ego needs.

Sensorimotor Skill Development.   Everything a child learns is dependent on sensorimotor skills. Sensorimotor refers to a combination of the input of sensations and the output of motor activity. It reflects the development of the central nervous system. To discover the functions of the body and its parts, the child will try all the possible muscular reactions, large muscle groups, and small muscle groups. Beginning at the head, muscle control moves to the foot in a systematic fashion. In addition, development takes place from the axis of the body outward to the periphery, the outer surfaces of the body.

The body can be used in a variety of ways during food preparation, thereby fostering the development of sensorimotor skills. Stirring, beating, slicing, roll-ing, breaking eggs, peeling, scrubbing, holding, spreading, and shaking are but a few of the movements that, with repetition, evidence gradual mastery and increased coordination (Figure 8–6).

Language Development—Receptive and Expressive.   Language development depends on past sensorimotor experiences and exposure to a variety of people,

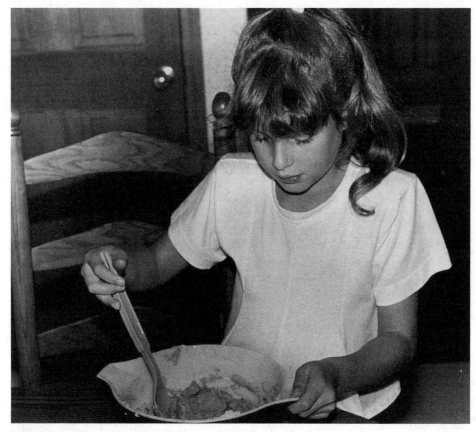

Figure 8–6 Sensory motor skills are developed in food preparation.
Photo by Janet K. Kniepkamp.

places, and things. Language is learned through imitation and reinforcement. Receptive language is language that is spoken or written by others and received by the individual. The receptive language skills are listening and reading. Expressive language is language that is used in communicating with other individuals. Speaking and writing are expressive language skills.

Between the ages of 3 and 4, children acquire the ability to comprehend most of the language they will use in conversation throughout their lives. At 3 years of age most children use 900 words; by 4 years they use about 1550.

Expressing emotions and ideas is also vital to language development. Provide stimulating situations in which the child has ample time to give opinions and to express creatively without being interrupted. Language skills will affect all endeavors in learning. Having acquired these abilities, the child will be ready to attempt other learning skills.

Food preparation and serving are heavily supported by communication. Communication begins between parent and child during feeding. Mealtime can be a prime time for language stimulation as children become older. As children

Figure 8–7   Expressive and receptive language development is facilitated while children prepare snacks.
Photo by Kevin French.

become involved in such situations as planning and preparing snacks and meals, receptive and expressive language are facilitated (Figure 8–7).

Perceptual-Cognitive Skill Development.   Cognitive learning prospers when a child is socially competent, emotionally stable, and physically healthy. Cognitive objectives represent an intertwining of creative arts, mathematics, and science skills. A young child is a natural explorer, with a built-in curiosity mechanism that wants to find out how and why. Using real situations, an adult will be able to teach mathematical and scientific concepts. The child will learn to reason and analyze, developing processes for ordering, sorting, spatial relationships, sequencing, and becoming aware of the physical environment.

Providing meaningful experiences in the three areas of creative arts—music, art, and drama—develops a child's creativeness and improves self-concept. The creative arts can also be used to develop and improve personal and social, sensorimotor, and language skills. A social skill that could be taught is distinguishing between happy and sad music; a sensorimotor skill would be clapping and marching to the beat of a song or kneading or patting bread to the sound of music. Music education should encourage all types of movements and sounds. Art allows children to exhibit their view of the world. Because children love to

Figure 8–8 Food preparation offers numerous perceptual discrimination opportunities. Photo by Robert E. Rockwell.

role-play at this stage, drama activities should be an integral part of the curriculum. Children should be allowed to express themselves by acting out a nursery rhyme or a fairy tale or putting on dress-up clothes. Food puppets can help children express feelings about food and what food contributes to their well-being.

Taking part in food preparation is a good way to help create an environment rich in perceptual stimulation and to encourage use of all sensory receptors (Figure 8–8). The smells, tastes, sounds, textures, and sights of food are varied. As children arrange raw vegetables and fruits on a plate, they are exposed to a variety of textures, shapes, colors, and odors, with unlimited opportunities to discriminate perceptually.

OBJECTIVES AND NUTRITION EDUCATION

A curriculum plan serves as a framework through which the staff can implement various approaches to achieving nutrition education goals.

Before writing any curriculum, the teacher must first possess basic knowledge and concepts of the chosen field. In this case, before attempting to write a nutrition curriculum, the care provider should know basic food and nutrition concepts (Chapters 1 to 6) and should have developed a basic educational approach.

When writing a curriculum, the teacher must take the lead in developing a plan or procedure to reach defined goals. This procedure is similar to the development of plays for a football game. In each instance, someone must do the planning, which includes identifying elements and recognizing the interrelationships that exist so that goals and objectives can be obtained at a specified time. A comprehensive system of steps in which all the elements are interrelated is vital. Steps in the system contribute to a common goal of improved nutrient intake through nutrition education.

Ten Steps

The following steps, essential in any curriculum, provide a systematic approach to instruction:

1. Developing objectives
2. Developing activities
3. Assessing entering skills
4. Choosing a teaching strategy
5. Organizing the group
6. Allocating time
7. Allocating space
8. Choosing teaching resources
9. Evaluating performance
10. Analyzing feedback

Developing Objectives.   The care provider first states in behavioral objectives what the learners should be able to do on completion of the curriculum. Learning objectives vary according to children's chronological age and developmental level. As was mentioned earlier, learning objectives are crucial to the development of an effective curriculum. The teacher must clearly define objectives for children not only to plan the curriculum but also to assess individual progress and to evaluate program effectiveness.

Early childhood programs must acknowledge developmental variability in children but be cognizant of objectives appropriate to their age level and toward which they should be progressing.

Developing Activities.   The care provider selects and develops activities that will help children attain the stated objectives. Content selection should include a variety of activities that are developmentally suitable for preschoolers.

Assessing Entering Skills.   The child's entering behavior must be evaluated. The teacher can make use of the previously developed behavioral objectives with a checklist to record the child's progress. Another approach is to develop an informal inventory to assess the child's existing knowledge of or skill in a particular area. This screening device might indicate a child's ability to define basic terms related to nutrition and the ability to describe basic concepts. For example, if all 3-year-olds can identify all the food items present, the care provider should progress to the next objective.

The essential question to be asked by the pretest is, To what extent has the child previously acquired the terms, concepts, and skills that are a part of this curriculum?

Choosing a Teaching Strategy. An approach should be chosen that will provide the teacher with a method to most effectively present learning activities. We have chosen the cognitive-interactionist approach previously discussed.

Organizing the Group. Group organization is determined by the objectives. Which objectives can be reached by the learner individually? Which objectives can be achieved only through interaction among the learners themselves? Which objectives can be achieved through a presentation by the teacher and interaction between the learners and the teacher?

Allocating Time. The teacher must estimate the time necessary to accomplish defined objectives, teaching strategies, and use of resources, considering the abilities and interest of the children. The teaching plan should take into account the estimated time for each type of activity. Yet no teacher should feel bound by any formula allocating time; rather, analyze the learning objectives and space availability and make the best use of each.

Allocating Space. Space allocation involves the decision to use or have available large spaces, small spaces, and independent learning spaces. Space should be allocated on the basis of meeting the objectives taught by the lesson.

Choosing Teaching Resources. While the teacher is the most important resource for the child, a variety of instructional materials also enable the learner to obtain knowledge.

Gerlach and Ely [12] classify resources into five general categories:

1. Real materials and people (care givers, cooks, parents, food, real things)
2. Visual materials for projection (videotapes, filmstrips, movie projectors, television, opaque projectors)
3. Audio materials (radio, recordings, tapes)
4. Printed materials (books, pictures, duplicating masters)
5. Display materials (food boxes, bulletin boards, flannel boards, chalk boards)

A good curriculum will make use of all these resource categories to provide a rich variety of learning experiences for the child.

Evaluating Performance. A vital component of the curriculum, performance evaluation asks the question, "Did the child meet the objective?" When evaluating a preschool curriculum, the teacher observes the child's behavior and actions. Evaluation by child observation is naturally enhanced by properly stated behavioral objectives.

Analyzing Feedback. The care provider asks, "Is this approach to teaching effective? Are all the elements working together as a unit to do what was originally proposed?" The care provider self-evaluates performance by continually analyzing the interaction of the children with the activities and by noting their performance evaluations. The teacher can observe not only the strong points the curriculum presents but also those areas that call for improvement. The teacher must be flexible enough to change activities or any step if the objectives are not being met.

Lesson Plans for Preschoolers

Now that you are familiar with a format for curriculum construction, you should be ready to begin the development of nutritional experiences that can be incorporated into the total early childhood program. The following plans follow the objective-oriented format. This formula can be adapted easily to any of the educational approaches previously detailed in this chapter. The activities are used with the interactionist approach, where routines are as tangible and concrete for the children as possible. An activity may be listed under one particular skill but could be applied to several.

Personal and Social Skills

Gross Motor Skills

ACTIVITY: Tacos
OBJECTIVE: Child is able to take turns and share.
MATERIALS: Taco shells, ground beef, taco seasoning and sauce, head of lettuce, cheddar cheese, onions, tomatoes.
PROCEDURE: Divide the children into five small groups. Each is responsible for a particular task in preparing the tacos. Group One—cook ground beef, adding sauce and seasoning. Group Two—heat taco shells for 10 minutes and shred the head of lettuce. Group Three—chop onions. Use a manual chopper, not a sharp knife. Group Four—shred cheese. Group Five—chop tomatoes. All children will then take turns filling the taco shells halfway with ground beef and adding toppings.
EVALUATION: Children are observed meeting the stated objectives.

Sensorimotor Development

Gross Motor Skills

ACTIVITY: Making butter
OBJECTIVE: Child moves body to rhythm of music while making butter from whipping cream.
MATERIALS: Record (any rhythm music), small jars with lids (baby food jars), whipping cream (at room temperature), salt (optional).
PROCEDURE:

1. Child or care provider pours 3 tablespoons of whipping cream into the small jars.
2. Child places lid on the jar.
3. The jar is shaken to the rhythm of the music until whipping cream turns to butter (5 to 10 minutes).
4. Liquid is poured off butter into container. Butter is put into bowl (stirring will take out additional liquid).

5. A pinch of salt is added to butter for taste.

6. Butter can be spread on crackers or bread for eating, and liquid can be drunk.

EVALUATION: Child can keep beat of music until butter is made.

Fine Motor Skills

ACTIVITY: No-bake cookies

OBJECTIVE: The child rolls, pounds, squeezes, and pulls dough.

MATERIALS: Bowl, large spoon, measuring cups, drawing-type recipe that children can read, ½ cup wheat germ, 1½ cups peanut butter, 1½ cups brown sugar, 3 cups dried milk, ¾ cup graham cracker crumbs, powdered sugar.

PROCEDURE:

1. Measure ingredients into bowl.
2. Mix ingredients with large spoon.
3. Take small amount of dough in hands and roll into small ball.
4. Roll balls in powdered sugar.

EVALUATION: Child is observed meeting the stated objective.

Kinesthetic Tactile Discrimination

ACTIVITY: Which food is missing?

OBJECTIVE: Child identifies food by touch.

MATERIALS: Ear of sweet corn, cauliflower, carrot (use items on menu), paper or cloth bag or covered can.

PROCEDURE:

1. Show children three types of food, and let them examine each by sight and touch.
2. Place the three foods in a bag or covered can.
3. Have the children remove the food you call for by touch identification only.
4. Replace the food and pass on to another group member.
5. Repeat the process.

EVALUATION: Child is observed meeting the stated objectives.

Taste-Olfactory Discrimination

ACTIVITY: Taste and touch

OBJECTIVE: Child discriminates between the following taste qualities: sweet, sour, and salty.

MATERIALS: Variety of foods to taste, including three tastes distinguishable by a preschooler (sweet—fruit; salty—apple slice with salt; and sour—pickle or lemon); pictures of food items; blindfold.

PROCEDURE:

1. Blindfold child.
2. Have child taste item.
3. Remove blindfold.
4. Have child describe what was tasted.
5. Have child find picture of what was tasted.

EVALUATION: Child is observed meeting the stated objectives.

Auditory Discrimination and Memory

ACTIVITY: Rotten potato
OBJECTIVE: The child carries out a series of three or more directions.
MATERIALS: One sheet of poster board, lined and cut into 64 equal pieces; 16 foods from each of the food groups on the cards to facilitate pairing.
PROCEDURE: Play "Rotten Potato" using the same pairing format used when playing "Go Fish."
EVALUATION: Children observed meeting the stated objective.

Visual Discrimination and Memory

ACTIVITY: Tell a story with pictures
OBJECTIVE: The child describes objects or experiences from memory.
MATERIALS: Sequence cards depicting nutritional activity.
PROCEDURES:

1. Give the child cards depicting a previous food activity.
2. Have the child arrange the cards in the proper sequence (Figure 8–9).
3. Have the child relate the story to other children.

EVALUATION: Child is observed meeting the stated objective.

Language Development (Receptive and Expressive)

ACTIVITY: Relating an experience
OBJECTIVE: Children dictate ideas in an organized, sequential pattern. This activity is to follow a field trip to an apple orchard.
MATERIALS: Newsprint, Magic Markers.
PROCEDURE: Following a trip to an apple orchard, the children dictate to the care provider their interpretation of the trip from its beginning until its end. The care provider records what the children say. This activity also helps children to listen and appreciate the contributions of others as well as enlarging their vocabulary. If the written material can be reproduced, parents enjoy seeing what the child has contributed.
EVALUATION: Children observed meeting the stated objectives.

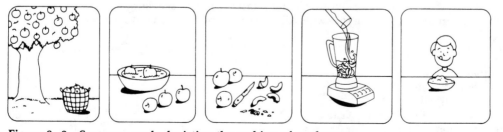

Figure 8–9   Sequence cards depicting the making of applesauce.

Cognitive Development

Mathematics and Science Skills

ACTIVITY: Outline matching
OBJECTIVE: The child matches, recognizes, and identifies a variety of shapes. The child also establishes a one-on-one correspondence through matching.
MATERIALS: Two 12 × 18 inch pieces of poster board, outlines of food items to match shapes outlined on poster board (e.g., apple, lemon, banana, grape, peanut, lettuce), small box.
PROCEDURE: Child takes food items out of box one at a time, names the item, and then attempts to place the object on its outline form. Teacher might say, "Can you find which shape this banana is on the answer board?"
EVALUATION: Child is observed meeting the stated objective.

Sets and Subsets

ACTIVITY: Choose a set
OBJECTIVE: The child identifies and constructs sets and subsets from 1 to 10.
MATERIALS: Pocket chart; numerals 1 through 5 written on top line of chart; index cards; pictures of basic food groups in 10 sets of 1, 10 sets of 2, 10 sets of 3, 10 sets of 4, and 10 sets of 5 glued on index cards.
PROCEDURE: The child counts the set on each card and matches the card with the appropriate numeral (i.e., child picks a card). Count five lemons and then place the card with five lemons on it in the pocket chart under the numeral 5.
EVALUATION: The child is observed using the number concepts.

Numeration and Place Value

ACTIVITY: Cans
OBJECTIVE: The child recognizes numerals 1 to 10.
MATERIALS: Ten tin cans, numerals 1 through 10 painted on cans, 55 peanuts in the shell.
PROCEDURE: Child puts the appropriate number of peanuts in the cans. Child then can arrange the cans in order 1 through 10.
EVALUATION: The child recognizes numerals.

Addition and Subtraction

ACTIVITY: Dry fruit mix
OBJECTIVE: The child adds by joining sets.
MATERIALS: Small paper plates for each child, dried fruit (e.g., banana slices, apricots, raisins, and apples).
PROCEDURE: Place small amounts of dried fruit mix on table in front of each child. Direct the child to put two apple slices on his plate. Now ask, "How many pieces of fruit are on your plate?" Next direct the child to add one banana slice. Then ask, "How many pieces of fruit do you have now?" or "How many pieces do you have all together?" Continue process by adding various sets according to the child's ability. When finished, let the child eat the fruit mix.
EVALUATION: Child is able to add or join sets.

Measurement

ACTIVITY: Cups
OBJECTIVE: Child identifies concepts of volume: full, half full, and empty.
MATERIALS: Clear plastic cups of various sizes, container for pouring material, pouring material (water, rice, navy beans, or cornmeal).
PROCEDURE: The teacher discusses and demonstrates the concepts of full, half full, and empty. The children are then given time to take a container and then pour the material following the teacher's or child's directions, "Give me a full cup," "Give me an empty cup," or "Give me a half-full cup." This activity can be reinforced at mealtime or snacktime.
EVALUATION: Child is observed meeting the stated objectives.

Fractions

ACTIVITY: Tangerines
OBJECTIVE: Child determines one-half of the whole or small group.
MATERIALS: Tangerines (one per child); graph with children's names, one per column, with a different color for each child's area to aid in their visualization of the graph (Figure 8–10).
PROCEDURE:

1. Have the children peel their tangerines.
2. Break the tangerines into sections.
3. Let the children count their sections and circle the corresponding number on the graph.
4. Teacher-child interaction includes comparisons: "How many in Tim's tangerine?" "How many in Mary's tangerine?" "How many pieces make a whole tangerine?" "How many pieces in half of a tangerine?"

EVALUATION: Child is observed meeting the stated objective.

**Figure 8–10
Graph for
visualizing number
concepts**

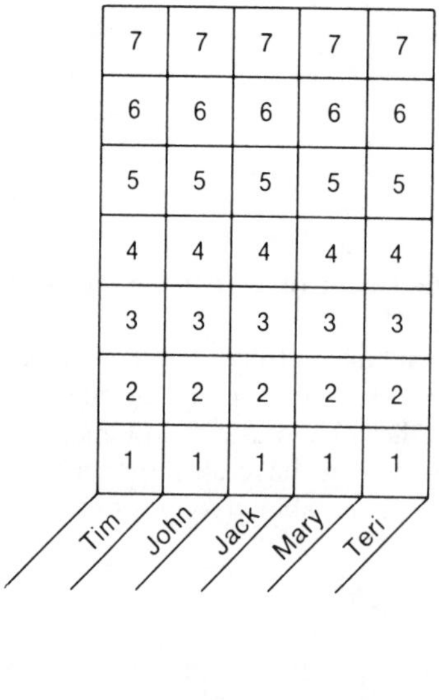

Tim	John	Jack	Mary	Teri
7	7	7	7	7
6	6	6	6	6
5	5	5	5	5
4	4	4	4	4
3	3	3	3	3
2	2	2	2	2
1	1	1	1	1

Geometry

ACTIVITY: Straight and curved
OBJECTIVE: The child recognizes straight and curved lines.
MATERIALS: An assortment of food-packaging materials (e.g., boxes, jars, cans, and bottles).
PROCEDURE:

1. The child examines the food packages.
2. The child separates the packages into two classifications—those with straight planes and those with curved planes.

EVALUATION: Child is observed meeting the stated objective.

Problem Solving

ACTIVITY: Use of a recipe
OBJECTIVE: Child uses the five senses to gather information and then communicates observations to others.
MATERIALS: Illustrated recipe, ingredients for recipe.
PROCEDURE: Give the child an illustrated recipe; see whether the child can "cook" from the recipe.
EVALUATION: Child is observed meeting the stated objective.

Creative Arts

ACTIVITY (ART): Drawing
OBJECTIVE: Child expresses a mental image, design, or happening from actual experience or verbal motivations. This activity follows a field trip to an apple orchard.
MATERIALS: Crayons (primary colors), newsprint.
PROCEDURE: Children are to draw and color their interpretations of the field trip highlights.
ADDITIONAL ACTIVITY: Children can make applesauce, then use the stems, seeds, and peelings to make a collage.
EVALUATION: Children are observed meeting the stated objective.

Sociodramatic Play

ACTIVITY: Fruit stand
OBJECTIVE: The child interprets realistic roles played by family and community members.
MATERIALS: Variety of fruits, shopping bags, a stand made from a refrigerator packing box or cardboard box of similar size, a scale.
PROCEDURE: Set up a fruit stand. Have some small boxes filled with a variety of fruits and set up a cash register, shopping bags, and a scale. After the children have purchased the fruit, they can use it as a snack.
EVALUATION: Children are observed meeting the stated objective.

As stated earlier, the curriculum serves as a guide for the teacher. Often curriculums are placed in folders, filed away, and used only when programs are evaluated or scrutinized by outside consultants. This should not be allowed to happen. A curriculum should always be open-ended. One should keep it updated with new activities and approaches.

RECIPES FOR NONREADERS

The menu, if planned with cooperation between food service personnel and care provider, is perhaps the best tool with which to teach nutrition education; creating a food product in the classroom is also exciting and fun for care provider and student. Often the first task in deciding what to cook is selecting a recipe. There are many cookbooks for children with illustrated recipes for nonreaders. However, any standard cookbook recipe may be used for cooking in the preschool center.

Use of a Recipe for Nonreaders

One of the most important lessons in reading readiness for the preschool student is that words have value. They tell us something. In a recipe, they tell us how to make something that we want to eat. The preschooler discovers that reading is something that can be personally exciting and useful.

By reorganizing, simplifying, and using illustrations, a recipe can be written so that a preschooler can read it nearly independently. A properly organized recipe gives the child such prereading skills as top-to-bottom and left-to-right sequencing. Most recipes as they appear in cookbooks do not do this. Usually the ingredients are listed, followed by a series of instructions. The teacher can rewrite the recipe on a large poster so that cooking can progress from the first to the last step in sequence (Figure 8–11). (These posters should be saved and used again and again.) After a few cooking experiences, the child will be able to help you to read the next step in sequence and will recognize the words that appear frequently on recipe posters.

The large recipe poster also teaches a variety of math concepts: numeral recognition, counting, measurement, and so on. Following the steps of a recipe gives an added dimension to the actual measuring the child is doing and gives the children who are waiting their turn something to refer to as they help count the ingredients being added. Figure 8–11 is a recipe for nonreaders for "Never-Fail Cookies," which can be made as follows:

EQUIPMENT: Cookie sheet; oven (preheat to 350° to 375° F); old newspapers for floor; waxed paper—approximately 12 × 12 inch pieces, one piece per child—or plastic bags; washcloth and water or hand-washing facilities nearby; deep cup and spoon; napkins or paper towels for eating cookies; at least 3 large bowls; 3 serving tablespoons; and 3 serving teaspoons.

INGREDIENTS: Margarine (shortening or fat); sugar (granulated or brown); flour (whole wheat) with 1 teaspoon baking powder per cup of flour; water or milk; decorative items such as raisins, coconut flakes, fruit, and nuts (chopped). Allow approximately 1½ ta-

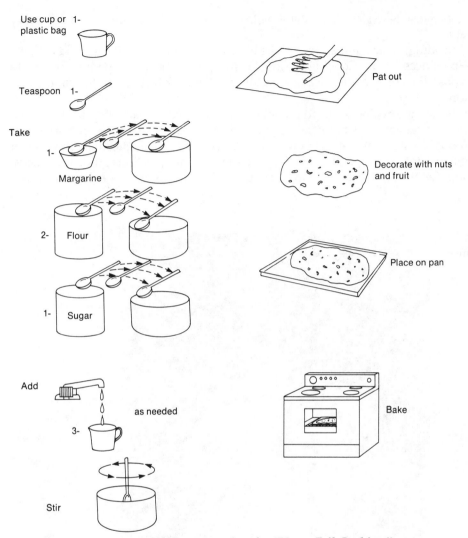

Use cup or plastic bag 1-

Teaspoon 1-

Take
1-
Margarine

2- Flour

1- Sugar

Add

3-

as needed

Stir

Pat out

Decorate with nuts and fruit

Place on pan

Bake

Figure 8–11 A recipe poster for nonreaders for "Never-Fail Cookies."

blespoons of the ingredient per child (e.g., 10 children = 1 cup fat, 1 cup sugar, and 1¼ cups flour).

PROCEDURE: The child takes a spoon of each of the ingredients from the bowls and places it on waxed paper. The child then makes one cookie and puts it on the cookie sheet. The teacher observes and adds more liquid or flour as needed. The cookies may be marked with a slip of paper. Have children help put cookies into oven. Bake 15 to 20 minutes. After cookies are cool, children can remove them to a plate. Sit at a table or in a circle to review activities for children, and let children explain what they have accomplished.

NOTE: A "never-fail muffin" can be made using the same principles. The child should add eggs (one or two), milk, and raisins, nuts, or fruit to the batter. The batter must be thinner, and the child uses bowl and spoon. Personal experiences with 3-year-olds indicate that they can accomplish this task! (No matter what the product looks like, they eat it!)

Reading, math, and science skills have much more value if the child actually experiences them. Cooking affords this opportunity. A recipe allows you to expose the child to a number of specific academic skills without formal instruction.

In using a recipe with preschoolers, do not belabor each step or insist that they understand each concept (Figure 8–12). Treat the recipe as a tool. For example, say, "Let's see what we do first." Ask occasional questions about what you are doing, and let the children's comments and questions guide the discussion. Let the equipment and ingredients be the tools to stimulate the discussion.

Figure 8–12 A child learns from experience.
Photo by Robert E. Rockwell.

COOKING IN THE CLASSROOM

Relatively few early childhood programs have child-sized cooking facilities; therefore, electrical appliances are frequently used. When using electrical appliances, be sure that the equipment is in proper working order. It is dangerous to allow children to stand on stools and chairs to do stove-top cooking in the kitchen. No matter where cooking is done or how, safety precautions must be emphasized, and supervision is imperative. Children can be taught the precautions to use around cooking equipment. Sharp knives should be kept by the teacher. The children can be taught how to use them properly for slicing, cutting, or chopping but only under close supervision. There will undoubtedly be some burns and cuts, but it is hoped that with adequate supervision these will not be serious. If a child should get burned or cut, administer first aid immediately.

Of course, along with food preparation comes cleanup. Children can and should be involved in the various cleanup chores, which vary from wiping counter tops and tables to washing, rinsing, and drying dishes. The degree of involvement in cleanup will depend on the facilities and legal requirements.

SUMMARY

- The development of thought and the process of learning are significantly influenced by a child's interactions with objects and persons in the environment. Nutrition may be learned through a curriculum that provides enriching experiences and materials and encourages interaction and exploration for the developing child.
- Four major approaches to early childhood education are cognitive-interactionist, academic skills, traditional nursery school, and perceptual-motor. Any of the methods can be used to successfully teach nutrition education concepts to children.
- The cognitive-interactionist method approaches cognitive ability as a process that develops in a predictable way. This process is separated into three major categories, according to Piaget. The sensorimotor stage ranges from birth to 24 months, the preoperational stage ranges from 2 to 6 years, and the concrete operations stage ranges from 7 to 11 years. Concepts play an important role in cognitive development. The care provider is extremely important in guiding and forming sound concepts.
- The cognitive development approach incorporates a variety of diverse types of programs. Common to all the approaches is the emphasis on the development of cognitive skills and abilities such as understanding and using language, concept formation, association, and discrimination, problem solving, and memory.

- There is no one best approach to learning for all children. Six important programmatic insights are presented as applicable to any approach to learning. The child-care worker is encouraged to choose and develop a program that will maximize the development of the group under consideration.
- The basic goal of the nutrition education program is to establish a lifetime pattern of eating a well-balanced daily diet.
- Teaching based on the food groups and the menu can help lead the child to accepting and eventually eating a wide variety of nourishing foods.
- The optimal time for teaching nutrition concepts directly to young children is just before a meal or snack, since the interest in food-related activities will be stronger.
- A hierarchical six-stage sequence for teaching a concept to young children was developed by Blank. The food and nutrition concepts may be taught through a modified version of this hierarchy. The six stages consist of giving a clear instance, giving a clear definition of the function or attribute of the instance, extending the concept to similar instances, extending the concept to less positive instances, considering negative instances, and extending the category.
- The very young child (birth to 18 months) can benefit from verbal stimulation provided by the care provider. Hearing the voice describe foods and eating utensils during mealtime enriches the eating experience of the young child. The older infant or toddler learns through observation of the care provider, who provides a model of appropriate nutrition and eating practices.
- By integrating food and nutrition concepts into various curriculum areas, the total early childhood curriculum can be used and enhanced.
- The menu can be considered the major raw material in planning and implementing learning activities in early childhood education.
- The major consideration in selecting a food for use in the curriculum should be the nutritional quality of the food.
- Curriculum objectives for preschool programs usually emphasize the following areas of development: personal and social, sensorimotor, language, and perceptual-cognitive.
- To write an effective nutrition curriculum, one must possess a knowledge of food and nutrition concepts.
- A systematic approach to instruction must be operational for a curriculum to be successful. The elements involved must be recognized as interrelated; steps in the system contribute to improved nutrient intake through nutrition education.
- Teaching preschoolers that words have value is very important for reading readiness. A recipe can be rewritten by simplifying, reorganizing, and including symbols or illustrations to facilitate the child's reading and understanding of it.

- An important component of nutrition education is safety during food preparation. Safety precautions should be emphasized, and supervision is imperative.

DISCUSSION QUESTIONS

1. Discuss the similarities and differences of the four programmatic approaches used in early childhood programs.
2. Name the program characteristics of the cognitive-interactionist approach.
3. List six programmatic insights to be gained in using any approach to learning.
4. What is the basic goal of the nutrition education program? Name an objective that would be representative of this goal.
5. Describe how the food groups can be used to present nutrition education activities in early childhood centers.
6. Using Blank's hierarchical stages, select and describe a nutrition concept as you would present it to a group of preschoolers.
7. List the activities that would be appropriate to teach good nutrition principles to the very young child (6 months to 2 years).
8. Explain how mealtime experiences can function as settings for nutrition education.
9. Why is the menu considered the major raw material in planning and implementing learning activities in early childhood education?
10. Discuss the importance of selecting foods high in nutrient density for use in the curriculum.
11. Name and explain the four developmental areas used to integrate food and nutrition activities into the learning environment.
12. List and describe the steps involved in a systematic approach to instruction.
13. How are learning objectives crucial to the development of an effective curriculum?
14. Explain how you would convert a recipe from a standard cookbook into one that would stimulate learning in preschoolers.
15. List some precautions to be observed when cooking in the classroom.

REFERENCES

1. Blank, M.: Teaching learning in the preschool—dialogue approach, Columbus, OH, 1983, Merrill/Macmillan Publishing Co.
2. Leeper, S. H., Witherspoon, R. R., and Day, D. B.: Good schools for young children, ed. 5, New York, 1984, Macmillan Publishing Co.
3. Spodeck, B., Saracho, O. N., and Davis, M. D.,: Foundations of early childhood education, teaching three, four and five year old children, ed. 2, Englewood Cliffs, NJ, 1991, Prentice-Hall, Inc.

4. Mayer, R. S.: A comparative analysis of preschool curriculum models. In Anderson, R. H., and Shane, H. G. (eds.): As the twig is bent, Boston, 1971, Houghton Mifflin Co.

5. Ginsberg, H., and Opper, S.: Piaget's theory of intellectual development, ed. 3, Englewood Cliffs, NJ, 1988, Prentice-Hall, Inc.

6. Flavell, J. H.: Concept development. In Mussen, P. H. (ed.): Carmichael's manual of child psychology, col. 3, vol. 1, New York, 1970, John Wiley & Sons, Inc.

7. Hohmann, M.: A study guide to young children in action, exercises in the cognitively oriented preschool curriculum, Ypsilanti, MI, 1983, The High Scope Press.

8. Morrison, G. S.: Early childhood education today, Columbus, OH, 1988, Merrill/Macmillan Publishing Co.

9. MacFadder, D. N. (ed.): Early childhood development programs and services: planning for action, Washington, DC, 1972 Publications, Department National Association for the Education of Young Children.

10. Lasser, G.: The need for diversity in day care. In Grotberg, E. (ed.): Day care: resources for decisions, Washington, DC, 1971, Office of Planning, Research, and Evaluation.

11. Clemens, B.: Presentation in elementary education 422 health and nutrition class, Edwardsville, 1976, Southern Illinois University.

12. Gerlach, V. S., and Ely, D. P.: Teaching and media: a systematic approach, ed. 2, Englewood Cliffs, NJ, 1980, Prentice-Hall, Inc.

SUGGESTED READINGS

Cook, R. E., Tessier, A., and Armbruster, V. B.: Adapting early childhood curricula for children with special needs, ed. 2, Columbus, OH, 1987, Merrill/Macmillan Publishing Co.

Elkind, D.: Child development and education—a Piagetian perspective, New York, 1976, Oxford University Press, Inc.

Hendrick, J.: The whole child, Columbus, OH, 1988, Merrill/Macmillan Publishing Co.

Hendrick, J.: Total learning: developmental curriculum for the young child, ed. 3, Columbus, OH, 1990, Merrill/Macmillan Publishing Co.

Margerey, A., Worsley, A., and Boulton, J.: Children's thinking about food: 1. Knowledge of nutrients, J. Nutr. 43:1, 2–8, 1986.

Margerey, A., Worsley, A., and Boulton, J.: Children's thinking about food: 2. Concept development and beliefs, J. Nutr. 43:1, 9–16, 1986.

Marotz, L., Rush, J., and Cross, M.: Health safety and nutrition for the young child, Albany, NY, 1989, Delmar Inc.

Rockwell, R. E., Sherwood, E. A., and Williams, R. A.: Hug a tree and other things to do outdoors with young children, Mt. Rainier, MD, 1983, Gryphon House, Inc.

Rockwell, R. E., Williams, R. A., and Sherwood, E. A.: Everybody has a body, science activities from head to toe, Mt. Rainier, MD, 1992, Gryphon House, Inc.

Sherwood, E. A., Williams, R. A., and Rockwell, R. E.: More mudpies to magnets—science activities for young children, Mt. Rainier, MD, 1990, Gryphon House, Inc.

Williams, R. A., Rockwell, R. E., and Sherwood, E. A.: Mudpies to magnets—a preschool science curriculum, Mt. Rainier, MD, 1987, Gryphon House, Inc.

Wolfgang, C., and Wolfgang, M. E.: School for young children, developmentally appropriate practices, Needham Heights, MA, 1992, Allyn Bacon.

9

Parent Involvement in Nutrition Education

LEARNING OBJECTIVES

Students will be able to:

- Describe the value of parent involvement in early childhood nutrition programs.
- List several methods of contacting parents regarding the nutrition education program.
- Identify and describe ways in which parents' contributions of time and talent can be used for nutrition education programs.
- Describe the need for evaluation of parent-involvement programs.
- Identify and describe methods of recognizing parent contributions of time and talent.

The child masters many skills during the first 8 years of life. Learning to eat is one of the most important. What the parent learns about nutrition, food, food preparation, and the importance of mealtime in the home all help to mold the child's food habits and attitudes.

Early childhood programs provide an excellent setting for nutrition education for the entire family. Therefore, it seems only practical that some ideas and approaches for working effectively with parents be discussed (Figure 9–1).

The increasing interest in parent involvement at both the preschool and elementary school levels has gained momentum over the past two decades. Involving parents in their children's education is hardly a new concept. Since at least the 1960s, the value of parental participation has been recognized in federal law, which mandated that parents be partners in a host of programs funded by the U.S. government. The Education of All Handicapped Children Act of 1975 gave parents a pivotal role in planning, implementing, and monitoring their children's education. The Federal Head Start initiative put parents in the classroom. Parents advisory councils also have been codified in such programs as Chapter I compensatory education. There is no question that federal programs have put and have continued to put parent involvement on the agenda of early childhood programs. The major focus of this emphasis has been founded on the theory that if the school and parents work together as partners, the result will be success for the child at school [1].

WHY INVOLVE PARENTS?

Parents and early childhood programs need to be involved with each other because they have a common element—children. The home and preschool are important functional areas for the young child. To assist the child and to provide

**Figure 9-1
Nutrition education
involves the entire
family.**
Courtesy of USDA.

the most effective learning environment, both preschool and home must be in cooperation, pulling together to benefit the child. Lack of cooperation and understanding between the two forces most instrumental in a young child's development can serve only to foster frustration and anxiety. Explicit conflict of purposes may result. When parents participate, the child knows the parents care enough to become involved. Lines of communication are open because there is an additional bond. The early childhood nutrition program can provide an avenue to unite parent and child in sound nutrition practices.

In a position statement on nutrition standards in day-care programs, the American Dietetic Association stresses, "Day care providers should develop and implement a nutrition education plan that will help children, parents, families, and personnel involved in the care of children make informal decisions affecting their health and well being"[2].

A by-product of parental involvement is that parents themselves benefit. The sense of being needed and useful is evident among those parents who have become involved in various center programs. There is a sense of giving of oneself. At the same time, parents learn how they may best help their youngsters at home, how they can provide a nutritious meal and snacks, or exciting ways in which they can introduce new foods.

Finally, the children's care providers benefit from parental involvement. For example, parent contributions of time and talent often free teachers for instruction and perhaps allow more time for individualization. In addition, parents provide a basis for a more thorough understanding of a child and the child's nutritional habits, thereby assisting the teacher in providing a stimulus to help the child acquire better food habits. The answer to why early childhood programs should seek to involve parents is to enhance the overall development of the children.

First Steps in Getting Parents Involved

If it is agreed that parent involvement is beneficial to children, how can early childhood educators encourage such parent participation in the nutrition program? Where does a teacher begin? Which methods may be worth trying? The following sections give several methods of initiating parent involvement. One or several of the methods may be used to motivate participation in children's learning experiences about food. Modifications and adaptations for specific neighborhoods and their specific needs must be made, of course, but taking advantage of these ideas should result in some forward movement in parent-teacher cooperation.

Informal Contacts.   Most of the initial contacts with parents can be made on an informal basis. Some will be incidental, a matter of taking advantage of a given situation. Perhaps when a parent stops by to pick up a child for a doctor appointment, if time permits, a teacher should move toward the door with a smile and at least say a few words about the eating activities of the child. In casual conversations so often parents say, "If there is anything I can do, please let me know." They do not really expect the teacher to say, "As a matter of fact, there is something you can do." But the gate is open, and a teacher or director can step in with a simple way in which that parent can assist the child or the program.

The same procedure of openness and friendly conversation can be used during a center open house, parent-teacher conference periods, and parent meetings. When parents feel at ease and get the idea that their child will benefit, they are more willing to contribute their time and talent.

Registration.   Another opportunity for the center to encourage parent participation occurs at registration. If a parent is asked to fill out a registration form, a simple and general statement such as "I will volunteer to help the center in food and nutrition activities (yes _____ no _____)" might be included. Or an open-ended statement such as "I will volunteer to assist my child in the program by _____" could be used. If a secretary or teacher fills out a registration form while interviewing the parents, willingness to help could be ascertained through casual conversation. However, the interviewer must be careful to broach the subject in a matter-of-fact way so that the parent feels no pressure to participate.

Telephone Calls.   Telephone calls offer an opportunity for personal conversation with the parents. Parents are often afraid when they receive calls from the teacher. This is the result of past experiences when only bad news was communicated from the school to the home [3]. This tradition can be changed by setting aside a short period each day to make phone calls to parents. Initial calls can include information about who you are, why you are calling, and a short personal anecdote about the child. Health and nutritional concerns can also be shared. Such phone calls take only a few minutes each, but they let the parents know of a teacher's or director's interest in and knowledge of their child [4].

Resource Person.   Once the children are in the classroom, the teacher should be alert to any comments they might make about what their parents do. For example, if a child casually mentions that his family has beehives in the backyard, the teacher should determine through reviews of the records or even a phone call to the parents whether the family would be willing to share their special interest. Perhaps the parents have some slides, a beehive, or just some frames with honey on them to show the children. They might enjoy bringing samples of honey for the children to taste or sitting and talking with the children about bees. The teacher might provide pictures or slides so the learning situation would be a cooperative effort. Many parents have skills or hobbies in which children are interested, and they might be flattered to be asked to share them in the center. It may be necessary for the teacher to reassure them and to preplan together, but parents are often fine resources for specific areas of study and should never be overlooked.

A Special Letter.   A direct way to find out whether parents are willing volunteers is to send a letter telling them that their help is needed. Specific tasks for which they could volunteer should be included in an interest inventory that accompanies the letter. The inventory should provide an open-ended section to enable the parent volunteer to suggest activities that may not have been listed. Frequently parents are most willing to volunteer their talents, but when asked to list them, they respond in a limited manner.

Notes and Happy-Grams.   Notes written by the teacher and carried home by the child are a most effective form of communicating with the home. These notes should never be hastily scratched criticisms of the child or his work. Notes are a useful means of communicating positive, personal observations and anecdotes about the child. Often meal-time conversations abound with items that can be shared with a parent; i.e., "Christine tried kiwi fruit today and loved it. She said, 'It tastes like strawberries and watermelon mixed together!' " [4].

Orientation.   Just a few days before the beginning of a program year, all parents may be invited to attend an informal "get-acquainted-with-our-room" program orientation. Each parent is invited to the center and meets with the teacher and all the other parents. The teacher presents the routine for activities as well as the food and nutrition program. During this time the teacher extends an invitation for parental assistance and has a prepared list of some kinds of activities for which help is needed. For example, if parent aides are to be used daily for eating activities, a sign-up sheet should be available. Those parents who would like to go on field trips or who could provide transportation could sign another sheet so labeled. The teacher might merely keep a list of those who say they would like to help and then determine later which specific contribution the parent might prefer. However, advanced planning helps parents commit their time.

Standardized Informational Techniques.   Techniques for exchanging information between the parents and the care provider must be standardized and clear, particularly in infant programs. Nutritional information passed between the home and center always involves the accurate recording of daily and nightly occurrences such as times of feeding and types and amounts of food. In addition, naps, diaper changes, amount of sleep, unusual behavior, and home routines are recorded on standardized forms (see Appendixes 9–A, 9–B, 9–C, 9–D, 9–E). Sharing information helps to establish a sense of trust and a partnership between the home and the center as it contributes to an accurate 24–hour record of the child's health and well-being.

Newsletter.   Another method of maintaining home-center contact is the newsletter. A monthly newsletter can include a copy of the menus and the activities that have been used to help children "get to know" the foods on the menu. The newsletter also provides an opportunity to list materials needed from home for classroom activities involving food, to present recipes used, and to solicit recipes parents have used with children. Nutrition information may also be included.

Parent Teacher Conferences.   Parent-teacher conferences provide the time and the opportunity for parents and teachers to consider together all aspects of a child's overall development including health and nutritional concerns. It is an opportunity that establishes or furthers a sense of working together with shared information and common goals. The teacher has the responsibility for setting the tone of a partnership at this meeting by preparing parents for their participatory role, guiding and encouraging them by the use of questions and active listening. Careful planning, evaluation, and follow-up of conferences all work together to make this a productive experience for both the parents and the teachers [4].

Home Visits.   The most time-consuming method of contact with parents, but probably the most successful and beneficial to all, is the home visit. It takes a special type of teacher—one who is extroverted and personable—to call on parents in the home. The first visit should be brief and introductory and should provide a basis for future participation and involvement in all aspects of the program. During such visits, which preferably are arranged ahead of time, it is imperative that the teacher convey understanding and interest in the child and his family. During the visit it may become apparent that the family does not have the financial resources to supply the child with a wide variety of food experiences, as has been advocated in earlier chapters. However, use of the food stamp or commodity program can help the family continue the nutrition education objectives of the center.

Ways in Which to Use Parent Contributions

Once parent-center contacts have been made—and this may be a continuing process throughout the year—initiation of actual involvement must begin. Parent contributions will be more meaningful if parents are given an opportunity to plan with the care provider those areas that they mutually believe can be of benefit to the program. One goal for the care provider is to be organized but not so static that parents think their suggestions and ideas are not welcomed. In presenting options to the parent, the care provider may wish to organize activities into the following categories. It should be noted that contributions listed in one area may also be pertinent to another category of parent-care giver cooperation.

1. Ways in which parents may assist children during center hours
2. Ways in which parents may work with materials and equipment during center hours
3. Ways in which parents may contribute time and effort to the program after center hours
4. Ways in which parents may participate without leaving their homes

Assisting Children During Center Hours.   The following listing offers some ideas for parental assistance with children in the child-care center. Some parents may want and need on-the-job training. Remember that some states may require a health examination for all persons helping with preparation of food. It is important to capitalize on parents' strengths, hobbies, and interests. For example, someone who has worked as a food service employee in a restaurant would have contributions to make concerning food preparation and occupational information about food. Parents may participate in the following ways:

1. Supervise and contribute to learning centers
    a. Talk with children to develop language skills; that is, discuss food concepts following procedure described in Chapter 8; supervise games; tell and read stories about foods to children; listen to children read aloud
    b. Demonstrate and supervise a garden plot
    c. Demonstrate and supervise a cooking center
    d. Lead and supervise science and mathematics as food-related activities
2. Share hobbies and demonstrate how they are done (as food related)
3. Share and demonstrate career information (as food related)
4. Prepare snacks and interact with children during eating times (Figure 9–2)
5. Prepare basic mixes with children (Chapter 7) or for food service personnel
6. Supervise bathrooms and handwashing, especially before mealtime and food preparation activities
7. Share cleanup of kitchen equipment, table, and chairs with the children, or assist food service personnel

Figure 9–2   Parents can assist and interact with children.
Photo courtesy of USDA.

Working with Materials and Equipment During Center Hours. There are many ways that parents can assist at the center during, before or after class hours; however, they will need a place to do their work. We suggest a parent resource room. This room is a place within the school where parents can meet, show information, work and relax. The room can be equipped with comfortable chairs, tables, coffee pot, hot plate, telephone, typewriter, and a bulletin board. Parents and teachers can plan together about how to design, stock, and use the room. Some suggested tasks might be:

1. Typing menus
2. Taking pictures of food and making food displays or scrapbooks
3. Laminating materials, such as food pictures, child developed recipe books, and recipe cards
4. Making food boxes for the center
5. Arranging for field trips to food-producing sites, manufacturers, and sellers.
6. Recruiting, orienting, and training parent volunteers
7. Typing and copying monthly menu and activity calendars

The parent room implies that parents are expected to be a part of the program. This is a place for them to stop and a base from which they can reach out in their involvement.

Contributing Time and Effort at School After Center Hours. One of the most common forms of parent-teacher contact takes place at parent-teacher conferences. However, informal committees, discussion groups, and personal phone calls may provide for parent-teacher cooperation, too. Workshops are especially enjoyable and provide an inviting format for the care provider to offer information regarding basic nutrition, how nutrition objectives are met in the center program, and how the parents can work cooperatively with the staff to achieve objectives.

Early in the year, possibly even before the program starts, a teacher should list a number of activities that parents might work on during workshops. The list should be long enough so that an element of choice is offered to the parents at each gathering. Some of the following ideas might be considered and specific tasks planned around them:

1. Inviting nutritionists and other health professionals from the local health department, hospitals, and other community agencies to discuss basic nutrition concepts. It is important that these discussions
   a. Be organized, with the presentation of basic nutrition concepts first as a home foundation to the use of food and nutrition.
   b. Directly involve parents with hands-on nutrition experiences (Appendix 9–F presents a guideline for preplanning, conducting, and evaluating a nutritionally oriented family workshop.)

2. Creating work jobs, games, and toys that can be used in nutrition education, for example, preparing pocket charts for categorizing and classifying
food items, pictures and designs for a food bulletin board, or taste jars (for
additional ideas, see Chapter 8)
3. Meeting with care givers and food service personnel to plan menus that
can demonstrate the teaching of specific nutrition concepts
4. Inviting parents to share with professionals the importance of physical
activities as related to food consumption
5. Sharing nutritious recipes, that is, recipes with high nutrient density
6. Sharing activities that parents have used to encourage their children to
accept a wide variety of foods

Parent Advisory Committee.   Some programs may find parent advisory boards
advantageous. This form of parent participation offers parents an opportunity to
become involved as joint decision-makers. This committee is in constant touch
with all phases of the program. It is critical that parents who serve as members
receive continuous training regarding relevant program information to enable
them to become knowledgeable as well as effective policy and decision makers.
The PAC is a credibility link—a positive step in successful communication and
collaboration between parents and staff members. Parents should be free to
suggest and recommend anything, but final authority and decision making
probably should remain with the professionals, those trained educators who are
responsible for all of the children at the center. This is particularly true of decisions about curriculum or specific individual behavior problems. In addition,
parents should not be allowed to have access to an individual child's records or
to discuss a specific child's problems, especially if names or the data being
discussed would identify the child. Those responsibilities must be retained by
the care givers and administrators.

Participating Without Leaving the Home.   One important way in which parents
may participate at home is to help the child with developmental activities. The
care provider may list activities or games that provide nutrition experiences and
readiness for later learning. For example, a care provider may suggest some of
the following for follow-up activities to strengthen nutrition principles learned
in the centers.

1. While walking through a store together, talk to your child about the various products and their uses.
2. Look around the house for objects or foods whose first letters sound
alike—cup, can, cap; pickle, pear, peach, pineapple.
3. Encourage your child to talk with you about food.
4. While preparing food, allow your child to help.
5. Let child share in cleanup activities.

6. Test new food activities at home. Provide feedback to teacher on strengths and weaknesses of activities.

Only imagination will limit the number of ways in which parents may help their children at home. The suggestions will vary from year to year and community to community, although some may be duplicated. Ideally, they would vary from child to child, so the suggestions would be geared to individual needs. Several short lists of ideas sent home at different times are more effective than one long list at the beginning of the year. Some of the same activities may be discussed during casual conversations or even at workshops, if parents express an interest. The purpose is to help parents realize they may take advantage of incidental learning opportunities as they arise.

Often parents are willing to help children in the center but cannot take time away from home. Perhaps they work full-time or have younger children at home. Perhaps a handicap prohibits them from coming to the center. Nonetheless, there are ways in which these parents may be encouraged to help provide a better learning environment for their children.

Lending Library.   A lending library provides educational toys, books, and activities for children and parents to use together. A lending library is similar to the public library concept with the exception that materials are selected for inclusion in the lending library to provide a broad range of learning activities related to school readiness, and/or it includes books, toys, cassette tapes, tape players, and manipulatives. Parents and teachers work together to choose items that will be developmentally appropriate and useful to the individual child. If a parent is unable to come into the library, he or she may telephone or send a note and the materials will be sent home with the child. The lending library can also include a parent resource section with books, magazines, and videotapes on various parenting issues. Some lending libraries also have TV/VCR units that can be loaned to parents to view parenting tapes. The lending library is an excellent means of providing nutrition awareness to the entire family [4].

Calendars.   An activity calendar can be sent home at the beginning of each month. It can include simple daily activities that the parents and the child can do at home. The activities correspond with what is happening in the daily curriculum. The daily menu for a one-month time frame can also be shared.

Snacks and Treats.   Teachers frequently request that parents provide snacks and treats for birthdays and holidays. High-calorie foods with few nutrients are most often sent. This problem can only be avoided by developing a policy that endorses the provision of nutritious foods for party times. Parents, teachers, and children can work together to develop the party snack list, which can be presented to parents in a letter or a parent handbook at the beginning of the school year. Appendix 9–G provides an example of a letter that can be sent to parents as well as a list of nutritious treats parents and children can prepare at home.

EVALUATION OF PARENT INVOLVEMENT

A simple method to help evaluate the effectiveness of parental participation is to keep attendance records from workshops, discussion groups, and programs. Of course, such statistics on attendance cannot indicate the quality of participation; they indicate only the number of participants. Although exposure of parents to program purposes and activities may be advantageous, evaluation should not be based exclusively on program turnout [5].

Evaluating the quality of participation is much more difficult than counting noses or calculating percentage of parent participation. Both long-range (perhaps yearly) and short-range (daily) objectives need to be considered. Observations and discussions between parents and care givers, possibly with checklists, are means of informal evaluation. Parent grievances to administrators and care givers may indicate areas toward which improvement efforts need to be directed. All these sources of evaluative information should be used.

Each area of parent-school involvement must be evaluated. For example, after a parent acts as a volunteer, the parent and the care giver should immediately review both positive and negative points of that particular day's activities. The aim is to improve the quality of interaction on succeeding days. Neither parent nor care provider should be afraid of criticism, which needs to be given and accepted in a positive way.

Evaluations of clerical tasks should be done in two ways, one aimed at the self-fulfillment of the participant and the other at the quality of work. Do the participants feel useful and needed? Excessive typographical errors cannot be tolerated, nor can equipment constantly in need of repair because of mishandling. If the clerical chores involve total class interruptions, then alternate methods of completing the tasks must be created. Wastefulness of materials might be noted, also. As with other areas of evaluation, any benefit must be a result of frank and open discussion between parent participant and care giver.

After workshops or programs, a short, informal checklist could be passed to each parent in attendance. They should be encouraged, but not required, to fill it out. Questions might include: "Was this gathering worth your time and effort? What did you like about it? What did you dislike about it? Was it too long? Too short? Just right? What would you like to do at a future meeting? How could our gatherings be improved?" (If there were an outside resource person or persons, a question such as, "Would you invite him or her back? Why not?" might be included.) Parents need not sign their names. From these informal instruments some worthwhile suggestions for improvement of a parent-participation program may be forthcoming.

The teacher and care provider might use a checklist to help evaluate their own involvement with parents. Such a list might be scanned several times a year as a reminder of some important points to remember when cooperating with parent volunteers [5].

1. Am I a good listener?
2. Do I try to make parents feel needed?
3. Have I given personal recognition in the form of compliments and notes to all participants? Have I had the children send thank-you notes? Would a year-end recognition coffee session be useful?
4. Do I try to learn about each parent's interests, hobbies, or work so that each may contribute according to his or her strengths and training?
5. Do I accept all suggestions for activity and discuss programs and problems openly?
6. Do I preplan alone or with the parents?
7. Am I a dictator?
8. Do I keep all meetings and workshops informal and encourage interaction?
9. Do I keep parents informed through meetings, newsletters, notes, or phone calls?
10. Do I provide baby-sitting and transportation services if needed for greater participation?
11. Have I elicited cooperation and understanding of the center administration?
12. Am I careful not to discuss children in front of their parents? Am I sure all records are confidential and unavailable to any parents?
13. Am I aware that some parents may force their views on others?
14. Do I believe there are too many interruptions in the center when parents are involved?
15. Do I expect every parent to be involved? Do I exploit their generosity of time, talent, and effort?

At the end of the year, suggestions for improving the program should be solicited from all parent participants—clerical aides, parent resources, and home participants. A letter could be sent home and returned with each child. Some portions of the programs may be dropped, others added, and some modified according to the combined responses of parents, children, director, and care giver.

RECOGNITION

Every parent volunteer, regardless of the time devoted to the program, should receive frequent praise and encouragement for service. Parents can gain much satisfaction when they believe they have been accepted as colleagues by their coworkers. Another form of satisfaction results when parents believe they have contributed to the progress and growth of an individual child or group of children. Teachers must make a continual effort to express their acceptance of the volunteers and the skills they are contributing.

A special "thank you" is in order for the parents. This can be done at a meeting where the main order of business is the public recognition of parents for their services. Some form of tangible recognition is recommended: a certificate of appreciation, a letter of congratulations, a "good egg award," a happy-gram. It should be something the volunteer can take as a memento of the experience [6]. Newspaper and television coverage of the awards and recognition ceremonies can be helpful in drawing public attention to the program.

Recognition, no matter which form it takes, is essential. A single thank-you as the parent volunteer leaves is a courtesy that will pay dividends. A parent volunteer who enjoys the work is thanked in many ways. The general reception and attitude that the staff expresses toward the volunteer is a form of recognition. In addition, the parent volunteer represents the people of the community. When we recognize the volunteer, we recognize the community.

Parents, care givers, and children may all benefit from effective participation based on clear-cut objectives and goals. It is natural that as the year progresses, more and more responsibility and freedom may be allowed parent participants, according to their responsiveness and abilities. Effective participation grows like a seed, a little each day. If properly nurtured, it produces fine fruit by the end of a growing season.

SUMMARY

- Children and their well-being are major concerns for parents and early childhood educators. Parent involvement in early childhood nutrition programs provides unity for the parent and child in sound educational experiences about food.
- Benefits of parent participation are realized by parents, early childhood care givers, and the children involved.
- Effectiveness of parent recruitment is maximized when several methods are used. Contacts can be made through informal conversation during various parent-teacher meetings, notes, letters, newsletters, telephone calls, lending libraries, home visits, advisory committees, and inclusion of appropriate questions on registration forms.
- To ensure maximum participation, parents should be given options for involvement. Suggested categories for contribution include (1) assisting children during center hours, (2) working with materials and equipment during center hours, (3) contributing time and effort to the program after center hours, and (4) participating without leaving the home.
- Ideas for parental assistance are vast; parents' strengths, hobbies, and interests should be explored. Parents can also serve as valuable resource persons for early childhood nutrition education.

- Evaluating the effectiveness of a parent involvement program is necessary to maintain and improve the quality of interaction. Suggested evaluation techniques are attendance records at various meetings, questionnaires, parent/care giver feedback, and self-evaluation by teachers concerning involvement with parents.
- Recognition of parent participation is vital. Frequent praise or other tangible expressions of appreciation provide encouragement and satisfaction for parents.

DISCUSSION QUESTIONS

1. Discuss the value of parent involvement in early childhood nutrition programs.
2. Briefly outline the methods of initiating parent involvement in a nutrition education program.
3. What purpose do home visits serve in nutrition education?
4. Describe four ways parents can contribute to the early childhood nutrition program during center hours.
5. Discuss opportunities for parents to contribute to the school's nutrition program after center hours.
6. List three suggestions for parents to use at home to reinforce nutrition concepts learned at school.
7. Discuss the necessity of evaluating a parent involvement program. Which aspects of the program should be evaluated?
8. Describe methods of recognizing parents for their involvement in early childhood nutrition programs. Why is this important?

REFERENCES

1. Gough, P. B.: Tapping parent power, Phi Delta Kappan 72:339,1991.
2. Position paper on nutrition standards in day care programs for children, J. Am. Diet Assoc. 87:502, 1987.
3. Berger, E. H.: Parents as partners in education, New York, 1990, Macmillan Publishing Co., p. 138.
4. Rockwell, R. E.: Parent involvement. In Howery, B.J. (ed.): Early childhood handbook, Springfield, IL, 1993, Illinois State Board of Education. Illinois Resource Center, Des Plaines, IL.
5. Rockwell, R. E., and Grafford, K. J.: Tips: teachers involve parent services, Edwardsville, 1977, Department of Curriculum and Instruction, Southern Illinois University.
6. Rockwell, R. E., and Comer, J. M.: School volunteer program, a manual for coordinators, midwest teachers corp network, Athens, OH, 1978, College of Education, Ohio University.

SUGGESTED READINGS

Bigner, J. J.: Parent-child relations: an introduction to parenting, New York, 1989, Macmillan Publishing Co.

Cataldo, C.Z.: Parent education for early childhood, New York, 1987, Teachers College Press.

Curran, D.: Working with parents, Circle Pines, MN, 1989, American Guidance Service.

Ferguson-Florissant School District: Parents as first teachers, Ferguson, MO, 1985, Ferguson-Florissant School District.

Shea, T. M., and Bauer, A. M.: Parents and teachers of exceptional students, Boston, 1991, Allyn and Bacon, Inc.

APPENDIX 9–A Center Feeding Chart

CENTER FEEDING CHART

Date: _March 23_   Sample:

		Time: 9:15		
	John	Solids Milk	1/2 j 8 oz.	1/4 j 6 oz.

Name	1st feeding Food prepared/eaten			2nd feeding Food prepared/eaten			3rd feeding Food prepared/eaten			4th feeding Food prepared/eaten		
Amy	Time: 9:40			Time: 1:10			Time:			Time:		
	formula cereal	8 oz. 3T	6 oz. all	milk fruit meat	4 oz. 4T 2T	all 2T 1T						
Cathie	Time: 9:30			Time: 11:36			Time: 3:15			Time:		
	juice cracker	4 oz. 1	all	sandwich milk fruit	½ 8 oz. ½ jar	¼ 6 oz. all	milk fruit	4 oz. ½ jar	1 oz. all			
Emmy	Time: 10:07			Time:			Time:			Time:		
	milk fruit	4 oz. 1 jar	2 oz. all									
Frances	Time: 10:05			Time: 12:37			Time: 3:04			Time:		
	cereal fruit	1 jar ½ jar	¾ j. all	meat veg. milk	1 jar ½ jar 6 oz.	½ jar all all	juice	8 oz.	6 oz.			
Kerry	Time: 11:45			Time:			Time:			Time:		
	meat veg. fruit	½ jar ½ jar ½ jar	all	juice	4 oz.	all						
Leigh	Time: 12:30			Time: 2:45			Time:			Time:		
	banana milk	1 4 oz.	⅔ 3 oz.	juice sandwich	8 oz. ½	all						
Leslie	Time: 10:09			Time: 1:15			Time:			Time:		
	milk cereal	6 oz. 2T	3 oz. ref.	juice sandwich	8 oz. ½	all						
Munro	Time: 1:13			Time:			Time:			Time:		
	sandwich cheese fruit milk	1 slice 1 jar 8 oz.	½ all all all									
Oliver	Time: 9:30			Time: 12:30			Time: 3:10			Time:		
	juice	6 oz.	all	meat + veg. fruit milk	1 jar ½ jar 4 oz.	all all	milk	8 oz.	all			

Source: Herbert-Jackson, E., O'Brien, M., Porterfield, J., and Risley, T. R.: The infant center, Baltimore, 1977, University Park Press.

APPENDIX 9–B   Notes for Parents of 3- to 18-Month-Old Infants

Parent Report   Date _____

Name _____   Leaving _____

Last fed: _____   Last slept from: _____ To: _____

Parent's instructions for today:

Medicines:

Give phone number if different from the one we have on file: _____

Center Report

Your baby slept from: Diapering

_____ to _____   _____   _____

_____ to _____   _____   _____

_____ to _____   _____   _____

_____ to _____   _____   _____

Your baby ate:

When   What
‾‾‾‾   ‾‾‾‾
1st

2nd

3rd

4th

Some of the activities your   Disposition:
baby participated in were:

Center Comments:

Source: St. Louis Community College at Florissant Valley, Child Development Center,
1988.

Notes for Parents of 18- to 24-Month-Old Toddlers

Name: _____

Date: _____

Did your child sleep
well last night?

Yes _____ No _____

Is your child having a
hard morning?

Yes _____ No _____

Reason:

Give phone number if
different: _____

Special instructions for
today:

FOOD INTAKE

+ = good

1 = one serving

0 = nothing

Breakfast _____

Lunch _____

Snack _____

SLEEPING

_____ to _____

_____ to _____

EXTRA COMMENTS:

OLDER
TODDLERS

DIAPERING (bowel movements)

L = Loose

H = Hard

N = Normal

_____

_____

_____

ACTIVITIES

Source: St. Louis Community College at Florissant Valley, Child Development Center, 1988.

San Antonio College
Child Development Center
Two-Year-Old Class

Parent Report

Day _____ Departure time _____ Child's name _____

Did your child sleep well last night? _____ Has your child had breakfast? _____

Any special instructions for today?   Phone number if different for today: _____

Today's play activities	**Meals**
Individual	√ = type of snack food served
Art or science	+ = ate lots
Large group	1 = ate one serving
Helping	0 = ate little
Outdoor	
Other	

	A.M. Snack	Lunch	P.M. Snack
Protein source			
Fruit/juice			
Vegetable			
Bread/cereal			
Milk product			

General disposition

Nap: Slept from _____ to _____

Potty: Number of accidents _____

Comments:

Permission to Give Medication

I authorize the Director or employed staff member to administer the following medication(s):

Medication or Prescription No.	Dosage	Hours of Day	Staff use only (Date, Time, Initials)

Parent's Signature

Date

Source: San Antonio College Child Development Center.

APPENDIX 9–E Sign In and Out Form

		St. Louis Community College at Florissant Valley Child Development Center Sign-in/Sign-out			

Classroom: _____ Date: _____

Child's Name	Parent's Signature	Arrival Time	Parent's Signature	Departure Time	Comments
1.					
2.					
3.					
4.					
5.					
6.					
7.					
8.					
9.					
10.					
11.					
12.					
13.					
14.					
15.					
16.					
17.					
18.					
19.					
20.					

Source: St. Louis Community College at Florissant Valley, Child Development Center, 1988.

WORKSHOP AGENDA

Workshop Title
Show, Tell, and Taste Snacks: a Fun Way to Eat for Nutrition

Theme
Nutritious snacks

Purpose

- To promote family togetherness
- To increase parents' awareness of what their children eat
- To teach children to choose, make, and enjoy nutritious food and snacks
- To help families choose nutritious snacks
- To suggest that children keep a record of the snacks they eat
- To know the difference between nutritious snacks and those that are not

Advance Preparation
Three weeks before:

1. Clear meeting with principal.
2. Secure authorization for room use.
3. Secure room for babysitting facility.
4. Make arrangements for several babysitters—one on "standby" status.
5. Form committee to make arrangements for possible transportation for parents.
6. Set up food committee with chairman. Pass out food sign-up sheet.

Two weeks before:

1. Make invitations.
2. Remind parents of food items they signed up for use as workshop material or refreshments.
3. Organize games (include extra one if time permits).

4. Prepare on paper physical arrangement of the room.

One week before:

1. Prepare name tags.
2. Prepare mixer.
3. Prepare evaluation form and box.
4. Organize material for workshop.
5. Check with food committee to see what items are still lacking.
6. Prepare and organize materials for snack kit.
7. Send invitations.

One day before:

1. Remind parents of meeting.
2. Check progress of food committee.
3. Remind baby-sitters of the date and time.
4. Check with transportation committee to verify rides for parents needing them.

Day of the meeting:

1. Set up tables and activity centers.
2. Put posters, name tags, handouts in place.

Mixer
Materials:

1. Poster of the Food Guide Pyramid
2. Paper plate with pictures depicting a balanced meal
3. Ten envelopes of food pictures
   a. Two envelopes of bread, cereal, rice, and pasta pictures
   b. Two envelopes of vegetable pictures
   c. Two envelopes of fruit pictures
   d. Two envelopes of milk, yogurt, and cheese pictures
   e. Two envelopes of meat, poultry, fish, dried beans, eggs, and nuts
4. Ten plates

Activity

1. Each person receives a food envelope and a paper plate.
2. Each person must ask others for food items to place on his/her plate until a balanced meal is received.

NAME TAGS

Name tags are cut in the shape of a glass from orange construction paper (orange juice) or white construction paper (milk) with space for a name to be written in marker.

WORKSHOP SCHEDULE

Time	Activity	Technique	Resources	Person Responsible
12:45–12:55	Welcome	Name tags Mixer	Paper, markers, pins Paper plates, tape, food pictures	Janet Susan
12:55–1:05	Introduction of meeting Purpose: Choosing nutritious snacks	Good nutrition is important. We can make nutritious food more interesting and fun to eat, especially snacks. This can be a family or child project.	Basic food groups posters	Donna
	Parents go to the six activity centers (see next section)	Explain each activity center. Look at the number on your name tag. Begin at that station and continue wherever your interest takes you.	Name tags Activity centers	Amanda
1:05–1:30	Activity centers 1. Peanut butter play dough	Follow recipe #1 in parent handout.	Peanut butter, dry milk	Amanda
	2. Bugs on a log	Follow recipe #2 in parent handout.	Peanut butter, celery, raisins	Donna
	3. Peanut butter fruitwich	Follow recipe #3 in parent handout.	Crushed cereal, banana, peanut butter	Erma
	4. Fruit face and variations	Follow recipe #4 in parent handout.	Apple slices, raisins, pineapple chunks, shredded carrots, orange	Susan
	5. Decorated crackers	Follow recipe #5 in parent handout.	Crackers, cheese spread in a can	Katie
	6. Bread cut-outs	Follow recipe #6 in parent handout.	Whole wheat bread, cookie cutters, cream cheese	Janet
1:30–1:45	Refreshments	Serve yourself juice; eat snacks prepared.	Fruit punch, bowl, cups	All
	Conclusion	Pass out evaluation sheet.	Pencils, parent handout	Katie

EVALUATION SHEET

We are interested in knowing whether you enjoyed our meeting this afternoon. Please put a check in the box below that best describes your feeling about the meeting. The space provided at the bottom of this page is for any suggestions you might have concerning our parent group meetings. We would be happy to hear from you, so feel free to comment!

Comments:

_____

_____

_____

_____

RECIPES FOR SNACKS PREPARED AT ACTIVITY CENTERS

#1 Peanut Butter Play Dough

(Meat and milk groups)
18 oz peanut butter
6 tbsp honey
Nonfat dry milk to right consistency
Cocoa (optional)
Mix together and form into shapes. Eat and enjoy!

#2 Bugs on a Log

(meat and fruit/vegetable groups)
Celery washed and cut into 4" lengths
Peanut butter
Raisins
Spread peanut butter in celery. Arrange 3 or 4 raisins on top of peanut butter.

#3 Peanut Butter Fruitwich

(fruit/vegetable and grain or meat groups)
Banana cut in half lengthwise
Peanut butter to spread on banana
Crushed cereal or nuts
Reassemble the bananas and roll in the crushed cereal or nuts. Slice in round if desired.

#4 Fruit Face

(fruit/vegetable group)
Apple, cut into quarters
Pineapple chunk
2 raisins
2 orange slices
½ C shredded carrots
Paper plate
Arrange ¼ apple below center of plate for mouth. Put two quarters on either side for ears. A pineapple chunk in the middle becomes the nose. Use two raisins for eyes and two orange slices for eyebrows. Shredded carrots at the top make hair. Substitute any fruit and vegetables you like.

#5 Decorated Crackers

(grain and milk groups)
Whole wheat or whole-grain crackers
Cheese in a can
Create designs, faces, animals with the cheese on the crackers, or spread cream cheese on preshaped crackers.

#6 Bread Cut-outs

(grain and milk groups)
Whole wheat bread
Cheese from a can or cream cheese
Cookie cutters
Cut shapes from a slice of whole wheat bread with cookie cutters. Decorate with cheese from a can. Or spread cream cheese on the bread with a knife.

ADDITIONAL RECIPES TO TRY AT HOME

#7 Pudding Finger Paint

1 package pudding mix, cooked type
2 C milk
Waxed paper, large sheet
Cook pudding according to package directions. Pour a small amount (¼ C) on the waxed paper. Make designs with fingers or spoon. Lick fingers as necessary. Eat remainder of "painting" with spoon.

#8 Meal Face

Hot dog, poached egg, or bacon strip fried for
  mouth
Carrot or celery slices for eyes and nose
Tomato slices for ears
Shredded cheese, lettuce, or slaw for hair
Paper plate
Assemble foods to make face. Or use any favorite foods to arrange a face on the plate.

#9 Sandwich Special

Cottage cheese and shredded carrots on whole
  wheat raisin bread
Peanut butter between apple rings
Honey butter (mix equal parts of honey and soft
  butter) between graham crackers (much better
  for a snack or dessert than cookies)
Chopped leftover meat (moisten with mayonnaise) and a lettuce slice
Peanut butter and alfalfa sprouts or tomato slices
  on whole wheat bread

#10 Banana Pops

Banana on a stick
Yogurt
Nuts, coconut, or granola
Dip banana in yogurt, then roll in nuts, coconut, or granola. Freeze.

#11 Crunchy Bananas
Banana cut into 1″ thick slices
Popsicle stick
Orange juice
Coconut, wheat germ, or chopped peanuts
Spear banana slices with stick, dip in juice, and roll in favorite topping.

#12 Homemade Granola
Unsweetened cereal, any variety
Raisins
Coconut
Peanuts
Mix all together.

#13 Banana Candle
Pineapple slice on a plate
Banana, peeled and cut in half
Maraschino cherry
Cut off ends of banana. Stand up the half banana in the pineapple ring. Put a cherry on top for the flame.

#14 Meat Kabobs
Vienna sausage rounds
Cherry tomato
Toothpick
Italian dressing
Thread sausage on toothpick with tomato. Marinate in Italian dressing if desired.

#15 Cheese Kabobs
Cubed cheese
Toothpicks
Fruit chunks, any variety
Thread cubes of cheese on toothpicks, alternating with fruit.

#16 Cheese Balls
Cream cheese
Milk
Chopped peanuts
Soften cream cheese with a little milk; form into balls. Roll in chopped peanuts.

#17 Cheese Crunchies
Cheese cubes
Pretzel sticks
Wheat germ

Spear cheese cube with pretzel stick and roll in wheat germ.

#18 Popcorn with Cheese
Popcorn, popped
Cheese melted or dried to sprinkle on popcorn

#19 Popcorn-peanut Nibbler
Popped corn
Roasted peanuts
Butter and salt
Mix and toast in oven approximately 10 minutes.

#20 Finger Jello (Knox Blox)
7 envelopes unflavored gelatin (or 4 envelopes unflavored gelatin and 3 envelopes flavored)
4 C boiling fruit juice (or 4 C boiling water)
Mix and pour into a 13″ × 9″ pan. Chill until firm and cut into approximately 100 squares.

#21 Toad-in-a-Hole
1 slice of bread
1 tbsp butter
1 egg
With a cookie cutter cut out a circle in the center of the bread. Melt butter in pan and brown bread on both sides. Break an egg in the hole. Cook covered until the egg doesn't jiggle.

#22 Bunny Salad
1 lettuce leaf
1 canned pear half
4 orange sections
1 maraschino cherry cut into 6 slices (or substitute pieces of apple or tomato for the cherry)
Put the lettuce leaf on the table. Put the pear half cut side down on the lettuce leaf. Add orange sections for ears. Use cherry or apple or tomato slices for eyes, nose, mouth and inside of ears.

#23 Mellow Yellow
2 slices of bread, buttered
1 slice of cheese between the bread slices
1 tbsp butter melted in a pan
Brown bread on both sides. Cut into triangles and share with a friend.

SNACKS

The following list is a list of simple, economical, and nutritious snack ideas you may find practical. Remember, to make snacks more tempting have them readily accessible and attractive for eyecatching appeal.

Milk Group

Flavored milk drink—½ C milk with ½ C any fruit juice
Cheese cubes
Ice cream

Meat Group

Sunflower seeds, pumpkin seeds
Toasted soybeans
Assorted nuts
Peanut butter
Peanut butter balls rolled in sesame seeds
Beef jerky
Eggs sliced with pickle

Walnut, pecan halves with soft cheese spread as filling.

Fruits and Vegetables

Using any fresh fruit or vegetable, experiment with imaginative shapes (minted or dilled cucumbers, radish fans, celery branches, pepper strips, carrot curls, or cauliflower buds).
Make fruit juice by rolling unpeeled orange between hands until soft; insert straw.
Cut apples into small wedges and place on toothpick with raisins.
Freeze orange juice on sticks in ice cube trays to make sunshine pops.

Grains

Chow mein noodles
Crackers—use cheese and whole-grain varieties
Unsugared, ready-to-eat cereal
Taco shells (broken into chips)

APPENDIX 9–G   Letter to Parents

Dear Parents,

If you panic when someone tells you to bring a "nutritious" snack, relax. Here are some guidelines for choosing and making nutritious snacks.

Use plain simple foods which are low in sugar, salt, and fat and high in food value.

Why low in sugar? Because sugar promotes tooth decay, is a concentrated source of calories with no nutrients, and displaces more nutritious foods in our diet.

Why low in salt? Because we consume 2 to 10 times more salt than we need and excessive salt intake may trigger hypertension in susceptible people.

Why low in fat? Because fat contains twice the calories of carbohydrate or protein and while we do need some fat in our diets, we generally get much more than we need.

Why high in food value? Because preschool appetites are quite variable from day to day, even meal to meal, and most young children cannot consume all the nutrients they need in three meals a day. Snacks become an important part of the child's nutrient intake so these foods need to be carefully chosen to balance the child's diet.

Why worry at this age? Because preschool children are establishing eating habits that will last a lifetime—hopefully, a long healthy lifetime.

This doesn't mean you must throw out your 5 lb. bag of sugar or empty the salt shaker into the trash can and serve dry toast in the morning. Moderation is a better idea.

It may interest you to know that nutrition surveys have revealed that most preschoolers do not get enough iron, calcium and vitamin A in their diets.

Snack time is an important time of the preschool day, a time of learning as well as physical satisfaction. Involving your child in snack preparation at home for class can be a meaningful and educational experience.

Thanks,

The Teachers

Source: Barbara L. Goldenhersh, Director of Presbyterian Community Preschool, Belleville, IL, 1988.

NUTRITIOUS SNACK SUGGESTIONS PRESBYTERIAN COMMUNITY PRESCHOOL

Fresh Fruit Kabobs
Cut bite-size pieces of melon, pineapple, grapes, strawberries, apples, etc. Place on a plastic straw. Dip in lemon juice to keep fresh.

Orange Smiles
Cut each orange into eight wedges. Leave peel on.

"Gorp"
Mixture of raisins, dried fruits, sunflower seeds, and nuts in small cups or sandwich bags.

Banana Bread, Pumpkin Bars, Blueberry Muffins
Home-made breads and muffins are always a special treat. These make excellent birthday snacks.

"Ants on a Log"
Spread celery pieces with peanut butter or cheese. Add raisins on top for the "ants."

Raw Veggies and Dip
Celery, cucumber, green pepper, cherry tomatoes, carrot sticks, broccoli "trees," and cauliflower "flowers" are great with dip. Dill dip is quite popular with preschoolers.

Popcorn
For variety sprinkle with cinnamon or Parmesan cheese.

Sandwiches
Peanut butter and jelly or honey, tuna, egg or chicken salad, and bologna sandwiches are fine snacks. A quarter or half sandwich per child is appropriate.

Rice Krispie Squares, Triangles, or Rectangles

Face Cookies
Spread peanut butter on graham cracker. Make a face with raisins.

Jello or Pudding
Make in small paper cups.

Celery and Pineapple Sticks
Mash two 8 oz packages of cream cheese. Add one large can of crushed pineapple drained. Mix and spread on celery pieces.

Dried Fruit Assortment
Mix an assortment of dried fruits: apricots, peaches, dates, apples, raisins, etc. Serve in small paper cups.

Happy Faces
Spread bread circles with peanut butter. Add raisins for features and grated carrots or cheese for hair.

Applewiches
Core an apple, slice into circles and dip in lemon juice to prevent discoloration. Spread peanut butter on apple slices and close to make sandwiches.

Popsicles
Blend one 6 oz can softened frozen juice (grape is excellent), 1 can water and 1 pint vanilla ice cream. Pour into molds or small paper cups, insert sticks, and freeze.

Orange Juice-icles
Mix one 6 oz can frozen orange juice, 3 cans cold water, 1 egg white and 2 tbsp honey in blender. Pour into molds or small paper cups, insert sticks, and freeze.

Source: Nutritious snack suggestions courtesy of Barbara L. Goldenhersh, Director of Presbyterian Community Preschool, Belleville, IL, 1988.

Appendixes

I.	Nutritive Values of the Edible Parts of Foods	316
II.	Recommended Dietary Allowances (RDA), Revised 1989	348
III.	Daily Values (DV)	350
IV.	Dietary Screening Aids	352
V.	Weight-for-Stature Charts for Prepubertal Girls and Boys	356
VI.	Sources of Funding for Food Service	361

APPENDIX I   Nutritive Values of the Edible Parts of Foods[1]

		Food energy	Protein	Fat	Fatty Acids		
					Saturated	Monoun- saturated	Polyun- saturated
BEVERAGES		Grams	Calories	Grams	Grams	Grams	Grams	Grams

		Grams	Calories	Grams	Grams	Grams	Grams	Grams
COLA REGULAR[2] .... 12 FL OZ		369	160	0	0	0.0	0.0	0.0
COLA DIET ASPRTAME + SACCHRN[2] .... 12 FL OZ		355	0	0	0	0.0	0.0	0.0
COLA DIET SACCHARIN ONLY[2] .... 12 FL OZ		355	0	0	0	0.0	0.0	0.0
COLA DIET ASPARTAME ONLY[2] .... 12 FL OZ		355	0	0	0	0.0	0.0	0.0
ORANGE SODA[2] .... 12 FL OZ		372	180	0	0	0.0	0.0	0.0
PEPPER-TYPE SODA[2] .... 12 FL OZ		369	160	0	0	0.0	0.0	0.0
ROOT BEER[2] .... 12 FL OZ		370	165	0	0	0.0	0.0	0.0
COFFEE BREWED .... 6 FL OZ		180	0	0	0	0.0	0.0	0.0
COFFEE INSTANT PREPARED .... 6 FL OZ		182	0	0	0	0.0	0.0	0.0
FRUIT PUNCH DRINK CANNED .... 6 FL OZ		190	85	0	0	0.0	0.0	0.0
LEMONADE CONCEN FRZEN DILUTED ...... 6 FL OZ		185	80	0	0	0.0	0.0	0.0
TEA BREWED .... 8 FL OZ		240	0	0	0	0.0	0.0	0.0
TEA INSTANT PREPRD UNSWEETEND .... 8 FL OZ		241	0	0	0	0.0	0.0	0.0
TEA INSTANT PREPARD SWEETENED .... 8 FL OZ		262	85	0	0	0.0	0.0	0.0
DAIRY PRODUCTS								
BLUE CHEESE .... 1 OZ		28	100	6	8	5.3	2.2	0.2
CAMEMBERT CHEESE .... 1 WEDGE		38	115	8	9	5.8	2.7	0.3
CHEDDAR CHEESE .... 1 OZ		28	115	7	9	6.0	2.7	0.3
CHEDDDAR CHEESE SHREDDED .... 1 CUP		113	455	28	37	23.8	10.6	1.1
COTTAGE CHEESE CREMD LRGE CURD ..... 1 CUP		225	235	28	10	6.4	2.9	0.3
COTTAGE CHEESE LOWFAT 2% .... 1 CUP		226	205	31	4	2.8	1.2	0.1
COTTAGE CHEESE UNCREAMED .... 1 CUP		145	125	25	1	0.4	0.2	0.0
CREAM CHEESE .... 1 OZ		28	100	2	10	6.2	2.8	0.4
PASTERZD PROCES CHEESE AMERICN ..... 1 OZ		28	105	6	9	5.6	2.5	0.3
PASTERZD PROCES CHESE FOOD AMR ..... 1 OZ		28	95	6	7	4.4	2.0	0.2

[1] Selected foods reprinted from Nutritive value of foods, U.S. Department of Agriculture, Home and Garden Bulletin No. 72.
[2] Mineral content varies depending on water source.
[3] With added ascorbic acid.

Choles-terol	Carbo-hydrate	Calcium	Iron	Potas-sium	Sodium	Vit. A Value (RE)	Thiamin	Ribo-flavin	Niacin	Ascorbic Acid
Milligrams	Grams	Milligrams	Milligrams	Milligrams	Milligrams	Retinol Equivalents	Milligrams	Milligrams	Milligrams	Milligrams
0	41	11	0.2	7	18	0	0.00	0.00	0.0	0
0	0	14	0.2	7	32	0	0.00	0.00	0.0	0
0	0	14	0.2	7	75	0	0.00	0.00	0.0	0
0	0	14	0.2	7	23	0	0.00	0.00	0.0	0
0	46	15	0.3	7	52	0	0.00	0.00	0.0	0
0	41	11	0.1	4	37	0	0.00	0.00	0.0	0
0	42	15	0.2	4	48	0	0.00	0.00	0.0	0
0	0	4	0.0	124	2	0	0.00	0.02	0.4	0
0	1	2	0.1	71	0	0	0.00	0.03	0.6	0
0	22	15	0.4	48	15	2	0.03	0.04	0.0	61[3]
0	21	2	0.1	30	1	10	0.01	0.02	0.2	13
0	0	0	0.0	36	1	0	0.00	0.03	0.0	0
0	1	1	0.0	61	1	0	0.00	0.02	0.1	0
0	22	1	0.0	49	0	0	0.00	0.04	0.1	0
21	1	150	0.1	73	396	65	0.01	0.11	0.3	0
27	0	147	0.1	71	320	96	0.01	0.19	0.2	0
30	0	204	0.2	29	176	86	0.01	0.11	0.0	0
119	1	815	0.8	111	701	342	0.03	0.42	0.1	0
34	6	135	0.3	190	911	108	0.05	0.37	0.3	0
19	8	155	0.4	217	918	45	0.05	0.42	0.3	0
10	3	46	0.3	47	19	12	0.04	0.21	0.2	0
31	1	23	0.3	34	84	124	0.00	0.06	0.0	0
27	0	174	0.1	46	406	82	0.01	0.10	0.0	0
18	2	163	0.2	79	337	62	0.01	0.13	0.0	0

		Food energy	Protein	Fat	Fatty Acids		
					Saturated	Monoun-saturated	Polyun-saturated
DAIRY PRODUCTS CONT.	Grams	Calories	Grams	Grams	Grams	Grams	Grams
HALF HALF AND HALF CREAM .... 1 TBSP	15	20	0	2	1.1	0.5	0.1
LIGHT COFFEE OR TABLE CREAM .... 1 TBSP	15	30	0	3	1.8	0.8	0.1
WHIPPING CREAM UNWHIPED HEAVY ...... 1 TBSP	15	50	0	6	3.5	1.6	0.2
WHIPPED TOPPING PRESSURIZED .... 1 CUP	60	155	2	13	8.3	3.9	0.5
MILK WHOLE 3.3% FAT .... 1 CUP	244	150	8	8	5.1	2.4	0.3
MILK LOFAT 2% NO ADDED SOLID .... 1 CUP	244	120	8	5	2.9	1.4	0.2
MILK LOFAT 1% ADDED SOLIDS .... 1 CUP	245	105	9	2	1.5	0.7	0.1
MILK SKIM ADDED MILK SOLIDS .... 1 CUP	245	90	9	1	0.4	0.2	0.0
BUTTERMILK FLUID .... 1 CUP	245	100	8	2	1.3	0.6	0.1
SWEETENED CONDENSED MILK CNND ...... 1 CUP	306	980	24	27	16.8	7.4	1.0
EVAPORATED MILK WHOLE CANNED ...... 1 CUP	252	340	17	19	11.6	5.9	0.6
EVAPORATED MILK SKIM CANNED .... 1 CUP	255	200	19	1	0.3	0.2	0.0
NONFAT DRY MILK INSTANTIZED .... 1 CUP	68	245	24	0	0.3	0.1	0.0
CHOCOLATE MILK REGULAR .... 1 CUP	250	210	8	8	5.3	2.5	0.3
CHOCOLATE MILK LOWFAT 2% .... 1 CUP	250	180	8	5	3.1	1.5	0.2
CHOCOLATE MILK LOWFAT 1% .... 1 CUP	250	160	8	3	1.5	0.8	0.1
COCA PWDR W/O NOFAT DRY MLK PRD .... 1 SERVNG	265	225	9	9	5.4	2.5	0.3
ICE CREAM VANLLA REGULR 11% .... 1 CUP	133	270	5	14	8.9	4.1	0.5
ICE CREAM VANLLA SOFT SERVE .... 1 CUP	173	375	7	23	13.5	6.7	1.0
ICE CREAM VANLLA RICH 16% FT .... 1 CUP	148	350	4	24	14.7	6.8	0.9
ICE MILK VANILLA SOFTSERV 3% .... 1 CUP	175	225	8	5	2.9	1.3	0.2
SHERBET 2% FAT .... 1 CUP	193	270	2	4	2.4	1.1	0.1
YOGURT W/ LOFAT MILK FRUIT FLV[6] .... 8 OZ	227	230	10	2	1.6	0.7	0.1
YOGURT W/ LOFAT MILK PLAIN .... 8 OZ	227	145	12	4	2.3	1.0	0.1
EGGS							
EGGS RAW WHOLE .... 1 EGG	50	75	6	5	1.6	1.9	0.7
EGGS RAW WHITE .... 1 WHITE	33	15	4	0	0.0	0.0	0.0
EGGS RAW YOLK .... 1 YOLK	17	60	3	5	1.6	1.9	0.7
EGGS COOKED HARD-COOKED .... 1 EGG	50	75	6	5	1.6	2.0	0.7
EGGS COOKED SCRAMBLED/OMELET ...... 1 EGG	61	100	7	7	2.2	2.9	1.3
FATS AND OILS							
BUTTER SALTED .... 1/2 CUP	113	810	1	92	57.1	26.4	3.4
BUTTER UNSALTED .... 1/2 CUP	113	810	1	92	57.1	26.4	3.4
BUTTER SALTED .... 1 TBSP	14	100	0	11	7.1	3.3	0.4

[4]With added vitamin A.
[5]Carbohydrate content varies widely because of amount of sugar added and solids content of added flavoring. Consult the label if more precise values for carbohydrate and calories are needed.
[6]Values for vitamin A are year-round average.

Choles-terol	Carbo-hydrate	Calcium	Iron	Potas-sium	Sodium	Vit. A Value (RE)	Thiamin	Ribo-flavin	Niacin	Ascorbic Acid
Milligrams	Grams	Milligrams	Milligrams	Milligrams	Milligrams	Retinol Equivalents	Milligrams	Milligrams	Milligrams	Milligrams
6	1	16	0.0	19	6	16	0.01	0.02	0.0	0
10	1	14	0.0	18	6	27	0.00	0.02	0.0	0
21	0	10	0.0	11	6	63	0.00	0.02	0.0	0
46	7	61	0.0	88	78	124	0.02	0.04	0.0	0
33	11	291	0.1	370	120	76	0.09	0.40	0.2	2
18	12	297	0.1	377	122	139	0.10	0.40	0.2	2
10	12	313	0.1	397	128	145	0.10	0.42	0.2	2
5	12	316	0.1	418	130	149	0.10	0.43	0.2	2
9	12	285	0.1	371	257	20	0.08	0.38	0.1	2
104	166	868	0.6	1136	389	248	0.28	1.27	0.6	8
74	25	657	0.5	764	267	136	0.12	0.80	0.5	5
9	29	738	0.7	845	293	298	0.11	0.79	0.4	3
12	35	837	0.2	1160	373	483[4]	0.28	1.19	0.6	4
31	26	280	0.6	417	149	73	0.09	0.41	0.3	2
17	26	284	0.6	422	151	143	0.09	0.41	0.3	2
7	26	287	0.6	425	152	148	0.10	0.42	0.3	2
33	30	298	0.9	508	176	76	0.10	0.43	0.3	3
59	32	134	0.1	257	116	133	0.05	0.33	0.1	1
153	38	236	0.4	338	153	199	0.08	0.45	0.2	1
88	32	151	0.1	221	108	219	0.04	0.28	0.1	1
13	38	274	0.3	412	163	44	0.12	0.54	0.2	1
14	59	103	0.3	198	88	39	0.03	0.09	0.1	4
10	43	345	0.2	442	133	25	0.08	0.40	0.2	1
14	16	415	0.2	531	159	36	0.10	0.49	0.3	2
213	1	25	0.7	60	63	95	0.03	0.25	0.0	0
0	0	2	0.0	48	55	0	0.00	0.15	0.0	0
213	0	23	0.6	16	7	320	0.03	0.11	0.0	0
213	1	25	0.6	63	62	280	0.03	0.26	0.0	0
215	1	44	0.7	84	171	119	0.03	0.27	0.0	0
247	0	27	0.2	29	933	852[6]	0.01	0.04	0.0	0
247	0	27	0.2	29	12	852[6]	0.01	0.04	0.0	0
31	0	3	0.0	4	116	106[6]	0.00	0.00	0.0	0

		Food energy	Protein	Fat	Fatty Acids		
					Saturated	Monoun-saturated	Polyun-saturated
	Grams	Calories	Grams	Grams	Grams	Grams	Grams

FATS AND OILS CONT.

		Grams	Calories	Grams	Grams	Grams	Grams	Grams
BUTTER UNSALTED	1 TBSP	14	100	0	11	7.1	3.3	0.4
BUTTER SALTED	1 PAT	5	35	0	4	2.5	1.2	0.2
BUTTER UNSALTED	1 PAT	5	35	0	4	2.5	1.2	0.2
FATS COOKING/VEGETBL SHORTENG	1 CUP	205	1810	0	205	51.3	91.2	53.5
FATS COOKING/VEGETBL SHORTENG	1 TBSP	13	115	0	13	3.3	5.8	3.4
LARD	1 CUP	205	1850	0	205	80.4	92.5	23.0
LARD	1 TBSP	13	115	0	13	5.1	5.9	1.5
MARGARINE REGULR HARD 80% FAT	1/2 CUP	113	810	1	91	17.9	40.5	28.7
MARGARINE REGULR SOFT 80% FAT	1 TBSP	14	100	0	11	1.9	4.0	4.8
CORN OIL	1 TBSP	14	125	0	14	1.8	3.4	8.2
OLIVE OIL	1 TBSP	14	125	0	14	1.9	10.3	1.2
SOYBEAN OIL HYDROGENATED	1 TBSP	14	125	0	14	2.1	6.0	5.3
SUNFLOWER OIL	1 TBSP	14	125	0	14	1.4	2.7	9.2
BLUE CHEESE SALAD DRESSING	1 TBSP	15	75	1	8	1.5	1.8	4.2
FRENCH SALAD DRESSING REGULAR	1 TBSP	16	85	0	9	1.4	4.0	3.5
ITALIAN SALAD DRESSING REGULAR	1 TBSP	15	80	0	9	1.3	3.7	3.2
MAYONNAISE REGULAR	1 TBSP	14	100	0	11	1.7	3.2	5.8
MAYONNAISE TYPE SALAD DRESSING	1 TBSP	15	60	0	5	0.7	1.4	2.7
TARTAR SAUCE	1 TBSP	14	75	0	8	1.2	2.6	3.9
1000 ISLAND SALAD DRSNG REGLR	1 TBSP	16	60	0	6	1.0	1.3	3.2
COOKED SALAD DRSSING HOME RCP[9]	1 TBSP	16	25	1	2	0.5	0.6	0.3
VINEGAR AND OIL SALAD DRESSING	1 TBSP	16	70	0	8	1.5	2.4	3.9

FISH AND SHELLFISH

CLAMS RAW	3 OZ	85	65	11	1	0.3	0.3	0.3
CLAMS CANNED DRAINED	3 OZ	85	85	13	2	0.5	0.5	0.4
CRABMEAT CANNED	1 CUP	135	135	23	3	0.5	0.8	1.4
FISH STICKS FROZEN REHEATED	1 STICK	28	70	6	3	0.8	1.4	0.8
HADDOCK BREADED FRIED	3 OZ	85	175	17	9	2.4	3.9	2.4
HALIBUT BROILED BUTTER LEM JU	3 OZ	85	140	20	6	3.3	1.6	0.7
OCEAN PERCH BREADED FRIED[10]	1 FILLET	85	185	16	11	2.6	4.6	2.8
OYSTERS RAW	1 CUP	240	160	20	4	1.4	0.5	1.4

[6]Values for Vitamin A are year-round average.
[7]For salted margarine.
[8]Based on average vitamin A content of fortified margarine. Federal specifications for fortified margarine require a minimum of 15,000 IU per pound.
[9]Fatty acid values apply to product made with regular margarine.
[10]Dipped in egg, milk, and bread crumbs; fried in vegetable shortening.

Choles-terol	Carbo-hydrate	Calcium	Iron	Potas-sium	Sodium	Vit. A Value (RE)	Thiamin	Ribo-flavin	Niacin	Ascorbic Acid
Milligrams	Grams	Milligrams	Milligrams	Milligrams	Milligrams	Retinol Equivalents	Milligrams	Milligrams	Milligrams	Milligrams
31	0	3	0.0	4	2	106[6]	0.00	0.00	0.0	0
11	0	1	0.0	1	41	38[6]	0.00	0.00	0.0	0
11	0	1	0.0	1	1	38[6]	0.00	0.00	0.0	0
0	0	0	0.0	0	0	0	0.00	0.00	0.0	0
0	0	0	0.0	0	0	0	0.00	0.00	0.0	0
195	0	0	0.0	0	0	0	0.00	0.00	0.0	0
12	0	0	0.0	0	0	0	0.00	0.00	0.0	0
0	1	34	0.1	48	1066[7]	1122[8]	0.01	0.04	0.0	0
0	0	4	0.0	5	151[7]	139[8]	0.00	0.00	0.0	0
0	0	0	0.0	0	0	0	0.00	0.00	0.0	0
0	0	0	0.0	0	0	0	0.00	0.00	0.0	0
0	0	0	0.0	0	0	0	0.00	0.00	0.0	0
3	1	12	0.0	6	164	10	0.00	0.02	0.0	0
0	1	2	0.0	2	188	0	0.00	0.00	0.0	0
0	1	1	0.0	5	162	3	0.00	0.00	0.0	0
8	0	3	0.1	5	80	12	0.00	0.00	0.0	0
4	4	2	0.0	1	107	13	0.00	0.00	0.0	0
4	1	3	0.1	11	182	9	0.00	0.00	0.0	0
4	2	2	0.1	18	112	15	0.00	0.00	0.0	0
9	2	13	0.1	19	117	20	0.01	0.02	0.0	0
0	0	0	0.0	1	0	0	0.00	0.00	0.0	0
43	2	59	2.6	154	102	26	0.09	0.15	1.1	9
54	2	47	3.5	119	102	26	0.01	0.09	0.9	3
135	1	61	1.1	149	1350	14	0.11	0.11	2.6	0
26	4	11	0.3	94	53	5	0.03	0.05	0.6	0
75	7	34	1.0	270	123	20	0.06	0.10	2.9	0
62	0	14	0.7	441	103	174	0.06	0.07	7.7	1
66	7	31	1.2	241	138	20	0.10	0.11	2.0	0
120	8	226	15.6	290	175	223	0.34	0.43	6.0	24

		Food energy	Protein	Fat	Fatty Acids		
					Saturated	Monoun-saturated	Polyun-saturated
FISH AND SHELLFISH CONT.	Grams	Calories	Grams	Grams	Grams	Grams	Grams
OYSTERS BREADED FRIED .... 1 OYSTER	45	90	5	5	1.4	2.1	1.4
SALMON CANNED PINK W/ BONES .... 3 OZ	85	120	17	5	0.9	1.5	2.1
SALMON BAKED RED .... 3 OZ	85	140	21	5	1.2	2.4	1.4
SALMON SMOKED .... 3 OZ	85	150	18	8	2.6	3.9	0.7
SARDINES ATLNTC CNNED OIL DRN .... 3 OZ	85	175	20	9	2.1	3.7	2.9
SHRIMP CANNED DRAINED .... 3 OZ	85	100	21	1	0.2	0.2	0.4
SHRIMP FRENCH FRIED[11] .... 3 OZ	85	200	16	10	2.5	4.1	2.6
TUNA CANND DRND OIL CHK LGHT .... 3 OZ	85	165	24	7	1.4	1.9	3.1
TUNA CANND DRND WATR WHITE .... 3 OZ	85	135	30	1	0.3	0.2	0.3
TUNA SALAD[12] .... 1 CUP	205	375	33	19	3.3	4.9	9.2
FRUITS AND FRUIT JUICES							
APPLES RAW UNPEELED 3 PER LB .... 1 APPLE	138	80	0	0	0.1	0.0	0.1
APPLE JUICE CANNED[13] .... 1 CUP	248	115	0	0	0.0	0.0	0.1
APPLESAUCE CANNED SWEETENED .... 1 CUP	255	195	0	0	0.1	0.0	0.1
APPLESAUCE CANNED UNSWEETENED ..... 1 CUP	244	105	0	0	0.0	0.0	0.0
APRICOTS RAW .... 3 APRCOT	106	50	1	0	0.0	0.2	0.1
APRICOT CANNED HEAVY SYRUP .... 1 CUP	258	215	1	0	0.0	0.1	0.0
APRICOT CANNED HEAVY SYRUP .... 3 HALVES	85	70	0	0	0.0	0.0	0.0
APRICOTS DRIED UNCOOKED .... 1 CUP	130	310	5	1	0.0	0.3	0.1
APRICOTS DRIED COOKED UNSWTN .... 1 CUP	250	210	3	0	0.0	0.2	0.1
APRICOT NECTAR NO ADDED VIT C .... 1 CUP	251	140	1	0	0.0	0.1	0.0
AVOCADOS CALIFORNIA .... 1 AVOCDO	173	305	4	30	4.5	19.4	3.5
AVOCADOS FLORIDA .... 1 AVOCDO	304	340	5	27	5.3	14.8	4.5
BANANAS .... 1 BANANA	114	105	1	1	0.2	0.0	0.1
BANANAS SLICED .... 1 CUP	150	140	2	1	0.3	0.1	0.1
BLACKBERRIES RAW .... 1 CUP	144	75	1	1	0.2	0.1	0.1
BLUEBERRIES RAW .... 1 CUP	145	80	1	1	0.0	0.1	0.3
CHERRIES SOURRED CANND WATER .... 1 CUP	244.00	90	2	0	0.1	0.1	0.1
CHERRIES SWEET RAW .... 10 CHERY	68	50	1	1	0.1	0.2	0.2
CRANBERRY JUICE COCKTAIL W/VIT C ...... 1 CUP	253	145	0	0	0.0	0.0	0.1
CRANBERRY SAUCE CANNED SWTND ...... 1 CUP	277	420	1	0	0.0	0.1	0.2

[11]Dipped in egg, breadcrumbs, and flour; fried in vegetable shortening.
[12]Made with drained chunk light tuna, celery, onion, pickle relish, and mayonnaise-type salad dressing.
[13]Also applies to pasteurized apple cider.
[14]Without added ascorbic acid. For value with added ascorbic acid, refer to label.
[15]With added ascorbic acid.

Cholesterol	Carbohydrate	Calcium	Iron	Potassium	Sodium	Vit. A Value (RE)	Thiamin	Riboflavin	Niacin	Ascorbic Acid
Milligrams	Grams	Milligrams	Milligrams	Milligrams	Milligrams	Retinol Equivalents	Milligrams	Milligrams	Milligrams	Milligrams
35	5	49	3.0	64	70	44	0.07	0.10	1.3	4
34	0	167	0.7	307	443	18	0.03	0.15	6.8	0
60	0	26	0.5	305	55	87	0.18	0.14	5.5	0
51	0	12	0.8	327	1700	77	0.17	0.17	6.8	0
85	0	371	2.6	349	425	56	0.03	0.17	4.6	0
128	1	98	1.4	104	1955	15	0.01	0.03	1.5	0
168	11	61	2.0	189	384	26	0.06	0.09	2.8	0
55	0	7	1.6	298	303	20	0.04	0.09	10.1	0
48	0	17	0.6	255	468	32	0.03	0.10	13.4	0
80	19	31	2.5	531	877	53	0.06	0.14	13.3	6
0	21	10	0.2	159	0	7	0.0	20.0	20.1	8
0	29	17	0.9	295	7	0	0.05	0.04	0.2	2[14]
0	51	10	0.9	156	8	3	0.03	0.07	0.5	4[14]
0	28	7	0.3	183	5	7	0.03	0.06	0.5	3[14]
0	12	15	0.6	314	1	277	0.03	0.04	0.6	11
0	55	23	0.8	361	10	317	0.05	0.06	1.0	8
0	18	8	0.3	119	3	105	0.02	0.02	0.3	3
0	80	59	6.1	1791	13	941	0.01	0.20	3.9	3
0	55	40	4.2	1222	8	591	0.02	0.08	2.4	4
0	36	18	1.0	286	8	330	0.02	0.04	0.7	2
0	12	19	2.0	1097	21	106	0.19	0.21	3.3	14
0	27	33	1.6	1484	15	186	0.33	0.37	5.8	24
0	27	7	0.4	451	1	9	0.05	0.11	0.6	10
0	35	9	0.5	594	2	12	0.07	0.15	0.8	14
0	18	46	0.8	282	0	24	0.04	0.06	0.6	30
0	20	9	0.2	129	9	15	0.07	0.07	0.5	19
0	22	27	3.3	239	17	184	0.04	0.10	0.4	5
0	11	10	0.3	152	0	15	0.03	0.04	0.3	5
0	38	8	0.4	61	10	1	0.01	0.04	0.1	108[15]
0	108	11	0.6	72	80	6	0.04	0.06	0.3	6

| | | | | | Fatty Acids | | |
		Food energy	Protein	Fat	Saturated	Monoun-saturated	Polyun-saturated
FRUITS AND FRUIT JUICES CONT.	Grams	Calories	Grams	Grams	Grams	Grams	Grams
DATES CHOPPED .... 1 CUP	178	490	4	1	0.3	0.2	0.0
FIGS DRIED .... 10 FIGS	187	475	6	2	0.4	0.5	1.0
FRUIT COCKTAIL CNND HEAVY SYRUP .... 1 CUP	255	185	1	0	0.0	0.0	0.1
FRUIT COCKTAIL CNND JUICE PACK .... 1 CUP	248	115	1	0	0.0	0.0	0.0
GRAPEFRUIT RAW WHITE .... 1/2 FRUT	120	40	1	0	0.0	0.0	0.0
GRAPEFRUIT RAW PINK .... 1/2 FRUT	120	40	1	0	0.0	0.0	0.0
GRAPEFRUIT CANNED SYRUP PACK .... 1 CUP	254	150	1	0	0.0	0.0	0.1
GRAPEFRUIT JUICE RAW .... 1 CUP	247	95	1	0	0.0	0.0	0.1
GRAPEFRUIT JUICE CANNED UNSWT ...... 1 CUP	247	95	1	0	0.0	0.0	0.1
GRAPEFRUIT JUICE CANNED SWTND .... 1 CUP	250	115	1	0	0.0	0.0	0.1
GRAPEFRT JCE FRZN CNCN UNSWTEN ..... 6 FL OZ	207	300	4	1	0.1	0.1	0.2
GRAPEFRT JCE FRZN DLTD UNSWTEN ...... 1 CUP	247	100	1	0	0.0	0.0	0.1
GRAPES EUROPEAN RAW THOMPSN .... 10 GRAPE	50	35	0	0	0.1	0.0	0.1
GRAPES EUROPEAN RAW TOKAY .... 10 GRAPE	57	40	0	0	0.1	0.0	0.1
GRAPE JUICE CANNED .... 1 CUP	253	155	1	0	0.1	0.0	0.1
KIWIFRUIT RAW .... 1 KIWI	76	45	1	0	0.0	0.1	0.1
LEMONS RAW .... 1 LEMON	58	15	1	0	0.0	0.0	0.1
LEMON JUICE RAW .... 1 CUP	244	60	1	0	0.0	0.0	0.0
LEMON JUICE CANNED .... 1 CUP	244	50	1	1	0.1	0.0	0.2
LEMON JUICE CANNED .... 1 TBSP	15	5	0	0	0.0	0.0	0.0
LEMON JUICE FRZN SINGLE-STRNGH .... 6 FL OZ	244	55	1	1	0.1	0.0	0.2
MANGOS RAW .... 1 MANGO	207	135	1	1	0.1	0.2	0.1
CANTALOUP RAW .... 1/2 MELN	267	95	2	1	0.1	0.1	0.3
HONEYDEW MELON RAW .... 1/10 MEL	129	45	1	0	0.0	0.0	0.1
NECTARINES RAW .... 1 NECTRN	136	65	1	1	0.1	0.2	0.3
ORANGES RAW .... 1 ORANGE	131	60	1	0	0.0	0.0	0.0
ORANGES RAW SECTIONS .... 1 CUP	180	85	2	0	0.0	0.0	0.0
ORANGE JUICE RAW .... 1 CUP	248	110	2	0	0.1	0.1	0.1
ORANGE JUICE CANNED .... 1 CUP	249	105	1	0	0.0	0.1	0.1
ORANGE JUICE FROZEN CONCENTRTE ..... 6 FL OZ	213	340	5	0	0.1	0.1	0.1
ORANGE JUICE FRZN CNCN DILUTED ...... 1 CUP	249	110	2	0	0.0	0.0	0.0
ORANGE + GRAPEFRUIT JUCE CANND ..... 1 CUP	247	105	1	0	0.0	0.0	0.0
PAPAYAS RAW .... 1 CUP	140	65	1	0	0.1	0.1	0.0
PEACHES RAW .... 1 PEACH	87	35	1	0	0.0	0.0	0.0
PEACHES RAW SLICED .... 1 CUP	170	75	1	0	0.0	0.1	0.1
PEACHES CANNED HEAVY SYRUP .... 1 CUP	256	190	1	0	0.0	0.1	0.1

[14]Without added ascorbic acid. For value with added ascorbic acid, refer to label.
[15]Sodium benzoate and sodium bisulfite added as preservatives.

Choles-terol	Carbo-hydrate	Calcium	Iron	Potas-sium	Sodium	Vit. A Value (RE)	Thiamin	Ribo-flavin	Niacin	Ascorbic Acid
Milligrams	Grams	Milligrams	Milligrams	Milligrams	Milligrams	Retinol Equivalents	Milligrams	Milligrams	Milligrams	Milligrams
0	131	57	2.0	1161	5	9	0.16	0.18	3.9	0
0	122	269	4.2	1331	21	25	0.13	0.16	1.3	1
0	48	15	0.7	224	15	52	0.05	0.05	1.0	5
0	29	20	0.5	236	10	76	0.03	0.04	1.0	7
0	10	14	0.1	167	0	1	0.04	0.02	0.3	41
0	10	14	0.1	167	0	31	0.04	0.02	0.3	41
0	39	36	1.0	328	5	0	0.10	0.05	0.6	54
0	23	22	0.5	400	2	2	0.10	0.05	0.5	94
0	22	17	0.5	378	2	2	0.10	0.05	0.6	72
0	28	20	0.9	405	5	2	0.10	0.06	0.8	67
0	72	56	1.0	1002	6	6	0.30	0.16	1.6	248
0	24	20	0.3	336	2	2	0.10	0.05	0.5	83
0	9	6	0.1	93	1	4	0.05	0.03	0.2	5
0	10	6	0.1	105	1	4	0.05	0.03	0.2	6
0	38	23	0.6	334	8	2	0.07	0.09	0.7	0[14]
0	11	20	0.3	252	4	13	0.02	0.04	0.4	74
0	5	15	0.3	80	1	2	0.02	0.01	0.1	31
0	21	17	0.1	303	2	5	0.07	0.02	0.2	112
0	16	27	0.3	249	51[16]	4	0.10	0.02	0.5	61
0	1	2	0.0	15	3[16]	0	0.01	0.00	0.0	4
0	16	20	0.3	217	2	3	0.14	0.03	0.3	77
0	35	21	0.3	323	4	806	0.12	0.12	1.2	57
0	22	29	0.6	825	24	861	0.10	0.06	1.5	113
0	12	8	0.1	350	13	5	0.10	0.02	0.8	32
0	16	7	0.2	288	0	100	0.02	0.06	1.3	7
0	15	52	0.1	237	0	27	0.11	0.05	0.4	70
0	21	72	0.2	326	0	37	0.16	0.07	0.5	96
0	26	27	0.5	496	2	50	0.22	0.07	1.0	124
0	25	20	1.1	436	5	44	0.15	0.07	0.8	86
0	81	68	0.7	1436	6	59	0.60	0.14	1.5	294
0	27	22	0.2	473	2	19	0.20	0.04	0.5	97
0	25	20	1.1	390	7	29	0.14	0.07	0.8	72
0	17	35	0.3	247	9	40	0.04	0.04	0.5	92
0	10	4	0.1	171	0	47	0.01	0.04	0.9	6
0	19	9	0.2	335	0	91	0.03	0.07	1.7	11
0	51	8	0.7	236	15	85	0.03	0.06	1.6	7

| | | Food energy | Protein | Fat | Fatty Acids | | |
					Saturated	Monoun-saturated	Polyun-saturated
FRUITS AND FRUIT JUICES cont.	Grams	Calories	Grams	Grams	Grams	Grams	Grams
PEACHES CANNED HEAVY SYRUP .... 1 HALF	81	60	0	0	0.0	0.0	0.0
PEACHES DRIED .... 1 CUP	160	380	6	1	0.1	0.4	0.6
PEACHES DRIED COOKED UNSWETND ...... 1 CUP	258	200	3	1	0.1	0.2	0.3
PEACHES FROZEN SWETNED W/VIT C ...... 10 OZ	284	265	2	0	0.0	0.1	0.2
PEACHES FROZEN SWETNED W/VIT C ...... 1 CUP	250	235	2	0	0.0	0.1	0.2
PEARS RAW BARTLETT .... 1 PEAR	166	100	1	1	0.0	0.1	0.2
PEARS CANNED HEAVY SYRUP .... 1 CUP	255	190	1	0	0.0	0.1	0.1
PEARS CANNED HEAVY SYRUP .... 1 HALF	79	60	0	0	0.0	0.0	0.0
PEARS CANNED JUICE PACK .... 1 CUP	248	125	1	0	0.0	0.0	0.0
PEARS CANNED JUICE PACK .... 1 HALF	77	40	0	0	0.0	0.0	0.0
PINEAPPLE RAW DICED .... 1 CUP	155	75	1	1	0.0	0.1	0.2
PINEAPPLE CANNED HEAVY SYRUP .... 1 CUP	255	200	1	0	0.0	0.0	0.1
PINEAPPLE CANNED HEAVY SYRUP .... 1 SLICE	58	45	0	0	0.0	0.0	0.0
PINEAPPLE CANNED JUICE PACK .... 1 CUP	250	150	1	0	0.0	0.0	0.1
PINEAPPLE CANNED JUICE PACK .... 1 SLICE	58	35	0	0	0.0	0.0	0.0
PINEAPPLE JUICE CANNED UNSWTN .... 1 CUP	250	140	1	0	0.0	0.0	0.1
PLUMS RAW 1-1/2-IN DIAM .... 1 PLUM	28	15	0	0	0.0	0.1	0.0
PLUMS CANNED HEAVY SYRUP .... 1 CUP	258	230	1	0	0.0	0.2	0.1
PLUMS CANNED HEAVY SYRUP .... 3 PLUMS	133	120	0	0	0.0	0.1	0.0
PLUMS CANNED JUICE PACK .... 1 CUP	252	145	1	0	0.0	0.0	0.0
PLUMS CANNED JUICE PACK .... 3 PLUMS	95	55	0	0	0.0	0.0	0.0
PRUNES DRIED .... 5 LARGE	49	115	1	0	0.0	0.2	0.1
PRUNES DRIED COOKED UNSWTNED .... 1 CUP	212	225	2	0	0.0	0.3	0.1
PRUNE JUICE CANNED .... 1 CUP	256	180	2	0	0.0	0.1	0.0
RAISINS .... 1 CUP	145	435	5	1	0.2	0.0	0.2
RAISINS .... 1 PACKET	14	40	0	0	0.0	0.0	0.0
RASPBERRIES RAW .... 1 CUP	12	60	1	1	0.0	0.1	0.4
RASPBERRIES FROZEN SWEETENED .... 10 OZ	284	295	2	0	0.0	0.0	0.3
RASPBERRIES FROZEN SWEETENED .... 1 CUP	250	255	2	0	0.0	0.0	0.2
RHUBARB COOKED ADDED SUGAR .... 1 CUP	240	280	1	0	0.0	0.0	0.1
STRAWBERRIES RAW .... 1 CUP	149	45	1	1	0.0	0.1	0.3
STRAWBERRIES FROZEN SWEETEND .... 10 OZ	284	275	2	0	0.0	0.1	0.2
STRAWBERRIES FROZEN SWEETEND .... 1 CUP	255	245	1	0	0.0	0.0	0.2
TANGERINES RAW .... 1 TANGRN	84	35	1	0	0.0	0.0	0.0
TANGERINES CANNED LIGHT SYRP .... 1 CUP	252	155	1	0	0.0	0.0	0.1
TANGERINE JUICE CANNED SWTNED .... 1 CUP	249	125	1	0	0.0	0.0	0.1
WATERMELON RAW .... 1 PIECE	482	155	3	2	0.3	0.2	1.0

Choles-terol	Carbo-hydrate	Calcium	Iron	Potas-sium	Sodium	Vit. A Value (RE)	Thiamin	Ribo-flavin	Niacin	Ascorbic Acid
Milligrams	Grams	Milligrams	Milligrams	Milligrams	Milligrams	Retinol Equivalents	Milligrams	Milligrams	Milligrams	Milligrams
0	16	2	0.2	75	5	27	0.01	0.02	0.5	2
0	98	45	6.5	1594	11	346	0.00	0.34	7.0	8
0	51	23	3.4	826	5	51	0.01	0.05	3.9	10
0	68	9	1.1	369	17	81	0.04	0.10	1.9	268
0	60	8	0.9	325	15	71	0.03	0.09	1.6	236
0	25	18	0.4	208	0	3	0.03	0.07	0.2	7
0	49	13	0.6	166	13	1	0.03	0.06	0.6	3
0	15	4	0.2	51	4	0	0.01	0.02	0.2	1
0	32	22	0.7	238	10	1	0.03	0.03	0.5	4
0	10	7	0.2	74	3	0	0.01	0.01	0.2	1
0	19	11	0.6	175	2	4	0.14	0.06	0.7	24
0	52	36	1.0	265	3	4	0.23	0.06	0.7	19
0	12	8	0.2	60	1	10	0.05	0.01	0.2	4
0	39	35	0.7	305	3	10	0.24	0.05	0.7	24
0	9	8	0.2	71	1	2	0.06	0.01	0.2	6
0	34	43	0.7	335	3	1	0.14	0.06	0.6	27
0	4	1	0.0	48	0	9	0.01	0.03	0.1	3
0	60	23	2.2	235	49	67	0.04	0.10	0.8	1
0	31	12	1.1	121	25	34	0.02	0.05	0.4	1
0	38	25	0.9	388	3	254	0.06	0.15	1.2	7
0	14	10	0.3	146	1	96	0.02	0.06	0.4	3
0	31	25	1.2	365	2	97	0.04	0.08	1.0	2
0	60	49	2.4	708	4	65	0.05	0.21	1.5	6
0	45	31	3.0	707	10	1	0.04	0.18	2.0	10
0	115	71	3.0	1089	17	1	0.23	0.13	1.2	5
0	11	7	0.3	105	2	0	0.02	0.01	0.1	0
0	14	27	0.7	187	0	16	0.04	0.11	1.1	31
0	74	43	1.8	324	3	17	0.05	0.13	0.7	47
0	65	38	1.6	285	3	15	0.05	0.11	0.6	41
0	75	348	0.5	230	2	17	0.04	0.06	0.5	8
0	10	21	0.6	247	1	4	0.03	0.10	0.3	84
0	74	31	1.7	278	9	7	0.05	0.14	1.1	118
0	66	28	1.5	250	8	6	0.04	0.13	1.0	106
0	9	12	0.1	132	1	77	0.09	0.02	0.1	26
0	41	18	0.9	197	15	212	0.13	0.11	1.1	50
0	30	45	0.5	443	2	105	0.15	0.05	0.2	55
0	35	39	0.8	559	10	176	0.39	0.10	1.0	46

		Food energy	Protein	Fat	Fatty Acids		
					Saturated	Monoun-saturated	Polyun-saturated
GRAIN PRODUCTS		Grams	Calories	Grams	Grams	Grams	Grams	Grams

		Grams	Calories	Grams	Grams	Grams	Grams	Grams
BARLEY PEARLED LIGHT UNCOOKD	1 CUP	200	700	16	2	0.3	0.2	0.9
BAKING PWDR BISCUITS HOME RECPE	1 BISCUT	28	100	2	5	1.2	2.0	1.3
BREADCRUMBS DRY GRATED	1 CUP	100	390	13	5	1.5	1.6	1.0
BOSTON BROWN BREAD W/WHTE CRNM[17]	1 SLICE	45	95	2	1	0.3	0.1	0.1
CRACKED-WHEAT BREAD	1 LOAF	454	1190	42	16	3.1	4.3	5.7
CRACKED-WHEAT BREAD	1 SLICE	25	65	2	1	0.2	0.2	0.3
FRENCH OR VIENNA BREAD	1 LOAF	454	1270	43	18	3.8	5.7	5.9
FRENCH BREAD	1 SLICE	35	100	3	1	0.3	0.4	0.5
VIENNA BREAD	1 SLICE	25	70	2	1	0.2	0.3	0.3
ITALIAN BREAD	1 LOAF	454	1255	41	4	0.6	0.3	1.6
ITALIAN BREAD	1 SLICE	30	85	3	0	0.0	0.0	0.1
MIXED GRAIN BREAD[17]	1 LOAF	454	1165	45	17	3.2	4.1	6.5
MIXED GRAIN BREAD[17]	1 SLICE	25	65	2	1	0.2	0.2	0.4
MIXED GRAIN BREAD TOASTED[17]	1 SLICE	23	65	2	1	0.2	0.2	0.4
RAISIN BREAD[17]	1 LOAF	454	1260	37	18	4.1	6.5	6.7
RAISIN BREAD[17]	1 SLICE	25	65	2	1	0.2	0.3	0.4
RAISIN BREAD TOASTED[17]	1 SLICE	21	65	2	1	0.2	0.3	0.4
RYE BREAD LIGHT[17]	1 LOAF	454	1190	38	17	3.3	5.2	5.5
RYE BREAD LIGHT[17]	1 SLICE	25	65	2	1	0.2	0.3	0.3
RYE BREAD LIGHT TOASTED[17]	1 SLICE	22	65	2	1	0.2	0.3	0.3
WHEAT BREAD[17]	1 LOAF	454	1160	43	19	3.9	7.3	4.5
WHEAT BREAD[17]	1 SLICE	25	65	2	1	0.2	0.4	0.3
WHITE BREAD[17]	1 LOAF	454	1210	38	18	5.6	6.5	4.2
WHITE BREAD SLICE 18 PER LOAF[17]	1 SLICE	25	65	2	1	0.3	0.4	0.2
WHITE BREAD TOASTED 18 PER[17]	1 SLICE	22	65	2	1	0.3	0.4	0.2
WHOLE-WHEAT BREAD[17]	1 LOAF	454	1110	44	20	5.8	6.8	5.2
WHOLE-WHEAT BREAD[17]	1 SLICE	28	70	3	1	0.4	0.4	0.3
WHOLE-WHEAT BREAD TOASTED[17]	1 SLICE	25	70	3	1	0.4	0.4	0.3
CORN GRITS CKD REG WHTE NO SALT	1 CUP	242	145	3	0	0.0	0.1	0.2
CORN GRITS CKD REG WHTE W/SALT	1 CUP	242	145	3	0	0.0	0.1	0.2
CORN GRITS CKD REG YLLW NOSALT	1 CUP	242	145	3	0	0.0	0.1	0.2
CORN GRITS CKD REG YLLW W/SALT	1 CUP	242	145	3	0	0.0	0.1	0.2
CORN GRITS COOKED INSTANT	1 PKT	137	80	2	0	0.0	0.0	0.1

[17] Made with vegetable shortening.
[18] Nutrient added.

Choles-terol	Carbo-hydrate	Calcium	Iron	Potas-sium	Sodium	Vit. A Value (RE)	Thiamin	Ribo-flavin	Niacin	Ascorbic Acid
Milligrams	Grams	Milligrams	Milligrams	Milligrams	Milligrams	Retinol Equivalents	Milligrams	Milligrams	Milligrams	Milligrams
0	158	32	4.2	320	6	0	0.24	0.10	6.2	0
0	13	47	0.7	32	195	3	0.08	0.08	0.8	0
5	73	122	4.1	152	736	0	0.35	0.35	4.8	0
3	21	41	0.9	131	113	0	0.06	0.04	0.7	0
0	227	295	12.1	608	1966	0	1.73	1.73	15.3	0
0	12	16	0.7	34	106	0	0.10	0.09	0.8	0
0	230	499	14.0	409	2633	0	2.09	1.59	18.2	0
0	18	39	1.1	32	203	0	0.16	0.12	1.4	0
0	13	28	0.8	23	145	0	0.12	0.09	1.0	0
0	256	77	12.7	336	2656	0	1.80	1.10	15.0	0
0	17	5	0.8	22	176	0	0.12	0.07	1.0	0
0	212	472	14.8	990	1870	0	1.77	1.73	18.9	0
0	12	27	0.8	56	106	0	0.10	0.10	1.1	0
0	12	27	0.8	56	106	0	0.08	0.10	1.1	0
0	239	463	14.1	1058	1657	0	1.50	2.81	18.6	0
0	13	25	0.8	59	92	0	0.08	0.15	1.0	0
0	13	25	0.8	59	92	0	0.06	0.15	1.0	0
0	218	363	12.3	926	3164	0	1.86	1.45	15.0	0
0	12	20	0.7	51	175	0	0.10	0.08	0.8	0
0	12	20	0.7	51	175	0	0.08	0.08	0.8	0
0	213	572	15.8	627	2447	0	2.09	1.45	20.5	0
0	12	32	0.9	35	138	0	0.12	0.08	1.2	0
0	222	572	12.9	508	2334	0	2.13	1.41	17.0	0
0	12	32	0.7	28	129	0	0.12	0.08	0.9	0
0	12	32	0.7	28	129	0	0.09	0.08	0.9	0
0	206	327	15.5	799	2887	0	1.59	0.95	17.4	0
0	13	20	1.0	50	180	0	0.10	0.06	1.1	0
0	13	20	1.0	50	180	0	0.08	0.06	1.1	0
0	31	0	1.5[18]	53	0	0	0.24[18]	0.15[18]	2.0[18]	0
0	31	0	1.5[18]	53	540	0	0.24[18]	0.15[18]	2.0[18]	0
0	31	0	1.5[18]	53	0	14	0.24[18]	0.15[18]	2.0[18]	0
0	31	0	1.5[18]	53	540	14	0.24[18]	0.15[18]	2.0[18]	0
0	18	7	1.0[18]	29	343	0	0.18[18]	0.08[18]	1.3[18]	0

		Food energy	Protein	Fat	Fatty Acids		
					Saturated	Monoun-saturated	Polyun-saturated
GRAIN PRODUCTS CONT.	Grams	Calories	Grams	Grams	Grams	Grams	Grams
CRM WHEAT CKD REG INST NO SALT ...... 1 CUP	244	140	4	0	0.1	0.0	0.2
CRM WHEAT CKD REG INST W/SALT .... 1 CUP	244	140	4	0	0.1	0.0	0.2
CRM WHEAT CKD QUICK NO SALT .... 1 CUP	244	140	4	0	0.1	0.0	0.2
CRM WHEAT CKD QUICK W/SALT .... 1 CUP	244	140	4	0	0.1	0.0	0.2
CREAM OF WHEAT CKD MIX N EAT .... 1 PKT	142	100	3	0	0.0	0.0	0.1
MALT-O-MEAL W/O SALT .... 1 CUP	240	120	4	0	0.0	0.0	0.1
MALT-O-MEAL WITH SALT .... 1 CUP	240	120	4	0	0.0	0.0	0.1
OATMEAL CKD RG QCK INST W/OSAL ...... 1 CUP	234	145	6	2	0.4	0.8	1.0
OATMEAL CKD RG QCK INST W/SALT .... 1 CUP	234	145	6	2	0.4	0.8	1.0
OATMEAL CKD INSTNT PLAIN FORTF .... 1 PKT	177	105	4	2	0.3	0.6	0.7
OATMEAL CKD INSTNT FLVRD FORTF ...... 1 PKT	164	160	5	2	0.3	0.7	0.8
ALL-BRAN CEREAL .... 1 OZ	28	70	4	1	0.1	0.1	0.3
CAP'N CRUNCH CEREAL .... 1 OZ	28	120	1	3	1.7	0.3	0.4
CHEERIOS CEREAL .... 1 OZ	28	110	4	2	0.3	0.6	0.7
CORN FLAKES KELLOGG'S .... 1 OZ	28	110	2	0	0.0	0.0	0.0
CORN FLAKES TOASTIES .... 1 OZ	28	110	2	0	0.0	0.0	0.0
40% BRAN FLAKES KELLOGG'S .... 1 OZ	28	90	4	1	0.1	0.1	0.3
40% BRAN FLAKES POST .... 1 OZ	28	90	3	0	0.1	0.1	0.2
FROOT LOOPS CEREAL .... 1 OZ	28	110	2	1	0.2	0.1	0.1
GOLDEN GRAHAMS CEREAL .... 1 OZ	28	110	2	1	0.7	0.1	0.2
GRAPE-NUTS CEREAL .... 1 OZ	28	100	3	0	0.0	0.0	0.1
HONEY NUT CHEERIOS CEREAL .... 1 OZ	28	105	3	1	0.1	0.3	0.3
LUCKY CHARMS CEREAL .... 1 OZ	28	110	3	1	0.2	0.4	0.4
NATURE VALLEY GRANOLA CEREAL .... 1 OZ	28	125	3	5	3.3	0.7	0.7
100% NATURAL CEREAL .... 1 OZ	28	135	3	6	4.1	1.2	0.5
PRODUCT 19 CEREAL .... 1 OZ	28	110	3	0	0.0	0.0	0.1
RAISIN BRAN KELLOGG'S .... 1 OZ	28	90	3	1	0.1	0.1	0.3
RAISIN BRAN POST .... 1 OZ	28	85	3	1	0.1	0.1	0.3
RICE KRISPIES CEREAL .... 1 OZ	28	110	2	0	0.0	0.0	0.1
SHREDDED WHEAT CEREAL .... 1 OZ	28	100	3	1	0.1	0.1	0.3
SPECIAL K CEREAL .... 1 OZ	28	110	6	0	0.0	0.0	0.0
SUPER SUGAR CRISP CEREAL .... 1 OZ	28	105	2	0	0.0	0.0	0.1
SUGAR FROSTED FLAKES KELLOGG .... 1 OZ	28	110	1	0	0.0	0.0	0.0
SUGAR SMACKS CEREAL .... 1 OZ	28	105	2	1	0.1	0.1	0.2
TOTAL CEREAL .... 1 OZ	28	100	3	1	0.1	0.1	0.3
TRIX CEREAL .... 1 OZ	28	110	2	0	0.2	0.1	0.1
WHEATIES CEREAL .... 1 OZ	28	100	3	0	0.1	0.0	0.2

[a]Nutrient added.
[b]Value based on label declaration for added nutrients.

Choles-terol	Carbo-hydrate	Calcium	Iron	Potas-sium	Sodium	Vit. A Value (RE)	Thiamin	Ribo-flavin	Niacin	Ascorbic Acid
Milligrams	Grams	Milligrams	Milligrams	Milligrams	Milligrams	Retinol Equivalents	Milligrams	Milligrams	Milligrams	Milligrams
0	29	54[19]	10.9[19]	46	5	0	0.24[19]	0.07[19]	1.5[19]	0
0	29	54[19]	10.9[19]	46	390	0	0.24[19]	0.07[19]	1.5[19]	0
0	29	54[19]	10.9[19]	46	142	0	0.24[19]	0.07[19]	1.5[19]	0
0	29	54[19]	10.9[19]	46	390	0	0.24[19]	0.07[19]	1.5[19]	0
0	21	20[19]	8.1[19]	38	241	376[19]	0.43[19]	0.28[19]	5.0[19]	0
0	26	5	9.6[19]	31	2	0	0.48[19]	0.24[19]	5.8[19]	0
0	26	5	9.6[19]	31	324	0	0.48[19]	0.24[19]	5.8[19]	0
0	25	19	1.6	131	2	4	0.26	0.05	0.3	0
0	25	19	1.6	131	374	4	0.26	0.05	0.3	0
0	18	163[19]	6.3[19]	99	285[19]	453[19]	0.53[19]	0.28[19]	5.5[19]	0
0	31	168[19]	6.7[19]	137	254[19]	460[19]	0.53[19]	0.38[19]	5.9[19]	0
0	21	23	4.5[19]	350	320	375[19]	0.37[19]	0.43[19]	5.0[19]	15[19]
0	23	5	7.5[19]	37	213	4	0.50[19]	0.55[19]	6.6[19]	0
0	20	48	4.5[19]	101	307	375[19]	0.37[19]	0.43[19]	5.0[19]	15[19]
0	24	1	1.8[19]	26	351	375[19]	0.37[19]	0.43[19]	5.0[19]	15[19]
0	24	1	0.7[19]	33	297	375[19]	0.37[19]	0.43[19]	5.0[19]	0
0	22	14	8.1[19]	180	264	375[19]	0.37[19]	0.43[19]	5.0[19]	0
0	22	12	4.5[19]	151	260	375[19]	0.37[19]	0.43[19]	5.0[19]	0
0	25	3	4.5[19]	26	145	375[19]	0.37[19]	0.43[19]	5.0[19]	15[19]
0	24	17	4.5[19]	63	346	375[19]	0.37[19]	0.43[19]	5.0[19]	15[19]
0	23	11	1.2	95	197	375[19]	0.37[19]	0.43[19]	5.0[19]	0
0	23	20	4.5[19]	99	257	375[19]	0.37[19]	0.43[19]	5.0[19]	15[19]
0	23	32	4.5[19]	59	201	375[19]	0.37[19]	0.43[19]	5.0[19]	15[19]
0	19	18	0.9	98	58	2	0.10	0.05	0.2	0
0	18	49	0.8	140	12	2	0.09	0.15	0.6	0
0	24	3	18.0[19]	44	325	1501[19]	1.50[19]	1.70[19]	20.0[19]	60[19]
0	21	10	3.5[19]	147	207	288[19]	0.28[19]	0.34[19]	3.9[19]	0
0	21	13	4.5[19]	175	185	375[19]	0.37[19]	0.43[19]	5.0[19]	0
0	25	4	1.8[19]	29	340	375[19]	0.37[19]	0.43[19]	5.0[19]	15[19]
0	23	11	1.2	102	3	0	0.07	0.08	1.5	0
0	21	8	4.5[19]	49	265	375[19]	0.37[19]	0.43[19]	5.0[19]	15[19]
0	26	6	1.8[19]	105	25	375[19]	0.37[19]	0.43[19]	5.0[19]	0
0	26	1	1.8[19]	18	230	375[19]	0.37[19]	0.43[19]	5.0[19]	15[19]
0	25	3	1.8[19]	42	75	375[19]	0.37[19]	0.43[19]	5.0[19]	15[19]
0	22	48	18.0[19]	106	352	1501[19]	1.50[19]	1.70[19]	20.0[19]	60[19]
0	25	6	4.5[19]	27	181	375[19]	0.37[19]	0.43[19]	5.0[19]	15[19]
0	23	43	4.5[19]	106	354	375[19]	0.37[19]	0.43[19]	5.0[19]	15[19]

		Food energy	Protein	Fat	Fatty Acids		
					Saturated	Monoun-saturated	Polyun-saturated
Grain Products cont.		Grams	Calories	Grams	Grams	Grams	Grams	Grams

		Grams	Calories	Grams	Grams	Grams	Grams	Grams
BUCKWHEAT FLOUR LIGHT SIFTED	1 CUP	98	340	6	1	0.2	0.4	0.4
BULGUR UNCOOKED	1 CUP	170	600	19	3	1.2	0.3	1.2
GINGERBREAD CAKE FROM MIX	1 PIECE	63	175	2	4	1.1	1.8	1.2
SHEETCAKE W/O FRSTNG HOME RECIP[20]	1 PIECE	86	315	4	12	3.3	5.0	2.8
SHEETCAKE W/ WH FRSTNG HOME RCIP[20] ...	1 PIECE	121	445	4	14	4.6	5.6	2.9
POUND CAKE FROM HOME RECIPE[21]	1 SLICE	30	120	2	5	1.2	2.4	1.6
CHOCOLATE CHIP COOKIES HME RCP[22]	4 COOKIE	40	185	2	11	3.9	4.3	2.0
CORNMEAL WHOLE-GRND UNBOLT DRY	1 CUP	122	435	11	5	0.5	1.1	2.5
CORNMEAL BOLTED DRY FORM	1 CUP	122	440	11	4	0.5	0.9	2.2
CORNMEAL DEGERMED ENRICHED DRY	1 CUP	138	500	11	2	0.2	0.4	0.9
CORNMEAL DEGERMED ENRCHED COOK ...	1 CUP	240	120	3	0	0.0	0.1	0.2
GRAHAM CRACKER PLAIN[23]	2 CRACKR	14	60	1	1	0.4	0.6	0.4
DOUGHNUTS CAKE TYPE PLAIN	1 DONUT	50	210	3	12	2.8	5.0	3.0
FRENCH TOAST HOME RECIPE	1 SLICE	65	155	6	7	1.6	2.0	1.6
MACARONI COOKED FIRM	1 CUP	130	190	7	1	0.1	0.1	0.3
MACARONI COOKED TENDER HOT	1 CUP	140	155	5	1	0.1	0.1	0.2
CORN MUFFINS HOME RECIPE	1 MUFFIN	45	145	3	5	1.5	2.2	1.4
NOODLES EGG COOKED	1 CUP	160	200	7	2	0.5	0.6	0.6
PANCAKES BUCKWHEAT FROM MIX	1 PANCAK	27	55	2	2	0.9	0.9	0.5
PANCAKES PLAIN HOME RECIPE	1 PANCAK	27	60	2	2	0.5	0.8	0.5
PIECRUST FROM HOME RECIPE	1 SHELL	180	900	11	60	14.8	25.9	15.7
PIECRUST FROM MIX	2 CRUST	320	1485	20	93	22.7	41.0	25.0
APPLE PIE	1 PIECE	158	405	3	18	4.6	7.4	4.4
BLUEBERRY PIE	1 PIECE	158	380	4	17	4.3	7.4	4.6
CHERRY PIE	1 PIECE	158.	410	4	18	4.7	7.7	4.6
CUSTARD PIE	1 PIECE	152	330	9	17	5.6	6.7	3.2
LEMON MERINGUE PIE	1 PIECE	140	355	5	14	4.3	5.7	2.9
PUMPKIN PIE	1 PIE	910	1920	36	102	38.2	40.0	18.2
PUMPKIN PIE	1 PIECE	152	320	6	17	6.4	6.7	3.0
PRETZELS STICK	10 PRETZ	3	10	0	0	0.0	0.0	0.0
RICE WHITE COOKED	1 CUP	205	225	4	0	0.1	0.1	0.1
RICE WHITE INSTANT COOKED	1 CUP	165	180	4	0	0.1	0.1	0.1
RICE WHITE PARBOILED COOKED	1 CUP	175	185	4	0	0.0	0.0	0.1
ROLLS DINNER COMMERCIAL	1 ROLL	28	85	2	2	0.5	0.8	0.6

[20]Cake made with vegetable shortening; frosting with margarine.
[21]Made with margarine.
[22]Made with vegetable shortening.
[23]Crackers made with enriched flour.

Choles-terol	Carbo-hydrate	Calcium	Iron	Potas-sium	Sodium	Vit. A Value (RE)	Thiamin	Ribo-flavin	Niacin	Ascorbic Acid
Milligrams	Grams	Milligrams	Milligrams	Milligrams	Milligrams	Retinol Equivalents	Milligrams	Milligrams	Milligrams	Milligrams
0	78	11	1.0	314	2	0	0.08	0.04	0.4	0
0	129	575	9.5	389	7	0	0.48	0.24	7.7	0
1	32	57	1.2	173	192	0	0.09	0.11	0.8	0
61	48	55	1.3	68	258	41	0.14	0.15	1.1	0
70	77	61	1.2	74	275	71	0.13	0.16	1.1	0
32	15	20	0.5	28	96	60	0.05	0.06	0.5	0
18	26	13	1.0	82	82	5	0.06	0.06	0.6	0
0	90	24	2.2	346	1	62	0.48	0.13	2.4	0
0	91	21	2.2	303	1	59	0.37	0.10	2.3	0
0	108	8	5.9	166	1	61	0.61	0.36	4.8	0
0	26	2	1.4	38	0	14	0.14	0.10	1.2	0
0	11	6	0.4	36	86	0	0.02	0.03	0.6	0
20	24	22	1.0	58	192	5	0.12	0.12	1.1	0
112	17	72	1.3	86	257	32	0.12	0.16	1.0	0
0	39	14	2.1	103	1	0	0.23	0.13	1.8	0
0	32	11	1.7	85	1	0	0.20	0.11	1.5	0
23	21	66	0.9	57	169	15	0.11	0.11	0.9	0
50	37	16	2.6	70	3	34	0.22	0.13	1.9	0
20	6	59	0.4	66	125	17	0.04	0.05	0.2	0
16	9	27	0.5	33	115	10	0.06	0.07	0.5	0
0	79	25	4.5	90	1100	0	0.54	0.40	5.0	0
0	141	131	9.3	179	2602	0	1.06	0.80	9.9	0
0	60	13	1.6	126	476	5	0.17	0.13	1.6	2
0	55	17	2.1	158	423	14	0.17	0.14	1.7	6
0	61	22	1.6	166	480	70	0.19	0.14	1.6	0
169	36	146	1.5	208	436	96	0.14	0.32	0.9	0
143	53	20	1.4	70	395	66	0.10	0.14	0.8	4
655	223	464	8.2	1456	1947	2493	0.82	1.27	7.3	0
109	37	78	1.4	243	325	416	0.14	0.21	1.2	0
0	2	1	0.1	3	48	0	0.01	0.01	0.1	0
0	50	21	1.8	57	0	0	0.23	0.02	2.1	0
0	40	5	1.3	0	0	0	0.21	0.02	1.7	0
0	41	33	1.4	75	0	0	0.19	0.02	2.1	0
0	14	33	0.8	36	155	0	0.14	0.09	1.1	0

	Food energy	Protein	Fat	Fatty Acids		
				Saturated	Monoun-saturated	Polyun-saturated
	Grams	Calories	Grams	Grams	Grams	Grams	Grams

GRAIN PRODUCTS cont.							
ROLLS HARD . . . . 1 ROLL	50	155	5	2	0.4	0.5	0.6
SPAGHETTI COOKED FIRM . . . . 1 CUP	130	190	7	1	0.1	0.1	0.3
WAFFLES FROM MIX . . . . 1 WAFFLE	75	205	7	8	2.7	2.9	1.5
WHEAT FLOUR ALL-PURPOSE SIFTD . . . . 1 CUP	115	420	12	1	0.2	0.1	0.5
CAKE OR PASTRY FLOUR SIFTED . . . . 1 CUP	96	350	7	1	0.1	0.1	0.3
SELF-RISING FLOUR UNSIFTED . . . . 1 CUP	125	440	12	1	0.2	0.1	0.5
WHOLE-WHEAT FLOUR HRD WHT STIR . . . . . . 1 CUP	120	400	16	2	0.3	0.3	1.1

LEGUMES, NUTS, AND SEEDS							
ALMONDS SLIVERED . . . . 1 CUP	135	795	27	70	6.7	45.8	14.8
ALMONDS WHOLE . . . . 1 OZ	28	165	6	15	1.4	9.6	3.1
GREAT NORTHN BEANS DRY CKD DRN . . . . . 1 CUP	180	210	14	1	0.1	0.1	0.6
LIMA BEANS DRY COOKED DRANED . . . . 1 CUP	190	260	16	1	0.2	0.1	0.5
PEA BEANS DRY COOKED DRAINED . . . . 1 CUP	190	225	15	1	0.1	0.1	0.7
PINTO BEANS DRY COOKED DRAINED . . . . . . 1 CUP	180	265	15	1	0.1	0.1	0.5
BEANS DRY CANNED W/FRANKFURTER . . . . . 1 CUP	255	365	19	18	7.4	8.8	0.7
BEANS DRY CANNED W/PORK +TOM SCE . . . 1 CUP	255	310	16	7	2.4	2.7	0.7
BRAZIL NUTS . . . . 1 OZ	28	185	4	19	4.6	6.5	6.8
CASHEW NUTS DRY ROASTED SALTD . . . . . . 1 CUP	137	785	21	63	12.5	37.4	10.7
CASHEW NUTS DRY ROASTD SALTED . . . . . . 1 OZ	28	165	4	13	2.6	7.7	2.2
PEANUTS OIL ROASTED SALTED . . . . 1 CUP	145	840	39	71	9.9	35.5	22.6
PEANUTS OIL ROASTED SALTED . . . . 1 OZ	28	165	8	14	1.9	6.9	4.4
PEANUT BUTTER . . . . 1 TBSP	16	95	5	8	1.4	4.0	2.5
PEAS SPLIT DRY COOKED . . . . 1 CUP	200	230	16	1	0.1	0.1	0.3
PECANS HALVES . . . . 1 CUP	108	720	8	73	5.9	45.5	18.1
PECANS HALVES . . . . 1 OZ	28	190	2	19	1.5	12.0	4.7
REFRIED BEANS CANNED . . . . 1 CUP	290	295	18	3	0.4	0.6	1.4
WALNUTS BLACK CHOPPED . . . . 1 CUP	125	760	30	71	4.5	15.9	46.9
WALNUTS BLACK CHOPPED . . . . 1 OZ	28	170	7	16	1.0	3.6	10.6
WALNUTS ENGLISH PIECES . . . . 1 CUP	120	770	17	74	6.7	17.0	47.0
WALNUTS ENGLISH PIECES . . . . 1 OZ	28	180	4	18	1.6	4.0	11.1

Cholesterol	Carbohydrate	Calcium	Iron	Potassium	Sodium	Vit. A Value (RE)	Thiamin	Riboflavin	Niacin	Ascorbic Acid
Milligrams	Grams	Milligrams	Milligrams	Milligrams	Milligrams	Retinol Equivalents	Milligrams	Milligrams	Milligrams	Milligrams
0	30	24	1.4	49	313	0	0.20	0.12	1.7	0
0	39	14	2.0	103	1	0	0.23	0.13	1.8	0
59	27	179	1.2	146	515	49	0.14	0.23	0.9	0
0	88	18	5.1	109	2	0	0.73	0.46	6.1	0
0	76	16	4.2	91	2	0	0.58	0.38	5.1	0
0	93	331	5.5	113	1349	0	0.80	0.50	6.6	0
0	85	49	5.2	444	4	0	0.66	0.14	5.2	0
0	28	359	4.9	988	15	0	0.28	1.05	4.5	1
0	6	75	1.0	208	3	0	0.06	0.22	1.0	0
0	38	90	4.9	749	13	0	0.25	0.13	1.3	0
0	49	55	5.9	1163	4	0	0.25	0.11	1.3	0
0	40	95	5.1	790	13	0	0.27	0.13	1.3	0
0	49	86	5.4	882	3	0	0.33	0.16	0.7	0
30	32	94	4.8	668	1374	33	0.18	0.15	3.3	0
10	48	138	4.6	536	1181	33	0.20	0.08	1.5	5
0	4	50	1.0	170	1	0	0.28	0.03	0.5	0
0	45	62	8.2	774	877	0	0.27	0.27	1.9	0
0	9	13	1.7	160	181	0	0.06	0.06	0.4	0
0	27	125	2.8	1019	626	0	0.42	0.15	21.5	0
0	5	24	0.5	199	122	0	0.08	0.03	4.2	0
0	3	5	0.3	110	75	0	0.02	0.02	2.2	0
0	42	22	3.4	592	26	8	0.30	0.18	1.8	0
0	20	39	2.3	423	1	14	0.92	0.14	1.0	2
0	5	10	0.6	111	0	4	0.24	0.04	0.3	1
0	51	141	5.1	1141	1228	0	0.14	0.16	1.4	17
0	15	73	3.8	655	1	37	0.27	0.14	0.9	0
0	3	16	0.9	149	0	8	0.06	0.03	0.2	0
0	22	113	2.9	602	12	15	0.46	0.18	1.3	4
0	5	27	0.7	142	3	4	0.11	0.04	0.3	1

						Fatty Acids	
		Food energy	Protein	Fat	Saturated	Monoun-saturated	Polyun-saturated
MEAT AND MEAT PRODUCTS	Grams	Calories	Grams	Grams	Grams	Grams	Grams
BEEF CKD CHUCK BLADE LEAN+FAT .... 3 OZ	85	325	22	26	10.8	11.7	0.9
BEEF CKD CHUCK BLADE LEAN ONLY ...... 2.2 OZ	62	170	19	9	3.9	4.2	0.3
BEEF CKD BTTM ROUND LEAN+FAT .... 3 OZ	85	220	25	13	4.8	5.7	0.5
BEEF CKD BTTM ROUND LEAN ONLY .... 2.8 OZ	78	175	25	8	2.7	3.4	0.3
GROUND BEEF BROILED LEAN .... 3 OZ	85	230	21	16	6.2	6.9	0.6
GROUND BEEF BROILED REGULAR .... 3 OZ	85	245	20	18	6.9	7.7	0.7
BEEF ROAST RIB LEAN+FAT .... 3 OZ	85	315	19	26	10.8	11.4	0.9
BEEF ROAST RIB LEAN ONLY .... 2.2 OZ	61	150	17	9	3.6	3.7	0.3
BEEF ROAST EYE O RND LEAN+FAT .... 3 OZ	85	205	23	12	4.9	5.4	0.5
BEEF ROAST EYE O RND LEAN .... 2.6 OZ	75	135	22	5	1.9	2.1	0.2
BEEF STEAK SIRLOIN BROIL LEAN+FAT .... 3 OZ	85	240	23	15	6.4	6.9	0.6
BEEF STEAK SIRLOIN BROIL LEAN .... 2.5 OZ	72	150	22	6	2.6	2.8	0.3
BEEF CANNED CORNED .... 3 OZ	85	185	22	10	4.2	4.9	0.4
BEEF DRIED CHIPPED .... 2.5 OZ	72	145	24	4	1.8	2.0	0.2
LAMB CHOPS ARM BRAISED LEAN+FAT .... 2.2 OZ	63	220	20	15	6.9	6.0	0.9
LAMB CHOPS ARM BRAISED LEAN .... 1.7 OZ	48	135	17	7	2.9	2.6	0.4
LAMB CHOPS LOIN BROIL LEAN+FAT ...... 2.8 OZ	80	235	22	16	7.3	6.4	1.0
LAMB CHOPS LOIN BROIL LEAN .... 2.3 OZ	64	140	19	6	2.6	2.4	0.4
LAMB LEG ROASTED LEAN+FAT .... 3 OZ	85	205	22	13	5.6	4.9	0.8
LAMB LEG ROASTED LEAN ONLY .... 2.6 OZ	73	140	20	6	2.4	2.2	0.4
PORK CURED BACON REGUL CKED .... 3 SLICE	19	110	6	9	3.3	4.5	1.1
PORK CURED HAM ROSTED LEAN+FAT ..... 3 OZ	85	205	18	14	5.1	6.7	1.5
PORK CURED HAM ROSTED LEAN .... 2.4 OZ	68	105	17	4	1.3	1.7	0.4
PORK CURED HAM CANNED ROAST .... 3 OZ	85	140	18	7	2.4	3.5	0.8
PORK LUNCHEON MEAT CANNED .... 2 SLICES	42	140	5	13	4.5	6.0	1.5
PORK CHOP LOIN BROIL LEAN+FAT ...... 3.1 OZ	87	275	24	19	7.0	8.8	2.2
PORK CHOP LOIN BROIL LEAN .... 2.5 OZ	72	165	23	8	2.6	3.4	0.9
PORK CHOP LOIN PAN FRY LEAN+FAT ..... 3.1 OZ	89	335	21	27	9.8	12.5	3.1
PORK CHOP LOIN PAN FRY LEAN .... 2.4 OZ	67	180	19	11	3.7	4.8	1.3
PORK FRESH HAM ROASTD LEAN+FAT ..... 3 OZ	85	250	21	18	6.4	8.1	2.0
PORK FRESH HAM ROASTD LEAN .... 2.5 OZ	72	160	20	8	2.7	3.6	1.0
PORK FRESH RIB ROASTD LEAN+FAT ...... 3 OZ	85	270	21	20	7.2	9.2	2.3
PORK FRESH RIB ROASTD LEAN .... 2.5 OZ	71	175	20	10	3.4	4.4	1.2
BOLOGNA .... 2 SLICES	57	180	7	16	6.1	7.6	1.4
FRANKFURTER COOKED .... 1 FRANK	45	145	5	13	4.8	6.2	1.2
PORK LINK COOKED .... 1 LINK	13	50	3	4	1.4	1.8	0.5
VEAL CUTLET MED FAT BRSD BRLD .... 3 OZ	85	185	23	9	4.1	4.1	0.6
VEAL RIB MED FAT ROASTED .... 3 OZ	85	230	23	14	6.0	6.0	1.0

²⁴Contains added sodium ascorbate. If sodium ascorbate is not added, ascorbic acid is negligible.

Choles-terol	Carbo-hydrate	Calcium	Iron	Potas-sium	Sodium	Vit. A Value (RE)	Thiamin	Ribo-flavin	Niacin	Ascorbic Acid
Milligrams	Grams	Milligrams	Milligrams	Milligrams	Milligrams	Retinol Equivalents	Milligrams	Milligrams	Milligrams	Milligrams
87	0	11	2.5	163	53	0	0.06	0.19	2.0	0
66	0	8	2.3	163	44	0	0.05	0.17	1.7	0
81	0	5	2.8	248	43	0	0.06	0.21	3.3	0
75	0	4	2.7	240	40	0	0.06	0.20	3.0	0
74	0	9	1.8	256	65	0	0.04	0.18	4.4	0
76	0	9	2.1	248	70	0	0.03	0.16	4.9	0
72	0	8	2.0	246	54	0	0.06	0.16	3.1	0
49	0	5	1.7	218	45	0	0.05	0.13	2.7	0
62	0	5	1.6	308	50	0	0.07	0.14	3.0	0
52	0	3	1.5	297	46	0	0.07	0.13	2.8	0
77	0	9	2.6	306	53	0	0.10	0.23	3.3	0
84	0	8	2.4	290	48	0	0.09	0.22	3.1	0
80	0	17	3.7	51	802	0	0.02	0.20	2.9	0
46	0	14	2.3	142	3053	0	0.05	0.23	2.7	0
77	0	16	1.5	195	46	0	0.04	0.16	4.4	0
59	0	12	1.3	162	36	0	0.03	0.13	3.0	0
78	0	16	1.4	272	62	0	0.09	0.21	5.5	0
60	0	12	1.3	241	54	0	0.08	0.18	4.4	0
78	0	8	1.7	273	57	0	0.09	0.24	5.5	0
65	0	6	1.5	247	50	0	0.08	0.20	4.6	0
16	0	2	0.3	92	303	0	0.13	0.05	1.4	6
53	0	6	0.7	243	1009	0	0.51	0.19	3.8	0
37	0	5	0.6	215	902	0	0.46	0.17	3.4	0
35	0	6	0.9	298	908	0	0.82	0.21	4.3	19
26	1	3	0.3	90	541	0	0.15	0.08	1.3	0
84	0	3	0.7	312	61	3	0.87	0.24	4.3	0
71	0	4	0.7	302	56	1	0.83	0.22	4.0	0
92	0	4	0.7	323	64	3	0.91	0.24	4.6	0
72	0	3	0.7	305	57	1	0.84	0.22	4.0	0
79	0	5	0.9	280	50	2	0.54	0.27	3.9	0
68	0	5	0.8	269	46	1	0.50	0.25	3.6	0
69	0	9	0.8	313	37	3	0.50	0.24	4.2	0
56	0	8	0.7	300	33	2	0.45	0.22	3.8	0
31	2	7	0.9	103	581	0	0.10	0.08	1.5	12[24]
23	1	5	0.5	75	504	0	0.09	0.05	1.2	12[24]
11	0	4	0.2	47	168	0	0.10	0.03	0.6	0
109	0	9	0.8	258	56	0	0.06	0.21	4.6	0
109	0	10	0.7	259	57	0	0.11	0.26	6.6	0

		Food energy	Protein	Fat	Fatty Acids		
					Saturated	Monoun- saturated	Polyun- saturated
MIXED DISHES AND FAST FOODS		Grams	Calories	Grams	Grams	Grams	Grams	Grams

BEEF AND VEGETABLE STEW HM RCP . . . . . . 1 CUP	245	220	16	11	4.4	4.5	0.5
BEEF POTPIE HOME RECIPE[26] . . . . 1 PIECE	210	515	21	30	7.9	12.9	7.4
CHICKEN POTPIE HOME RECIPE[25] . . . . 1 PIECE	232	545	23	31	10.3	15.5	6.6
CHILI CON CARNE W/ BEANS CNND . . . . 1 CUP	255	340	19	16	5.8	7.2	1.0
MACARONI AND CHEESE HOME RCPE[26] . . . . . 1 CUP	200	430	17	22	9.8	7.4	3.6
SPAGHETTI TOM SAUCE CHEE HM RP . . . . . . 1 CUP	250	260	9	9	3.0	3.6	1.2
SPAGHETTI MEATBALLS TOM SA HM RP . . . . 1 CUP	248	330	19	12	3.9	4.4	2.2

POULTRY AND POULTRY PRODUCTS							
CHICKEN FRIED BATTER BREAST[27] . . . . 4.9 OZ	140	365	35	18	4.9	7.6	4.3
CHICKEN FRIED BATTER DRMSTCK[27] . . . . . . 2.5 OZ	72	195	16	11	3.0	4.6	2.7
CHICKEN FRIED FLOUR BREAST[27] . . . . 3.5 OZ	98	220	31	9	2.4	3.4	1.9
CHICKEN FRIED FLOUR DRMSTCK[27] . . . . 1.7 OZ	49	120	13	7	1.8	2.7	1.6
CHICKEN ROASTED BREAST . . . . 3.0 OZ	86	140	27	3	0.9	1.1	0.7
CHICKEN ROASTED DRUMSTICK . . . . 1.6 OZ	44	75	12	2	0.7	0.8	0.6
CHICKEN CANNED BONELESS . . . . 5 OZ	142	235	31	11	3.1	4.5	2.5
CHICKEN FRANKFURTER . . . . 1 FRANK	45	115	6	9	2.5	3.8	1.8
CHICKEN ROLL LIGHT . . . . 2 SLICES	57	90	11	4	1.1	1.7	0.9

SOUPS, SAUCES, AND GRAVIES							
CLAM CHOWDER NEW ENG W/ MILK . . . . 1 CUP	248	165	9	7	3.0	2.3	1.1
CR OF CHICKEN SOUP W/ MLK CNND . . . . . . 1 CUP	248	109	7	11	4.6	4.5	1.6
CR OF MUSHROM SOUP W/ MLK CNND . . . . . 1 CUP	248	205	6	14	5.1	3.0	4.6
TOMATO SOUP WITH MILK CANNED . . . . 1 CUP	248	160	6	6	2.9	1.6	1.1
BEAN WITH BACON SOUP CANNED . . . . 1 CUP	253	170	8	6	1.5	2.2	1.8
BEEF BROTH BOULLN CONSM CNND . . . . 1 CUP	240	15	3	1	0.3	0.2	0.0
CHICKEN NOODLE SOUP CANNED . . . . 1 CUP	241	75	4	2	0.7	1.1	0.6
CLAM CHOWDER MANHATTAN CANND . . . . . . 1 CUP	244	80	4	2	0.4	0.4	1.3
CR OF MUSHROM SOUP W/ H2O CNND . . . . . 1 CUP	244	130	2	9	2.4	1.7	4.2
MINESTRONE SOUP CANNED . . . . 1 CUP	241	80	4	3	0.6	0.7	1.1
PEA GREEN SOUP CANNED . . . . 1 CUP	250	165	9	3	1.4	1.0	0.4
TOMATO SOUP W/ WATER CANNED . . . . 1 CUP	244	85	2	2	0.4	0.4	1.0
VEGETABLE BEEF SOUP CANNED . . . . 1 CUP	244	80	6	2	0.9	0.8	0.1
VEGETARIAN SOUP CANNED . . . . 1 CUP	241	70	2	2	0.3	0.8	0.7

[26]Crust made with vegetable shortening and enriched flour.
[26]Made with shortening.
[27]Fried in vegetable shortening.

Cholesterol	Carbohydrate	Calcium	Iron	Potassium	Sodium	Vit. A Value (RE)	Thiamin	Riboflavin	Niacin	Ascorbic Acid
Milligrams	Grams	Milligrams	Milligrams	Milligrams	Milligrams	Retinol Equivalents	Milligrams	Milligrams	Milligrams	Milligrams
71	15	29	2.9	613	292	568	0.15	0.17	4.7	17
42	39	29	3.8	334	596	517	0.29	0.29	4.8	6
56	42	70	3.0	343	594	735	0.32	0.32	4.9	5
28	31	82	4.3	594	1354	15	0.06	0.18	3.3	8
44	40	362	1.8	240	1086	232	0.20	0.40	1.8	1
8	37	80	2.3	406	955	140	0.25	0.18	2.3	13
89	39	124	3.7	665	1009	159	0.25	0.30	4.0	22
119	13	28	1.8	281	385	28	0.16	0.20	14.7	0
62	6	12	1.0	134	194	19	0.08	0.15	3.7	0
87	2	16	1.2	254	74	15	0.08	0.13	13.5	0
44	1	16	0.7	112	44	12	0.04	0.11	3.0	0
73	0	13	0.9	220	64	5	0.06	0.10	11.8	0
41	0	5	0.6	106	42	8	0.03	0.10	2.7	0
88	0	20	2.2	196	714	48	0.02	0.18	9.0	3
45	3	43	0.9	38	616	17	0.03	0.05	1.4	0
28	1	24	0.6	129	331	14	0.04	0.07	3.0	0
22	17	186	1.5	300	992	40	0.07	0.24	1.0	3
27	15	181	0.7	273	1047	94	0.07	0.26	0.9	1
20	15	179	0.6	270	1076	37	0.08	0.28	0.9	2
17	22	159	1.8	449	932	109	0.13	0.25	1.5	68
3	23	81	2.0	402	951	89	0.09	0.03	0.6	2
0	0	14	0.4	130	782	0	0.00	0.05	1.9	0
7	9	17	0.8	55	1106	71	0.05	0.06	1.4	0
2	12	34	1.9	261	1806	92	0.06	0.05	1.3	3
2	9	46	0.5	100	1032	0	0.05	0.09	0.7	1
2	11	34	0.9	313	911	234	0.05	0.04	0.9	1
0	27	28	2.0	190	988	20	0.11	0.07	1.2	2
0	17	12	1.8	264	871	69	0.09	0.05	1.4	66
5	10	17	1.1	173	956	189	0.04	0.05	1.0	2
0	12	22	1.1	210	822	301	0.05	0.05	0.9	1

		Food energy	Protein	Fat	Saturated	Monoun- saturated	Polyun- saturated
						Fatty Acids	
Sugars and Sweets		Grams	Calories	Grams	Grams	Grams	Grams	Grams

		Grams	Calories	Grams	Grams	Grams	Grams	Grams
CARAMELS PLAIN OR CHOCOLATE	1 OZ	28	115	1	3	2.2	0.3	0.1
MILK CHOCOLATE CANDY PLAIN	1 OZ	28	145	2	9	5.4	3.0	0.3
FUDGE CHOCOLATE PLAIN	1 OZ	28	115	1	3	2.1	1.0	0.1
GUM DROPS	1 OZ	28	100	0	0	0.0	0.0	0.1
HARD CANDY	1 OZ	28	110	0	0	0.0	0.0	0.0
MARSHMALLOWS	1 OZ	28	90	1	0	0.0	0.0	0.0
GELATIN DESSERT PREPARED	1/2 CUP	120	70	2	0	0.0	0.0	0.0
HONEY	1 TBSP	21	65	0	0	0.0	0.0	0.0
JAMS AND PRESERVES	1 TBSP	20	55	0	0	0.0	0.0	0.0
JELLIES	1 TBSP	18	50	0	0	0.0	0.0	0.0
SUGAR BROWN PRESSED DOWN	1 CUP	220	820	0	0	0.0	0.0	0.0
SUGAR WHITE GRANULATED	1 CUP	200	770	0	0	0.0	0.0	0.0
SUGAR WHITE GRANULATED	1 TBSP	12	45	0	0	0.0	0.0	0.0
SUGAR WHITE GRANULATED	1 PKT	6	25	0	0	0.0	0.0	0.0
SUGAR POWDERED SIFTED	1 CUP	100	385	0	0	0.0	0.0	0.0
SYRUP CHOCOLATE FLVRED FUDGE	2 TBSP	38	125	2	5	3.1	1.7	0.2
MOLASSES CANE BLACKSTRAP	2 TBSP	40	85	0	0	0.0	0.0	0.0
TABLE SYRUP (CORN AND MAPLE)	2 TBSP	42	122	0	0	0.0	0.0	0.0

Vegetables and Vegetable Products								
ASPARAGUS CKD FRM RAW DR CUT	1 CUP	180	45	5	1	0.1	0.0	0.2
ASPARAGUS CKD FRM RAW DR SPER	4 SPEARS	60	15	2	0	0.0	0.0	0.1
ASPARAGUS CKD FRM FRZ DR SPER	4 SPEARS	60	15	2	0	0.1	0.0	0.1
ASPARAGUS CANNED SPEARS W/SALT	4 SPEARS	80	10	1	0	0.0	0.0	0.1
ASPARAGUS CANNED SPEARS NO SALT	4 SPEARS	80	10	1	0	0.0	0.0	0.1
LIMA BEANS THICK SEED FRZN CKD	1 CUP	170	170	10	1	0.1	0.0	0.3
LIMA BEANS BABY FRZN CKED DRN	1 CUP	180	190	12	1	0.1	0.0	0.3
BEAN SPROUTS MUNG RAW	1 CUP	104	30	3	0	0.0	0.0	0.1
BEAN SPROUTS MUNG COOKD DRAN	1 CUP	124	25	3	0	0.0	0.0	0.0
BEETS COOKED DRAINED DICED	1 CUP	170	55	2	0	0.0	0.0	0.0
BEETS COOKED DRAINED WHOLE	2 BEETS	100	30	1	0	0.0	0.0	0.0
BEETS CANNED DRAINED W/ SALT	1 CUP	170	55	2	0	0.0	0.0	0.1
BEETS CANNED DRAINED NO SALT	1 CUP	170	55	2	0	0.0	0.0	0.1
BROCCOLI RAW COOKED DRAINED	1 CUP	155	45	5	0	0.1	0.0	0.2
BRUSSELS SPROUTS RAW COOKED	1 CUP	155	60	4	1	0.2	0.1	0.4
CABBAGE COMMON RAW	1 CUP	70	15	1	0	0.0	0.0	0.1
CABBAGE COMMON COOKED DRNED	1 CUP	150	30	1	0	0.0	0.0	0.2

Cholesterol	Carbohydrate	Calcium	Iron	Potassium	Sodium	Vit. A Value (RE)	Thiamin	Riboflavin	Niacin	Ascorbic Acid
Milligrams	Grams	Milligrams	Milligrams	Milligrams	Milligrams	Retinol Equivalents	Milligrams	Milligrams	Milligrams	Milligrams
1	22	42	0.4	54	64	0	0.01	0.05	0.1	0
6	16	50	0.4	96	23	30	0.02	0.10	0.1	0
1	21	22	0.3	42	54	0	0.01	0.03	0.1	0
0	25	2	0.1	1	10	0	0.00	0.00	0.0	0
0	28	0	0.1	1	7	0	0.10	0.00	0.0	0
0	23	1	0.5	2	25	0	0.00	0.00	0.0	0
0	17	2	0.0	0	55	0	0.00	0.00	0.0	0
0	17	1	0.1	11	1	0	0.00	0.01	0.1	0
0	14	4	0.2	18	2	0	0.00	0.01	0.0	0
0	13	2	0.1	16	5	0	0.00	0.01	0.0	1
0	212	187	4.8	757	97	0	0.02	0.07	0.2	0
0	199	3	0.1	7	5	0	0.00	0.00	0.0	0
0	12	0	0.0	0	0	0	0.00	0.00	0.0	0
0	6	0	0.0	0	0	0	0.00	0.00	0.0	0
0	100	1	0.0	4	2	0	0.00	0.00	0.0	0
0	21	38	0.5	82	42	13	0.02	0.06	0.1	0
0	22	274	10.1	1171	38	0	0.04	0.06	0.8	0
0	32	1	0.0	7	19	0	0.00	0.00	0.0	0
0	8	43	1.2	558	7	149	0.18	0.22	1.9	49
0	3	14	0.4	186	2	50	0.06	0.07	0.6	16
0	3	14	0.4	131	2	49	0.04	0.06	0.6	15
0	2	11	0.5	122	278	38	0.04	0.07	0.7	13
0	2	11	0.5	122	3	38	0.04	0.07	0.7	13
0	32	37	2.3	694	90	32	0.13	0.10	1.8	22
0	35	50	3.5	740	52	30	0.13	0.10	1.4	10
0	6	14	0.9	155	6	2	0.09	0.13	0.8	14
0	5	15	0.8	125	12	2	0.06	0.13	1.0	14
0	11	19	1.1	530	83	2	0.05	0.02	0.5	9
0	7	11	0.6	312	49	1	0.03	0.01	0.3	6
0	12	26	3.1	252	486	2	0.02	0.07	0.3	7
0	12	26	3.1	252	78	2	0.02	0.07	0.3	7
0	9	71	1.8	253	17	218	0.13	0.32	1.2	97
0	13	56	1.9	491	33	111	0.17	0.12	0.9	96
0	4	33	0.4	172	13	9	0.04	0.02	0.2	33
0	7	50	0.6	306	29	13	0.09	0.06	0.3	36

		Food energy	Protein	Fat	Fatty Acids		
					Saturated	Monoun- saturated	Polyun- saturated
VEGETABLES AND VEGETABLE PRODUCTS cont.		Grams	Calories	Grams	Grams	Grams	Grams	Grams
CABBAGE CHINESE PAK-CHOI CKD .... 1 CUP	170	20	3	0	0.0	0.0	0.1
CABBAGE CHINESE PE-TSAI RAW .... 1 CUP	76	10	1	0	0.0	0.0	0.1
CABBAGE RED RAW .... 1 CUP	70	20	1	0	0.0	0.0	0.1
CABBAGE SAVOY RAW .... 1 CUP	7	20	1	0	0.0	0.0	0.0
CARROTS RAW WHOLE .... 1 CARROT	72	30	1	0	0.0	0.0	0.1
CARROTS RAW GRATED .... 1 CUP	110	45	1	0	0.0	0.0	0.1
CARROTS COOKED FROM RAW .... 1 CUP	156	70	2	0	0.1	0.0	0.1
CARROTS COOKED FROM FROZEN .... 1 CUP	146	55	2	0	0.0	0.0	0.1
CARROTS CANNED DRN W/ SALT .... 1 CUP	146	35	1	0	0.1	0.0	0.1
CARROTS CANNED DRND W/O SALT ...... 1 CUP	146	35	1	0	0.1	0.0	0.1
CAULIFLOWER COOKED FROM RAW ...... 1 CUP	125	30	2	0	0.0	0.0	0.1
CAULIFLOWER COOKED FROM FROZN ...... 1 CUP	180	35	3	0	0.1	0.0	0.2
CELERY PASCAL TYPE RAW STALK .... 1 STALK	40	5	0	0	0.0	0.0	0.0
CELERY PASCAL TYPE RAW PIECE .... 1 CUP	120	20	1	0	0.0	0.0	0.1
COLLARDS COOKED FROM RAW .... 1 CUP	190	25	2	0	0.1	0.0	0.2
CORN COOKED FROM RAW YELLOW .... 1 EAR	77	85	3	1	0.2	0.3	0.5
CORN COOKED FROM RAW WHITE .... 1 EAR	77	85	3	1	0.2	0.3	0.5
CORN COOKED FRM FROZN YELLOW ...... 1 EAR	63	60	2	0	0.1	0.1	0.2
CORN COOKED FRM FROZN YELLOW ...... 1 CUP	165	135	5	0	0.0	0.0	0.1
CORN CNND CRM STL YLLW W/SALT ...... 1 CUP	256	185	4	1	0.2	0.3	0.5
CORN CNND CRM STL YLLW NO SAL ...... 1 CUP	256	185	4	1	0.2	0.3	0.5
CORN CNND CRM STL WHIT W/SALT ...... 1 CUP	256	185	4	1	0.2	0.3	0.5
CORN CNND CRM STL WHIT NO SAL ...... 1 CUP	256	185	4	1	0.2	0.3	0.5
CUCUMBER W/ PEEL .... 6 SLICES	28	5	0	0	0.0	0.0	0.0
LETTUCE BUTTERHEAD RAW HEAD .... 1 HEAD	163	20	2	0	0.0	0.0	0.2
LETTUCE CRISPHEAD RAW HEAD .... 1 HEAD	539	70	5	1	0.1	0.0	0.5
LETTUCE LOOSELEAF .... 1 CUP	56	10	1	0	0.0	0.0	0.1
MUSHROOMS CANNED DRND W/SALT ...... 1 CUP	156	35	3	0	0.1	0.0	0.2
OKRA PODS COOKED .... 8 PODS	85	25	2	0	0.0	0.0	0.0
ONIONS RAW CHOPPED .... 1 CUP	160	55	2	0	0.1	0.1	0.2
ONIONS RAW SLICED .... 1 CUP	115	40	1	0	0.1	0.0	0.1
ONIONS RAW COOKED DRAINED .... 1 CUP	210	60	2	0	0.1	0.0	0.1
ONIONS SPRING RAW .... 6 ONION	30	10	1	0	0.0	0.0	0.0
PARSLEY RAW .... 10 SPRIG	10	5	0	0	0.0	0.0	0.0
PARSNIPS COOKED DRAINED .... 1 CUP	156	125	2	0	0.1	0.2	0.1
PEAS EDIBLE POD COOKED DRNED .... 1 CUP	160	65	5	0	0.1	0.0	0.2
PEAS GREEN CNND DRND W/ SALT .... 1 CUP	170	115	8	1	0.1	0.1	0.3
PEAS GREEN CNND DRND W/O SALT .... 1 CUP	170	115	8	1	0.1	0.1	0.3
PEAS GRN FROZEN COOKED DRANED ...... 1 CUP	160	125	8	0	0.1	0.0	0.2

Choles-terol	Carbo-hydrate	Calcium	Iron	Potas-sium	Sodium	Vit. A Value (RE)	Thiamin	Ribo-flavin	Niacin	Ascorbic Acid
Milligrams	Grams	Milligrams	Milligrams	Milligrams	Milligrams	Retinol Equivalents	Milligrams	Milligrams	Milligrams	Milligrams
0	3	158	1.8	631	58	437	0.05	0.11	0.7	44
0	2	59	0.2	181	7	91	0.03	0.04	0.3	21
0	4	36	0.3	144	8	3	0.04	0.02	0.2	40
0	4	25	0.3	161	20	70	0.05	0.02	0.2	22
0	7	19	0.4	233	25	2025	0.07	0.04	0.7	7
0	11	30	0.6	355	39	3094	0.11	0.06	1.0	10
0	16	48	1.0	354	103	3830	0.05	0.09	0.8	4
0	12	41	0.7	231	86	2585	0.04	0.05	0.6	4
0	8	37	0.9	261	352	2011	0.03	0.04	0.8	4
0	8	37	0.9	261	61	2011	0.03	0.04	0.8	4
0	6	34	0.5	404	8	2	0.08	0.07	0.7	69
0	7	31	0.7	250	32	4	0.07	0.10	0.6	56
0	1	14	0.2	114	35	5	0.01	0.01	0.1	3
0	4	43	0.6	341	106	15	0.04	0.04	0.4	8
0	5	148	0.8	177	36	422	0.03	0.08	0.4	19
0	19	2	0.5	192	13	17	0.17	0.06	1.2	5
0	19	2	0.5	192	13	0	0.17	0.06	1.2	5
0	14	2	0.4	158	3	13	0.11	0.04	1.0	3
0	34	3	0.5	229	8	41	0.11	0.12	2.1	4
0	46	8	1.0	343	73	25	0.06	0.14	2.5	12
0	46	8	1.0	343	8	25	0.06	0.14	2.5	12
0	46	8	1.0	343	730	0	0.06	0.14	2.5	12
0	46	8	1.0	343	8	0	0.06	0.14	2.5	12
0	1	4	0.1	42	1	1	0.01	0.01	0.1	1
0	4	52	0.5	419	8	158	0.10	0.10	0.5	13
0	11	102	2.7	852	49	178	0.25	0.16	1.0	21
0	2	38	0.8	148	5	106	0.03	0.04	0.2	10
0	8	17	1.2	201	663	0	0.13	0.03	2.5	0
0	6	54	0.4	274	4	49	0.11	0.05	0.7	14
0	12	40	0.6	248	3	0	0.10	0.02	0.2	13
0	8	29	0.4	178	2	0	0.07	0.01	0.1	10
0	13	57	0.4	319	17	0	0.09	0.02	0.2	12
0	2	18	0.6	77	1	15	0.02	0.04	0.1	14
0	1	13	0.6	54	4	52	0.01	0.01	0.1	9
0	30	58	0.9	573	16	0	0.13	0.06	1.1	20
0	11	67	3.2	384	6	21	0.20	0.12	0.9	77
0	21	34	1.6	294	372	131	0.21	0.13	1.2	16
0	21	34	1.6	294	3	131	0.21	0.13	1.2	16
0	23	36	2.5	269	139	107	0.45	0.16	2.4	16

				Fatty Acids		
	Food energy	Protein	Fat	Saturated	Monoun- saturated	Polyun- saturated
	Grams	Calories	Grams	Grams	Grams	Grams	Grams

VEGETABLES AND VEGETABLE PRODUCTS cont.							
POTATOES BAKED FLESH ONLY .... 1 POTATO	156	145	3	0	0.0	0.0	0.1
POTATOES BOILED PEELED AFTER .... 1 POTATO	136	120	3	0	0.0	0.0	0.1
POTATOES BOILED PEELED BEFOR .... 1 POTATO	135	115	2	0	0.0	0.0	0.1
POTATOES FRENCH-FRD FRZN OVEN .... 10 STRIP	50	110	2	4	2.1	1.8	0.3
POTATOES FRENCH-FRD FRZN FRIED ...... 10 STRIP	50	160	2	8	2.5	1.6	3.8
POTATO CHIPS .... 10 CHIPS	20	105	1	7	1.8	1.2	3.6
PUMPKIN CANNED .... 1 CUP	245	85	3	1	0.4	0.1	0.0
RADISHES RAW .... 4 RADISH	18	5	0	0	0.0	0.0	0.0
SAUERKRAUT CANNED .... 1 CUP	236	45	2	0	0.1	0.0	0.1
SPINACH COOKED FR FRZEN DRND .... 1 CUP	190	55	6	0	0.1	0.0	0.2
SPINACH CANNED DRND W/ SALT .... 1 CUP	214	50	6	1	0.2	0.0	0.4
SPINACH CANNED DRND W/O SALT .... 1 CUP	214	50	6	1	0.2	0.0	0.4
SQUASH SUMMER COOKED DRAIND .... 1 CUP	180	35	2	1	0.1	0.0	0.2
SQUASH WINTER BAKED .... 1 CUP	205	80	2	1	0.3	0.1	0.5
SWEETPOTATOES BAKED PEELED .... 1 POTATO	114	115	2	0	0.0	0.0	0.1
SWEETPOTATOES BOILED W/O PEEL .... 1 POTATO	151	160	2	0	0.1	0.0	0.2
SWEETPOTATOES CANDIED .... 1 PIECE	105	145	1	3	1.4	0.7	0.2
SWEETPOTATOES CNNED VAC PACK ...... 1 PIECE	40	35	1	0	0.0	0.0	0.0
TOMATOES RAW .... 1 TOMATO	123	25	1	0	0.0	0.0	0.1
TOMATOES CANNED S+L W/ SALT .... 1 CUP	240	50	2	1	0.1	0.1	0.2
TOMATOES CANNED S+L W/O SALT .... 1 CUP	240	50	2	1	0.1	0.1	0.2
TOMATO JUICE CANNED WITH SALT ...... 1 CUP	244	40	2	0	0.0	0.0	0.1
TOMATO JUICE CANNED W/O SALT .... 1 CUP	244	40	2	0	0.0	0.0	0.1
TURNIPS COOKED DICED .... 1 CUP	156	30	1	0	0.0	0.0	0.1
TURNIP GREENS COOKED FROM RAW ...... 1 CUP	144	30	2	0	0.1	0.0	0.1
TURNIP GREENS CKED FRM FROZEN .... 1 CUP	164	50	5	1	0.2	0.0	0.3

MISCELLANEOUS ITEMS							
CATSUP .... 1 CUP	273	290	5	1	0.2	0.2	0.4
CATSUP .... 1 TBSP	15	15	0	0	0.0	0.0	0.0
CHILI POWDER .... 1 TSP	2	10	0	0	0.1	0.1	0.2
CHOCOLATE BITTER OR BAKING .... 1 OZ	28	145	3	15	9.0	4.9	0.5
MUSTARD PREPARED YELLOW .... 1 TSP	5	5	0	0	0.0	0.2	0.0
OLIVES CANNED GREEN .... 4 MEDIUM	13	15	0	2	0.2	1.2	0.1
OLIVES CANNED RIPE MISSION .... 3 SMALL	9	15	0	2	0.3	1.3	0.2
PICKLES CUCUMBER DILL .... 1 PICKLE	65	5	0	0	0.0	0.0	0.1
PICKLES CUCUMBER SWT GHERKIN .... 1 PICKLE	15	20	0	0	0.0	0.0	0.0

Choles-terol	Carbo-hydrate	Calcium	Iron	Potas-sium	Sodium	Vit. A Value (RE)	Thiamin	Ribo-flavin	Niacin	Ascorbic Acid
Milligrams	Grams	Milligrams	Milligrams	Milligrams	Milligrams	Retinol Equivalents	Milligrams	Milligrams	Milligrams	Milligrams
0	34	8	0.5	610	8	0	0.16	0.03	2.2	20
0	27	7	0.4	515	5	0	0.14	0.03	2.0	18
0	27	11	0.4	443	7	0	0.13	0.03	1.8	10
0	17	5	0.7	229	16	0	0.06	0.02	1.2	5
0	20	10	0.4	366	108	0	0.09	0.01	1.6	5
0	10	5	0.2	260	94	0	0.03	0.00	0.8	8
0	20	64	3.4	505	12	5404	0.06	0.13	0.9	10
0	1	4	0.1	42	4	0	0.00	0.01	0.1	4
0	10	71	3.5	401	1560	4	0.05	0.05	0.3	35
0	10	277	2.9	566	163	1479	0.11	0.32	0.8	23
0	7	272	4.9	740	683	1878	0.03	0.30	0.8	31
0	7	272	4.9	740	58	1878	0.03	0.30	0.8	31
0	8	49	0.6	346	2	52	0.08	0.07	0.9	10
0	18	29	0.7	896	2	729	0.17	0.05	1.4	20
0	28	32	0.5	397	11	2488	0.08	0.14	0.7	28
0	37	32	0.8	278	20	2575	0.08	0.21	1.0	26
8	29	27	1.2	198	74	440	0.02	0.04	0.4	7
0	8	9	0.4	125	21	319	0.01	0.02	0.3	11
0	5	9	0.6	255	10	139	0.07	0.06	0.7	22
0	10	62	1.5	530	391	145	0.11	0.07	1.8	36
0	10	62	1.5	530	31	145	0.11	0.07	1.8	36
0	10	22	1.4	537	881	136	0.11	0.08	1.6	45
0	10	22	1.4	537	24	136	0.11	0.08	1.6	45
0	8	34	0.3	211	78	0	0.04	0.04	0.5	18
0	6	197	1.2	292	42	792	0.06	0.10	0.6	39
0	8	249	3.2	367	25	1308	0.09	0.12	0.8	36
0	69	60	2.2	991	2845	382	0.25	0.19	4.4	41
0	4	3	0.1	54	156	21	0.01	0.01	0.2	2
0	1	7	0.4	50	26	91	0.01	0.02	0.2	2
0	8	22	1.9	235	1	1	0.01	0.07	0.4	0
0	0	4	0.1	7	63	0	0.00	0.01	0.0	0
0	0	8	0.2	7	312	4	0.00	0.00	0.0	0
0	0	10	0.2	2	68	1	0.00	0.00	0.0	0
0	1	17	0.7	130	928	7	0.00	0.01	0.0	4
0	5	2	0.2	30	107	1	0.00	0.00	0.0	1

		Food energy	Protein	Fat	Fatty Acids		
					Saturated	Monoun-saturated	Polyun-saturated
MISCELLANEOUS ITEMS CONT.		Grams	Calories	Grams	Grams	Grams	Grams	Grams

RELISH SWEET .... 1 TBSP	15	20	0	0	0.0	0.0	0.0
SALT .... 1 TSP	5	0	0	0	0.0	0.0	0.0
VINEGAR CIDER .... 1 TBSP	15	0	0	0	0.0	0.0	0.0
YEAST BAKERS DRY ACTIVE .... 1 PKG	7	20	3	0	0.0	0.1	0.0
YEAST BREWERS DRY .... 1 TBSP	8	25	3	0	0.0	0.0	0.0

Choles-terol	Carbo-hydrate	Calcium	Iron	Potas-sium	Sodium	Vit. A Value (RE)	Thiamin	Ribo-flavin	Niacin	Ascorbic Acid
Milligrams	Grams	Milligrams	Milligrams	Milligrams	Milligrams	Retinol Equivalents	Milligrams	Milligrams	Milligrams	Milligrams
0	5	3	0.1	30	107	2	0.00	0.00	0.0	1
0	0	14	0.0	0	2132	0	0.00	0.00	0.0	0
0	1	1	0.1	15	0	0	0.00	0.00	0.0	0
0	3	3	1.1	140	4	0	0.16	0.38	2.6	0
0	3	17	1.4	152	10	0	1.25	0.34	3.0	0

Category	Age (years) or Condition	Weight† (kg)	Weight† (lb)	Height† (cm)	Height† (in)	Protein (g)	Fat-Soluble Vitamins Vita-min A (μg RE)‡	Vita-min D (μg)§	Vita-min E (mg α-TE)‖	Vita-min K (μg)
Infants	0.0–0.5	6	13	60	24	13	375	7.5	3	5
	0.5–1.0	9	20	71	28	14	375	10	4	10
Children	1–3	13	29	90	35	16	400	10	6	15
	4–6	20	44	112	44	24	500	10	7	20
	7–10	28	62	132	52	28	700	10	7	30
Males	11–14	45	99	157	62	45	1,000	10	10	45
	15–18	66	145	176	69	59	1,000	10	10	65
	19–24	72	160	177	70	58	1,000	10	10	70
	25–50	79	174	176	70	63	1,000	5	10	80
	51+	77	170	173	68	63	1,000	5	10	80
Females	11–14	46	101	157	62	46	800	10	8	45
	15–18	55	120	163	64	44	800	10	8	55
	19–24	58	128	164	65	46	800	10	8	60
	25–50	63	138	163	64	50	800	5	8	65
	51+	65	143	160	63	50	800	5	8	65
Pregnant						60	800	10	10	65
Lactating	1st 6 months					65	1,300	10	12	65
	2nd 6 months					62	1,200	10	11	65

*The allowances, expressed as average daily intakes over time, are intended to provide for individual variations among most normal persons as they live in the United States under usual environmental stresses. Diets should be based on a variety of common foods in order to provide other nutrients for which human requirements have been less well defined. See text for detailed discussion of allowances and of nutrients not tabulated.

†Weights and heights of Reference Adults are actual medians for the U.S. population of the designated age, as reported by NHANES II. The median weights and heights of those under 19 years of age were taken from Hamill et al. (1979) (see pages 16–17). The use of these figures does not imply that the height-to-weight ratios are ideal.

Water-Soluble Vitamins							Minerals						
Vita-min C (mg)	Thia-min (mg)	Ribo-flavin (mg)	Niacin (mg NE)**	Vita-min B_6 (mg)	Fo-late (μg)	Vitamin B_{12} (μg)	Cal-cium (mg)	Phos-phorus (mg)	Mag-nesium (mg)	Iron (mg)	Zinc (mg)	Iodine (μg)	Sele-nium (μg)
30	0.3	0.4	5	0.3	25	0.3	400	300	40	6	5	40	10
35	0.4	0.5	6	0.6	35	0.5	600	500	60	10	5	50	15
40	0.7	0.8	9	1.0	50	0.7	800	800	80	10	10	70	20
45	0.9	1.1	12	1.1	75	1.0	800	800	120	10	10	90	20
45	1.0	1.2	13	1.4	100	1.4	800	800	170	10	10	120	30
50	1.3	1.5	17	1.7	150	2.0	1,200	1,200	270	12	15	150	40
60	1.5	1.8	20	2.0	200	2.0	1,200	1,200	400	12	15	150	50
60	1.5	1.7	19	2.0	200	2.0	1,200	1,200	350	10	15	150	70
60	1.5	1.7	19	2.0	200	2.0	800	800	350	10	15	150	70
60	1.2	1.4	15	2.0	200	2.0	800	800	350	10	15	150	70
50	1.1	1.3	15	1.4	150	2.0	1,200	1,200	280	15	12	150	45
60	1.1	1.3	15	1.5	180	2.0	1,200	1,200	300	15	12	150	50
60	1.1	1.3	15	1.6	180	2.0	1,200	1,200	280	15	12	150	55
60	1.1	1.3	15	1.6	180	2.0	800	800	280	15	12	150	55
60	1.0	1.2	13	1.6	180	2.0	800	800	280	10	12	150	55
70	1.5	1.6	17	2.2	400	2.2	1,200	1,200	320	30	15	175	65
95	1.6	1.8	20	2.1	280	2.6	1,200	1,200	355	15	19	200	75
90	1.6	1.7	20	2.1	260	2.6	1,200	1,200	340	15	16	200	75

‡Retinol equivalents. 1 retinol equivalent = 1 μg retinol or 6 μg β-carotene. See text for calculation of vitamin A activity of diets as retinol equivalents.

§As cholecalciferol. 10 μg cholecalciferol = 400 ɪᴜ of vitamin D.

‖α-Tocopherol equivalents. 1 mg d-α tocopherol = 1 α-ᴛᴇ. See text for variation in allowances and calculation of vitamin E activity of the diet as α-tocopherol equivalents.

**1 ɴᴇ (niacin equivalent) is equal to 1 mg of niacin or 60 mg of dietary tryptophan.

Source: Food and Nutrition Board, National Academy of Sciences—National Research Council: Recommended dietary allowances, revised 1989.

APPENDIX III Daily Values (DV)

The new label reference value, Daily Value (DV), comprises two new sets of dietary standards: Reference Daily Intakes (RDIs) and Daily Reference Values (DRVs). Only the Daily Value term will appear on the label to make label reading less confusing.

The RDIs replace the term "U.S. RDAs," which was introduced in 1973 as a label reference value for vitamins, minerals, and protein. The name change was sought because of confusion with "RDAs" (Recommended Dietary Allowances). The values for the new RDIs follow in Table III–1 and are the same as the old U.S. RDAs introduced in 1973. During 1994, FDA plans to propose new values.

Daily Reference Values (DRVs) are being introduced for sources of energy—fat, carbohydrate (including fiber), and protein—and for cholesterol, sodium, and potassium, which do not contribute calories. DRVs for nutrients are based on the number of calories consumed per day. A daily intake of 2,000 calories has been established as the reference. This level was chosen because it has the greatest public health benefit for the nation.

DRVs for the energy-producing nutrients are calculated as follows:

- Fat based on 30% of calories.
- Saturated fat based on 10% of calories.
- Carbohydrate based on 60% of calories.
- Protein based on 10% of calories.
- Fiber based on 11.5 g of fiber per 1,000 calories.

Because of current recommendations, DRVs for the following nutrients represent the uppermost limit that is considered desirable. The DRVs for fats and sodium are:

- Total fat: less than 65 g.
- Saturated fat: less than 20 g.
- Cholesterol: less than 300 mg.
- Sodium: less than 2400 mg.

Table III–1   Reference Daily Intakes (RDIs)

Nutrient	Unit of Measurement*	Adults and Children 4 or more Years of Age	Children Less than 4 Years of Age†	Infants‡	Pregnant Women	Lactating Women
Vitamin A	Retinol equivalents§	875	400	375	800	1,300
Vitamin C	Milligrams	60	40	33	70	95
Calcium	Milligrams	900	800	500	1,200	1,200
Iron	Milligrams	12	10	8.0	30	15
Vitamin D	Micrograms‖	6.5	10	9.0	10	10
Vitamin E	α-Tocopherol equivalents	9.0	6.0	3.5	10	12
Vitamin K	Micrograms	65	15	7.5	65	65
Thiamin	Milligrams	1.2	0.7	0.4	1.5	1.6
Riboflavin	Milligrams	1.4	0.8	0.5	1.6	1.8
Niacin	Niacin equivalents§	16	9.0	5.5	17	20
Vitamin B_6	Milligrams	1.5	1.0	0.5	2.2	2.1
Folate	Micrograms	180	50	30	400	280
Vitamin B_{12}	Micrograms	2.0	0.7	0.4	2.2	2.6
Biotin	Micrograms	60	20	13	65	65
Pantothenic acid	Milligrams	5.5	3.0	2.5	5.5	5.5
Phosphorus	Milligrams	900	800	400	1,200	1,200
Magnesium	Milligrams	300	80	50	320	355
Zinc	Milligrams	13	10	5.0	15	19
Iodine	Micrograms	150	70	45	175	200
Selenium	Micrograms	55	20	13	65	75
Copper	Milligrams	2.0	0.9	0.6	2.5	2.5
Manganese	Milligrams	3.5	1.3	0.6	3.5	3.5
Fluoride	Milligrams	2.5	1.0	0.5	3.0	3.0
Chromium	Micrograms	120	50	33	130	130
Molybdenum	Micrograms	150	38	26	160	160
Chloride	Milligrams	3,150	1,000	650	3,400	3,400

*The following abbreviations are allowed: "mg" for "milligram"; "mcg" for "micrograms"; "µg RE" for "retinol equivalents"; "mg α-TE" for "α-tocopherol equivalents"; "mg NE" for "niacin equivalents."

†The term "children less than 4 years of age" means persons 13 through 47 months of age.

‡The term "infants" means persons not more than 12 months of age.

§1 retinol equivalent = 1 microgram retinol or 6 micrograms β-carotene; 1 α-tocopherol equivalent = 1 milligram d-α-tocopherol; 1 niacin equivalent = 1 milligram niacin or 60 milligrams of dietary tryptophan.

‖As cholecalciferol.

24-HOUR RECALL

Name _____

Date and time of interview _____

Length of interview _____

Date of recall _____

Day of the week of recall (1—M, 2—T, 3—W, 4—Th, 5—F, 6—Sat, 7—Sun) ____

"I would like you to tell me everything you (your child) ate and drank from the time you (he) got up in the morning until you (he) went to bed at night and what you (he) ate during the night. Be sure to mention everything you (he) ate or drank at home, at work (school), and away from home. Include snacks and drinks of all kinds and everything else you (he) put in your (his) mouth and swallowed. I also need to know where you (he) ate the food, and now let us begin."

What time did you (he) get up yesterday? _____

Was it the usual time? _____

What was the first time you (he) ate or had anything to drink yesterday morning?   (list on the form that follows)

Where did you (he) eat? (list on form that follows)

Now tell me what you (he) had to eat and how much?

(Occasionally the interviewer will need to ask:)

   When did you (he) eat again? Or, is there anything else?

   Did you (he) have anything to eat or drink during the night?

Was intake unusual in any way? Yes _____ No _____

(If answer is yes) Why? _____

                In what way? _____

What time did you (he) go to bed last night? _____

Do(es) you (he) take vitamin or mineral supplements?

            Yes _____ No _____

(If answer is yes) How many per day? _____

            Per week? _____

What kind? (Insert brand name if known)

Multivitamins _____

Ascorbic acid _____

Source: From Screening children for nutritional status: suggestions for child health programs, Washington, DC, 1971, U.S. Government Printing Office.

24-HOUR RECALL—cont'd

Vitamins A and D _____

Iron _____

Other _____

Suggested Form For Recording Food Intake

Time	Where Eaten*	Food	Type and/or Preparation	Amount	Food Code†	Amount Code†

*Code

H—Home

R—Restaurant, drugstore, or lunch counter

CL—Carried lunch from home

CC—Child-care center

OH—Other home (friend, relative, baby-sitter, etc.)

S—School, office, plant, or work

FD—Food dispenser

SS—Social center (e.g., Senior Citizen, etc.)

†Do not write in these spaces.

DIETARY QUESTIONNAIRE FOR CHILDREN

Name _____

Date _____

1. Does the child eat at regular times each day? _____

2. How many days a week does he eat?

   A morning meal? _____

   A lunch or midday meal? _____

   An evening meal? _____

   During the night?* _____

3. How many days a week does he have snacks?

   In midmorning? _____

   In midafternoon? _____

   In the evening? _____

   During the night? _____

*Include formula feeding for young children.

DIETARY QUESTIONNAIRE FOR CHILDREN—cont'd

4. Which meals does he usually eat with your family?

 None _____ Breakfast _____ Noon meal _____ Evening meal _____

5. How many times per week does he eat at school, child-care center, or day camp?

 Breakfast _____ Lunch _____ Between meals _____

6. Would you describe his appetite as Good? _____ Fair? _____ Poor? _____

7. At what time of day is he most hungry?

 Morning _____ Noon _____ Evening _____

8. What foods does he dislike? _____

 _____

9. Is he on a special diet now? Yes _____ No _____

 If yes, why is he on a diet? (Check)

 _____ For weight reduction (own prescription)

 _____ For weight reduction (doctor's prescription)

 _____ For gaining weight

 _____ For allergy, specify _____

 _____ For other reason, specify _____

 If no, has he been on a special diet within the past year? Yes _____ No _____

 If yes, for what reason? _____

10. Does he eat anything that is not usually considered food? Yes _____ No _____

 If yes, with his fingers? _____ With a spoon? _____

11. Can he feed himself? Yes _____ No _____

 If yes, with his fingers? _____ with a spoon? _____

12. Can he use a cup or glass by himself? Yes _____ No _____

13. Does he drink from a bottle with a nipple? Yes _____ No _____

 If yes, how often? _____ At what time of day or night? _____

14. How many times per week does he eat the following foods (at any meal or between meals)? Circle the appropriate number:

Bacon _____	0 1 2 3 4 5 6 7 >7, specify _____
Tongue _____	0 1 2 3 4 5 6 7 >7, specify _____
Sausage _____	0 1 2 3 4 5 6 7 >7, specify _____
Luncheon meat _____	0 1 2 3 4 5 6 7 >7, specify _____
Hot dogs _____	0 1 2 3 4 5 6 7 >7, specify _____
Liver—chicken _____	0 1 2 3 4 5 6 7 >7, specify _____
Liver—other _____	0 1 2 3 4 5 6 7 >7, specify _____
Poultry _____	0 1 2 3 4 5 6 7 >7, specify _____
Salt pork _____	0 1 2 3 4 5 6 7 >7, specify _____
Pork or ham _____	0 1 2 3 4 5 6 7 >7, specify _____
Bones (neck or other _____	0 1 2 3 4 5 6 7 >7, specify _____
Meat in mixtures (stew, tamales, casseroles, etc.) _____	0 1 2 3 4 5 6 7 >7, specify _____
Beef or veal _____	0 1 2 3 4 5 6 7 >7, specify _____
Other meat _____	0 1 2 3 4 5 6 7 >7, specify _____
Fish _____	0 1 2 3 4 5 6 7 >7, specify _____

DIETARY QUESTIONNAIRE FOR CHILDREN—cont'd

15. How many times per week does he eat the following foods (at any meal or between meals)? Circle the appropriate number:

Fruit juice _____ 0 1 2 3 4 5 6 7 >7, specify _____
Fruit _____ 0 1 2 3 4 5 6 7 >7, specify _____
Cereal—dry _____ 0 1 2 3 4 5 6 7 >7, specify _____
Cereal—cooked or instant _____ 0 1 2 3 4 5 6 7 >7, specify _____
Cereal—infant _____ 0 1 2 3 4 5 6 7 >7, specify _____
Eggs _____ 0 1 2 3 4 5 6 7 >7, specify _____
Pancakes or waffles _____ 0 1 2 3 4 5 6 7 >7, specify _____
Cheese _____ 0 1 2 3 4 5 6 7 >7, specify _____
Potato _____ 0 1 2 3 4 5 6 7 >7, specify _____
Other cooked vegetables _____ 0 1 2 3 4 5 6 7 >7, specify _____
Raw vegetables _____ 0 1 2 3 4 5 6 7 >7, specify _____
Dried beans or peas _____ 0 1 2 3 4 5 6 7 >7, specify _____
Macaroni, spaghetti, rice, or noodles 0 1 2 3 4 5 6 7 >7, specify _____
Ice cream, milk pudding, custard, 0 1 2 3 4 5 6 7 >7, specify _____
   or cream soup _____
Peanut butter or nuts _____ 0 1 2 3 4 5 6 7 >7, specify _____
Sweet rolls or doughnuts _____ 0 1 2 3 4 5 6 7 >7, specify _____
Crackers or pretzels _____ 0 1 2 3 4 5 6 7 >7, specify _____
Cookies _____ 0 1 2 3 4 5 6 7 >7, specify _____
Pie, cake, or brownies _____ 0 1 2 3 4 5 6 7 >7, specify _____
Potato chips or corn chips _____ 0 1 2 3 4 5 6 7 >7, specify _____
Candy _____ 0 1 2 3 4 5 6 7 >7, specify _____
Soft drinks, Popsicles, or Kool-Aid _ 0 1 2 3 4 5 6 7 >7, specify _____
Instant Breakfast _____ 0 1 2 3 4 5 6 7 >7, specify _____

16. How many servings per day does he eat of the following foods? Circle the appropriate number:

Bread (including sandwich), toast,
   rolls, muffins
   (1 slice or 1 piece is 1 serving) ___ 0 1 2 3 4 5 6 7 >7, specify _____
Milk (including on cereal or other
   foods)
   (8 ounces is 1 serving) _____ 0 1 2 3 4 5 6 7 >7, specify _____
Sugar, jam, jelly, syrup (1 tsp is 1 0 1 2 3 4 5 6 7 >7, specify _____
   serving)

17. What specific kinds of the following foods does he eat most often?

Fruit juices _____

Fruit _____

Vegetables _____

Cheese _____

Cooked or instant cereal _____

Dry cereal _____

Milk _____

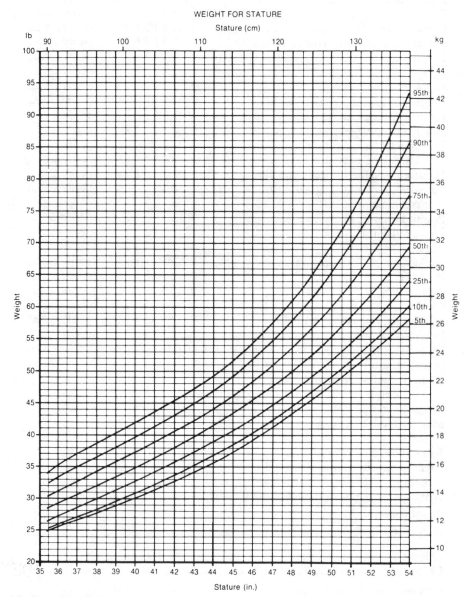

WEIGHT FOR STATURE

Prepubertal girls from 2 to 10 years
Source: U.S. Department of Health, Education and Welfare, National Center
for Health Statistics, 1979.

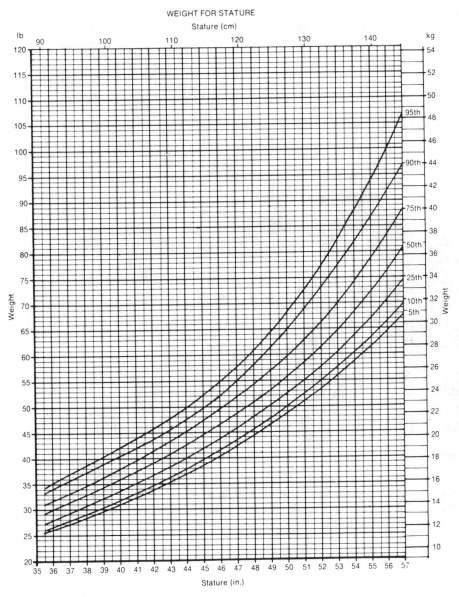

WEIGHT FOR STATURE

Prepubertal boys from 2 to 11½ years
Source: U.S. Department of Health, Education and Welfare, National Center for Health Statistics, 1979.

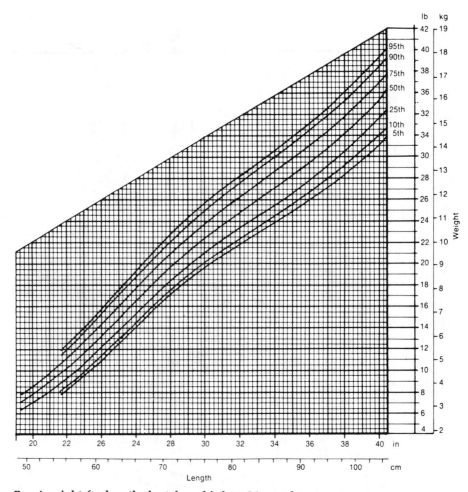

Boys' weight-for-length chart from birth to 36 months
Source: U.S. Department of Health, Education and Welfare, National Center for Health Statistics, 1979.

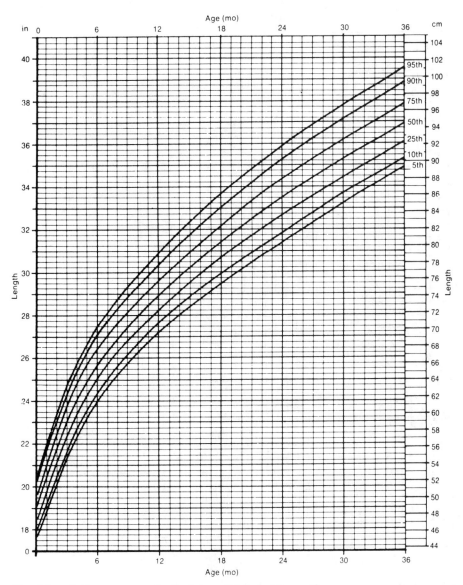

Boys' length-for-age growth chart from birth to 36 months
Source: Department of Health, Education and Welfare, National Center for
Health Statistics, 1979.

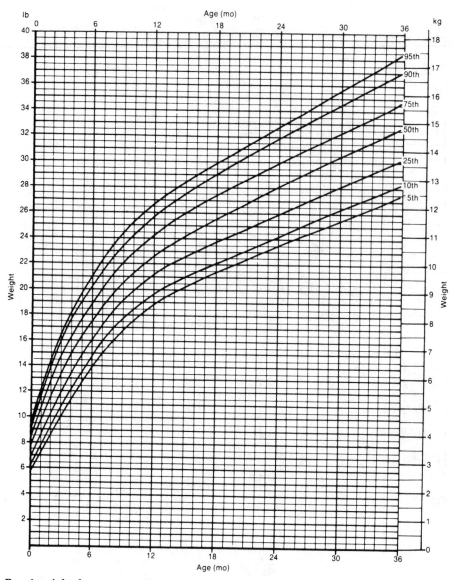

Boys' weight-for-age growth chart from birth to 36 months
Source: U.S. Department of Health, Education and Welfare, National Center for Health Statistics, 1979.

APPENDIX VI Sources of Funding for Food Service

SOURCES OF FUNDING FOR FOOD SERVICE—CHILD CARE FOOD PROGRAM

The Child Care Food Program was begun in 1968 by the U.S. Department of Agriculture and was known as the Special Food Service Program for Children. Designed originally to serve especially needy children, the program provided assistance to nonresidential child-care centers serving children from low-income areas or from areas with significant numbers of working mothers.

In October 1975 new child nutrition legislation, Public Law 94–105, expanded and refocused the program. The law extended eligibility to all nonprofit daycare centers—those serving nonneedy as well as needy areas. It also opened participation to family and group day-care homes, allowing them to join under the sponsorship of a qualifying institution or organization.

Many centers would qualify but are unaware of the services. The following facts are presented to clarify the program:

The Child Care Food Program (CCFP) provides nutritious meals to children enrolled in child-care centers or day-care homes throughout the country. It also introduces young children to many different types of foods and helps teach them good eating habits.

Who Can Participate

The Program is limited to public and private nonprofit organizations providing licensed or approved nonresidential day-care services. Such organizations include, but are not limited to, day-care centers, outside-school-hours care centers, day-care homes, and institutions providing day-care services for handicapped children. Also, private for-profit centers may qualify if they receive compensation under Title XX of the Social Security Act for at least 25% of the children who are receiving nonresidential day care.

Child-care centers and outside-school-hours care centers can operate in the program either independently or under the auspices of a sponsoring organization, which accepts final administrative and financial responsibility for the program. Family day-care homes must participate under a sponsoring organization; they cannot enter the CCFP directly.

Children 12 and younger are eligible to participate in the program (except that for children of migrant workers, the age limit is 15 years). Physically or mentally handicapped people can participate regardless of age, if they receive care at a center or home where the majority of the enrollees are 18 or under.

Eligibility Requirements

All private institutions (except for-profit Title XX organizations) must have tax-exempt status under the Internal Revenue Code of 1954, or must have applied to the Internal Revenue Service (IRS) for it at the time they apply for the Child Care Food Program. If an institution takes part in other federal programs for which it needs nonprofit status, it already meets this requirement. Family daycare homes are not required to be tax exempt, but their sponsoring organizations must have tax-exempt status if they are private. Local IRS offices can provide information on how to obtain tax-exempt status.

All institutions, except sponsoring organizations, must have child care *licensing or approval*. The administering agency can provide information on how to obtain a license or approval.

Meal Service

All participating institutions must serve meals that meet U.S. Department of Agriculture nutritional standards. Institutions may receive reimbursement for up to three meals per child per day. However, one of these meals must be a snack.

Available Assistance

The CCFP provides financial assistance to child-care centers and sponsoring organizations of day-care homes so that they can provide nutritious meals to the children enrolled for care.

Generally, program payments to child-care centers and outside-school-hours care centers are limited to the number of meals served to enrolled children multiplied by the appropriate rates for reimbursement. The rate of payment varies according to the family size and income of children participating in the program. Increased reimbursement is provided for needy children. Some state administering agencies may base reimbursement on the maximum rates or actual costs, whichever is less.

Meals served by day-care homes under the CCFP are reimbursed at different rates for each type of meal served that meets program requirements. The sponsoring organization must pass the full food service payment to the home, unless the sponsoring organization provides part of the home's food service. Day-care home providers receive reimbursement for meals served to their own children only when (1) their children meet the family size and income standards for free and reduced-price meals, and are participating in the CCFP, and (2) other nonresident enrolled children are present and participating in the program. Separate administrative funds are provided to sponsoring organizations based on the number of homes they administer.

Civil Rights

The CCFP is available to all eligible children regardless of race, color, national origin, sex, age, or handicap. If you believe that you have been treated unfairly in receiving food services for any of these reasons, write immediately to the Secretary of Agriculture, Washington, DC 20250. More information may be obtained from the Office of Equal Opportunity, U.S. Department of Agriculture, Washington, DC 20250.

Administering Agency

In most states, the program is administered by the State Department of Education. Where states do not administer the program, Food and Nutrition Service Regional Offices operate it directly.*

*From Facts about the Child Care Food Program, Food and Nutrition Service, INS-242, Aug. 1983.

Glossary

absorption   The process by which digestive products are transferred from the gastro-intestinal tract into the blood or lymphatic system.

acid   A "sour" compound capable of reacting with an alkali.

acid-base balance   The equilibrium or relationship between acidic and alkaline compounds in the body.

additives (food)   Substances incorporated accidentally or intentionally in processed foods.

adipose tissue   Storehouse of fat in the body; chemically active tissue containing protein and other substances as well as fat.

alkaline substance   Any substance that can neutralize acids; basic in reaction.

amino acid   Organic molecule containing carbon, hydrogen, oxygen, and nitrogen; the structural unit of protein; contains an amino group (– NH2) and a carboxyl or acidic group (– COOH).

anemia   Term literally meaning without blood; condition in which red blood cell and/or hemoglobin level is below normal.

anorexia   Disease state characterized by self-starvation; sometimes seen in achievement-oriented adolescents, particularly girls.

antacids   Substances that neutralize acidity, especially in the digestive tract. Common antacids include calcium carbonate, aluminum hydroxide, and sodium bicarbonate (baking soda).

antibodies   Proteins capable of combining with foreign substances (antigens) such as viruses, rendering them inactive or harmless.

antioxidant   Substances such as vitamin E that help prevent oxidative (oxygen-caused) destruction of body tissues and food substances.

appetite   Desire or craving for food that often occurs in the absence of hunger.

arteriosclerosis   Disease characterized by hardening and thickening of the walls of the arteries.

aspartame   A low-calorie, nutritive sweetener used as an additive in cold breakfast cereals, chewing gum, and other food products.

assessment   An evaluation of a child's knowledge, skills, behavior, and/or progress.

B vitamins   Group of water-soluble vitamins originally considered to be a single essential factor and now known to consist of eight separate vitamins.

base   An alkaline substance that can react with acids to neutralize the acid.

behavioral objective   Identifies exactly what the teacher will do, provide, or restrict, describes the learner's observable behavior, and defines how well the learner must perform.

bulimia   Condition characterized by binge eating or the compulsive ingestion of large amounts of food (as many as 5000 to 20,000 kcal) over a short period, and often followed by self-induced vomiting.

Calorie   The heat required to raise the temperature of 1 kg water (at 1 atmosphere of pressure) 1 centigrade degree; also called a kilocalorie.

carbohydrates   Organic compounds composed of carbon, hydrogen, and oxygen. The hydrogen/oxygen ratio is that of water.

carbon   Chemical element present in all substances designated as organic, including proteins, carbohydrates, and fats. When a compound containing carbon combines with oxygen in the body, energy is liberated, and carbon dioxide is formed. Compounds that do not contain carbon are classified as inorganic.

carbon dioxide   Compound that is formed when carbon combines with oxygen. It leaves the body chiefly when air is exhaled from the lungs.

carotene   Yellow pigments that act as provitamin A; that is, they are converted into vitamin A in the body.

cell   Smallest structural unit of living material.

cellulose   A polysaccharide that provides roughage but is not digested by humans.

Child Care Food Program (CCFP)   Provides nutritious meals to children enrolled in child-care centers or day-care homes throughout the country (Federal Register, Vol. 47, No. 162, Aug. 20, 1982).

cholesterol   A steroid alcohol.

coenzyme   A component of an enzyme system (usually containing a vitamin) that is required for the activity of the enzyme.

cognition   All forms of knowing, including perceiving, imagining, reasoning, and judging.

cognitive development   The progression of an individual through a sequence of stages where thoughts, knowledge, interpretations, understandings, and ideas are developed.

comprehensive care   Care for children that encourages their social, emotional, physical, and intellectual growth.

coronary heart disease (CHD)   Arteriosclerosis in the arteries feeding the heart muscle.

curriculum   All of the specific features of a master teaching plan that have been chosen by a particular teacher for his or her classroom. Curricula may vary widely from school to school, but each curriculum reflects the skills, tasks, and behaviors that a school has decided are important for children to acquire.

dental caries   Tooth decay.

dextrose   See **glucose.**

dietary guidelines   Set of general dietary recommendations formulated by the U.S. Department of Agriculture and the Department of Health and Human Services. It advocates dietary measures to prevent disease in terms that the average consumer can understand.

dietitian   Person who by taking college courses in nutrition, food science, food management, and related physical, biological, and social sciences and through formal work experience in an approved (usually clinical) setting has qualified to become a member of the American Dietetic Association.

digestion   Process of breaking down food into molecules that can be absorbed in the bloodstream.

disaccharide   Carbohydrate that breaks down to two monosaccharide molecules during digestion. Examples are sucrose, maltose, and lactose.

electrolyte   Any substance that dissociates into ions when dissolved.

element   Any one of the fundamental atoms of which all matter is composed.

energy   Capacity to do work against resistance.

enrichment   Addition of nutrients to food products.

enzyme   Proteins that catalyze reactions in the body. The names of enzymes frequently end with the suffix -*ase*, such as sucrase, the enzyme that effects the breakdown of sucrose.

essential amino acid   An amino acid needed for growth and maintenance of the body. It must be supplied in the diet.

essential fatty acid   Linoleic acid and possibly linolenic acid; a fatty acid that is a dietary essential.

evaluation   The process of analyzing and determining whether the desired objectives were achieved.

expressive language   Language used in communicating with other individuals.

fat-soluble vitamins   Vitamins A, D, E, and K; vitamins that dissolve in fat but not in water.

fatty acid   An organic acid that can combine with glycerol.

feedback   Any kind of information being returned from a source that is useful in regulating behavior.

fiber (crude)   Insoluble organic material remaining from plants after prolonged acid and base hydrolysis.

fiber (dietary)   Generic term that includes those plant constituents, mostly carbohydrates, that are not digestible by humans.

fine motor skills   Activities with the fingers and hands.

Food and Drug Administration   Agency associated with the U.S. Department of Health and Human Services that has jurisdiction over the safety of food shipped interstate.

food guide   Diet plan devised by the U.S. Department of Agriculture and U.S. Department of Health and Human Services. Used in this text to refer to the Guide to Daily Food Choices the Food Guide Pyramid. The Guide provides specific amounts of foods from food groups to help plan a diet for groups or individuals.

Food Guide Pyramid   An educational tool for use with the Guide to Daily Food Choices.

Food and Nutrition Board   Group of scientists in food and nutrition or related fields who act in an advisory capacity to the National Research Council of the National Academy of Sciences.

fortification   Addition of one or more nutrients to a food item that is not normally a good source of the nutrient, such as the addition of iodine to salt or vitamin D to milk.

fructose   A monosaccharide found in fruits and corn.

galactose   A monosaccharide or simple sugar with a chemical formula identical to that of glucose but with a different structure; component of lactose (milk sugar) and seldom found in nature uncombined.

genetics   The study of heredity and its variations.

glucose   A monosaccharide; the sugar of the blood.

goals   General statements that tell what teaching is expected to accomplish; for example, "to improve Mary's fine motor skills."

gross motor skills   Activities using large muscles such as ruuning, climbing, throwing, and jumping.

hemoglobin   The oxygen-carrying pigment of red blood cells. Normal hemoglobin (Hb) values for adults are about 14 to 16 g/100 mL. Values for children will vary depending on the age of the child. In general after 6 months of age a hemoglobin value of log/100 mL or greater is desirable.

hormone   A compound secreted by an endocrine gland that influences the functioning of an organ in another part of the body.

hunger   Complex of unpleasant sensations felt after prolonged food deprivation that will impel an animal or human to seek, work for, or fight for immediate relief by ingestion of food.

hydrogenation   The controlled addition of hydrogen to an unsaturated fatty acid. This process changes the melting point, thus producing solid fats from oils, depending on the extent of hydrogenation.

hydrolysis   The breaking apart of chemical bonds during digestion with the addition of water.

hyperactivity   A set of behavioral symptoms such as restlessness, excitability, short attention span, and a need for instant gratification.

hypertension   Abnormally high blood pressure.

inorganic   Pertaining to chemical compounds that do not contain carbon.

integration   Nutrition activities taking place in a variety of curricular areas, such as mathematics, science, music, motor skills, art, and social studies.

interest inventory   Identifies specific tasks for which parents can volunteer.

intrinsic factor   Substance produced in the stomach and needed for the absorption of vitamin B_{12} from the small intestine.

ketogenesis   Formation of ketones from fatty acids and some amino acids.

kilocalorie   The amount of heat required to raise 1 kg of water (at 1 atmosphere of pressure) 1 centigrade degree; same as a Calorie.

kinesthetic tactile   A combination of muscles, tendons, joints, and touch receptors yielding information about objects as well as the position of the body in space.

lactase   Enzyme that breaks down lactose in milk to glucose and galactose.

lactoovovegetarian   Person who consumes dairy products and eggs in addition to plant foods but no meat.

lactose   Milk sugar; a disaccharide that is a combination of glucose and galactose.

lactovegetarian   Person who consumes plant foods and dairy products but no meat or eggs.

low birth weight   A birth weight of less than 2500 g or about 5½ pounds.

linoleic acid   Polyunsaturated fatty acid that is an essential nutrient.

lipids   Organic compounds composed of carbon, hydrogen, and oxygen and generally immiscible with water; fats or fatlike substances.

lipoprotein   Compound composed of a lipid and a protein.

lipoprotein (high density)   Blood lipoproteins that help protect against coronary heart disease, probably by helping prevent cholesterol deposition in the tissues and blood vessels.

lipoprotein (low density)   Blood lipoprotein that carries large amounts of cholesterol to the tissues, where it is deposited.

macrominerals   Minerals present in the body in relatively large amounts.

megadose   Usually an intake of a vitamin or a mineral that exceeds recommended levels by about 10 times.

membrane   Thin, soft, pliable layers of animal or vegetable tissue, usually composed of layers of protein and lipid.

metabolism   All the chemical changes that occur from the time nutrients are absorbed until they are built into body substances or eliminated from the body.

microminerals   Minerals present in the body in relatively small amounts; also called trace elements.

monosaccharide   Carbohydrate in its simplest form. Examples are fructose, glucose, and galactose.

monounsaturated fatty acid   Fatty acid containing one double bond.

National Research Council (NRC)   Group of leading scientists appointed by the National Academy of Sciences to coordinate the efforts of major scientific and technical societies of the United States advising the government.

natural foods   Used loosely for foods made from ingredients of plant or animal origin that are altered as little as possible and do not contain artificial ingredients or additives.

nutrition labeling   Mandatory nutrition information carried on packages of all foods shipped interstate for which a nutritional claim is made, as well as on other foods at the discretion of the manufacturer. Mandatory information includes serving size, kilocalories, protein, carbohydrate, and fat content per serving and percentage of the U.S. RDA provided by the eight leading nutrients.

nutritional assessment   Determination of a person's or a group's nutritional status by means of (1) dietary analysis, (2) anthropometric measures (height, weight, skinfold thickness), (3) physical examination, and (4) determination of nutrient or metabolite levels in blood and urine.

obesity   Condition of being 20% or more above desirable or standard weight.

osteomalacia   Vitamin D deficiency disease of adults characterized by bone demineralization.

osteoporosis   Prolonged chronic reduction in bone mass in which reduced bone formation and or accelerated reabsorption may occur.

overweight   Body weight 10% above desirable or standard weight.

oxalate   Substance present in some plant foods such as spinach that binds calcium and various other minerals in the digestive tract and prevents their absorption.

oxidation   The loss of electrons; also combining with oxygen or removal of hydrogen.

pH   Negative logarithm of the effective hydrogen ion concentration; a means of expressing relative acidity or alkalinity, with pH 7 representing neutrality. Numbers lower than 7 indicate acidic; numbers greater than 7 indicate alkaline.

pantothenic acid   One of the B vitamins.

perception   The process of interpreting what is received by the five senses.

perceptual-motor interaction   The interaction of various channels of perception with motor activity; for example, the act of kicking is a perceptual-motor interaction between sight and gross motor responses.

performance objective   See **behavioral objective.**

peristalsis   Motions of the alimentary tract to move the food through the tract.

phospholipid   A fat containing phosphate and a nitrogenous substance in place of one of the fatty acids.

physiological   Refers to the science of physiology, which deals with functions of living organisms or their parts.

phytates   Substances often found with fiber in plant foods that bind zinc, calcium, and other minerals.

picture recipe   A recipe designed especially for nonreaders using illustrations rather than words.

plaque   Sticky film that forms on teeth; the lipid-containing substance that deposits on the inner walls of blood vessels.

plasma   Colorless fluid portion of the blood from which the cells have been removed.

polysaccharide   Complex carbohydrate molecule often consisting of 10,000 or more monosaccharides.

polyunsaturated fatty acid (PUFA)   Fatty acid with two or more double bonds in its carbon chain; present in large amounts in plant oils and liquid at room temperature.

protein   Class of nutrients made up of amino acids.

Public Law 94-142   The Education for All Handicapped Children Act (Federal Register, Vol. 42, No. 163, Aug. 23, 1977).

Recommended Dietary Allowances (RDA)   Quantities of specified vitamins, minerals, and protein needed daily that have been judged adequate for maintenance of good nutrition in the U.S. population, developed by the Food and Nutrition Board of the National Academy of Sciences—National Research Council.

satiety   Cessation of desire for further nourishment.

saturated fatty acid   Fatty acid in which the carbons in its interior chain each have two hydrogens attached to them; present in large amounts in animal fats and usually solid at room temperature.

sensorimotor   Relating to a combination of input of sense organs and output of motor activity.

serum (blood serum)   Fluid portion of the blood that separates from the blood cells after clotting.

single-parent family   A family composed of children living with only one parent.

staff/child ratio   The number of child-care staff required in proportion to the number of children present. This ratio is necessary to ensure the safety and proper care of the children at all times.

starch   Polysaccharide consisting of many glucose molecules bonded together in both branched and straight chains; found in plant foods such as potatoes and corn.

sucrose   A disaccharide made up of glucose and frutose; table sugar.

supplements (dietary)   Substance or mixture of substances found in food but isolated in pure form or present in proportions untypical of a natural food product.

synthesis   Process by which a new substance is formed from its individual parts.

toxicity   Quality of a substance that makes it poisonous or toxic. It sometimes refers to the degree of severity of the poison or the possibility of being poisonous.

unsaturated fatty acid   Fatty acid with one or more sets of adjacent carbons held together with double bonds.

U.S. Recommended Daily Allowance (U.S. RDA)   A standard set of daily quantities of specified vitamins, minerals, and protein judged to be essential in human nutrition by the Food and Drug Administration. Values are taken from the Recommended Dietary Allowances developed by the Food and Nutrition Board of the National Academy of Sciences—National Research Council; used as a standard for nutrient labeling.

vegan   Person who does not consume animal products.

vitamin B_6   Water-soluble B vitamin.

vitamins   Organic nutrients that act as regulators of metabolic processes and are needed in the diet in small amounts.

volunteers   Unpaid personnel who usually work on a part-time basis performing important tasks that supplement, but do not replace, the work of employed staff.

whole-grain cereal   Cereal that contains all parts of the kernel of the grain from which it was made.

Index

Note: Page numbers followed by f indicate figures; page numbers followed by t indicate tables.

Academic skills approach to early childhood education, 248–249
Acesulfame-K, 165
Acquired Immune Deficiency Syndrome (AIDS), 195–196
Additives, 171, 172–173t
AIDS. *See* Acquired Immune Deficiency Syndrome (AIDS)
Alcohol, 17–18, 42
Allergies, 89, 195
Amino acids, 16
Anemia
  iron-deficiency, 29, 70, 88, 127–128, 149
  from lack of folacin, 157
Anorexia nervosa, 4
Antioxidant, 22
Appetite, decreased, 195–196
Ascorbic acid. *See* Vitamin C
Aspartame, 165, 171
Autonomy, in toddlers, 108

Baby bottle tooth decay, 90–91
Baby-Cise, 137
Bag lunches, 224
Beans, 118
Body shape, 7–8
Bottle-feeding
  of infants, 77–82
  of toddlers, 122
Botulism, 235

Breads
  calories in, 162t
  Child and Adult Food Program requirements for, 212–214
  iron value of, 162t
  for preschoolers, 155–156
  for toddlers, 119, 121
Breast-feeding, 71–77
  assistance with, 74–75, 93
  benefits of, 72
  constipation from, 89
  exercise during, 76
  incidence of, 72–73, 74t
  and infant growth, 69
  limitations of, 75
  nutrition during, 76–77
  resources about, 97
Breast milk, care of, 74
Breast pumps, 74, 75, 75f, 76f
Brown sugar, 165
Bulimia, 4
B vitamins, 22

Cafeteria style food service, 224
Calcium, 25–26, 39–40
  for preschoolers, 148–149
  sources of, 111, 112t
  for toddlers, 111
Caloric need, 6–7. *See also* Energy
  of infants, 86t

Caloric need, *continued*
of preschoolers, 147–148
of six- to eight-year-olds, 184
of toddlers, 110–111
Cancer, and vitamins, 19, 22
Carbohydrates, 13–16
function of, 14
and link between sugar and disease, 16
sources of, 14–16
Cardiovascular disease prevention
in six- to eight-year-olds, 194–195
in toddlers, 135
Caregiver role, in toddler's eating, 121–127
Caries
nursing bottle, 90–91, 134
in six- to eight-year-olds, 193–194
in toddlers, 134–135
Cavities. *See* Caries
Cellulose gel, 13
Center-prepared foods, for infants, 208–209
Cereals
for infants, 83, 84
for preschoolers, 155–156
for toddlers, 119, 120t, 121
Chewing
in infants, 60
in toddlers, 106
Child and Adult Food Program (CACFP)
foods not meeting requirements of, 212t
questions about, 209–215
bread and bread alternate component, 212–214
fruit/vegetable component, 214
meat/meat alternate component, 214–215
milk component, 209–212
required meal pattern for, 210–211t
Child nutrition labeling, 229, 230f
Cholesterol, 11, 41
food substitutions for lowering of, 12t
and heart disease, 119, 135, 194, 195
Clostridium organisms, 234–235
Cognitive-interactionist approach to early childhood education, 246–248
Colon disease, fiber and, 14–15
Commercially prepared foods
for infants, 208
for toddlers, 123
Complex carbohydrates, 13–14

Computer programs, for dietary data analysis, 44–45, 50, 52f
Concepts
and cognitive development, 247–248
nutrition, teaching of, 253–256
Concrete operations stage of development, 247
Constipation
and fluid intake, 30
in infants, 89, 90
Cooking
classroom, 279
with recipes for nonreaders, 276–278
Coronary heart disease, prevention of, 195
Cow's milk, 78–80
Culture, and food, 2–3
Cup drinking
by infants, 87
by toddlers, 122
Curriculum plans for nutrition education, 267–276
Cycle menus, 224–229

Dairy products
calcium in, 149, 163t
calories in, 163t
for preschoolers, 156
for toddlers, 121
Day care centers, policies of, 92–93
Dehydration, from diarrhea, 90
Descriptors, on food labels, 48
Desirable body weight, 6, 7t, 40–41
Diarrhea, infant, 90
Dietary Guidelines for Americans, 35
Dietary laws, religious, 2
Dietitians, 241
Diet record, 49–50

Early childhood education, approaches to, 246–250
Eating behavior
of preschoolers, 157–161
of toddlers, 125–127
Eating disorders, 3–4
Eating equipment
for preschoolers, 159–160
for toddlers, 125
Eating patterns, influences on, 189–192
Eating problems, 3
Economics, and food, 2

Education, nutrition. *See* Nutrition education
Emotional factors, and food, 3
Energy, 6–8. *See also* Caloric need
  exercise and, 53, 55
  preschoolers' need for, 147–148
  toddlers' need for, 110–111
Equipment
  eating, 125, 159–160
  exercise, 179–180
Estrogen therapy, for calcium loss, 26
Ethnic foods, 2, 3, 230–231
Exercise
  for children, 55
  and energy, 53, 55
  for infants, 91–92
  objectives for, 41
  for preschoolers, 172–175
  for six- to eight-year-olds, 196–198
  for toddlers, 136–138
Exercise equipment, for preschoolers, 179–180
Exercise record, 49

Family style food service, 224
Fast food, 164, 166–167t
Fat(s), 8–13
  cholesterol and. *See* Cholesterol
  dietary reduction of, 185, 186f, 188t
  food substitutions for lowering of, 12t
  for preschoolers, 148
  proportion of, in girls, 183
  recommendations for intake of, 11–12
  reduced intake of, 41
  for six- to ten-year-olds, 184–185, 186f, 188t
  in snack foods, 192t
  sources of, 8–11
  substitutes for, 12–13
  toddler consumption of, 119, 135
Fat substitutes, 12–13
Fatty acids, 9, 10f
Feeding schedule, for infants, 205
Feingold diet, for hyperactivity, 171
Fiber, 14–16
Finger foods, for infants, 86
Fluoride
  for infants, 77, 82
  for preschoolers, 157
  for toddlers, 113, 135
Folacin, 38, 39t, 157
Food additives, 171

Food allergies, 89
Food groups, teaching of, 251–253
Food Guide Pyramid, 36–37
Food handling guidelines, 238–239f
Food labeling, 39, 45–48
  child nutrition, 229, 230f
Food patterns. *See also* Meal patterns
  cultural, 230–231
Food plan, for infants, 205–209
Food poisoning, 235
Food service, 203
  dietitians and, 241
  for preschoolers, 209
  sanitary practices for, 233–240
  styles of, 224–229
  for toddlers, 209
Food service personnel
  hygiene of, 235–236, 238, 240
  training of, 241–242
Formula, infant, 77–78
  composition of, 80t
  preparation of, 81, 205, 207
Fruits
  Child and Adult Food Program requirements
    for, 214
  educational opportunities from, 164t
  increased consumption of, 41
  for preschoolers, 153
  for toddlers, 117

Goiter, 29
Grains, 41
Gross motor development, 173–175
Growth charts, 64–65
  for boys, 132f, 133f
  for girls, 65f, 66f, 67f, 104f
  interpretation of, 68–69, 103, 105
  for toddlers, 101–102
Guide to Daily Food Choices, 36–38
  sample diet compared to, 50, 51t, 52f
Gymboree, 137–138

HDL cholesterol, 11
Health objectives, 39–44
Healthy People 2000, 39, 42, 43, 44, 45, 73
Height. *See also* Length
  of preschoolers, 145t
  of six- to eight-year-olds, 183, 184t
  of toddlers, 102–103

Hematocrit, and nutritional status, 70
Hemoglobin, and nutritional status, 70
High chairs, 125
High-density lipoprotein (HDL), 11
High-fructose corn syrup, 14
Hydrogenated vegetable fat, 11
Hydrogenation, 11
Hygiene, of food service personnel, 235–236,
    238, 240
Hyperactivity, diet and, 171–172
Hypercarotenemia, 19
Hypertension, and salt intake, 27

Infant centers, policies of, 92–93
Infant feeders, 84
Infants
    bottle-feeding of, 77–82
    breast-feeding of, 71–77
    cup drinking by, 87
    developmental stages of, 60, 61–63t
    diet evaluation of, 87–88
    eating by, with utensils, 87
    exercise for, 91–92
    feeding schedule for, 205
    finger foods for, 86
    food allergies in, 89
    food plan for, 205–209
    gastrointestinal tract disturbances in, 89–90
    guide to amounts of food for, 85t
    iron-deficiency anemia in, 88
    lactose intolerance in, 88–89
    measurement of, 60, 64–67
    nursing bottle caries in, 90–91, 135
    nutritional needs and diet for, 86t
    physical characteristics of, related to food, 59
    RDA for, 79t
    solid foods for, 83–86
Iodine, 29
Iron, 28–29
    food sources of, 113, 114t, 149
    in formula, 77, 82, 88
    in fruits and vegetables, 154t
    for infants, 82, 88
    in molasses, 165
    during pregnancy, 71
    for preschoolers, 149
    for toddlers, 112–113
Iron-deficiency anemia. See Anemia,
    iron-deficiency

Kilocalories, 5

Labeling. See Food labeling
Lactase, 88, 89, 136
Lactation. See Breast-feeding
Lactose intolerance
    in infants, 88–89
    in toddlers, 135–136
La Leche League International, 74
Language development, 264–266
LDL cholesterol, 11
Lead contamination, 81
Learning, approaches to, 245–250
Length. See also Height
    of infants, 60, 64
    of toddlers, 102–103
Lesson plans, for preschooler nutrition
    education, 270–276
Lipids, 8
Lipoprotein, 11
Locomotor movement abilities, 174
Low-density lipoprotein (LDL), 11

Macrominerals, 23, 24t, 25–28
Magnesium, 38, 39t
Manipulative movement abilities, 174
Meal patterns
    daily food choices in, 204t
    infant, 206t
Meat
    Child and Adult Food Program requirements
        for, 214–215
    for preschoolers, 153, 155
    for toddlers, 118–119
Meat alternates
    Child and Adult Food Program requirements
        for, 214–215
    for preschoolers, 153, 155
    for toddlers, 118
Menopause, calcium loss during, 26
Menu, in nutrition education, 259–267
Menu planning, 217–223
    and availability of foods, 218
    checklist for, 220–223t, 231–232
    cycle, 224–229
    food service supervisor's contribution to, 217
    management principles for, 232–233
    parents' contribution to, 240–241
    teacher's contribution to, 218–219

Menu planning, *continued*
  worksheet for, 225f
Messages, on food labels, 48
Microminerals, 23, 24–25t, 28–29
Microwaving
  guidelines for, 239–240
  of infant food, 81–82
Milk
  calcium in, 111, 112t, 148–149, 163t
  calories in, 163t
  Child and Adult Food Program requirements
      for, 209–212
  composition of, 80t
  cow's, 78–80
  low-fat, 80
  for preschoolers, 156
  skim, 80–81
  for toddlers, 121
Milk products. *See* Dairy products
Minerals, 23–29
  for preschoolers, 148–150
  supplementary. *See* Supplements
  for toddlers, 111–113
Modified family style food service, 224
Molasses, 165, 171
Monosaccharides, 13
Monounsaturated fatty acids, 9
Movement abilities, 174–175

National health objectives, 39–44
Natural foods, 169–171
Nonlocomotor movement abilities, 174–175
Nursing bottle caries, 90–91, 135
Nutbutters, 118
NutraSweet. *See* Aspartame
Nutrient Dietary Data Analysis System, 44–45
Nutrients
  classes of, 4
  definition of, 1
  function of, 4–5
  teaching about, 256–258
Nutrition
  cultural factors and, 2–3
  definition of, 1
  economic factors and, 2
  emotional factors and, 3
  social factors and, 1
Nutritional deficiencies, in vegetarians, 169

Nutrition education
  for children, 251–258
  curriculum plan for, 267–276
  goals and objectives for, 250–251
  menu in, 259–267
  objectives for, 42
  parent involvement in, 240–241, 284–299
  strategies for incorporating, 258
Nutrition Labeling and Education Act, 45
Nutrition objectives, 39–44

Obesity, 4
  in six- to eight-year-olds, 196
  in toddlers, 128–137
Olestra, 13
Organic foods, 169–170
Organisms in food, 234–235
Osteomalacia, 26
Osteoporosis, 26
Overeating, 3

Parent involvement
  in menu planning, 240–241
  in nutrition education, 284–299
    benefits of, 285–287
    evaluation of, 295–296
    options for, 290–295
    recognition of, 296–297
    recruitment techniques for, 287–290
Pattern for daily food choices, 204t
Peas, 118
Perceptual-cognitive skill development, 266–
    267
Perceptual-motor approach to early childhood
    education, 249
Perry Preschool High/Scope Curriculum,
    248
Personal development, 264
Pest infestations, 235
Phosphorus, 26–27
Physical education classes, frequency of, 196–
    198
Physical fitness. *See* Exercise
Picnic style food service, 224
Play materials, for preschoolers, 179–180
Polysaccharides, 13
Polyunsaturated fatty acids, 9
Potassium, 28
Pregnancy, weight gain during, 71
Preoperational stage of development, 247

Preschoolers
  cycle menus for, 226–228t
  developmental skills of, 145, 146t
  diet-related concerns for, 161–168
    fast food, 164, 166–167t
    snack foods, 161–164
    sweeteners, 164–165, 168
  eating behavior of, 157–161
  energy needs of, 147–148
  food needs of, 150–156
    breads, 155–156
    cereals, 155–156
    fruits, 153
    meat and meat alternates, 153, 155
    milk and milk products, 156
    recommended intake, 151t
    vegetables, 153
  growth of, 144–145
  nutritional needs of
    fat, 148
    minerals, 148–150
    protein, 148
    vitamins, 149–150
  nutrition lesson plans for, 270–276
  play materials for, 179–180
  RDA for, 147–148, 147t
  vegetarianism among, 168–169, 170t
Proteins, 16–17
  function of, 17
  for preschoolers, 148
  sources of, 17
  for toddlers, 111
  for vegetarians, 168, 169f
Psychological factors, and food, 3

Recipes, for nonreaders, 276–278
Recommended Dietary Allowances (RDA), 44–45
  for preschoolers, 147–148, 147t
  for six- to eight-year-olds, 184, 185t
  for toddlers, 110t, 147t
Regional foods, 3
Regurgitation, by infants, 90
Religion, and food, 2

Saccharin, 165, 168
Salicylates, and hyperactivity, 171
Salmonella organisms, 234
Sanitation in food preparation, 233–240

Saturated fatty acids, 9
Scurvy, 22
Selenium, 29
Sensorimotor skill development, 264
Sensorimotor stage of development, 246
Serving size
  guidelines for, 37–38, 46, 48
  for toddler food, 123–124
Shame, in toddlers, 108
Simplesse, 12–13
Six- to eight-year-olds
  energy needs of, 184
  exercise for, 196–198
  food needs of, 186, 187–188t
  growth of, 183, 184t
  influences on eating patterns of, 189–192
  nutrient needs of, 184–186
  nutrition-related health concerns, 193–196
    AIDS, 195–196
    allergies, 195
    cardiovascular diseases, 194–195
    dental caries, 193–194
    obesity, 196
  RDA for, 184, 185t
Skinfold thickness, in assessment of children's nutrition, 69, 70f
Snack foods
  for parties, 294–295
  for preschoolers, 161–164
  for six- to eight-year-olds, 190–192
  for toddlers, 126
Social development, 264
Social factors, and food, 1
Sodium, 27, 41–42, 119
Solid foods, for infants, 83–86, 207–208
Sorbitol, 165
Special Supplemental Food Program for Women, Infants and Children (WIC), 98–99, 128
Spitting up, by infants, 90
Spoon feeding, of infants, 87
Staphylococcus organisms, 234
Starvation, 4
Stature. *See* Height; Length
Stellar, 13
Sterols, 11
Stomach cancer, and salt intake, 27
Stools, infant, 89–90

Strained foods, for infants, 207–208
Sucking, in infants, 60
Sucrose. *See also* Sugar
  and hyperactivity, 171
Sugar, 14, 16, 164–165, 171
Sunette, 165
Supplements
  for infants, 82, 93
  for preschoolers, 156–157
  recommendations for, 31
  for six- to eight-year-olds, 185–186
  for toddlers, 113
Sweeteners, 164–165, 168
Sweet One, 165

Teeth, eruption of, 106
Temperature, and food sanitation, 235, 236f
Thyroid gland, and iodine, 29
Toddlers
  autonomy versus shame in, 108
  and cardiovascular disease, 135
  care provider's role in eating by, 121–127
  dental caries in, 134–135
  developmental skills of, 105–106
  developmental stages of, 107t
  eating behavior of, 125–127
  exercise for, 136–138
  food guide for, 114–121
    breads, 119, 121
    cereals, 119, 120t, 121
    fruits, 117
    meat and meat alternates, 118–119
    milk and milk products, 121
    nutrient analysis, 116f
    recommended intake, 115t
    vegetables, 117
  growth of, 101–105
  iron-deficiency anemia in, 127–128
  lactose intolerance in, 135–136
  and loss of interest in food, 108–109
  nutritional needs of, 109–114
    energy, 110–111
    minerals, 111–113
    protein, 111
    supplementation, 113
  obesity in, 128–137
  psychological characteristics of, 106, 108–109
  RDA for, 110t, 147t
  social characteristics of, 106, 108–109

weaning of, 122
Tooth decay. *See* Caries
Trace elements. *See* Microminerals
Traditional nursery school approach to
    childhood education, 249
Twenty-four-hour dietary recall, 49, 50

Utensils
  for infant feeding, 87
  for preschoolers, 158–159
  for toddlers, 125

Vegetables
  Child and Adult Food Program requirements
      for, 214
  educational opportunities from, 164t
  increased consumption of, 41
  for preschoolers, 153
  for toddlers, 117
Vegetarianism, 3
  guidelines for, 53–54
  among preschoolers, 168–169, 170t
  supplementation with, 157
Very low density lipoprotein (VLDL), 11
Vitamin A
  sources of, 19
  for toddlers, 113, 117
  toxicity from, 23, 157
Vitamin B_6, 38, 39t
Vitamin B_{12}, 157
Vitamin C
  in fruits, 153, 154t
  for iron absorption, 28, 29
  for preschoolers, 149–150
  sources of, 22–23
  for toddlers, 113, 117
  in vegetables, 153, 154t
Vitamin D
  for infants, 82
  sources of, 19, 22
  toxicity from, 157
Vitamin E, 22, 38, 39t
Vitamin K, 22
Vitamins, 18–23. *See also specific vitamins*
  fat-soluble, 19, 20t, 22
  supplementary. *See* Supplements
  toxicity from, 23
  water-soluble, 20–21t, 22–23
VLDL cholesterol, 11

Vomiting, by infants, 90

Water, 30, 81
Weaning, 122
Weight
  of infants, 64
  during pregnancy, 71
  of preschoolers, 144–145
  of six- to eight-year-olds, 183, 184t

  of toddlers, 102t, 103
  variation of, in infants, 69
WIC (Special Supplemental Food Program for
    Women, Infants and Children), 98–99,
    128

Xylitol, 165

Zinc, 29, 38, 39t, 150